FUNDED BY

KISD
Köln International School
of Design

Technology
Arts Sciences
TH Köln

The responsibility for the content of the publication lies with the authors. We have made every effort to obtain all image rights for the publication of third-party materials. If, in individual cases, copyrights have not been clarified, please contact the editors.

All rights reserved. This work is protected by copyright. Any use other than that legally permitted is not approved without the prior written consent of the publisher.

© 2023
Published by adocs
Produktion und Verlag GmbH
Annenstraße 16
20359 Hamburg
www.adocs.de

Technische Hochschule Köln (https://www.th-koeln.de)
Köln International School of Design (https://kisd.de)

This publication is available as open access at the following address:

Design:
Layout: Jost Goldschmitt (https://jostgoldschmitt.de/)
Coverdesign: Philipp Pätzold (https://www.instagram.com/philipppaetzold/)
Typeface: Marguerite by Charlotte Rohde (https://charlotterohde.de/)

Printing: KERSCHOFFSET, Zagreb

Language Editing: Jacob Watson (https://www.translabor.de)

This work is licensed under a Creative Commons License (CC BY-SA 4.0). https://creativecommons.org/licenses/by-sa/4.0/

This license allows reusers to distribute, remix, adapt, and build upon the material in any medium or format, so long as attribution is given to the creator. If you remix, adapt, or build upon the material, you must license the modified material under identical terms.

Permissions beyond the scope of this license are administered by adocs publishing. Information on how to request permission may be found at: https://adocs.de/en/contact

ISBN (Book): 978-3-943253-62-7
ISBN (PDF): 978-3-943253-72-6
DOI: https://doi.org/10.53198/9783943253726

Attending [to] Futures

Matters of Politics
in Design Education,
Research, Practice

Edited by
Johanna Mehl
Carolin Höfler

ACKNOWLEDGMENTS

We would like to thank the authors of this book for their perspectives, research, and expertise and for sharing their work twice – first at the *Attending [to] Futures* conference in November 2021 and now here in this collection. The conference took place at the Köln International School of Design (KISD) of TH Köln (Cologne University of Applied Sciences) and invited designers, scholars, activists, artists, practitioners, and researchers to "engage in a political reprogramming of design!" – to quote from our website.[1] The chapters you'll read here are carefully revised manuscripts, workshop protocols, or lecture notations, and we are incredibly grateful to be able to bring together such diverse approaches to matters of politics in design. We are thankful for the author's openness to discuss their work and the radical design futures they envision through their practices. We are honored to be part of such a critical, hopeful, and active group of people.

[1] https://www.attendingtofutures.de

Making this book was an intense process that involved the support of many people along the way. We would like to express our deep gratitude to our language editor, Jacob Watson. We are beyond happy about this collaboration, his enthusiasm for the project, his mindful engagement with every chapter, and his flexibility and patience during the review process. We also want to thank Moritz Ingwersen for his additional set of eyes, open ears, words of encouragement, and his unmatched sense for sentence flow.

We want to use this opportunity to thank the students that were involved in the conference back in 2021. Without their engagement in the coordination, organization, preparation, and realization, and without their ideas and work, the event would not have been possible. They moderated the keynotes, organized and built the exhibition space, took care of the technical setup to make the workshops and talks hybrid, designed all online and print visuals, coded the conference website, prepared meals and snacks for the guests, looked for sponsors, and helped with the budgeting. To these students, we want to say: Thank you for your incredible work, team spirit, critical engagement, and love for this project. It was a year of being constantly reminded of what you are capable of.

Some of the students that were part of the conference team also contributed to this publication. We would like to thank and applaud Philipp Pätzold and Jost Goldschmitt, who were part of the conference's graphic design team, for the layout of this book. Philipp designed the cover and backside, Jost was responsible for laying out the content pages. We are so grateful for the time and effort they poured into this project, their eye for details, colors, type, and their reliability in the process of making this book. We also would like to thank Jiye Kim, Sally Loutfy, and Tomás Ignacio Corvalán Azócar who were conference team members as well as moderators at the conference, for the interview that opens this volume and for their encouragement, openness, and sharp-witted comments throughout the publication process. Another former conference student team member we are greatly indebted to is Jule Schacht. Her energy and clarity were indispensable during the event as well as the editing process. We'd like to thank her for her meticulous work on the bibliographies and catching those errors that are bound to happen when the letters already begin to dance on the screen from being looked at for too long.

Thank you to KISD and TH Köln. Without their funding for language editing, layout, and open access fees this publication would not be possible. We would like to express our gratitude to the TH Köln President Stefan Herzig, the Vice Presidents Sylvia Heuchemer, Klaus Becker and Ursula Löffler, as well as the Dean of the Faculty of Cultural Studies, Regina Urbanek. Making this book publicly available and free was one of our priorities and we want to especially thank Kerstin Klein at the university library for her tireless support during the application stage for the Open Access Publication Fund.

We are beyond grateful to our publisher, adocs, who recently launched an open access program and supported this project from day one. Special thanks goes out to the adocs team, especially Oliver Gemballa, for making communication easy and for always being transparent, optimistic, and open, and for making it possible that this book will also be published as a small print edition.

There are some people we want to personally say thanks to for various reasons, be it an open ear, good advice, encouraging words, or other forms of support: Michael Gais, Michaela Büsse, Anthony Burton, Michelle Pfeifer, Nelly Y. Pinkrah, Celia Brightwell, and Leon Vogler.

Finally, this volume is indebted to the work of many activists, theorists, designers, artists, scholars, and (former) students that preceded, ignited, informed, and guided the event as well as the publication. These pages are embedded in and surrounded by their thoughts and arguments. You will find them in the references, footnotes, and bibliographies throughout the following pages.

(Johanna Mehl) (Carolin Höfler)

ACKNOWLEDGMENTS 5

FOREWORD: ATTENDING [TO] FUTURES 13
Matters of Politics in Design Education, Research, Practice
(Johanna Mehl) (Carolin Höfler)

TABLE OF CONTENTS

PART 1: INSTITUTIONS

I DISAGREE WITH YOU SUPER POLITELY
A Reflection of Attending [to] Futures, One Year Later
Johanna Mehl · Jiye Kim · Tomás Ignacio Corvalán Azócar · Sally Loutfy
23

(IM)POSSIBLE EXITS, SILENCED AFFECTS
Design Futures and Disciplinary Mobilities
Imad Gebrael
31

A LIST OF LONGINGS
Luiza Prado
41

RESONANCE AND ONTOLOGICAL DESIGN
On Facilitating and Obstructing Transformative Teaching and Learning Experiences in Design Education
Lisa Baumgarten
51

DWELLINGS IN ETHERNITY
Designing and Unraveling the Patadesign School
Isabella Brandalise · Henrique Eira · Søren Rosenbak
59

COMMITTED TO PRESENTS
A Break at Attending [to] Futures
Dorsa Javaherian · Abigail Schreider
73

PART 2: HISTORIES

POLITICAL ECONOMY PUSHES BACK
How Structures of Power Govern our Design History Narratives
Bonne Zabolotney
83

DESIGNING THE DESIGNER
Publicity and Immutability as Colonial and Capitalist Design Imperatives

Chris Lee

95

PATIO DESIGN AND CRAFTS
Building Encounters

Zoë Rush   Patio International

111

TOWARDS A DEMOCRATIC FUTURE
Art and Education at Black Mountain College

Ina Scheffler

119

EMBRACING EQUIVOCATIONS
An Attempt to Attend When Design Has Never Been Modern

Marius Förster

127

EASTBOUND
A Decolonial Approach to Relocating Vietnamese Design History

ngọc triệu

137

PART 3: SCENARIOS

WICKED RITUALS OF CONTEMPORARY DESIGN THINKING

Carmem Saito   Frederick M. C. van Amstel   Bibiana Oliveira Serpa   Rafaela Angelon

151

UNIVERSAL SPECIES SUFFRAGE

Jaione Cerrato   Jon Halls

163

DESIGN OF UNREST
Right-wing Metapolitics – Paralogy – Knowledge Spaces – Chaos

Tom Bieling   Frieder Bohaumilitzky   Anke Haarmann   Torben Körschkes

169

MAKING ROOM FOR ABOLITION

Lauren Williams

183

OUT OF STOCK
Notations on a Speculative Journal for Fashion and Design

Edith Lázár

191

MEXICO 44 AND LATINOFUTURISMO 203
César Neri

MARIAH 209
Acts Of Resistance, Legally "Trespassing" in The Metaverse

Adam DelMarcelle   Heather Snyder Quinn

PART 4: NARRATIVES

DESIGN NARRATIVES AND THE WHITE SPATIAL IMAGINARY 219
Becky Nasadowski

MATRIARCHAL DESIGN FUTURES 231
A Collective Work in Progress

Heather Snyder Quinn   Ayako Takase

WEIRD PROBLEMS 243
Rethinking Privileged Design?

Sven Quadflieg

CHANGING THE HOW 253
First Steps Towards Critical Design Pedagogy

Mira Schmitz

AN OPTICAL DECOY FOR THE MACHINE 259
Automatic Policing of Trademarks Online

Chris Hamamoto   Federico Pérez Villoro

VARIANT OF CYBERFEMINISM(S) 273
Mindy Seu

BIO NOTES 283

FOREWORD: ATTENDING [TO] FUTURES

Matters of Politics in Design Education, Research, Practice

Johanna Mehl   Carolin Höfler

In response to the prevailing idea that design reacts to a situation *that is* and turns it into a situation that *should be*,[1] this book presents an understanding of design as a culturally embedded and context-specific material practice and knowledge culture. Design, in this perspective, actively shapes our perception of the world and affects lived realities. With a focus on education, research, and practices, this volume explores how design both reflects and influences the social and environmental conditions of our time, while also considering how it shapes our collective imagination of possible futures. By breaking down the book's title, the following passages delve into its core themes, exploring the layers of design approaches and perspectives it encompasses.

Matters of Politics in Design

Paying attention to the underlying politics of design practices requires examining the multiplicity of actors, from institutional norms and regulations, pedagogies, curricula, tools, materials, architectural environments, and discursive conventions to the very mechanics and protocols by which we imagine. From the programs we work with and the languages in which we code to the aesthetic dogmas we follow and seminars we attend, all of the elements that make design are fundamentally structured by social power dynamics and guided by ideologies. In many ways, this book is about the politics that inform what we design long before we even set foot in a design school. On the one hand, it investigates inherited biases that are habitually normalized and missed because they are encoded in design practices, internalized in common design narratives and encapsulated in the built environment that surrounds us.[2] Specifically, authors attend to the discriminatory, exclusionary, oppressive, and ecologically untenable systems that a lot of common design practices build on and perpetuate. On the other hand, authors in this book resist and critically reflect on the ideological, geographical, and temporal boundaries that are persistently drawn by proponents of a design history canon despite a critical rethinking of historiography across the sciences and humanities. Some discussions of design histories in this book proceed from design's entanglements with Euro-Western capitalist modernity and hetero-patriarchal normativity,[3] not to insist on the centrality of these ideologies for all design histories, presents, and futures, but to recognize and reckon with the role design plays in forging global power structures. It is a key element of this book, however, to contextualize these entanglements within broader historical and cultural frameworks. The aim is not to establish

1 While this phrasing is a nod towards Herbert Simon's well-cited proclamation that „[e]veryone designs who devises courses of action aimed at changing existing situations into preferred ones" (*The Sciences of the Artificial* 1969), it references the institutionalized framing of design as problem-solving based on the perpetual recital of canonical texts by Euro-Western design theorists and historians.

2 Initiatives such as the "Decolonising Design" group, "Decentering Whiteness in Design History Resources," or "Depatriarchise Design" mobilize the prefix "de-" to acknowledge, address, resist, and disrupt such reproductions of oppression through design.

3 The entanglements of western design history with structural violence and oppression based on race, gender, ethnicity, sexuality, and dis/ability are interrogated by a growing number of critical design scholars, including many authors of this book. For further reference see for example: *Feminist Futures of Spatial Practices* (Schalk et al., editors, AADR Spurbuchverlag 2017), *The Responsible Object: A History of Design Ideology for the Future* (van Helvert, Marjanne, editor, Valiz 2016), *Critical Fabulations* (Rosner, Daniela, MIT Press 2018), *Design History Beyond the Canon* (Kaufmann-Buhler, Jennifer et al., editors., Bloomsbury 2019), or visit *futuress*, a learning community space and platform that focuses on publishing writing at the intersection of "feminism, design, and politics" (https://futuress.org [accessed June 2023]).

[4] This mutually constituting relation and co-evolution of "[what] we make and what (we think) we are" is central to feminist science & technology studies scholars such as N. Katherine Hayles (quoted here is her article "Unfinished Work: From Cyborg to Cognisphere". *Theory, Culture & Society*, vol. 23, no. 7–8, Dec. 2006, pp. 159–66.). In this context, design scholars such as Anne-Marie Willis and Arturo Escobar are well-cited for their theorization of ontological design. See Escobar quoting Willis: "We design tools, and these tools design us back. 'Design designs' is the apt and short formula given to this circularity by Anne-Marie Willis: 'we design our world, while our world acts back on us and designs us' (2006, 80)." (*Designs for the Pluriverse*, Duke University Press 2018, 110; see Willis, Anne-Marie (2006) "Ontological Designing." *Design Philosophy Papers*: Vol. 4, No. 2, pp. 69-92)

[5] This is a reference to Gayatri Chakravorty Spivak's concept of "unlearning" to emphasize the complexity of learning processes and the entanglements between education and power. Education is not only the transmission of knowledge but also a cultural practice that shapes collectives of students in specific ways. Education enables agency – which can then be used to examine one's own prejudices, beliefs, worldviews, and positionality within systems of privilege and oppression.

[6] The dimensions of design as future-making have been elaborated in publications such as *Design as Future-Making* (Yelavich; Adams, Bloomsbury 2014), or *Designs for the Pluriverse* (Escobar, Duke University Press 2018). For World-making, a term frequently used with respect to the activist potential of speculative fiction, see for example *Staying with the Trouble* (Haraway, Duke University Press 2016) or *As We Have Always Done: Indigenous Freedom through Radical Resistance* (Betasamosake Simpson, University of Minnesota Press 2017): "It became clear to me that *how* we live, *how* we organize, *how* we engage in the world – the process – not only frames the outcome, it is the transformation. *How* molds and then gives birth to the present. The *how* changes us. *How* is the theoretical intervention" (emphases in original).

or restate a hegemonic, universally applicable critique, but rather to embrace and navigate uneasy tensions and understand that how we practice design is not only made by politics but makes politics.[4]

Attending [to] Futures

If "design" is the lens through which we glimpse into possible futures, this volume asks: What are the futures we are capable of imagining? As a subject of study, design is enabled and constrained by educational institutions and academic traditions. As a profession it is conditioned by systems of labor. As a creative activity it is shaped by what tools are programmed to do. As a field of study it is contoured by inherited customs and ways of conducting design. Authors in this book challenge common ways of knowing, being, and doing in design with regard to the futures they facilitate and interrogate the role, responsibility, and potential of a plurality of design practices in confrontation with social and environmental crises. In this way, this volume does not only ask about designed futures, but also the futures of design: What are the consequences drawn from a critical examination of the histories and politics underlying normative renderings of design? What are steps towards more equitable education, research, and practice? How can we disrupt the perpetuation of biases and reification of social injustices? How can existing problematic narratives be effectively challenged and unlearned?[5]

The title of this book "Attending [to] Futures" articulates a collective practice and presence of agency and worldmaking or future-making in design.[6] It is a move from perception to relation and from participating to pushing forward. The prepositional "to" inquires into the conditions of attending not only speculative futures but the physical and mental places in which they take shape. Who has access and who is denied entry? What are the hiring policies in design agencies or the conditions of admission to design schools? What are the metrics that designed objects, interactions, and spaces appeal to? How do design practices account for the interdependencies between building the material world and establishing cultural norms, including their capacities to enable, exclude, encourage, condemn, or sanction certain values and worldviews? Authors attend to these questions responsibly and with care, in some cases reversing in other cases resisting entrenched design narratives, and exposing the ongoing systems of white supremacy, (settler-)colonialism, heteropatriarchy, racism, and ableism. Drawing on their own background and experiences, the authors assembled in this book not only examine design and its socio-political systems, but also envision alternative scenarios and propose pathways towards multiple, inclusive, and just futures. In papers and project documentations that include workshop reflections, personal stories, critical inquiries and analysis using modes of queer-feminist critique and activist research creation, contributors are both attending and attending to the future of design. The personal in many of these accounts becomes political and an expression of an embodied and situated engagement that is explicit about the stakes and commitments necessary for theorizing and materializing design.

This book contributes to a growing body of literature that specifically addresses matters of politics in design such as *Design Struggles* (Mareis; Paim, Valiz 2021), *Design Justice* (Costanza-Chock, MIT Press 2020), *Graphic Design Is Not Innocent* (Offermanns, Valiz 2022), *Design Anthropological Futures* (Smith et al., Bloomsbury 2016), *Social Matter, Social Design* (Boelen; Kaethler, Valiz 2020), Design in Crisis (Fry; Nocek, Routledge 2021), *Economies of Design* (Julier, SAGE 2017) or *Extra Bold – A Feminist Inclusive Anti-Racist Non-Binary Field Guide For Graphic Designers* (Lupton et al., Princeton Architectural Press 2020), to name but a few recent publications. The authors in *Attending [to] Futures* link up with disciplines such as cultural studies, sociology, anthropology, media studies, and philosophy and conceptually draw from critical theory, including feminist science & technology studies, intersectional feminisms, critical race theory, critical dis/ability studies, and decolonial theory. Self-reflexively engaging their own experiences and work, they interrogate design in all its convoluted modalities: as activism, practice, discipline, way of knowing, field of study and set of objects.

Education, Research, Practice

All of these matters were at the heart of the *Attending [to] Futures* conference convened at the Köln International School of Design (KISD) of TH Köln (Cologne University of Applied Sciences) in November 2021. It gathered designers, scholars, activists, artists, and students online and on site for talks, workshops, and performances – many of which were transformed into the papers or project documentations that make up this volume. As a continuation and expansion of the lectures and conversations held at this event, this book brings together multiple approaches and diverse formats that are clustered in four parts: **INSTITUTIONS, HISTORIES, NARRATIVES,** and **SCENARIOS.** While these categories certainly extend, overlap and deeply relate to one another, they allow for the chapters to mutually amplify one another.

PART 1 contains investigations and critiques of the conditions of design education as well as perspectives on how to navigate and challenge the pressures and restrictions that come with educational, academic, and non-academic design **INSTITUTIONS.** It opens and closes with two critical reflections of the *Attending [to] Futures* conference from the perspective of (former) design students of its host university. In a moderated interview student team members **Sally Loutfy, Jiye Kim,** and **Tomás Ignacio Corvalán Azócar** reflect on their positionality as design students, while KISD alumni **Dorsa Javaherian** and **Abigail Schreider** look back on a roundtable they hosted, which created a space for students to voice how ongoing structures of racism, sexism, xenophobia, and eurocentrism affect their studies and lives as design students in Germany.

These critiques resonate with the first-hand experiences as educators made by **Imad Gebrael, Luiza Prado,** and **Lisa Baumgarten,** who in their chapters observe and address an institutional turn from the dismissal of "conversations on gender equality, racism, disability, and decolonization" (Prado), towards adoptions of and a focus on socio-political matters in design curricula. Yet, the observation of such a turn is compounded with caution: too often these discourses are implemented superficially and come without the willingness "to deal with any form of accountable change" (Gebrael) or consideration of the challenges and pressures of students that Lisa Baumgarten traces to the Bologna Process. Subsequently **Isabella Brandalise, Henrique Eira,** and **Søren Rosenbak** reflect on a series of self-initiated, international workshops that mobilized and estranged the structural implications of a school to radically rethink common models of design education "in search for plural, critical, and experimental alternatives."

In **PART 2** authors revisit and rethink design **HISTORIES** written from a Euro-Western perspective that universalize an exclusionary set of methods, knowledges, traditions, materials, and tools while neglecting the underlying politics that continue to shape the trajectory of design practices. **Zoë Rush** revisits the workshop conducted by the design collective *Patio International,* which explored past encounters between design and craft and critically asked about the dangers of commodification in interdisciplinary collaborations that seek to find "common ground in a system in which one is centralized and the other is 'other'". Authors **Chris Lee** and **Bonne Zabolotney** both address the ways in which design histories or historiography regulate and delineate who is and who is not a designer, and what counts or doesn't count as design. Through different lenses, they explore modes of operating beyond Euro-centric paradigms and opening up the canon. A critical engagement with canonical design literature is an elemental aspect throughout all chapters in part 1. While **Marius Förster** mobilizes Bruno Latour to imagine design beyond modern ontologies, **Ina Scheffler** encourages us to revisit the Black Mountain College, a central node in the history of western design education, and its forgotten contexts as a historical site that calls for reevaluation. Lastly, **ngọc triệu** offers an account of Vietnamese design history and explains how the presentation of an exclusively Euro-Western-centric design history as the whole story continues to colonize design futures and delegitimizes non-hegemonic practices, histories, and identities.

The design **SCENARIOS** described in **PART 3** offer different ways of approaching matters of politics through speculative design futures, fictional worlds, or discursive spaces established via various forms of media from 2D and 3D visualizations, artifacts and films, to interactive games, AR mobile applications, and a speculative online journal.

César Neri and **Lauren Williams** reflect on their recent installations in which they narrate a fictional future via objects and spatial installations. While Lauren Williams' exhibition *Making Room for Abolition* rehearses a world without police, prisons, and capitalism, Cesar Neri's speculative design intervention *Mexico 2044* employs a latinX-futurist lens to envision "a future of mass-commodified Indigenous identity in the face of a fully Westernized and hyper-capitalist State" (Neri). The online journal *Out of Stock* edited by **Edith Lázár** assembles speculative approaches in fashion design to think rebelliously about possible futures with a focus on Eastern-European subjectivities and urgencies. In her chapter, she contextualizes the artworks presented in the journal as counter-narratives to stereotypes, violence, and toxicity perpetuated by the (fashion) design industry.

Tom Bieling, Frieder Bohaumilitzky, Anke Haarmann, and **Torben Körschkes** elaborate on their collaborative short film *Design of Unrest,* employing a non-linear approach to story-telling that undermine what they call epistemological seriousness to address designs entanglements with oppressive social and cultural systems. Other design scenarios discussed in this part are created collaboratively with an audience, but through different modes of interactive play and participation. **Carmem Saito, Frederick M. C. van Amstel, Bibiana Oliveira Serpa,** and **Rafaela Angelon** reflect on and contextualize their online *Forum Theater* staged at the conference, in which participants were invited to communicate with digitally augmented performers that represented and personified the pitfalls of working in the design industry. Employing a different form of audience participation, the *Universal Species Suffrage* workshop—conceptualized by **Jaione Cerrato** and **Jon Halls**—uses roleplaying to create fictional scenarios in which participants shift perspectives and vote in the name of other species in speculative geo-political decision-making processes. Finally, **Adam DelMarcelle** and **Heather Snyder-Quinn** share what motivated them to explore augmented reality as a means of digital protest in their project documentation for their AR and film project *Mariah*.

PART 4 is about the cultural design **NARRATIVES** that not only subconsciously shape designed products, systems, and services, but that are intentionally (re-)produced in order to sell products, systems, and services in higher quantities or at higher prices. In this way, **Chris Hamamoto** and **Federico Pérez Villoro** address the mechanisms of branding, namely creating narratives as added value to consumer products, by exploring Chinese physical and digital replica markets. **Mira Schmitz** proposes ways of unlearning communication design strategies, which frequently mobilize and perpetuate racial, gendered, and age-related stereotypes in creating ads that appeal to a specific target audience. The reliance on and reproduction of stereotypical and discriminatory narratives about normative forms of embodiment, identity, and sexuality through design is discussed throughout the chapters in part 4. Specifically, authors analyze design's tendency to create exclusive spaces–physical, virtual, and social–by centering and catering to predominantly white, male, able-bodied, and Western demographics. **Becky Nasadowski** examines how design contributes to a white spatial imaginary that influences racialized patterns of habitation, while **Sven Quadflieg** analyzes the consequences of standardized products and design processes for marginalized social groups, ethnicities, or people with disabilities. The chapters by **Mindy Seu** as well as **Heather Snyder-Quinn** and **Ayako Takase** ask what it would mean to employ a feminist lens when practicing design, e.g., in order to rehearse matriarchal design futures in re-telling the histories of design technologies.

Ultimately, contributions within this book scrutinize unchallenged disciplinary norms and call for a shift in how we approach teaching and learning design. They emphasize the need for a design education that enables future designers to engage with the political implications of their work, by cultivating literacy of the conditions and contingencies that shape their practice. This process should not be mistaken as yet another problem to be solved by design. Responses to contemporary social and political challenges presented in this book are culturally specific, and they involve addressing ambiguities, complexities, and uncertainties. The authors engage in an ongoing, reflexive, critical, hopeful, and messy process that entails a plurality of approaches and perspectives, without tokenizing or simply adding new vocabulary to processes that at their core remain the same. Notably, this is a collection of work by not only researchers but also practitioners in various design disciplines and beyond, people with different jobs and at different stages in their personal and professional lives, making this book a situated, perforated, always unfinished, contemporary commentary from within and about the playing fields of design. It is not representative of all the ways in which design operates, a universally applicable critique, or a manual for good design practices, but a meshwork of thoughts that connect to each other. Drawing from and contributing to a body of theoretical and practical work that addresses political matters of design, authors attend to the ways we tell design histories, practice design in the present, and how we envision design in the future.

PART 1 contains investigations and critiques of the conditions of design education as well as perspectives on how to navigate and challenge the pressures and restrictions that come with educational, academic, and non-academic design **INSTITUTIONS.**

1

INSTITUTIONS

Acknowledgements

Thank you to Valentina Stahnke and Abies Robinson for the transcript.

I DISAGREE WITH YOU SUPER POLITELY

A Reflection of Attending [to] Futures, One Year Later

(Johanna Mehl)   (Jiye Kim)   (Tomás Ignacio Corvalán Azócar)   (Sally Loutfy)

On October 25, 2022—roughly one year after the event—conference organizer Johanna Mehl interviewed student members of the conference team Jiye Kim, Tomás Ignacio Corvalán Azócar, and Sally Loutfy. This is part of their conversation.

Johanna: Hi Everyone! Would you like to introduce yourselves and briefly explain your role in the conference?

Jiye: My name is Jiye Kim (she/her) and I was born and raised in Seoul, South Korea. I go by the name "Jane" too. I have been on a journey of finding my own identity as a designer since moving from Korea to the United Kingdom, and am now living in Köln, Germany. My identity has been slowly changing due to several multicultural experiences and constant self-reflection. I joined the M.A. Program, Integrated Design at Köln International School of Design (KISD) in March, 2021, and will graduate in February 2023 with a M.A. thesis that focuses on ethical design processes for technological services. During the *Attending [to] Futures* conference, I mainly participated in the "content" team and also moderated keynotes on the stage.

Tomás: My name is Tomás (they/he), I think of myself as a design and research enthusiast, design practitioner, and facilitator—with a strong focus on queer feminisms and critical approaches to design and academia. Born and raised in Santiago de Chile, I graduated from Design at Pontificia Universidad Católica de Chile. In 2019 I moved to Germany and about a year later I started my M.A. at KISD. At the moment, I am finishing my M.A. thesis, an exploratory approach to design academia and learning, situated somewhere between textiles, participation, design theory and queer feminist approaches. My main contributions to the *Attending [to] Futures* conference were as a member of the "food" team and "content" team. You can picture me mixing vegetables for a soup one minute and the next sprinting to the stage to moderate a keynote.

Sally: My name is Sally. I am a Lebanese architect and designer interested in the influence of human psychology in architecture and urban space. I was born and raised in Beirut, Lebanon, a place that I share a bitter-sweet relationship with. My country and the experiences I've had there influence my design works in a major way. I came to Germany in 2021 to pursue my M.A. Degree at KISD in Integrated Design research. My academic work focuses on the effects of trauma and political conflict on the ways in which we design for our built environment. At the moment I am working as a 3D Innovation Architect in Berlin. During the *Attending [to] Futures* conference, I was involved in the social media campaign and moderated a keynote in the "content" team. As a member of the "rooms" team, I co-organized the space on-site.

Johanna: What motivated you to participate in the conference project?

Tomás: I used to do textiles back in Chile and for my undergraduate studies I started exploring the intersections of textiles and gender theory. I was more interested in the political side of design than praxis. When I first saw the conference's full name "*Attending [to] Futures*, Matters of Politics in Design" which is followed by "Education, Research, and Practice"— I immediately thought 'Hey! Something is happening here that is, hmm, not very often talked about with students'. Coincidentally, my interest in design and politics and how design can be political was one of the reasons why I wanted to get a M.A. degree in design in the first place.

Sally: We came here during Covid. So, we didn't know anyone at all and felt like there was something missing. We hardly knew each other! To be honest, I had a specific idea of what coming to Germany would mean and how it was an opportunity for me to study design differently. When I finally arrived, I felt like I was pulled into the very loop that I was trying to avoid. When I saw this conference I thought there is finally a chance for me to see that other people are experiencing the same things as I do. The main thing that attracted me to the conference was that it provided a space for critical questioning within the design world with likeminded people.

Jiye: As a non-European person, once I saw the announcement of *Attending [to] Futures*, I thought it would be interesting to participate in a project about what needs to be unlearned in design education. I wanted to learn how to organize and structure a conference, as well as deep-dive into diverse academic perspectives from a range of international people. I got my bachelor's degree in South Korea, which has a different educational system than Germany and other western countries. Experiencing the conference was meaningful for me because it made me aware of things I never deeply thought about or acted upon before. Also, a motivation was that I wanted to do something with peers together at KISD and immerse myself in the school after Covid.

Tomás: I think it was very critical to do something together. In that sense, I feel the conference project managed to implement its content into its structure. The students were participating not only to move chairs or make coffee. We were involved, we were chatting with the speakers, we curated the space, we were part of the selection committee, we were in charge of moderations. And we had this team spirit. We were all committed to this equally. There wasn't really a hierarchy. I think that was the core value for me, and this experience affects my work a lot.

Sally: This lack of hierarchy is really unusual in the design world; both academically and professionally. Even though the conference was an accredited project and curricula activity, I did not feel an obligation to perform or compete, but rather wanted this experience to be as wholesome as possible. The problem is that this competitive design culture is rooted in many of us and it also stems from educational systems. In my bachelor studies we always had this underlying culture of 'I don't want to show you my work before it's done'. In this conference, however, I learned how to not be competitive but rather develop my strengths. This was the first project that I had at KISD in person, and I think it's the only one I ever had where I felt like there was nothing to compete about. And I was proud of what we were doing.

Jiye: I totally agree with Sally. In my experience, design education systems provoke competitiveness among students, for instance, when it's about who gets more acknowledgement for their work or who gets promised a bright future in the industry. Students easily lose their trust in each other. In my opinion, the most valuable thing of the conference was making time and space for and with students who collaboratively contributed. This experience shaped my personal perspective and also my M.A. thesis topic, which explores ways of envisioning 'good design processes'. The talks, workshops, and discussions among the participants inspired me throughout my studies.

Johanna: As design students currently studying in an educational institution in Europe, what do you think needs to change? What do you see changing in design or maybe in yourselves?

Jiye: Expecting radical changes in design education through a few events would be unrealistic, as this is not only about design, but also about social and cultural structures.

While the conference included international speakers and students from a variety of cultures and backgrounds, when it comes to my own experiences in design institutions in both South Korea and Germany, my projects and seminars were not as inclusive or diverse. Even though it seems like all designers talk about inclusivity and diversity nowadays, we need to act to make it more diverse and inclusive. It is good to talk about it, but we really need to find out how to change the curriculum accordingly. Personally, I would love to see more awareness of these shortcomings. *Attending [to] Futures* was a joint effort towards that. It was like planting a seed in participants.

In terms of what needs to change, I can not speak for all non-European students, however, I can say that I often felt like an outsider in design projects and lectures. I had thoughts like 'Would non-European perspectives be valuable for them?'. I often had mixed feelings. 'Did I learn something wrong as someone from a non-Western and non-European country?', 'Am I wrong?'. I do feel certain judgment.

Tomás: I think everything needs to change. Everything has to change in order for us to understand new things. I'm thrilled that we represent diverse identities in this conversation. Because so far my design education and my perspective on design education has been so utterly European. The school in Chile, where I did my undergrad, was reformed under the lead of Joseph and Anni Albers. I don't understand a design that is not European. Now I am trying to embrace and bring back some things from my own culture. And I am so happy to have the supervisors that I have, who facilitate a path for me to do that.

We need to stop arguing if something is design or not, or that this type of research is design, and this isn't. Who cares? We can change everything. We have the right to change it. But it will not change until those in positions of power are willing to make the necessary changes. And that is the hard part. For example, in a school where the teaching staff is predominantly male and exclusively white, I would say we need to change the people who are sitting there. And I'm not saying we should kick people out; perhaps it's a matter of generational turnover. I believe it will only change once the domino effect becomes large enough. In 15 years, when one of us has a professorship or some of us are giving a keynote at a conference; people like us who were able to take part in a collaborative project in our first years of design education, we'll be a bit closer.

Sally: Design is still being taught based on a canon that is outdated. The world is moving so rapidly and opening up to itself. There are tools and means that allow us to learn about different cultures, societies, techniques, and the variety of doing things alternatively. But when the topic revolves around design and its education, we tend to resort back to these "pillars" that lack relevance. It feels like the motto is 'We have to go back a hundred years and have to look at how design was studied, taught, and done in the West'. Even though a generational turnover will definitely benefit design education, there needs to be a fundamental acknowledgment of what is going wrong now. What is lacking in design education for me is having people who have a different point of view and are aware of their relevance. Talking about "primitive" or "traditional" non-design can not be tolerated anymore and coming from a different part of the world, I should no longer be perceived as "different". Design needs to be more accepting. Right now it is still lacking this self-reflexive criticism, even though we consider ourselves to be a very critical field.

Johanna: This is a crucial point, I think. Curiously, the general narrative about art and design schools is that they offer a particularly critical and politically engaged environment. Currently, the task for art and design schools may be to turn claims to "progressive" education into self-reflexive critique and an attention to the politics and ideologies of our field's histories and practices.

Jiye: In my opinion, the essential point is that you have to re-think design before you design. In my design education so far, there has been no such self-reflexive step, or discussion about implicit biases. But we need to be more sensitive towards that.

Sally: Since the conference I have been really interested in rethinking design education, but I feel that it's a very small community. I'm immersed in this community because I search for it, but it's not really a big space, if you are looking at it from the outside. The topics of design colonization and appropriation, for example, can be non-existent in some educational institutions if there aren't any people advocating for them. This demotivates me a little bit. When you are immersed in these topics you feel like you're changing the world – but as I get more exposed to different design institutions, I am discovering that people are not even aware of the very basic problems. There were many discussions during and after the conference where people highlighted the fact that they were completely unaware that the majority of the world feels misrepresented and appropriated in design. This needs to be tackled in design education but I don't know if it is. To some extent, I think, this critical bubble is becoming smaller and smaller. What is changing? How is it changing? I don't know if it is, because arguing and debating with people who are only interested in aggressively opposing you is often frustrating. I would prefer discussing these topics in a safe space rather than discussing it with someone who refuses to acknowledge that there is a problem.

Tomás: I disagree with you super politely. Because yeah, we are a bubble but we have more and more little bubbles that are going to have more and more little bubbles itself. In a way, it's spreading into different realms. And that makes it even nicer. It's like a self-replicating organism of knowledge that is going around.

Johanna: The conference, for example, did not emerge out of thin air but was itself a coming together of many such bubbles. Not just the contributions but also the questions and discussions that went into planning this event are informed by social movements such as Black Lives Matter, #MeToo, or Fridays for Future as well as a rich history and community of scholars, activists, and artists who have been pushing for equity and social justice inside and outside of academia. But I think both of your positions can be true at the same time and are equally part of an experience that probably most of the conference attendees share.

Sally: Coming to KISD the day after the conference made me feel like everything was a dream. The next day I woke up and everything was back to normal. I had this energy of ideas and things that I needed to discuss but everyone was just continuing as usual with their day and wanting to grab lunch with me. And in my head I was like: What lunch?! Were you here yesterday?!

Jiye: I think that is a good point, Sally. Personally, I would like to believe that design education can help design students to understand the role of design in larger contexts. Movements like Black Lives Matter or #MeToo for example are not from designers – they come from citizens. So design students and designers have a responsibility to open up their spaces and collaborate to help drive these social movements. And I see that people working in design academia are trying to build networks and think about design justice outside of their design bubbles. Sometimes, I feel like designers don't have much power to change things systemically, but at the very least we are capable of making small and "bubbly" yet significant steps. This leads to questions like 'What would be essential in order to change design education so that it is more aligned with the lived realities of people?'

Tomás: Speaking about change, I think we do have power as designers—a lot of power: we can design academia, we can design curricula, we can design change, and design our attitude towards change. From an activist point of view we can understand our positioning in the world. Some change is going to be having a coffee with a very conflicted colleague, sometimes it's going to be a course. Our role as activists and our actions can be designed. I am also super happy if someone who was at this conference or who I have been teaching will five years later work in marketing and branding with a more feminist perspective.

Sally: I completely agree. But the initial task is to incorporate critical theory in design institutions. We need to teach and learn how to question design practice with regard to its politics. How do we include these issues into this curriculum? How do we put these topics into this institution? Critical conversation often requires someone or something to ignite it. This conference highlighted the need for both a practical and theoretical rethinking of our own field, but the conversation needs to continue now.

Johanna: So … what's next for you?

Sally: The first thing that comes to mind, is discussing these topics with the next design generations. In January for example, Tomás and I are given the opportunity to teach a class in the M.A. program. We are proposing an open and critical space for discussion. We want to give the new students the chance to think about the very things that we just discussed because we never had that chance in an academic context. This is something that was a direct effect of the conference. We are given complete freedom to discuss what we think needs to be said and in a way, this is a start of change. And hopefully we can be a part of it positively.

Tomás: What's next? Our class, which is like an echo of the conference. What I think is good for us about this class is the experience of being told: 'Okay, you have 12 hours with the new M.A. students, go for it!' What we wanted to do with this was super open. We, as students who one year ago were organizing and thinking about the concepts of the conference, are now in the process of digesting and seeing how this continues. This openness continues in my M.A.s thesis work. My supervisors and I are not discussing if something is design or not design, we are saying 'yes' and 'let's see what happens'. That is part of the research. So that's what is next for me? Finishing my M.A. thesis and hopefully starting a PhD in the future.

Jiye: For me, what's next or what changed in my practice maybe … I'm now learning about both theoretical and practical design ethics for my M.A. thesis, and I'm hoping to bring meaningful findings from it. From the ongoing reflection after the conference finished, I realized that I want to become a person who is sensitive and critical towards matters of politics in design.

Every time I talk about ethics with people for my research—even professional designers—they make a face like 'What are you talking about?' or 'What is ethical design supposed to be?' I see some challenges to overcome and opportunities to engage with both designers and non-designers in participatory approaches for better design processes, either in business or public matters. *Attending [to] Futures* helped me a lot to re-think my capabilities and interests in my field—service design. And in the future, my dream is that we care about talking about a variety of topics that came from the conference more and more.

(IM)POSSIBLE EXITS, SILENCED AFFECTS

Design Futures and Disciplinary Mobilities

(Imad Gebrael)

This chapter is a child of 2021: troubled, emotional, and sporadically uncertain. It is entangled with a backdrop of turbulent social and political events, during which, communities I identify with have lost—and gained—substantial support, having to continuously defend a basic right of breathing on indigenous land. Within "critical design" circles, limitations of presumed intersectional solidarity became evident in the wake of global antiracist movements, such as Black Lives Matter or protests against displacement of families in Sheikh Jarrah, Palestine, and the following attacks on Gaza in May of 2021.

Self-identified decolonial and feminist design scholars faced the urgency of actionable solidarity: to speak up or to remain silent. Alas, it was their silence that spoke volumes on a field in turmoil, where engagement is often challenged by—and rarely challenges—neoliberal practices. Facing this disciplinary turmoil, plotting an exit route beyond apolitical programs and volatile design engagements, becomes a necessity. The potentials for this exit are discussed within the scope of this chapter under the term *disciplinary mobilities.* Thinking through disciplinary mobilities, I aim to induce the multiple potentials of a design exit, with a growing number of designers seeking refuge in other disciplines and design students resisting from within: continuously silenced in their demands for diversity, for actionable change, for unions, and for decolonization. This essay challenges divergent imaginations of future-makings by questioning: Whose futures? Whose pasts? Whose guilt? Whose design? Who is attending and who is attended to? Who is silenced and who is silent? Who is affecting and who is affected? Who is to stay and who is to exit performative design structures?

This chapter is a child of 2021: born in Germany to an Arab migrant. While initially presented during the design conference *Attending [to] Futures*, it is written and edited with a feeling of unsafety lurking in the background. This feeling is not necessarily caused by any of the conference organizers or attendees—for whom I feel nothing but gratitude—, but rather caused by my heightened engagement with design, research, and education during the last three years of total disruption. In less palatable words, by disappointment.

The political events of May 2021 remain very present. In fact, another round of attacks on Gaza is happening as I sit to edit this piece for publishing; it is August 2022, a moment producing further classifications of civilized/uncivilized war refugees and explicitly racist discussions on border regimes and deservability. While writing this piece, the growing frog in my throat might obstruct the airflow at times. I ask you to share this obstruction. This frog might do some typing on my behalf, a line here and there, some shade, some bitterness. Frogs can be loud and slippery, much like affects we cannot contain. They stick, they slip, they jump, they grunt. Ribbit.

This chapter is a child of 2021: it questions my alterity in a field I have invested a lot in and recalls moments of fragile solidarity and loud silences, cynically of course, as cynicism and indirectness have been inherently present in thinking through Arabic, my mother tongue. I am not writing to apologize for cynicism or indirectness for I find them beautifully poetic at times, but to ask you to read vulnerability through the discomfort that this piece might inflate. I invite you as I invite myself to sit with this discomfort, to allow it to brew, to transform. I invite you as I invite myself to host an aquaculture of frogs in our throats without seeking solutions, as hard as that might sound to an audience of designers molded by transactional solutionism since the conception of the discipline. I have assertively decided to foreground vulnerability, in line with Ruth Behar who advocates for acknowledging the heart by claiming that "when we write vulnerably, others respond vulnerably" (Behar 1997, 16) and this is indeed the response I hope for. I invite you to experience this piece as an investment in critical discomfort as formulated by Wayne Modest (Oswald and Tinius 2020, 65–74); a kind of critical discomfort about the taken-for-granted-ness we have of ourselves (Oswald and Tinius 2020, 65-74). Modest, whose work is driven by a concern for more historically contingent ways of understanding the present, especially in relation to material culture and museum collections, claims that much of the narrative of the constitution of Europeanness is that taken-for-granted-ness: "This is who we are. This is what we are. This is what we should be" (ibid., 72). While he addresses museums to participate in this critical discomfort, this shaking up, I urge designers and design educators to join this demand to see and understand otherwise, and in relation. "There is a world out there and we share it" (ibid.).

(Im)possible Exits: Uncertain Futures

A critical turn took place in the early 1970s among scholars in the humanities and social sciences to make cultures, criticality, decoloniality, and plural relations the foci of contemporary debates, whilst also demonstrating a shift in emphasis toward meaning and away from a positivist epistemology.[1] Design is only 50 years late to this debate. The field is in need of a shift into a new era outside of the art academy, away from solutionism and design-positivism.[2]

In my attempt to unpack such entangled relations, I will start by introducing *The Design Exit,* a project that negotiates possible or impossible repositionings of design outside of the art school system—precisely in the European context—while discussing the overdue critical turn in design education as a form of alter-reality.

The Design Exit was launched as a series of digital roundtables during the autumn of 2020 which I hosted with a generous group of guest participants, including Ahmed Ansari, Chris Lee, Eva Gonçalves, Maya Ober, Nadine Rotem, Nina Paim, Sara Kaaman, Sérgio Miguel Magalhães, and Zoy Anastassakis. The aim was to start an active, open-ended debate about design, design education, and disciplinary repositioning. The project was conceived as a response to multiple complaints by friends, colleagues, and students who could at the time trace a deceiving pattern of political engagement within design programs across multiple European countries.

---

1 Also referred to as "positivism," this refers to the school of research thought that sees observable evidence as the only form of defensible scientific findings. Positivist epistemology, therefore, assumes that only "facts" derived from the scientific method can make legitimate knowledge claims. It also assumes the researcher is separate from and not affecting the outcomes of research. "What Is Positivist Epistemology," IGI Global, accessed May 12, 2021, https://www.igi-global.com/dictionary/positivist-epistemology/23062

2 A common jargon promoting design as a problem-solving discipline, amplified by subfields like design thinking and innovation labs. Such understandings of design—when intersecting with Othered communities—create volatile, void, and apolitical outcomes favoring design (and designers) over accountable, sustainable engagement.

What became apparent in the roundtables was that academic structures within design education were increasingly seen as abstract and impossible to navigate, especially for international students who face challenges beyond discursive positioning. While looking for higher design education, prospective students—often with too much at stake—walk a dangerous minefield, continuously misled by programs trying to tick multiple boxes but rarely delivering on their promises. For fellow Lebanese designers that seek opportunities to leave Lebanon after the total collapse of the political and economic system, for example, a design program is sometimes a way out, an unclaimed, unlabeled, unofficial asylum-seeking process for individuals struggling with different forms of oppression, wanting an exit route that is not necessarily terminal. Such bodies present a lucrative market opportunity as well as a diversity token for design academies seeking international student investments. However, art schools housing design programs promoting criticality lack a basic infrastructure allowing for critical thinking, as well as adequate exposure to theoretical frameworks, political discussions, and access to different forms of research. Curating a selection of Metahaven publications is nothing but lacking, if we were to reflect on the selective and often-apolitical engagements with socioeconomic structures within European art-schools.

Knowledge is buildable; design students operating within the bubble of their often remote and mystical Harry-Potter campuses need to access other institutions, events, collaborations, discussions, dissertations, libraries, mobilization groups, and communities. Designers have the potential to advance a pre-existing body of research and contribute (to) transdisciplinary research methods but they are often trapped in a vacuum. The vacuum created by art schools across Europe promotes "critical design" while it simultaneously focuses on excessive production. Such systemic contradictions are often designed and sustained by a teaching body seeking a ticket to the hype-train without wanting to deal with any form of accountable change. Speed-boarding, stress-free. This volatility often fuses selective politics within academic curricula to mediate a brand I call *Engagement™*.

Engagement™ cynically denotes a trend among designers and design programs engaging with sociopolitical matters and addresses design's historical complicity in building structures of inequality. Especially visible on social media platforms, *Engagement™* performers embody a shift from celebrating the "creative (European male) genius" and the focus on function, value, and quality, to centering criticality. This trend, aiming at resurrecting the field from its ashes, manifests itself in emerging design programs. A quick look at design master's programs in Germany and the Netherlands shows a massive emergence of disciplines like social design, critical studies, visual cultures, situated design, geo-design, gender design, contextual design, and ecology futures, to name but a few. Master programs keep on rebranding on a yearly basis in hopes of attracting student-investors to the business model of European design education and its gated art school system. This fluctuation of performative engagement points to deeper problems, questioning the tight operational structures within the art-school system and calling for a radical design-exit, as discussed within the scope of this chapter.

Let me restate that I am not arguing against design programs experimenting with their positioning and seeking to advance their political content.

In fact, I am all for open access to criticality and for mainstreaming theoretical debates even at the risk of emptying them from their "presumed," exclusive value. Recent debates on decolonization have gained momentum in design education and decolonial scholars raised valid concerns against the volatile engagement of design with decolonization and the dangers of using such frameworks as thematic topics, or even as metaphors favoring settler futures (Tuck and Yang 2012, 1–40). With such concerns in mind, I still stand in favor of mainstreaming knowledge processes for they were never meant to live in exclusive academic structures.

Moving beyond the notion of the "broken world" (Fry n.d., 1–2), I suggest an approach meeting the social sciences, anthropology to be exact, somewhere in a liminal futuristic space where design students are taught qualitative and quantitative research methods and can therefore access different disciplines. I am not promoting anthropology as a solution (this essay is clearly anti-solutionism, as stated earlier) but as a potential ground for elements of para-siting,[3] co-laboration,[4] and multimodality[5] within the broken, colonial university system. I am all for abolishing disciplines, to begin with for *The Master's Tools Will Never Dismantle the Master's House* as Audre Lorde (2018) so perfectly states, but until then, I suggest occupying space from "without" (the art school).

I am calling for leaving the art school campus behind, for it to dwell in its mysticism, its constant pursuit of the contemporary and its stigma of the misunderstood creative genius, and focus on a space where designers are in exchange with historians, scientists, data analysts, journalists, sociologists, and anthropologists. Where designers work in—and with—the field rather than at it. In that ethnographic approach, designers are not expected to reproduce ethnography's colonial history, nor its exclusive focus on the problem, but rather address problems collaboratively and systemically, as the verve for design's approach to solving problems can stand in the way of addressing the complex systems that create the problem in the first place (Chin 2016).

During the aforementioned *Design Exit* conversations, the group discussed the tight grid of hesitations when negotiating a complete repositioning of design programs and curricula. A very subjective selection of such discussions reveals two main problematic clusters identified as "present bodies", including those directing and occupying the academy through reenacting its power dynamics, and "absent histories", of those invited as tokens, subjects, themes, and offered precarious teaching opportunities. Entanglements of the bodies blocking access and those resisting, intensify design's ontological turn and move the positioning debate from a housing crisis (inside/outside of the art school) into structural impossibilities: the European art school—as we know it—is in fact no longer habitable.

Disciplinary Mobilities: Gated Futures

While reflecting on futures created by and through design practices, as well as the futures created within design itself at times of heightened skepticism, a pattern reveals itself. In the last year, a number of design research colleagues and I decided to continue our research in anthropology with varying degrees of overlapping with design-adjacent matters. These overlapping experiences draw a momentum of disciplinary migration extending

---

3   Refers to collaboration between multiple sites of knowledge: a type of field situation that neither takes the shape of horizontal relations nor implies the erasure of (disciplinary) differences. On the contrary, the parasitical collaboration… is often brought into existence against a background of disciplinary frictions, differing knowledges, epistemic diversity and social misunderstandings. Estalella, Adolfo, and Tomás Sánchez Criado, eds.. *Experimental Collaboration: Ethnography Through Fieldwork Devices.* Berghahn Books, 2018.

4   Co-laborative: joint epistemic work aimed at producing disciplinary reflexivities not interdisciplinary shared outcomes. Jouhki, Jukka, and Tytti Steel, eds. "Co-laborative anthropology: Crafting reflexivities experimentally." In *Ethnos*, translated by Jörg Niewöhner , 81-125. 2016. https://edoc.hu-berlin.de/bitstream/handle/18452/19241/Niewoehner2016-Co-laborative-anthropology.pdf

5   Multimodality and its (occasional) double, multisensoriality, as terms that have recently been utilized in anthropology for thinking about and with the media ecologies—that is, the multiple media(tions)—in which we live. Dattatreyan, E. Gabriel, and Isaac Marrero-Guillamón. "Introduction: Multimodal Anthropology and the Politics of Invention." *American Anthropologist* 121, no. 1 (2019): 220-228.

transdisciplinary interests and maturing into a series of routes leading to potential elsewheres (Mittermaier 2012, 247–65).

Like most migratory journeys, they start from a place of need. They are often symbolizing a neck stretching high, desperately seeking air. Suffocation is not a metaphor, it is a direct result of oppressive structures leading to voluntary or involuntary exiles. Experiences collide and so do migratory routes in constant renegotiation with mobility regimes, but what largely unites migrant bodies like my own, for example, is a shadow of loneliness that journeys with and sticks to them; a thin attachment to abandoned homes and potential futures, quoting Omar Kasmani (2019, 1–36) as he affectively writes the city. Inasmuch as attachment in Kasmani's work refers to possibilities of contact and modes of attunement, the term "thin" in his work does not denote weak or watered-down relations. Instead, it is "a figure of potential … amid bare conditions of porosity, thin reminds us that there is a clearing outside linear time, that every now and then, an opening is created for feeling and knowing, knowing by feeling" (ibid., 35).

On the lookout for such porous openings away from design as a field of excessive solutions, I embarked on a journey towards a field of excessive inquiry: anthropology. I felt exiled for a while but I was eager to think rather than do, in a field that is not necessarily less guilty of upholding coloniality for, in fact, anthropology stems from colonization and was the main tool for its sustenance for a long time. Weeks later, I started noticing parallel stories occurring in "critical design" circles. A number of colleagues are in fact actively looking for potential futures outside of design. This growing number is finding shelter in anthropology as the latter develops a fascination for design and designerly ways wof making. One could argue that this entanglement has always been there, taking on different names: from visual and digital anthropology to multimodal anthropology, a rapidly growing and highly criticized sub-discipline in active exchange with design processes.

Designers, however, still resist a detachment from design despite their oftentimes harsh criticism of it. One could talk extensively about toxic relationships, but the focus of this chapter remains on disciplinary mobilities.

Brazilian curator, design researcher, and co-founder of *Futuress* Nina Paim was one of the scholars working on a doctoral project at the laboratory of Design and Anthropology at Esdi/Lada in Brazil. Paim's decision does not come from a place of leaving design behind, however, but from a wish to share space with people who are thinking interesting and urgent things in her mother tongue and cultural context. It stems from an urge to hold space and learn from-and-with them. She sees her partial disciplinary migration, as I would call it, as an excuse—or a bridge—to be on both shores at the same time. Design "the land of epistemic ignorance" as she identifies it, makes part of her, a part of her flesh, "whether I like it or not" she states (Nina Paim, personal e-mail, May, 2021). In Paim's case, it is not about abandoning the field, but rather about staying *with* the trouble of design, or *troubling* design (ibid.).

Activist, educator, designer, and researcher Maya Ober is on a similar journey. After running *Depatriarchise Design* which recently merged with *Futuress,* Ober started a PhD project in anthropology. Since her research is concerned with the everyday feminist practices of design education, anthropological perspectives came into play. Ober sees disciplinary divisions as a way of controlling knowledge production and gatekeeping:

> By crossing the disciplinary boundaries and working within and across multiple sites and modes of knowledge production, we can disturb the status quo and destabilize existing practices of knowing, as M. Jacqui Alexander puts it… (Maya Ober, personal e-mail, May, 2021).

expresses Ober, who identifies herself as an insider-outsider, neither anthropologist nor designer, rather *both* and *and*.

More pragmatic variables gain importance in pursuing rather precarious research at a doctoral level. Design is often excluded from lists of eligibility when applying for research grants, which prohibits designers from researching within design systems and facilitates their migration to the social sciences as their next logical habitat where funding structures *precariously* exist. Ober positions the two fields in different temporalities while refusing to idealize either of them for their obvious historical engagements with colonialism and aspires to contribute to their transformation by working from *within* (ibid.).

Swiss-Egyptian graphic designer and researcher Mayar El Bakry seeks a different route as she looks for alternatives to a field that cannot attend to past, present, and future problems of neoliberalism. El Bakry turned to a food-based practice because it is one of the few things that connect us: "we all need to nourish ourselves" she rightfully exclaims (Mayar El Bakry, personal e-mail, May, 2021).

The recent trend of design's fascination with anthropology is not a one-sided love story. Anthropology has been for years flirting with designerly ways of making, researching, and producing. The recent culmination of this fondness is called *multimodality*. By definition, multimodality offers a line of flight for an anthropology yet to come:

> Multisensorial rather than text-based, performative rather than representational, and inventive rather than descriptive. This reimagined anthropology requires a move away from established forms of authorship, representation, and academic publishing toward projects that experiment with unanticipated forms, collaborations, audiences, and correspondences. (Dattatreyan and Marrero-Guillamón 2019, 220–8)

In other terms, it is the culmination of critical design projects of the last few years, repackaged for scientific academic consumption.

Multimodal debates align with critical design discourses on decolonization and claims for an ontological turn in design (Ahmed Ansari, personal communications, September, 2020). Proponents of multimodal anthropology argue for method and knowledge production that can grow to encompass and move through other modes, media, and technologies—particularly those that are rooted in cultures of the Global South or, as Elizabeth Chin says, "beyond whiteness." (Hannabach 2018) The multimodal approaches Chin is arguing for, then, urge researchers to expand beyond Eurocentric, colonialist, and ableist ways of doing what we do, with or without technology (ibid.).

Multimodal courses are taught by anthropologists, however, often ignoring "critical design" perspectives and catering to anthropological ways of generating relations through solutionism, a discourse that has been continuously problematized by designers. Multimodal anthropologists continuously promote the political potentials of "making" without adequately problematizing overproduction and accessibility, while often focusing on the binary of the "textual" versus the "multimodal," ironically working through text to challenge the hegemony of textual output.

This disciplinary exchange highlights a clear power imbalance: design is welcome in academia but designers often remain excluded. The two fields are already communicating in absurdly divergent monologues. The problem is that they either cannot or do not want to hear each other because a fruitful dialogue has the potential to radically challenge disciplinary borders and threaten academic chair hoarders. Gatekeeping is not new to academic structures often reproducing precarious conditions and limiting access.

Silenced Affects: Troubling Futures

Engaging with potential exits of design towards other academic disciplines does not aim at discrediting the ongoing subversive efforts to trouble and disrupt the field from within. The art academy, despite its countless flaws, currently houses an increasing number of feminist killjoys (to borrow Sara Ahmed's term, 2010). This growing interest in political work that crosses the boundaries of the educational system and challenges its stagnant conservatism represents the light at the end of the dark tunnel I am yearning for in this piece. Stories of hopeful mobilizations from *within* are thriving. They are often led by student groups against various forms of oppression: self-organized, fearless, and undoubtedly louder than the excruciating silence of their educators.

Compelled to respond to the urgency of the moment instigated by the occupation in Palestine in May and June 2021, art and design students engaged in various forms of activism: they self-organized, visualized, mediated, published, wrote statements, challenged institutions, demonstrated, refused, resisted algorithmic discrimination, found creative solutions against digital shadow-banning, and went on multiple strikes. Art and design student groups understood the rather obvious matters of liberation as an unconditional stance against the cruelties of occupation, despite the private and public insistence on dismissing their demands under one claim: "it's complicated." Such claims do nothing but reinforce the silence.

The example of the M.A. Disarming Design students of Sandberg Institute is one of many hopeful nucleons of possible future-makings within design education. The following sentences are a direct quote from their statement addressing the executive board of the Gerrit Rietveld Academy:

> In light of the current international liberation movement for Palestine, and the historical and monumental reclamation of established discourses and narratives, we … find it immoral that Sandberg and Rietveld have remained publicly silent so far. Your claim to teach decolonial theory and yet have failed to take the smallest of action in solidarity with Palestine… (Disarming Design 2021).

Soon after their statement, the university reacted with the following lines:

> We want to speak out against violence and oppression, and condemn all actions that violate human rights. We stand in solidarity with our

> Palestinian students and the people of Palestine in their fight for freedom, self-determination, equality and justice against forced dispossession, settler-colonialism and apartheid. (Sandberg Instituut and Gerrit Rietveld Academie 2021)

Similar statements were released by numerous other student groups as well as artists' and designers' collectives calling for solidarity, while reactions ranged between silent and silencing.

Silencing students after complaints is not atypical to institutions pre-social media but is becoming increasingly harder at times of effective and affective digital activism, often dismissed by the intellectual class as Instagram clicktivism. Recent waves of clicktivism have reclaimed decade-old narratives. We experienced students-as-teachers in the post-institutional digital space where disciplinary boundaries do not matter and "discipline" comes closer to its genealogy: an oppressive structure made to instill power asymmetries.

During that period and despite the extreme fatigue and isolation of the pandemic, students found creative ways to support communities in their collective political reclaimings. As tech-giants used algorithmic tools to ban or hide political content in Arabic, native speakers found a trick to get around the so-called "technical glitches" by writing Arabic without dots (also known as *nuqat* or diacritic points), for example, as the Arabic script was born dotless and remains readable as it morphs back and forth in its own temporalities. Such creative attempts were supported by numerous designers and design students who volunteered to provide additional tools for tricking and calling out algorithmic discrimination to counteract institutional silence.

As empowering as it sounds, this process that invokes multiple affects from silence, disappointment, refusal, and fatigue, all the way to liberation and hope, is not devoid of emotional labor. It lingers, sticks, suffocates, burdens, exhausts, violates, and even breaks. Student mobilizations as emotional labor are undoubtedly a form of complaint that, following Sara Ahmed, "teach us something, the truth even, the truth about violence, institutional violence, the violence directed towards those who identify violence, who say *no* to violence" (Ahmed 2021). It is a truth about surviving violent structures because "if we need to transform institutions to survive them, we still need to survive the institutions we are trying to transform" (ibid).

In this chapter, I argue for honest and self-reflexive criticism of disciplinary mobilities to potentially harness the wider prospects of design as a field in constant influx. Such possibilities are challenged by systemic, structural hurdles that might render critical future imaginations rather impossible.

Through reporting on recent student mobilization movements, I try to offer a hopeful thread that aspires to resist the loud silence of academic institutions facing political events. Such examples do not aim to romanticize political mobilization but to rather subvert hierarchies through speaking out, for I have personally witnessed the uncertainty, loneliness, and choking that this process might entail. Is it not fascinating how choking, speaking out, and spitting are tightly related opposites?

This chapter might have diverged from its track into a messy, meta-piece on criticism, but I doubt that criticism is enough. I am trying to engage with criticism as catharsis, one that emerges from and connects my sorrows to yours. I go full-circle here and end as I started with Ruth Behar on criticism: "we need other forms of criticism, which are rigorous yet not disinterested; forms of criticism which are not immune to catharsis; forms of criticism which can respond vulnerably, in ways we must begin to try to imagine" (1997, 175). It is precisely with cynical criticism, vulnerability, and discomfort that I invite you to reflect on the aquaculture of frogs inhabiting this piece as they were patiently waiting for you to read between the lines in hopes of futures that are less still, less stagnant, and undoubtedly less silent. Ribbit.

BIBLIOGRAPHY

Ahmed, Sara. "Feminist Killjoys (And Other Willful Subjects)." *The Scholar and Feminist Online* 8, no. 3 (Summer 2010). https://sfonline.barnard.edu/polyphonic/print_ahmed.htm.

Ahmed, Sara. 2021. "Complaint as Feminist Pedagogy." *Feminist Killjoys Blog*. Last modified June 16, 2021. https://feministkilljoys.com/2021/06/16/complaint-as-feminist-pedagogy/.

Behar, Ruth. *The Vulnerable Observer Anthropology That Breaks Your Heart*. Boston: Beacon Press, 1997.

Chin, Elizabeth. 2016. "Collaboration: Deviation." Correspondences, *Fieldsights*. Last modified October 10, 2016. https://culanth.org/fieldsights/collaboration-deviation.

Dattatreyan, E. Gabriel, and Isaac Marrero-Guillamón. "Introduction: Multimodal Anthropology and the Politics of Invention." *American Anthropologist* 121, no. 1 (2019): 220-228.

Disarming Design. 2021. "For Palestine." Accessed May 31, 2021. https://disarm.design/.

Estalella, Adolfo, and Tomás Sánchez Criado, eds.. *Experimental Collaboration: Ethnography Through Fieldwork Devices*. Berghahn Books, 2018.

Fry, Tony. n.d. "Design Education in a Broken World." *The Studio at the Edge of the World*. Accessed May 31, 2021. http://www.thestudioattheedgeoftheworld.com/uploads/4/7/4/0/47403357/fry-designeducation.pdf.

Hannabach, Cathy. "Elizabeth J. Chin on Dancing Beyond Whiteness." Interview by Cathy Hannabach. Imagine Otherwise, Ideas on Fire, January 2018. Audio, 14:28-26:46. https://ideasonfire.net/56-elizabeth-chin/.

IGI Global. "What Is Positivist Epistemology." Accessed May 12, 2021. https://www.igi-global.com/dictionary/positivist-epistemology/23062.

Jouhki, Jukka, and Tytti Steel, eds.. "Co-laborative anthropology: Crafting reflexivities experimentally." In *Ethnos*, translated by Jörg Niewöhner, 81-125. 2016. https://edoc.hu-berlin.de/bitstream/handle/18452/19241/Niewoehner2016-Co-laborative-anthropology.pdf.

Kasmani, Omar. "Thin Attachments: Writing Berlin in Scenes of Daily Loves." *Capacious: Journal for Emerging Affect Inquiry* 1, no. 3 (2019): 1-36.

Lorde, Audre. *The Master's Tools Will Never Dismantle the Master's House*. Penguin Modern. London, England: Penguin Classics, 2018.

Mittermaier, Amira. "Dreams from Elsewhere: Muslim Subjectivities beyond the Trope of Self-Cultivation." *Journal of the Royal Anthropological Institute* 18, no. 2 (2012): 247—265.

Oswald, Margareta V., and Tinius Jonas, eds.. *Museums are Investments in Critical Discomfort: Across Anthropology. Troubling Colonial Legacies, Museums, and the Curatorial*. Leuven University Press, 2020.

Sandberg Instituut and Gerrit Rietveld Academie. n.d. "Homepage." Accessed October 18, 2022. https://sandberg.nl/statement-rietveld-sandberg-and-gerrit-rietveld-academie.

Tuck, Eve, and K. Wayne Yang. "Decolonization is not a metaphor." *Decolonization: Indigeneity, Education & Society* 1, no. 1 (2012): 1-40.

A LIST OF LONGINGS

(Luiza Prado)

1. Shattering Futures

A blank sheet of paper. A text cursor blinks in the white background with unnerving regularity. Paint slowly dries on a brush. A pencil sits, untouched. Time is now measured in terms of infection rates, incubation periods, and statistics of death. There are no plans, no travel, no certainties; there is no tomorrow, only today. The present stretches out into the unknown.

    For the past year and a half, the COVID-19 pandemic has led the world through a series of exhausting and seemingly endless cycles of openings and closings of public life. As the virus made its way through the global routes of human movement, what many had been accustomed to understand as normality came to a standstill: from hugging loved ones to walking down the street to work, to sharing a closed, unventilated space with other human beings. No aspect of life remains impervious to the pandemic's gravitational pull: streets empty, restaurants and bars closed, gatherings banned; re-openings that simultaneously bring senses of relief and dread, excitement with a side of social burnout. The first few days of lockdown dragged into weeks, then months; now, a year and a half on, the initial sense of uncanniness and dread reshapes itself as alternating waves of numbness, exhaustion, burnout, fear, recklessness. As the ebbs and flows of lockdowns and re-openings crash over each other, tethering ourselves to a stable sense of reality feels as fugitive a state as water held in the palm of one's hand.

    In many ways, the pandemic feels like a suspension of time: a breath caught in the throat, the unbearable tension that builds up before exhalation. Perhaps time stopped when notices of postponements, cancellations, and redundancies started arriving—an ominous litany of unpredictable duration and deep repercussions for those of us navigating the precarious life of freelancing, zero-hour contracts, gig work, migration, and displacement. Perhaps it stopped when people yearning for closeness, for exchange, for collective experience, found themselves scattered around cities, countries, continents. Perhaps it stopped when borders started ossifying further and further, the walls of countries, states, cities, neighborhoods, buildings, apartments and houses resonating, louder and louder, the structures of power they were always meant to materialize. Perhaps time stopped when loss started creeping closer and closer, and even being together in mourning became impossible.

    Insurmountable distances, amplifying the sound of shattered, uncertain futures. An uncertainty that has, however, not weighed equally upon all. Resonating long established power structures, it is those most vulnerable that continue to pay the steepest price for the global crisis we are facing, amongst a dire lack of material, financial, and logistic support. The conservative governments of countries like the Netherlands or the United Kingdom initially tried to adopt the approach known as "herd immunity" which, instead of focusing on containing the virus by all means possible, starts from the premise that allowing the infection to spread in a controlled manner will create widespread resistance throughout the population. In Brazil, where I am from, a genocidal authoritarian government recklessly denied the gravity of the pandemic and the deadliness of the virus, withheld information and spread lies about proper prevention and treatment, and later on tried its best to prevent access to life-saving vaccines. Implicit in all of these strategies—from the UK to the Netherlands to Brazil—is the idea that the loss of human life is a fair price to pay for oiling the gears of the economy; that the immense suffering inflicted on the most vulnerable is the coin that pays for a semblance of normality for the wealthier sectors of a capitalist society. Ultimately, this is of course is part of a broader political project meant to normalize the perception of certain lives as disposable, sacrifices at the altar of productivity and capital; a strategy designed to delegate disaster to an Other. To those of us with ties to the Global South, this is not news. Denial and delegation, however, cannot contain a pandemic. In an article published last year on Al Jazeera, historian of science and epidemics Dr. Edna Bonhomme remarks:

> Pandemics do not materialise in isolation. They are part and parcel of capitalism and colonisation. ... products of capitalism—from war to migration to mass production and increased travel—contribute massively to the proliferation of diseases.
>
> In the world that we live in, where capitalism and the remnants of colonialism fuel wars, unprecedented migration waves, public health crises and an increasing dependency on international and intercontinental travel, epidemics are inevitable. And, as the COVID-19 outbreak makes crystal clear, no countries, including the members of the Global North, are immune to these outbreaks. (Bonhomme 2020)

When I wrote the first words in this speech, at the height of the first lockdown in Berlin, the pandemic had begun a mere two and a half months prior. At the time, I thought surviving the pandemic would require the explosive force of a sprinter. I was entirely wrong; instead, the decisions made by powerful political and economic actors over the past year have created a situation where we need, instead, the determined resilience of a marathon runner, keeping pace amongst the ruins of shattered futures.

As we speak, as this conference is taking place, less than half of the world's population has been vaccinated. Amongst all of the available vaccines, Germany recognizes only five—creating a political and economic border that further hinders the mobility of people from the Global South into this country, this continent. As we speak, those most vulnerable in this capitalist world—from precarious workers to Indigenous communities, from those who are homeless to those who are displaced—have borne the brunt of the impact caused by this pandemic. As we speak, Human Rights Watch reports that about 75% of all available vaccines have been distributed in merely 10 countries (Hegarty 2021).

As we speak, rich countries hoard vaccines and distribute booster shots—whilst leaving much of the world in a state of vaccine poverty. As we speak, rich countries have been hoarding millions of vaccine surpluses that they don't need—of which 241 million doses might soon go to waste due to lack of use, according to an BBC article published in September 2021 (ibid.). As we speak, these same countries get praise when they, seemingly admitting that there is indeed a vaccine inequality issue, donate insufficient, poverty doses to the Global South. As we speak, studies on vaccine manufacturing and rollout predict that, in a best-case scenario, at least a fifth of the world's population will not have access to a single dose until 2022. And so, the virus is successfully inserted into structures designed to maintain colonial order; a pathogen weaponized to further ossify borders, to maintain the most vulnerable in a state of economic, political, and infrastructural dependency. A delegation of disaster that leaves us—some of us—living amongst the ruins of shattered futures.

2. Scarce Justice is No Justice at All

It is within this context of crisis that, earlier this year, I was invited by the organizers of this conference to give this keynote, my first one in an academic conference. For about a decade now, I have been thinking and writing about the future in my work. For about a decade now, I have been thinking and writing about education, as well as teaching. A year and a half into the pandemic, and with another wave of infections now engulfing much of Germany, the ways in which we need to approach learning, exchange, and education have been changed for the foreseeable future, and most likely permanently. Futures have shattered, surely; but, I stress, that has not taken place in quite the same way for all.

This invitation came within the context of a trend I had been observing in recent years: As conversations on gender equality, racism, disability, and decolonization became more and more prominent in the public sphere over the past few years—thanks to the tireless work of committed activists and thinkers—, universities and art institutions found themselves in a situation where their usual course of action—ignoring, stifling, and censoring these topics—became increasingly difficult. As my friend and fellow member of Decolonising Design Danah Abdulla mentioned in her talk yesterday, the landscape was very different when we founded Decolonising Design as eight PhD students, in 2016. For so long, I felt we had been swimming against the current, trying to push conversations we knew were fundamental whilst weathering attacks from people with far more power than ourselves. We were ridiculed, bashed, told that our concerns were not valid, that our scholarship lacked acuity of thought and scholarly relevance. For me, the group was not only a way to exchange ideas, references, and push each other forward; it was also a fundamental source of emotional support, without which I would have been unable to withstand the pressure and most likely given up on my research.

But slowly, painfully slowly, things seemed to change. For these institutions, new courses of action were needed to maintain relevance; and so, the invitations started coming, to me and to peers who had long been working in similar and related topics. Invitations to be part of panels; invitations to write critical pieces examining an institution's inner workings; invitations to be part of diversity committees; invitations to give guest lectures. Often, these invitations came from the same institutions that had, not so long before, enacted and covered up all sorts of violences towards minority students and staff. Often these invitations came WHILE these institutions were engaged in such harmful, violent practices.

These invitations came as part of efforts to rehabilitate the public image of these very institutions, whilst the structural issues that caused problems in the first place remained unaddressed. Institutional leadership and power still remain in the hands of those who are white, mostly male, cis-gendered; they remain in the hands of those who are citizens, able-bodied, wealthy.

Fleeting contact with discussions on topics like decoloniality, gender equality, anti-racism, disability, or classism are seen as enough; a guest lecture, a panel, an exhibition, a symposium. Never a professorship, never a full course, never a reconsideration of hiring practices and leadership roles. Never a reconsideration of the very role of the institution in maintaining that which it now claims to question. When we demand these things, it's all too hard: The rules and regulations don't allow it. You need to understand. Be patient, your turn will come; for now, take this opportunity and be grateful for it. Our futures are an afterthought; addressing their destruction remains at the very bottom of the list of priorities. There is always something more urgent, more important; and so, we walk amongst ruins.

For the institution, however, these moments of fleeting contact are framed as a recognition that there is, indeed, a problem. But a recognition of what is wrong is not enough. We must enact systemic and structural change, or else we will grow accustomed to walking amongst ruins. Writing on the significance of institutional speech acts, scholar Sara Ahmed identifies a pattern of response that she calls the politics of admission: the idea that by admitting to being implicated in the enactment of injustices—such as institutional racism—one automatically becomes exempt of guilt. She points out the misguided notion that this act of admission is a solution in itself; an easy way out, because if one admits to have been unjust in a past, it is implied that this is not the case anymore. The utterance becomes the solution, an act that brings with it automatic absolution. Ahmed writes:

> The paradoxes of admitting to one's own racism are clear: saying "we are racist" becomes a claim to have overcome the conditions (unseen racism) that require the speech act in the first place. ... What is important here is that the admission converts swiftly into a declarative mode: the speech act, in its performance, is taken up as having shown that the institution has overcome what it is that the speech act admits to. Simply put, admissions of racism become readable as declarations of commitment to antiracism. What does this conversion of admission into commitments do? (Ahmed 2004)

Additionally, this injustice becomes depersonalized, ascribed to the institution, thus deflecting guilt from the individuals that have enacted said injustice. With the admission of guilt, it's like the problem is magically solved: There, we admitted to it, therefore we don't need to do anything anymore. And, mirroring the patterns of vaccine disparity we have witnessed during the pandemic, poverty doses of recognition are seen as enough. Just enough to appease us, to keep us waiting for the next dose, for the next donation of a little time and a little space; waiting for the next act of apparent generosity and care.

3. Walking Amongst These Ruins

The most sacred duty of an educational space is to protect those who come to it to learn. Here, I approach "learning" as a two-way process, where all involved in the educational process are both teachers and students—an understanding that is deeply indebted to the work of Brazilian educator Paulo Freire. And of course, learning doesn't happen in a vacuum; education cannot be removed from the context in which it unfolds because learning is a process of responding to the world. During the pandemic and the multiple, echoing crises of the past year and a half, moving towards online learning formats was far from a simple task. This shift had to come with a full revision of courses and contents, as well as a significant readjustment in the expectations of both students and staff. This, obviously, is a difficult transition across all disciplines and approaches— and one that had, as we know, to take place at a moment's notice. Sadly, but unsurprisingly, in many cases this transition happened at the expense of minority students and staff.

The shift to online teaching meant the loss of a certain spontaneity, a certain fluidity to in-class interactions and conversations; speaking to a computer simply does not feel the same as speaking while sitting together in the same room, sharing the same space. There is, therefore, an additional workload that becomes necessary if one is to develop truly engaging formats of learning—a workload that goes unpaid and unrecognized in the case of untenured staff working on temporary contracts with German universities, for instance. These contracts only pay for hours spent in class, and not for preparation time. These contracts are also seldom renewed, preventing the further advancement of discourse and research within the institution. This is often the only way to develop some kind of teaching experience for young academics—especially for those coming from marginalized positions, who will seldom be offered more just opportunities, especially if they lack previous teaching experience.
And since I believe it is fundamental to be clear in these conversations, let me offer an example: last year, for an entire semester of guest teaching during the first lockdown, I was paid 900 euros by a German university under these contract conditions. In order to pay for the time and effort it took to develop this course during the economic chaos caused by the pandemic, I worked on a number of other projects, to the point of exhaustion. The group of students I was teaching/learning with was absolutely extraordinary; sharp minds and open hearts that I believe will continue to enact deep changes in the landscapes of art, design, and curatorial practices over the course of their careers. I believed, and still believe, it was all worth it—but this feeling is entirely directed towards the students, not the institution itself.

Listening to the perspective of students in this context was, too, fundamental to develop a better understanding of how learning had been (and would continue to be) affected by multiple, overlapping crises. In an interview conducted with students from an art institution during the first lockdown in 2020, students expressed to me that teaching at this institution traditionally works in a very face-to-face manner—a dynamic that was brought into disarray by the pandemic. Online teaching thus required from them a complete reshuffling of established structures; adding to that, they were worried about online privacy, particularly considering the fraught political moment we are currently living throughout most of the world. Some were worried about what topics could be safely discussed in online platforms susceptible to surveillance—particularly students coming from places where their political views might put them in vulnerable positions.

There were, too, concerns about access: one cannot assume that all students own or can use adequate equipment for a seemingly simple online teaching session. In an informal conversation, a professor at an architecture course in Germany told me that, in the beginning of the first lockdown, he created a poll for his students with the intent of assessing their learning and working conditions from home. He was taken aback in realizing that a significant amount of his students did not, in fact, have a computer of their own, and either relied on the institution's equipment in order to be able deliver their work, or had to share a computer with others in their household. Over the past several months, I've heard similar accounts from professors in a number of different institutions, fields, and countries; my own students also recounted similar stories during the two courses I taught in 2020. For students in fields where access to specific (and often expensive) equipment, materials, and technical supervision is vital, this question becomes even more pressing. How is it possible, then, to continue one's education within this context?

Furthermore, regardless of discipline or interests, all students had to deal with a variety of issues relating to their living and working conditions—from lack of privacy at home to the loss of access to libraries and quiet study rooms, to loss of income during lockdowns. A long list of hurdles, with far-reaching consequences and no solution in immediate sight. How do processes of mutual learning amongst peers—part of the very foundation of education—take place within the parameters imposed by a still-ongoing pandemic? How do we work around the limitations of this new context and learn to circumvent its hurdles? How do we nurture caring, healing learning environments at a time when most people—from staff to students—suddenly find themselves under enormous amounts of pressure? How can an educational institution support its students in face of future-shattering events that actively cause enormous amounts of human suffering, and for which there is no set end in sight? How do we hold space for the grief, fear, and anxiety inherent to this situation?

For many students and staff at art institutions I have spoken to for this piece since last year, the COVID-19 crisis has also gained deeply personal contours. Many might have seen a parent or other relative fall ill, and felt the deep fear of loss compounded by the weight of distance. Some were directly affected by loss, touched by the particularly cruel contours that grief acquires through distance and isolation. Those of us who are of migrant experience like myself might be keenly aware of the fact that the reduced recognition of vaccines developed, manufactured, and distributed in the Global South means that traveling to be with one's family and loved ones has become significantly more complicated.

A sneeze or a cough, things that ordinarily would not incite any particular worry, might have caused anyone to become suddenly, sharply aware of our breathing, of the rhythm of our bodies, wondering if we were infected—or if we had infected someone else. Some might have, indeed, become sick. Many might have realized how deeply and fundamentally we rely on touch, on human connection and presence. And many, faced with the sudden expectation of a return to normality, might have struggled with social burnout and a lack of space to process the trauma of the past year and a half.

There are, additionally, a number of practical anxieties associated with the expectations and results of the educational process. For students set to graduate in the next months, especially for those whose research interests rely on field work, this means a profound uncertainty in relation to how their projects will be completed, as well as how and when the graduation could potentially take place. There is the anxiety of graduating in the context of an economic depression, where positions in academia and in the market, as well as funding for arts and culture, are set to shrink significantly. For immigrant students, the pandemic compounds the inherent difficulties of a change of environment and the subsequent process of adaptation. For many, this also entails learning to deal with new manifestations of xenophobia, sexism, and racism, specific and contextual to this new reality. Being away from one's family, friends, and place of origin is difficult in the best of circumstances; during a pandemic, this physical distance acquires an almost unbearable weight. Furthermore, there is a palpable frustration in not being able to enjoy the environment of the university—with all the spontaneous exchanges that it entails—as well as being suddenly separated from friends and peers that, typically, offer a fundamental emotional support system.

There is, too, the—often internal—pressure that many feel, an impulse to extract as much knowledge and experience as possible from a course in which they have invested significant amounts of time, effort, and money. In our interview, students at this institution remarked that the uncertainty and anxiety caused by this seem particularly present due to the lack of a contingent plan of action that could offer pupils a way to make up for lost course time when the crisis breaks. Enrolling at a higher education institution in the Netherlands isn't cheap—especially for non-EU citizens. There was, at the time, no option for pausing enrollment at the institute until the pandemic was over or controlled; the general attitude seemed to tend towards a certain asceticism, an attempt to weather this turbulence for as long as possible.

Indeed, the economic question is a pressing one. In our interview, students also expressed the feeling that the initial institutional response to the crisis privileged EU citizens. Many students—particularly those for whom employment options are limited due to visa restrictions—rely on gig work, zero-hour contracts, unregistered jobs, and other similar occupations to fund their studies. With the COVID-19 crisis, the source of income for many was wiped out from one day to the next, and the emergency financial assistance offered by the government—a non-renewable 250-euro monthly fund, to be paid for a total of three months—felt insufficient. Non-EU citizens often don't have access to the full spectrum local social support programs; this, compounded with the fact that many of these students may have less of a safety net—due to distance from families and relatives or economic conditions in their home countries, amongst other factors—makes them particularly vulnerable. The tuition alone at this institution amounted to thousands of euros a year; add to that the steep housing costs of living in a major city, food, and other basic expenses, and a genuinely alarming scenario is set. The two students with whom I spoke were careful to clarify that they did not know what was the financial situation of the institution itself at that moment, and that more transparency in relation to what is happening would have helped them feel more in touch with the process—and, most importantly, more qualified to make informed decisions about their future.

Yet, in spite of all these difficulties, I still noticed a deep sense of collectivity and camaraderie amongst the student body. Self-organization, pupils told me, has always been present in the dynamic of the institution; indeed, a few weeks before our conversation, the students had come together to write an open letter to the board of directors, demanding clarification and a clear position on these pressing issues. In our May 2020 interview, two students described this gesture as a way to demand more transparency from the institution about the next steps to be taken in relation to the pandemic. They felt that their voices, as students, were not being considered in the institution's negotiations with the government; additionally, due to the relative independence with which departments operate, there was uncertainty amongst the student body on whom to communicate their needs and concerns to.

This labor of organization is something the wonderful Imad Gebrael also mentioned in his brilliant earlier keynote, referencing the work of Sara Ahmed on the power of complaint. Now, I want to stand alongside Imad here, reinforcing the importance of Sara Ahmed's words, and linking them further to the work of Paulo Freire. In his influential book Pedagogy of the Oppressed (2005), Freire remarks that, very often, oppressions become sedimented, imprinted into the oppressed's own mind; this, according to Freire, is part of the process through which they are stripped of their humanity and agency. The pedagogy of the oppressed, Freire states, is a humanist approach to learning which must be formed "with, not for the oppressed (whether individuals or peoples) in the incessant struggle to regain their humanity" (2005, 48). Such a pedagogy "makes oppression and its causes objects of reflection by the oppressed," (ibid.) fostering the political engagement that constitutes the necessary foundation for liberation. Freire warns us that emancipation and liberation cannot, however, be bestowed by others; rather, they must emerge as a result of the oppressed's conscientização (ibid., 67)—that is, the process of gaining conscience about one's humanity, even in face of adverse circumstances. He remarks:

> … not even the best-intentioned leadership can bestow independence as a gift. The liberation of the oppressed is a liberation of women and men, not things. Accordingly, while no one liberates himself by his own efforts alone, neither is he liberated by others. (Ibid., 66).

4. A List of Longings

What does it mean, then, to attend to futures, particularly at a moment when so many of us walk amongst the ruins of what could have been? What does liberation mean in the landscape of art and design education?

To attend is to be present; to look after; to care for. Yet, in spite of vehement public diversity statements, design institutions have failed, and continue to fail those they outwardly claim to want to protect and support; those whose lives and livelihoods have been, and continue to be, most directly impacted by its decisions. How do these institutions, then, look after those whose futures have been shattered by multiple, devastating, sustained crises—from pandemics to conflicts to hunger to economic insecurity? What is present amongst the detritus of what could have been? How to care for those most affected by the forced suspensions of time enacted by these crises we have witnessed over the past few years?

As I reflect on these questions, I am overcome by a deep sense of gratitude towards the speakers who have contributed to this conference so far. The conversations I have had the privilege to witness here yesterday and today are urgent and fundamental; being able to hear and engage with thinkers who are making and will continue to make key contributions to design and art, as well as many other disciplines over the next years, is always exciting. But I am also compelled to stress, addressing the institution who is hosting this event: These conversations cannot end here. A conference with this lineup and focusing on these questions is a great first step, but it is only a first step. Alongside these public acts of commitment to radical work, there must be a commitment to a radical change from within; otherwise, nothing will truly change. The interviews and conversations that informed this keynote included some with students of color from this very institution, who recounted to me instances of discrimination that took place within these very walls. Yet, there was also a sense of hope; a sense that things could change, and that this event could help catalyze and articulate these changes.

So, in closing, let us share that sense of hope, that sense of possibility and impending change. Let us work towards rebuilding that which has been shattered, moving with the knowledge that we will not accept anything but justice—full and abundant justice.

I want to conclude this keynote with the words of Algerian poet Anna Gréki. Each single line in this poem, which she wrote while incarcerated for fighting for Algerian independence, feels to me like the most beautiful list of longings; longings to rebuild shattered futures. She writes:

> I press you against my breast my sister
> Builder of liberty and tenderness
> And I say to you await tomorrow
> For we know
> The future is soon
> The future is for tomorrow.
>
> — Anna Gréki.

BIBLIOGRAPHY

Ahmed, Sara. "The Nonperformativity of Antiracism." *Meridians* 7, no. 1 (2006): 104–26. Accessed 10 July 2023, http://www.jstor.org/stable/40338719.

Bonhomme, Edna. 2020. "What coronavirus has taught us about inequality." Aljazeera. Last modified March 17, 2020. https://www.aljazeera.com/opinions/2020/3/17/what-coronavirus-has-taught-us-about-inequality/.

Freire, Paulo. *Pedagogy of the Oppressed*. Continuum, 2005.

Hegarty, Stephanie. 2021. "Covid vaccine stockpiles: Could 241m doses go to waste?" BBC News. Last modified September 21, 2021. https://www.bbc.com/news/world-us-canada-58640297.

> **Acknowledgements**
>
> The following chapter is strongly inspired and influenced by shared experiences and conversations with Paul Steinmann, Mara Recklies, Anja Neidhardt, and Julia Meer.

RESONANCE AND ONTOLOGICAL DESIGN

On Facilitating and Obstructing Transformative Teaching and Learning Experiences in Design Education

(Lisa Baumgarten)

Prelude

In October 2021, when I read Sarah Ahmed's (2021) latest book about complaints, I decided to start this paper with a selection of complaints by students. The snippets were sent to me as a reaction to a theory seminar called *Messy History*[1] I offered digitally over the past year and a half.[2]

> "Dear Lisa,
> after I had been very reluctant to work on the course assignments, I got to the bottom of it and thought about where this demotivation was coming from. I felt pressured and confused.
> ...
> The situation overwhelms me quite a bit. The various tools and channels (which have to be checked daily), the deadlines scattered throughout the week and deadlines for every single step of the task demotivate me personally. Somehow this constant checking reminds me unpleasantly of school …. The rushed feeling of constantly missing something … triggers a restlessness that makes this already challenging situation very uncomfortable. And we are only talking about one of seven seminars here."

> "Dear Lisa,
> I find it very difficult at the moment to maintain a relaxed private life alongside university, because it is constantly assumed that one is available."

> "Dear Lisa,
> there is also a lack of clarity in the course regarding compulsory attendance. Is there any?"

> "Dear Lisa,
> the deadlines breathing down our necks, but hardly any personal interaction with you, leads to latent stress building up."

> "Dear Lisa,
> the scope of the current task is too big … how are the tasks assessed?"

> "Dear Lisa,
> In terms of content, there is a desire for an introduction to scientific work in the context of art history. And for an overview of 'mainstream design history,' as it will certainly be relevant in our professional practice as designers. Critical examination is indeed the most thorough form of working with sources. It's just that our knowledge of art and design history is not yet so extensive that one wants to happily indulge in critiquing. Hence, we'd appreciate a canon excursus. There was also a wish for a traditional lecture format."

> "Dear Lisa,
> Please don't encourage us next time you'll introduce a text. It leads to frustration and anger because I expected the text to be easier."

1 In the seminar *Messy History*, we looked at dominant narratives of canonical design historiography from an intersectional-feminist and decolonial perspective and discovered, among other things, that "history is not the past" (Munslow 2018). We approached highly topical issues such as neo-colonialism, gender difference, sustainability, and cultural appropriation and showed their connection to the design practice. Instead of linear narratives, dates, and name-dropping, this course focused on the approaches and tools for working with design history. Together we read, discussed, researched, practiced factual and logical argumentation, and overturned many of our preconceptions about design in the process.

2 I was trained as a communication designer and have been working in the field since 2014. In 2017, I started working as an adjunct lecturer [Lehrbeauftragte] and have been teaching design at multiple universities since then. I will use the term 'teaching' throughout this lecture and refer to myself as an educator. However, I would describe my practice in design education more that of a "critical design mediator" [*kritische Designvermittlerin*] who facilitates and mediates rather than "teaches" or "educates" in a classical sense. The seminar was initially conceived in collaboration with Julia Meer for the summer term 2020.

I have to admit it was, partially, very hard for me to read—as you can imagine. Especially the demand for a canonical design history and traditional lecture formats were tough ones for me because the seminar foregrounded perspectives on design history that canonical literature structurally leaves out.

I tried to facilitate the seminar together with the students, offering the space to bring in their own questions and sharing responsibility. I tried to embody my critical perspective by structuring the class around interaction and dialogue instead of a one-way lecture. I purposefully did not make attendance mandatory to cater to the students' various living situations at the time. It was our first digital semester, and I introduced the course concept as "experimental" and prepared a thorough outline of the course content to guide the students through the seminar on their own time. There was only Zoom, as the primary channel for communication, questions, and feedback. Reading the students' complaints, it felt like there was a huge discrepancy between what I intended and what the students assumed I intended. What was happening?

Even though some of those complaints were hard to digest, I was thankful that the students felt safe to voice them. Those complaints gave me a chance to improve my teaching practice in the framework the art university provided. But they also changed my perspective on design education. It became clear—over time and also looking back from post-pandemic times—that the student's observations and experiences weren't isolated incidents. They were a manifestation of an institutional structure that I have encountered in different shapes and forms throughout my teaching career. Talking to other educators about my experience made me realize that I was not alone.

As an educator in design in German higher education, I encounter similar complaints particularly often in programs which are characterized by extremely tightly timed, detailed curricula and modules that hardly allow students to breathe between seminars and assignments. The curriculum that has to be completed gets between the teachers and the students (Rosa 2016). Due to the time pressure and lack of time, students hardly seem to have a chance to figure out which areas they find particularly interesting or suit them best. Along with that comes the impression that there is an "authorized knowledge" that gets passed from an educator as knower to the learner as not-knower (see Sternfeld 2010, 15). Because students feel driven and rushed, the likelihood of building a connection to the content decreases—and with it the interest and the sense of self-efficacy.

The so-called "time of contact" between educator and student is usually low. I learned from a course leader responsible for the admission procedure that each student—or "intake" as she called them—is entitled to a calculated amount of contact time with teachers, determined by university management.

As a critical design mediator working in German design education for years, I keep on bumping into the same issues over and over again. Echoed in many conversations with colleagues and students, the core issue seems to be the curricula and structure it dictates.

The material to be taught or the tools to be learned, which the module description specifies, are mostly too extensive. The result is that students do not feel well trained; instead, they feel insecure, and teachers feel frustrated and harbor a sentiment of being "never enough" because little "comes back" from the students. The pressure is particularly high for students who depend on study grants linked to a certain grade point average and/or the study is only funded for a standard period. The complaints that I shared in the beginning of this chapter confirmed my impression that structures which were already precarious before the pandemic were exacerbated during the pandemic.

But why? Why do I keep bumping into the same things over and over again? Why do BA and MA design programs feel so limiting? Why does it feel so frustrating sometimes? What can be learned from those student complaints? Or to say it with Sarah Ahmed's (2017) words: What do I have to come up against?

Looking at these problems through the magnifying glass of digital teaching, I searched for ways to critically assess what and how we teach design. I stumbled upon two researchers and two concepts that—in dialogue—didn't necessarily gave me answers and actionable guidelines but did provide me with the vocabulary to voice my concerns and helped me make sense of them: the theory of "resonance" by the sociologist Hartmut Rosa (2016) and the concept of "ontological design" by Arturo Escobar (2018).

Both concepts emphasize that the relationship between humans and their environment is reciprocally constitutive. They each use this idea of relationality to explain the state of modernity and its institutions.

In order to critically reflect on design programs in Germany and productively process the background of the students' grievances, I will relate my research on design education to Escobar and Rosa to argue that the social theory of a mutually constitutive resonance between humans and the world around us is a prerequisite for understanding design as a world-shaping practice.

Ontological Design

Ontological design is a way of thinking and practicing design centered on the awareness that design's world-building capacities can be used to actively shape human–environment relations and generate "structures of possibility" (Escobar 2018, 111). That includes the acknowledgement of design's role in shaping modernist ideals, exposing the ways in which design has always been and continues to be complicit in world-destroying practices. Here, the political implication of the ontological dimension of design becomes apparent, for as Escobar states: No matter at what point we determine the beginning of design "from the outset, [it] has been inextricably tied to decisions about the lives we live and the worlds in which we live them …" (Escobar 2018, 33).

This relational understanding of the world vis-à-vis its human and non-human actors is relevant when thinking about design education as a place where a future designer's understanding of the design discipline is shaped. As the emergence of design is inextricably intertwined with the value system of modernity and was developed within patriarchal structures, it is significantly involved in the creation and reproduction of power relations, which are then perpetuated in design education. An ontological perspective on design suggests not only a critical stance but also a responsibility that comes with designing (ibid., 32). Teaching design as ontological becomes crucial to disrupt these conditions. What students learn about design opens the horizons of their imagination and paves the way for their future practice. In terms of teaching design, this entails teaching literacy of its entangled histories to understand that the worlds design makes indeed concern us.

In order to relate to the world, however, we need to feel like the world concerns us—we need to experience "resonance" (Rosa 2016).

Resonance

The political scientist and sociologist Hartmut Rosa observes that human life and human experiences are defined by uncontrollability [*Unverfügbarkeit*]. Truly encountering the world, experiencing and feeling alive emerges through resonating with the world, through encountering what is uncontrollable—what can't be made available by force (Rosa 2020, 2). Included here are both interpersonal encounters, but also encounters with things and activities. Resonance, as explained by Rosa, is not just a metaphor but a mode of relation that can be defined by four characteristics:

(1) *Being affected* describes the moment in which we are "affected by the world, ... *touched* or *moved* in such a way as to develop an intrinsic interest in [that particular] segment of world [that we encounter] and to feel somehow 'addressed'" by it (ibid., 32). It's a moment in which we resonate with—are "inwardly" touched by another person, an idea, a song, a landscape. This affection has no instrumental value; it can't be commodified (ibid.).
(2) *Self-efficacy* as a second characteristic is the ability to actively respond to being addressed. When we are able to reach out to the world, feel connected, heard, and addressed by a responding voice, we are in return experiencing that our own voice has an effect (ibid., 32f).
(3) The moment we encounter other human beings in a resonant way holds the potential for *adaptive transformation*. Encounters between people are included here, but also encounters with objects and practices. Rosa (2020, 34) says, "Experiencing resonance transforms us, and it is precisely this transformation that makes us feel alive."
(4) *Uncontrollability* is the central aspect of a resonant relation to the world and at the same time—as indicated by its name—the one that is uncontrollable. There is no tool-kit or guideline which can make sure we resonate with other humans or things (ibid., 36). One peculiarity of resonance, writes Rosa, is therefore that it can neither be forced to happen nor assured against (ibid., 37). However, resonance is not only unavailable in its moment of emergence, but also in its transformative effect and thus constitutively open-ended.

As a social theory, resonance describes a mutually enriching relationship with the world as the basis for a good life. Rosa contrasts resonance with relationships based on the attitude that the world, human, and non-human actors can be instrumentalized, alienated, or dominated. He also mobilizes resonance theory to explore the specific social, historical, cultural, political, or geographical conditions that enable successful human–world relations and diagnoses capitalist modernity as being in a fundamental state of alienation. He argues that, in order to maintain its formative status quo, modern societies have to keep in a constant state of dynamization and acceleration through comprehensive processes of expansion, growth, innovation, production, consumption, and keeping up (Rosa 2016, 14). Through the compulsion to make the world controllable at all levels, feeling alive and authentically encountering the world—the prerequisite for resonance—always seems to slip away from us (Rosa 2020, 4).

Resonance is fundamentally in tension with both the social logic of relentless acceleration and optimization and the concomitant attitude of constantly perceiving the world as a point of aggression (ibid., 37). As described above, the four domains of mastering the world—making it visible, accessible, manageable, and useful—are firmly embedded in educational institutions (ibid., 17), the very institutions that shape the foundation of modern society.

Institutionalized Design Education as Point of Aggression

What if we understand design education as such a point of aggression? As an institutionalized process deeply interwoven with the logics of modernity, it becomes an object that we have to "know, attain, conquer, master, or exploit." hence make controllable (Rosa 2020, 4).

At the level of institutionalized education, control is being enforced through parameterization, which means by making educational processes measurable (ibid., 67) and comparable in the interests of neoliberal commitments to "quality" (Higgins in Davies and Bansel 2010, 12). If one understands "education as the acquisition of certain skills" (Rosa 2020, 67)—an understanding of education that, according to Rosa, currently dominates in science and politics—qualitatively measurable also means controllable, comparable, and, above all, optimizable (ibid.).

In many ways Rosa's assessments can help make sense of the developments in the German educational system. At least since the 1960s, studies and curricula in Germany are officially slanted towards economic interests, as stated by social scientist Martin Winter (2015a). The introduction of the modular, two-tier system through the Bologna reform in the 1990s eventually became the most significant policy contributing to the management of higher education, changing art universities at various levels. Initiated by education policy-makers to "harmonise higher education" (ibid.) in Europe, the further goal of the reform was "to be able to admit more people to a shorter course of study with roughly the same capacities" (Winter 2015b). As a result, universities today have more entrants than ever, but this is proving to be unsustainable. While more students enter university, at the same time more students are dropping out of their studies than ever before (see Rößler 2019). The shorter duration of studies in the BA/MA system was intended to make study costs more calculable and thus—as a third reform goal—make studying more accessible to so called "educationally deprived" (see Winter 2015b). However, as a result of the Bologna reform, access to Bachelor's and Master's programs "has in fact become more restrictive; universities are increasingly selecting their students themselves by defining requirements for admission to studies" (ibid.).

Even though design degree programs at most art universities in Germany are comparatively small and thus—in most cases—cannot be counted among the "mass degree programs," they still manifest shortcomings that have arisen as a result of the Bologna reform. Those shortcomings include: access to higher education still being significantly easier for people from a privileged social background through a linking of factors such as the admission procedure, external presentation, curricular structures, course content, representation, and stress triggered by increased financial pressure (see Futuress 2020).

Education is, according to Rosa, "at best, [a] semi-controllable process of establishing resonance between subject and world or between [student] and a certain segment of world" (2020, 67f). A resonant learning experience can only occur when student and teacher are touched [affiziert] by the course content which is only possible if the university framework allows for it. As I have tried to exemplify with sharing the student's complaints, this notion of a resonating education stands in contrast to a reality in which module descriptions with detailed learning objectives, made comparable through evaluations in order to be subsequently optimized, actually leading to "measurable" skills becoming the preferred content of the study programs (ibid., 68).

Resonance as Precondition for *Ontological Design*

As we have learnt, the increasingly tight-knit curricula and controlled learning environments are alienating students and teachers from each other and from the content of their studies. The optimization strategies described above aim to move as many students as possible through the education sector as quickly as possible, instead of building sustainable relationships. These relationships are now primarily focused on gaining structural advantages instead of building a caring relationality to the world and to each other. In other words, the more "we" want to make the world controllable, the more we deprive ourselves of the possibility of entering into resonant and thus mutually transformative relations with it.

The pandemic was a disruption enhancing pre-existing problematic structures in art universities. Students seemed to have the impression that they could get more out of the time—e.g, attain more ECTS—that was mostly spent at home anyway, while digital tools like Zoom, Miro, and Slack wiped away the already porous boundary between private and student life. The "fear of having less and less" (Rosa 2020, 10), which Rosa describes as a structuring characteristic of modernity, led—in the educational context during the pandemic—to a manic consumption and appropriation of knowledge. According to critical art mediator Nora Sternfeld, this is expressed through a "fear of not knowing" (2010, 15). For students, the fear of not knowing is deeply impactful as the worries voiced in their complaints make clear. Not knowing means that potential outcomes are unpredictable, which is contrary to the need to invest one's time in studying in the most efficient and profitable way. This need to make the learning process controllable leads to the process of learning from and with each other taking a back seat. The possibility of pursuing one's own interest in specific aspects becomes more difficult. As a result, experiencing resonance—and its transformative potential—becomes nearly impossible.

Even though Rosa and Escobar look at society from two different cultural perspectives and humanities disciplines, they share one fundamental observation: We are in a crisis—because of the destructive way we late-modern people are within the world and to the world (see Escobar 2018, 113f and Rosa 2016, 14).

Both concepts foreground that the relation between humans and their environment is mutually constitutive. Relationality, characterized by trust, love, and reciprocal stimulation can transform both sides. However, the condition of modernity, its institutions and ways of being—which are based on acceleration, expansion, and a narrative of progress—stand in strong contrast to a caring, solidary collectivity. Design education in Germany exemplifies this tension. As design is deeply entangled with industrial and capitalist modernity, it is complicit in world-destroying practices that need to be addressed in order to dis-entangle the design discipline from its legacies.

As Escobar shows, we can only care for the world if we can relate to the world. In order to relate to the world, however, we need to feel like the world concerns us, as Rosa points out. It takes encounter and experience, being in touch with oneself, each other and the world. In short, it requires resonance—to feel empowered, to feel agency for transformative (design) practices.

Foregrounding relationality and resonance in design education could be helpful in making sense, articulating, and countering those legacies. Design education has the potential to elevate design's world-building capacities and by that open up a space to envision an alternative way of doing design in a careful way.

I'd like to finish by asking: What kind of relationship to the world and to design are we mediating here? How can any transformative potential of design unfold if it is mediated and learned under those circumstances? What kind of design education would allow for resonant experiences? What institutional structures would be needed?

BIBLIOGRAPHY

Ahmed, Sara. *Complaint!*. Duke University Press, 2021.

———. *Living a Feminist Life*. Duke University Press, 2017.

Escobar, Arturo. *Designs for the Pluriverse: Radical Interdependence, Autonomy, and the Making of Worlds.* Duke University Press, 2018.

Futuress, depatriarchise design. 2020. "Diversity Issues – Teachers and students voice their grievances around discrimination in Swiss design schools". Futuress. Last modified December 4, 2020. Accessed July 29, 2022. https://futuress.org/magazine/diversity-issues/.

Higgins, Winton. "Globalization and Neoliberal Rule." *Journal of Australian Political Economy,* 57 (2006): 5–30, 9. Quoted in: Bronwyn Davies and Peter Bansel. "Governmentality and Academic Work Shaping the Hearts and Minds of Academic Workers." *Journal of Curriculum Theorizing 26,* (2010): 11.

Munslow, Alun. *Narrative and History*. Bloomsbury Publishing, 2018.

Rosa, Hartmut. *Resonanz: Eine Soziologie der Weltbeziehung*. Suhrkamp Verlag, 2016.

———. *The uncontrollability of the world*. John Wiley & Sons, 2020.

Rößler, Nele. 2019. "Wenn Studenten psychisch krank werden." Deutschlandfunk. Last modified October 6, 2019. Accessed July 29, 2022. www.deutschlandfunk.de/aengste-depressionen-studienabbruch-wenn-studenten.724.de.html?dram:article_id=460415.

Sternfeld, Nora. *Das pädagogische Unverhältnis – Lehren und lernen bei Rancière, Gramsci und Foucault*. Turia+Kant, 2010.

Winter, Martin. 2015a. "Bologna – vom politischen Prozess in Europa zur Studienreform in Deutschland". Bundeszentrale für politische Bildung. Last modified March 31, 2015. Accessed July 29, 2022. www.bpb.de/gesellschaft/bildung/zukunft-bildung/204059/bologna-politischer-prozess?p=all.

———. 2015b. "Bologna – die ungeliebte Reform und ihre Folgen". Bundeszentrale für politische Bildung. Last modified March 31, 2015. Accessed July 29, 2022. www.bpb.de/gesellschaft/bildung/zukunft-bildung/204075/bologna-folgen.

Acknowledgements

We would like to thank the participants, guests, and collaborators of the first edition of the Patadesign School: Zenobio Almeida, Xaviera Sánchez de la Barquera Estrada, Thomas Mical, Stacey Joy Rossouw, Ruby Quail, Rogério Camara, PNUL, Pedro Ribs, Milagros Fonrouge, Max Mollon, Marina de Sá, Luiz Jales, Lucas Vaqueiro, Leandro Pasini, Lauren Dark, Lara Silva Santos, Kate McEntee, Kalyani Tupkary, Julia Lozzi Teixeira, Jon Günther, Jamer Hunt, Guilherme A. de Almeida, Gabriel Lyra Chaves, Flávio Silva, Deborah Nogueira, Daniel Charkow, Daan de Loor, ReFluxus Olympic Committee (Karina Dias, Gê Orthof, Cecilia Mori), Coe Douglas, Clive Dilnot, Anne Mendes, Ana Maria Maccagnan, Ana Cecília Schettino, Amruta Supate, and Aly DiSalvo.

DWELLINGS IN ETHERNITY

Designing and Unraveling the Patadesign School

(Isabella Brandalise)   (Henrique Eira)   (Søren Rosenbak)

Authors have contributed equally to the publication and are listed alphabetically.

1. Before Anything Else

This is a school where your immediate vicinity is suddenly nothing but exceptional occurrences. This is a school where guest speakers naturally receive appropriate certificates of exceptional revelation for their illuminative appearances. This is a school where your athletic performance is being evaluated and scored by a most rigorous anti-Olympics committee. This is a school where the student ID you receive on your first day comes with an inspirational .gif gifted from a classmate. This is a school where messages reach you time and time again from Ethernity.

    This chapter focuses on the first instantiation of the Patadesign School, an exceptional school of exceptions. The Patadesign School proposes to highlight the pataphysical dimension of design and offer a critical response—in the form of questions and provocations—to the role of design in the age of the artificial. As such, the School had to design itself into existence. It was founded by three designers who practice and research precisely patadesign, or possible alignments between pataphysics, the most exceptional of sciences, and design understood from a critical, expanded, and experimental perspective. The first edition of the School brought together 21 people, located in nine different countries, to experience patadesign through five sessions over the course of two weeks in the month Absolute, year 149, of the Pataphysical Era (or September 2021 in the vulgar calendar).
    The goal of this chapter is to share the inspirations and motivations for creating the Patadesign School, to dwell in contradictions and possibilities related to a pataphysical educational institution and to dive into the specificities of its first manifestation in the inaugural edition and later unraveling. We discuss the format adopted and present results and reflections, in dialogue with plural, critical, and experimental possibilities of practice and teaching in design. We organized this text based on materials generated from the School, our reflections during and after the experience, in addition to spontaneous comments and evaluations sent by the participants. We begin by presenting pataphysics and the concept of patadesign, followed by a description and conceptualization of the Patadesign School and the institution as such. We then move on to the presentation of the first edition of the School, themed *Ethernity,* and reflections on the results obtained, ending with considerations on the pataphysical making and unmaking of institutions.

2. Pataphysics? Patadesign?

> "Patadesign is a branch of design which we have invented and for which a crying need is generally experienced." (Brandalise et al. 2022, 22)

Although a timeless impulse, pataphysics was formulated at the beginning of the 20th century by the French poet and playwright Alfred Jarry. The author defined pataphysics as the science of imaginary solutions and as the science of the particular (and not of the general rule) or that which examines the laws that govern exceptions ([1911] 1996). Thus, it is a kind of reverse science that appropriates the positivist terms and ways of the generalist, traditional science and academia, experiencing them from the point of view of absurdity, uselessness, humor, and ambiguity.

Pataphysics, as formulated by Jarry, arrived at a time in Western history when science was not only immensely powerful as a discipline but also on the brink of overriding itself, soon splintering its foundational building blocks, by way of the arrival of quantum mechanics, Einstein's theories of relativity, and other such leaps forward. Once banished from the world of supposed perfection and complete integrity, uncertainty and possibility now crept back into the inner workings of science itself. In this light, metaphysics started to look less like the singular truth that hovered above our very existence, and more like an imaginary solution to a time that viewed the world as a predictable unfolding of events, a set of cogs in a machine that was supremely governed by one set of eternal laws.

Jarry's ideas influenced the early twentieth-century European avant-garde, such as Dada and Surrealism, as well as later International Situationism. In 1948 the Collège de 'Pataphysique was founded in Paris, with members such as Boris Vian, Marcel Duchamp, Joan Miró, Eugène Ionesco, among other notable artists. The institution is dedicated to the investigation of the science of sciences and covers subjects ranging from Aesthetic Mechanics and Comparative Graphology to Crocodilogy, and its activities include banquets at the Polidor Restaurant, publications of written materials in different formats, as well as practical work.

Everything is pataphysics. However, in a still timid manner, we are witnessing a growing conscious recognition of the pataphysical infusion in design, mainly from pedagogical experiences and research projects, including the ones organized by the founding team of the School and authors of this chapter, such as an elective course at the University of Brasília (Brandalise and Eira 2020), the publication of a book with reflections based on patadesign principles (Eira and Brandalise 2019), and the doctoral thesis of Søren Rosenbak (2018), documenting and discussing the prototyping of a pataphysically infused design practice.

We refer to pataphysical design as *patadesign,* and view it as an appropriate imaginary solution to the problem of how one goes about emphasizing the pataphysical dimension of design in a conscious, explicit manner. Crucially, we also see patadesign as a critical response to the role of design today, as humanity finds itself in the Anthropocene, a geological epoch defined by the human impact on the planet itself. Clive Dilnot has extensively argued for the supreme role of artifice in this setting – not simply as artificial things in an otherwise natural world, but really as the "horizon, medium and prime condition of our lives" (2014, 187). In this sense, we too live in the age of the artificial. This is a condition that is characterized by uncertainty and the fact that anything and everything could be otherwise, since there are no laws that determine that these things need to be as they are. While Dilnot (2021) has argued that human beings, as a kind of failed animals, always seek to transform the world rather than existing in it contently, Nelson and Stolterman (2014) have also argued that human beings didn't invent fire, they indeed designed it. While artifice, as the "horizon, medium and prime condition of our lives," is the very antithesis to the notion of modernity (Dilnot 2014), its trademark of being contingent and uncertain in the extreme speaks profoundly to pataphysics, as a way of making sense of the world, and design, as a way of manipulating it. We take patadesign to be a way for design to consciously engage pataphysically with the artificial domain, or in other words, to deal with the artificial condition on its terms, terms which Dilnot argues are really the only terms that matters for our day and age: "How can we live with uncertainty, dependency, interrelationality, and do all this through mediation and the negotiation of absolutely incommensurable requirements and needs?" (Dilnot 2021). Where else to direct our attention to this task than from the foggy clarity offered by Ethernity?

With this in mind, we find potential energy in the pataphysical approach to exceptions, circumstantial events that negotiate with local rules, expanding the space of the possible (Badiou 2009 in Dilnot 2014). Patadesign also emerges as an opportunity to push ourselves towards unique ways of teaching and producing knowledge of design itself, recognizing a diversity of knowledge and worlds that coexist, both in theoretical and practical terms, rather than subscribing to the Western "One-World World" (Law 2011 in Escobar 2018).

3. Patadesign School

> "Does not the word teaching imply usefulness or pretensions to usefulness? Does not the word usefulness imply seriousness? Does not the word seriousness imply antipataphysics? All these terms are equivalent (profound sensation)." (Sandomir 1948)

With a shared interest in consciously examining, formulating and experimenting with ways in which pataphysics and design can go for a walk together, and inspired by other pataphysical organizations around the world, we founded a school. The Patadesign School is defined as an exceptional school of exceptions (Patadesign School, 2021) and is an autonomous institution that revolves around an unfolding patadesign practice. A significant part of this practice is collective pedagogical experimentation, developed with a focus on situated practices. Furthermore, despite adopting the rules of a school, with programs, lectures, classes and exercises, the Patadesign School paradoxically seeks to avoid becoming an established rule itself and, in doing so, commits to maintaining its exceptional character. This means operating, on a temporary basis, through a particular edition, an instantiation that not only acts as an exception from the largely modernistic design education offering in the 21st century, but also as an exception from itself, meaning past and future editions of the School. The proposal is to interact with topics in a creative and open way, instead of trying to fit them into pre-established structures and formats. In a profound sense, the School in this way also seeks to *show forth* one of its fundamental learning outcomes (rather than simply lecture *on it*), namely its insistence on remaining an exception. Just like everything in this world is an exception, so too is the School.

In each edition and in proper pataphysical fashion, the School adopts equivalence between all the exceptions that make up the world, celebrating their diversity and not prioritizing a specific profile in detriment of another. This also means explicitly inviting participants from different design backgrounds and regions of the world. We particularly encourage the participation of historically vulnerable and marginalized groups, as voices which are underrepresented in design education and consequently in the dance between the real and the imagined. While the School itself ran completely on a "pay what you like" model, we also reserved spots for completely free participation. Economically speaking, the voluntary fees paid by most participants were intended to be just enough to cover the costs of running the first edition of the School. In this way we wanted to secure and guard the exceptional nature of the first edition, avoiding its pollution with implicit projections around any kind of institutional growth or hardening beyond the here and now.

Fig. 1. Patadesign School's website

The visual identity of the School—as presented in official visual products such as the institution's website, social media communication, students' IDs and diplomas, and other ethereal material manifestations—is designed to perform in a pataphysical manner. Combining found illustrations with visual references to Jarry's time with contemporary typography that resemble a mix of different historical periods, vibrant RGB colors and elements that are constantly moving in and out of focus, the visual manifestation of the School offers materiality—albeit ethereal—to the institution, placing it as existing in this time but also in Ethernity. With this, we wanted to offer a clear example of the negotiation of incommensurabilities that is part and parcel of design (Dilnot 2021; Nelson and Stolterman 2014). We observe how this work with tying these disparate knots together into a whole, a design configuration, was done in a way that comically pointed to its own negotiation.

We frequently see other design institutions seeking to create a sharp unified visual identity, often to the effect of giving it a credibility pertaining to its age and tradition, heritage, craft and respectability. Counter to this process of willed or circumstantial solidification of institutions, which as an effect increasingly conveys that they couldn't have been otherwise, the Patadesign School actively sought to resist this very solidification process from its inception. It did so by insisting on its own artificial nature, and leaving its own negotiation of incommensurabilities open, even on its very surface, through its design language. The reasons for this were threefold. First, this is a concrete example of the argument about the School showing forth the fact that it too is an exception. The novel combination of its highly divergent constituent parts into a whole clearly marked it as such. Second, through comical juxtapositions we hoped to trigger a smile on the lips of our audience. While we did have a website, an Instagram account, spreadsheets, an application process etc., we also sought to suspend the institution in a slight state of disbelief. Thirdly, the openness of configuration, and the high degree of attention, which this delicate state forced us to apply in order to uphold the various constituents making the School, maintaining a sort of wicked equilibrium, also allowed us not only to resist the solidification process of institutions but also to unravel the School's institutional weight with a level of precision befitting the exception in question. In a sense, it is a school that exists both as a solution and dissolution into ether—as its own identity graphically turns into fog. This is the condition which enabled us to place the School simultaneously in the real, as a fully designed entity, while at the same time occupying Ethernity. Not as a bridge between two realms, but in the sense that Dilnot refers to as the "!?" (an interrobang), being simultaneously propositional and actual, in a sense collapsing the false modernistic dichotomy between the real world out there and the world of pure fantasy.

4. Inaugural Edition

The first edition of the Patadesign School took place between 1–15 Absolute 149 P.E. (September 8–22, 2021, vulg.), and had as its theme *Ethernity*—a pataphysical concept that merges the attributes of the luminiferous ether and eternity. Over the course of two weeks, we held five synchronous virtual sessions, interspersed with practical exercises in the physical locations of each participant. In order for the event to take place, in addition to the main team, we had an extended team, taking care of sound, regulations, memory making, advertising and more; and we adopted English as the official bureaucratic language.

As a result of an open call posted on the institutional website, followed by an intricate selection process, we had a group of 21 highly talented participants located in nine countries (Brazil, Argentina, United States, Portugal, England, Denmark, Netherlands, India and Australia) and approaching design from diverse perspectives and experience levels. We received applications from both undergraduates and experienced academics, and not only self-professed designers but also from a shoemaker, a sound ethnographer, and a coach. We created a system with options for registration fees so that each person could choose to pay the amount closest to their condition, acknowledging the exceptional nature of these as well. We especially encouraged the registration of women, people with disabilities, black and indigenous people, and LGBTQIA+ people, by offering five free spots for representatives of such groups.

As the prospective participants' first serious touch point with the School, we also carefully made sure to design the application process as an integral part of the aforementioned design configuration of the School. Besides the standard section with contact details, and questions around motivation for applying and the like, we also invited applicants to share their obsessions, tell us something about them that is not on the internet, and send us a recent imaginary solution of theirs. We wanted this moment to be as much an experience of one of the School's assignments, as a small playful rift of possibility opening up in that very moment of sitting down and writing an application, offering a taste of what might come, rather than a form about the School.

We defined the themes of each of the five sessions following possibilities offered by the letters that form the word *E-T-H-E-R:* 1) Exhaustive Explanations; 2) Turbulent Topographies; 3) Hilarious Hierarchies; 4) Ethereal Exceptions; and 5) Rarefied Rest. In each online session, the participants interacted in a moment of sharing perceptions and experiences about exercises and readings carried out since last session. In a second moment, we used stimuli in the form of audio clips sent to us from Ethernity, lectures, performances and discussions with guests—Clive Dilnot, Jamer Hunt and the ReFluxus Olympic Committee.

Fig. 2. First Edition program

D1: Exhaustive Explanations	D2: Turbulent Topographies	D3: Hilarious Hierarchies	D4: Ethereal Exceptions	D5: Rarefied Rest
Sep 9, 2021 *vulg.*	Sep 13, 2021 *vulg.*	Sep 17, 2021 *vulg.*	Sep 20, 2021 *vulg.*	Sep 22, 2021 *vulg.*
8–10:30am (Brasília) 1–3:30pm (Copenhagen) 9–11:30pm (Melbourne)	8–10:30am (Brasília) 1–3:30pm (Copenhagen) 9–11:30pm (Melbourne)	8–10:30am (Brasília) 1–3:30pm (Copenhagen) 9–11:30pm (Melbourne)	8–10:30am (Brasília) 1–3:30pm (Copenhagen) 9–11:30pm (Melbourne)	10:59am–12:30pm (B) 3:59–5:30pm (C) 11:59pm–1:30am (M)
PATADESIGN?	ON SCALE	NEW RITUALS	EXCEPTIONS	FEAST!
Scale: Earth *Guest:* Clive Dilnot *Exercise:* Student ID	*Scale:* City *Guest:* Jamer Hunt *Exercise:* Spiriform walking expedition	*Scale:* Home *Guest:* ReFluxus Olympic Committee *Exercise:* Anti-Olympics	*Scale:* Bodies *Exercise:* A slippery catalog of exceptions	*Scale:* Atom *Exercise:* Scenario for diploma ceremony in Ethernity

Over the course of the School sessions, our attention was dedicated to matters from the scale of the Earth to that of an atom, radically shrinking with time. Throughout the journey, we approached topics such as the artificial, culture, fog, humor, uselessness, exceptions, silence, School, and we proposed exercises such as the documentation of a spiral-shaped walk, the performatic participation in domestic Olympic modalities and the creation of a collective catalogue of exception specimens. The focus was on experiencing such topics through generative assignments, allowing for both a critical and creative engagement that goes beyond unified experiences of merely expository sessions. The School actually started with a holiday dedicated to the *Nativity of Alfred Jarry,* and the last session, which took place on the day of the *Feast of Ethernity* (September 22, vulg.), was celebrated with a virtual banquet and the diploma award ceremony.

5. Anti-Results and Dwellings in Ethernity

After the first edition of the School, we can highlight some reflections, related to the event itself—circumstances, methods, participants—and also to the pedagogical institution created—rules, paradoxes, unfoldings.

Regarding the first edition, the fact that it was held during the COVID-19 pandemic, an exceptional event in itself, required the creation of an infrastructure for participation that allowed both online exchanges and interactions that concerned the local specificities of each participant. Ethernity emerged as an all-encompassing fog that was capable of situating the School and its participants, engulfing an exceptional situation in an exceptional substance. As much as the possibility of physical and more spontaneous exchanges between participants was lost, the restriction of holding remote sessions allowed the participation of people from different places and time zones, and the acutely present condition of uncertainty made participants adapt the exercises to their own needs and situation, using constraints as a creative opportunity. We attempted to open this window of possibility as much as possible, by scheduling our collective activities in a time zone friendly manner, allowing for early risers in Brazil and late-night dreamers in Australia to interact with each other and everyone in-between.

Online interactions began even before the School itself, with the creation of a gift for another participant in .gif format—a gif(t). The gif(t) was delivered as a stamp or seal on that person's student ID, which arrived as part of a digital welcome package. Throughout the School, interactions took place in a variety of different formats, including conversations with the whole group and guests, discussions in smaller groups, listening to audio recordings, moments of communal silence and contemplation, among others. Some difficulties included getting everyone to be present at all sessions, as many were reconciling school activities with their daily work and study activities, in addition to the burden added by the pandemic situation itself. Another challenge was facilitating the understanding of all participants, who did not always have English as their first language. We tried to get around this by offering translations of written and audio materials, as well as subtitles for live interactions.

As mentioned earlier, one of the decisions we had to make was the language in which the sessions would be conducted. In order to reach a large number of participants from different nationalities, we chose to use English as a bureaucratic language, and to use the original languages of selected texts, the languages of the participant countries and our own languages throughout the whole school as part of didactic material and exercise results. We believe that the polyphony of languages was one of the strengths of the edition, and contributed to complex and rich exchanges, in addition to showing how languages too are particular exceptions, which can and should be playfully subverted.

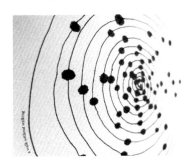
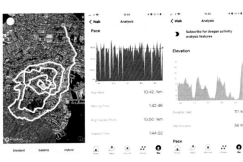

Fig. 3. Participants' work for the spiriform walk exercise

In preparation for the Turbulent Topographies session, we posed the exercise of going on a spiriform walk around their surroundings and documenting that walk. The spiral, which decorates Ubu's belly (one of Jarry's most emblematic characters), is one of the main symbols of pataphysics, containing within itself the coexistence of opposites—or a movement and its opposite, orientation and disorientation, what is and what is not. The spiral, in eternal rotation, is averse to the idea of linear progress and can be understood as the purest form of movement (Klee 1961). We then united the primary idea of walking (Gros 2021) with the vertigo of the spiral. From different spiral typologies and directionalities—"Am I being released from the center in a movement that is becoming more and more free? Or: are my movements more and more linked to the center, which in the end will engulf me?" (Klee 1961, 399)—and inspired by the work of artists such as Robert Smithson, people traveled through their neighborhoods and recorded the encounters through footstep monitoring apps, videos, photos, drawings, audio recordings, image manipulation and others. One person, facing a high risk of contamination from COVID-19, made a meditative and introspective spiral walk through her own dreams and thoughts, without leaving home.

Beyond spirals, the activities focused on accidents, coincidences and swerves, challenging both traditional ways of teaching and learning, as well as the sources of inspiration in design education, which are often anchored in case studies and universalist modernist models from the Global North. In the evaluation of the first edition, one of the participants stated that in many cases the source of inspiration for the patadesign exercises came from an attentive and sensitive observation of private everyday life and intimate domestic spaces, their objects, surfaces, rules and micro-epiphanies.

This last point can be seen in the collective exercise of building a slippery catalogue of exceptions (part of the Ethereal Exceptions session), in which participants gathered in groups to find and document exceptions within a 5-meter radius of the center of the bed in which each person slept that night. Each group documented one type of exception for each of the four pataphysical exception categories—anomaly, something different in a homogeneous system; clinamen, an accident, error or swerve; syzygy, an exceptional alignment of bodies in a system; and antinomy (plus-minus), the coexistence of opposites in the same being (Bök 2002). The results included drawings of imaginary alignments and contradictions, overlapping audio recordings and photographs of errors, distortions and crossings of objects and beings.

Fig. 4. Slippery Catalogue of Exceptions

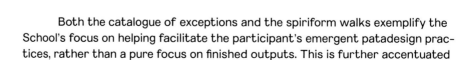

Both the catalogue of exceptions and the spiriform walks exemplify the School's focus on helping facilitate the participant's emergent patadesign practices, rather than a pure focus on finished outputs. This is further accentuated by the way in which an output such as the slippery catalogue points to its own absurd status, not unlike Jorge Luis Borges' (2007) taxonomy of animals from the *Celestial Emporium of Benevolent Knowledge*. It is a catalogue that mocks itself as a format, undermining its own taxonomy by explicitly acknowledging its slipperiness, and yet existing as a catalogue.

The session on Hilarious Hierarchies presented a structure that was an exception (as all sessions did, after all), guided by the guests of the ReFluxus Olympic Committee, composed of Cecilia Mori, Gê Orthof and Karina Dias, artists and professors from the University of Brasília. At the previous session, participants had received instructions and inspiration for the ReFluxus Olympics, with the aim of preparing their performances for the live evaluation during this session. Performances could be delivered in image or video format of up to one minute and had to correspond to an entry in each of the three domestic Olympic modalities: Eyelash Backlash, Rock-a-Chair and Dancing Days. On the day of the session, each entry was projected on the screen and immediately evaluated by the Committee, using a different evaluation system for each of the three modalities.

Fig. 5. Evaluation systems by the ReFluxus Olympic Committee

The experience of this anti-Olympic session was permeated by humor, a pataphysical quality that, momentarily and imperturbably, suspends the laws that organize the world, in addition to the traditional pedagogical logic itself. Through humor, we can say the opposite of what we mean, in elaborate expressions of reality. At the ReFluxus Olympics, the premise was that the worst performers would be crowned winners, and the grandiose Olympic torch naturally materialized as a tiny green candle, in another reference to a pataphysical symbol, for example, as encountered in Jarry's Ubu Roi ([1896] 2021). The displacement of familiar objects and beings from their usual situations, so that they could be reconfigured in performances for the proposed modalities, in many cases generated comic estrangement.

By interrupting the mundane reality and entering the intimate space of the house, the games allowed the experience of alternative possibilities, in a collective and shared way. Furthermore, by using non-oral and non-numerical evaluation systems, mixing silence and subtle sounds with facial expressions, tensions, words, images and overlapping meanings, the ReFluxus Committee played with the arbitrariness of evaluation systems and proposed other ways of relating to the work. The issue of language once again appeared, in a cacophony of simultaneous expressions and multiple possible layers of communication. Jamer Hunt, as part of the discussion following his presentation in the Turbulent Topologies session, offered another reflection on this point in relation to his own patadesign journey: "What I learned so far that is important about pataphysics as a practice is that it is not about knowing, it is about being comfortable with unknowing; and it is not about getting concepts right, but about productive mistranslations" (Hunt 2021). As a recurrent element in our sessions, we listened to audio messages sent to us from Ethernity. They were carefully and randomly included in-between activities, and too appeared in a multitude of languages, presenting ample reminders of the importance of not knowing.

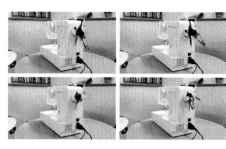

Fig. 6. Participants' performances at the ReFluxus Olympics

At the Ethereal Exceptions session, towards the end of the first edition, we also invited everyone to participate in the School's Inaugural Disassembly, an exercise of collectively creating rules for the School based on lived experience. Each person had to think of a rule for the Patadesign School that started with each letter of its name—P, A, T, A, D, E, S, I, G, N, S, C, H, O , O, L—resulting in an extensive list of 158 rules. For the letter A, for example, the rules included "Always alternate between seriousness and play," "Art is in the exceptions" and "Abandon all rules," while for the letter D they included "Draw the invisible," "Dance!" and "Deviate from order". With this exercise, we question the paradoxical character of creation and the impossibility of the School—an institution that creates its own rules so that it can exist and, at the same time, because there are so many rules, makes its own existence impossible. We also think of this moment as another exercise in the bringing together of incommensurables, as in creating a highly bureaucratic structure which for a moment was able to hold together a set of rules in which apparently opposite postulates coexist.

This moment could be read as a crescendo on the earlier point concerning the deliberately open configuration of the School, as was also discussed in the context of the design language of the School. As a collective moment, co-created with all participants in a performative, ritualistic setting, it stressed that delicate balance between imagination (the School can be whatever you want it to be, as everything can be otherwise) and the real (these are literally the rules of the School, which determine its functioning and dysfunctioning). The moment had a profound effect on our thinking about the School, as it made us reflect on the end of the first edition, not in terms of pattern and repetition, but as a provisional unraveling. In a pataphysical attitude, we carefully dismantled the fabric that was woven in Ethernity and remain with the threads. In other words, the open configuration of the School was stretched into a state where the actual whole disappeared back into possibility. The dismantling or unraveling mechanism itself, its method and meaning, is something that we are interested in exploring further.

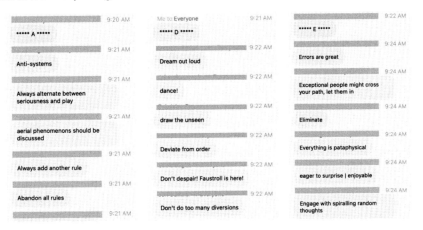

Fig. 7. Examples of rules created at the Inaugural Disassembly

We see these processes of making and unmaking, designing and unraveling (or perhaps undesigning), as a critical way of engaging with that delicate "!?" balance between the actual and propositional, the real and the imaginary, which exists in any exception. More specifically, the entangling and untangling of the imaginary and real aspect of the Patadesign School, in the careful and explicit way we have described in this chapter, points to how both of these aspects are present in any other design school. They are a reminder that all institutions are, after all, imaginary and therefore could be otherwise, regardless of how solid, timeless, universal and finished they claim to be. Further, the process of solidification seen in most design schools—an ironical resistance to facing their imaginary dimension and in a deeper sense artificiality—is a choice more than anything else.

The ethereal materialization of the first edition of the Patadesign School and its ephemeral existence open up possibilities for reflection and practice in contemporary design education. A school that belongs to this One-World World (Law 2011 in Escobar 2018), and therefore obeys to the rules of this world, and at the same time operates as an exception that stretches this very world and expands the field of the possible. Paradoxically—and we understand that appropriately—we chose to interrogate the institutionality of education precisely through an education institution (Illich 1971).

6. Unraveling

In this chapter, we discussed the first edition of the Patadesign School, an exceptional school of exceptions, as a patadesign response to design education in the age of the artificial. The Patadesign School is an experiment that allows us to investigate possibilities for both design practice and teaching, in search of engaged, experimental and critical processes (hooks 2020; Freire 2013). Overall, the configuration of the five sessions, alternating moments of discussion and sensorial experience, allowed the exploration of concepts with diversity and nuance, in a perspective of experiencing rather than explaining pataphysics (which would be a useless and impossible endeavor).

As they reported at the end of the School, participants, even with different contexts and occupations, felt that they had a space to explore alternatives to dominant design practices, while actively contributing to the construction of instances and understandings of patadesign. The experience was described by one of the participants as a way to be aware of the surrounding environment and to elevate ordinary things to an extraordinary scope. Another person highlighted the originality of the methodology used, which makes us deconstruct or question various practices and rules that we have internalized. The diversity of participants and the exchange with people from such different contexts and points of view was also one of the most highlighted points about the School, with the potential to maintain a community of exchanges and practices.

In addition to the feedback offered by the participants themselves, we also produced a zine to broaden the reverberations of this experiment. The publication (Brandalise et al. 2022) documents some of the contents, reflections, exercises and provocations found in Ethernity. The zine offered itself as a most suitable format for capturing the School. A real, yet provisional type of publication, which transgressed Ethernity into the participants' letterboxes, a lasting reminder that the real is imaginary and the imaginary too is real.

Just like the School designed itself into existence, responding to a crying need for the invention of patadesign, the School too unraveled itself as a natural consequence to this calling which we heard loud and clear. At this point, having published the zine, the first edition is officially fully dismantled, yet remains open as a gaping possibility. From the collective unraveling, we keep the threads that will weave new editions and new spaces to experience plural and exceptionally equivalent alternatives of thinking and making in design.

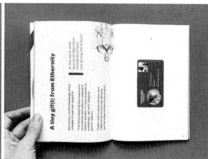

Fig. 8. Spreads from the printed copy of the zine

BIBLIOGRAPHY

Badiou, Alain, and Slavoj Zizek. *Philosophy in the Present*. John Wiley and Sons Ltd, 2009.

Bök, Christian. *'Pataphysics: The Poetics of an Imaginary Science*. Evanston: Northwestern University Press, 2002.

Borges, Jorge Luis. "O idioma analítico de John Wilkins." In *Outras inquisições*. Translated by Davi Arrigucci Jr. São Paulo: Companhia das Letras, 2007.

Brandalise, Isabella, and Henrique Eira. "Patadesign: A Pedagogical Experiment on Design of Exception, Absurd Artifacts, and Imaginary Interfaces." *Dearq*, no. 26 (January 2020): 36–43. https://doi.org/10.18389/dearq26.2020.04.

Brandalise, Isabella, Henrique Eira, and Søren Rosenbak. *Patadesign School 1: Ethernity*. Brasilia, Copenhagen and Melbourne: RMIT University, 2022.

Dilnot, Clive. "Exhaustive Explanations Talk." Presented at the Patadesign School, Ethernity, 2021.

———. "Reasons to Be Cheerful 1, 2, 3…" in *Design as Future-Making*, edited by Susan Yelavich and Barbara Adams, 185–97. London: Bloomsbury, 2014.

Eira, Henrique, and Brandalise, Isabella. *Patadesign: notas pendentes de soluções imaginárias*. Brasília: Estereográfica, 2019.

Escobar, Arturo. *Designs for the Pluriverse: Radical Interdependence, Autonomy, and the Making of Worlds*. New Ecologies for the Twenty-First Century. Durham: Duke University Press, 2018.

Freire, Paulo. *Pedagogia Do Oprimido*. Rio de Janeiro: Paz e Terra, 2013.

Gros, Frédérik. *Caminhar: Uma Filosofia*. Translated by Célia Euvaldo. São Paulo: Ubu Editora, 2021.

hooks, bell. *Ensinando Pensamento Crítico: Sabedoria Prática*. São Paulo: Elefante, 2020.

Hunt, Jamer. "Turbulent Topographies Talk." Presented at the Patadesign School, Ethernity, 2021.

Illich, Ivan. *Deschooling Society*. Harper & Row, 1971.

Jarry, Alfred. *Exploits & Opinions of Doctor Faustroll, Pataphysician: A Neo-Scientific Novel*. Translated by Simon Watson Taylor. Boston, MA: Exact Change, 1996.

———. *Ubu Rei Ou Os Poloneses*. Translated by Bárbara Duvivier and Gregório Duvivier. São Paulo: Ubu Editora, 2021.

Klee, Paul. *Notebooks*. Vol. 1: The Thinking Eye. London and Bradford: Lund Humphries, 1961.

Law, John. "What's Wrong with a One-World World." *heterogeneities* (September 25, 2011). http://www.heterogeneities.net/publications/Law2011WhatsWrongWithAOneWorldWorld.pdf.

Nelson, Harold, and Erik Stolterman. *The Design Way: Intentional Change in an Unpredictable World*. 2nd ed. Cambridge: MIT Press Academic, 2014.

Patadesign School. 2021. "Patadesign School" Accessed September 7, 2022. http://www.patadesignschool.com.

Rosenbak, Søren. *The Science of Imagining Solutions: Design Becoming Conscious of Itself through Design*. Umeå: Umeå University, Umeå Institute of Design, 2018.

Sandomir, Irénée-Louis. "Inaugural Harangue." Presented at the Collège de 'Pataphysique, Paris, 1948.

IMAGES AND ILLUSTRATION

Figure 1: Patadesign School, Patadesign School's website, Ethernity, September 2021.

Figure 2: Patadesign School, First Edition program, Ethernity, September 2021.

Figure 3: Patadesign School, Participants' work for the spiriform walk exercise, Ethernity, September 2021.

Figure 4: Patadesign School, Slippery Catalogue of Exceptions, Ethernity, September 2021.

Figure 5: Patadesign School, Evaluation systems by the Refluxus Olympic Committee, Ethernity, September 2021.

Figure 6: Patadesign School, Participants' performances at the ReFluxus Olympics, Ethernity, September 2021.

Figure 7: Patadesign School, Examples of rules created at the Inaugural Disassembly, Ethernity, September 2021.

Figure 8: Patadesign School, Spreads from the printed copy of the zine, Ethernity, September 2021. Photo: Henrique Eira.

Gratitude

We want to thank the speakers whose words became shelters for our thoughts as we are eager to reimagine design education otherwise beyond institutional norms and familiar pedagogies. We are grateful for your words and generous exchanges. Thank you for equipping us with the language and examples we need to actually do the work.

Thanks Johanna Mehl for being a students' ally and for initiating the conference at KISD. Thanks Nina Paim and Maya Ober for listening to us and opening the doors. Thanks also to all the students who worked for and at the conference. And everyone who joined the roundtable.

COMMITTED TO PRESENTS

A Break at Attending [to] Futures

(Dorsa Javaherian) (Abigail Schreider)

A few years after graduating from the M.A. program at Köln International School of Design, we, Abigail and Dorsa, revisited our former university to envision Committed to Presents—a roundtable concept at the *Attending [to] Futures* conference hosted by KISD in 2021. The roundtable invited participants to reflect on their lived experience as design students.

    As much as it sparked eagerness to critically engage with design education, the conference's open call also resonated with questions about our own experiences. How might we contribute to a collective and bottom-up effort to acknowledge the colonial roots and false neutrality of design education? How could we leverage those critical conversations and anchor them at Köln International School of Design? How could we create a legacy of transformation towards a more inclusive design education for future design students? Our heads boiling with these questions, we facilitated conversation between students, alumni, one faculty member, conference speakers, and participants to foster collective reflection, elevate students' situated knowledge and experiences, and expose entrenched ways of conducting design education in need of reformation.

In recent years, more and more students worldwide have begun to address a long-neglected topic at the margins of design academia: equity and justice in design education. Rather than design institutions—such as art schools and universities—para-institutional spaces, such as *Decolonizing Design, Depatriarchise Design,* and *Futuress,* have been pivotal in vocalizing critique and resounding actions toward more just and equitable classrooms. Furthermore, student bodies are increasingly demanding a transformation in design curricula and faculties towards a more inclusive educational environment. Students' *work* echoes the need for safer learning spaces and more diverse study courses, perspectives, and practices in design. As students coming from the Global South, we also longed for that.

From Teheran and Buenos Aires, where we packed up our lives, stuffed it into big suitcases and bought euros despite spiking rates of the Iranian rial and Argentinian peso, we came to Germany to pursue Master degrees, attracted by the design school's international reputation. However, our joy didn't last long as international students. The reality we experienced as newly arrived immigrant students differed from our idealized image.

    Very soon, we felt *alienated* and *exhausted* from navigating through the institutional structure; *disconnected* from a school that did not represent perspectives and diversity in its faculty members; *gaslighted,* when we were called *passionate* and *romantic* whenever we incorporated questions of equity and justice in design in our semester projects; *disoriented,* when we were reminded that we are not social scientists and therefore unable to criticize white supremacy within institutional design spaces; *detached from our education,* when we began to find peers confronted with similar situations in different schools, structures, and countries.

Our problems and feelings did not exist in a vacuum; they were extensions of our intersectional identities growing into the educational context. The Argentinian movement #niunamenos had already broken into the institutions. The South African #RhodesMustFall student-led demonstrations and actions questioned the glorification of colonialism while the *Black Lives Matter* movement gained international attention. #MeToo testimonies accumulated globally while Polish women fought on the streets to prevent the most restrictive abortion law in Europe. Indeed, these are only a few examples of many movements we witnessed.

Our intersectional feminist approach to design was informed by feelings of exhaustion during our time as Master students. Carrying on our common struggle, we wanted *Committed to Presents* to become a safe space to talk about our experiences as international students and design practitioners living in design academia, either short term or long term. Our primary goal was to reflect on reciprocity and commitments to do the work, to make preferred futures happen.

An "International" School

Early 2021 KISD announced hosting *Attending [to] Futures,* a conference that called out the necessity of anti-colonial and feminist design education, research, and practice and invited students, scholars, and practitioners of design and adjacent fields to address, examine, and critique institutional structures. Against the backdrop of our own experiences, we wanted to be part of the conversation that the conference sparked in its host institution, and witness fields of research that so far had systematically been rejected move in the center of the spotlight.

We proposed the roundtable because we wanted to listen to the voice of students, amplify their thoughts, and make space to ask those same questions we had as students years before. We opened the debate with the question "What has changed that design is more and more interested in feminism and decolonization?" It didn't take long until the conversation burst open like a floodgate: *"We have heard about feminism but we haven't talked about it in classrooms, with each other."* one student said. She continued: *"We haven't talked about decolonization even though we have a huge body of students that are not German and come from other educational systems, other countries."* Many testimonies reflected on the lack of decolonial lenses within their education, something that echoes a habitual neglect of Germany's colonial past in public discourse as well as educational institutions from high schools to universities. Another student pointed out that socially important topics tend to be addressed superficially: *"Sometimes I still feel lonely because it's not really deep, it's just—ok we have these topics (like Black Lives Matter) and it's important cause it's in the media. But when I have some questions or really want someone to speak about this, there's a limit."* Not recognizing those limits can be threatening for students whose design research and work is significantly shaped and impacted by personal confrontations with structural racism and sexism. Testimonies at the roundtable showed the difficulty to raise critical questions in classrooms and projects: *"We had this project about Decolonizing Everything and I was critical about it. I don't feel confident to address having experienced racism with someone who maybe never experienced it. In the end I got support, not from the professors but from people who were accepting my criticism, but I never had an answer."*

The students' comments underline the importance of representing critical thinking, questions of race, gender, disability, and other intersecting social identities in their education. They want this change to go beyond seminar topics by making intersectional identities an integral part of the institutional structure via designating positions and reforming hiring policies that do justice to the academic fields and critical practices that require their expertise, nuance, and space in the curriculum.

During the conference, many of the keynote lecturers spotlighted the lack of representation and diversity among the faculty members in European design schools. In most cases, non-European professors or guest lecturers are rarely invited to participate in curriculum development, or they are only involved in extracurricular and parallel spaces and one-time events. Building upon students' comments during the roundtable, this observation could hold institutions back to attune their structure to diverse student bodies' interests and ambitions.

Attending [to] Futures featured experienced and emerging academics from multiple and diverse backgrounds (majority from the Global South) in a conference hosted within an institution with 100% white and European professors. The presence of the conference's diverse lecturers in the roundtable enabled students to speak up and encouraged them to engage critically with their environment. Also, speakers who joined the roundtable highlighted the urgency of diversifying the teaching body in design schools in order to create forces to push the boundaries and challenge and transform the status quo from within.

A Safe Space

The roundtable centered the voices and concerns of the students, mostly those with marginalized identities whose needs and expectations too often remain unseen. We presumed that the setting and constellation of participants were going to influence group dynamics. Among peers, some of the keynote speakers, one KISD professor and us as the roundtable moderators, the students opened up and shared stories about how they rarely felt that someone was on their side when they proposed to approach matters of politics in design. For some of them it feels more like surviving despite the institution: *"I feel comfortable now because speakers are here, I feel you have our backs and feel your support. But tomorrow you guys are not here anymore,"* they continued, *"If I imagine this conversation with professors and students, I don't really know if I want to. It would be really exhausting. You feel like I have to defend myself, it doesn't feel safe."* The feeling of constantly having to defend yourself is something we are very familiar with. Oftentimes the structure of educational spaces prevent its own students from learning what could empower them simply because those lessons challenge the structure that they are built on. It is not so hard to imagine that students might not want to share experiences of racism or sexism with professors who are known to question their personal stories. To put students' needs at the center means acknowledging that the lack of diversity within the institution is a disservice to a very diverse body of students, many of them migrants who are already juggling with bureaucracy and who end up exhausted from having to justify their very presence in an oppressive environment. The demand placed upon those students is labor that multiplies when they additionally have to educate professors and peers, while enduring their insensitivity towards lived realities of migrants and international students.

Reciprocity

Building networks of support and care becomes an imperative; the well-being of each individual student slowly becomes a political act of self-care that they perform when choosing when and with whom to take the conversation further, as one student pointed: *"I don't know how we can come together because when I try to talk to professors, they don't understand what I'm saying. I constantly have to explain why what I'm experiencing at KISD is legitimate. For him it's my problem if I feel uncomfortable in this space, not recognizing that it's an institutional problem and I cannot tell him because I'm a student and in his eyes I'm a black student and a woman. What can I do? I really think we need a mediator."*

The roundtable was a constant back and forth between testimonies, complaints, and suggestions on how to change things. The idea of a mediator or "someone who would support students" came back time and again. As former international students we could relate to the importance of having someone back you up in an environment that you are not accustomed to and that requires a specific literacy of culturally coded gestures, non-verbal contracts, tacit understandings, or social cues.

Students often struggle to navigate their host institution and fulfill the requirements, which could be misapprehended in many cases as a lack of commitment to adopt. In the roundtable, it became clear that the KISD, and many other institutions, are based on the idea that students are expected to be fully responsible for casting their educational experience, from organizing projects independently to contributing to the future curriculum. The professor who joined the roundtable explained the faculty's perspective: *"KISD is a platform for you to explore yourself, experiment, and come up with your own ideas. That is what we would like to serve: a safe space where you can do nearly everything and find your partners."* Under these premises, students are responsible for new curriculum design, co-organizing projects, contributing to hiring processes, learning about political discussions on their own, and that is all in addition to carrying out their duties as students, such as attending the courses and performing successfully in examinations. However, these seemingly open-structured curricula privilege those who can operate with self-reliance. Consequently, only those who are achnored, networked, and have tacit knowledge can profit from so-called unstructured structures, as it is much easier for them to explore, take risks, do things alone, complain, or feel entitled to access.

Furthermore, that DIY spirit sometimes covers a lack of interest or willingness to engage with what international students bring to the table. As one former student said, *"There's been a lot of talk about giving the students the power. I witnessed that myself in some courses where we would come in and nothing happened. It's easy to say, 'you have the power, you can do whatever you want,' but as a student you don't know what you are supposed to do and I didn't even know we had the power in the first place."* Referring to student autonomy is a weak attempt at critical design education if there's a lack of infrastructure to support them plus a lack of transparency on how to enforce student initiatives.

The roundtable showed that it mattered that the conference was co-organized and co-run by students and faculty members. According to their personal interests, students took on key roles in the event, such as chairing panels, moderating discussion rounds, organizing the exhibition and talks on site, or introducing keynote speakers.

It mattered that students were part of the selection committee that greenlighted the roundtable—a format that promised to spark heated discussions and address uncomfortable truths.

Committed to Doing the Work

We hosted the roundtable to expose and start the work that is needed, in order for institutions to be accountable for their own transformation towards a more equitable and inclusive educational system. Investigating and addressing institutional injustices is a first step that the roundtable and many lectures and workshops at the conference contributed to. Consequently, the commitment to listen to those critiques can be very vital to heal and strengthen the infrastructures of building trust and reciprocity between student body and faculty members. The students articulated a need that they want their educators to embark on a transformative journey along with them, as part of their responsibility of being a design education advocate. A speaker who had joined the roundtable summarized it so, *"...to speak to this idea of what you need for decolonial work to develop is that commitment and that accountability and to see it as not abstract but practical."* Practical exercise could be to actively hire and give space to scholars, professors, and practitioners that have different backgrounds, learning paths, and experiences. Such educators often have to work under very precarious conditions such as short-term contracts, and BiPOC scholars are disproportionately affected by this.

When thinking about how to make the work stick it was rather unclear whose responsibility it would be to propagate the conference's key learnings in the institution. Is it the one professor who joined the roundtable? Is it the strategic hire with a short-term contract? The few professors and faculty members who got involved with the conference? The students? All of them together? How do you guarantee a ripple effect of work that is not sustained by paid positions?

It is urgent to reflect on how, if we continue to contribute to places in which is normal not to be paid for work, we cast votes towards a future in which only those who are economically privileged would remain and join the conversation, take the time to talk to students in a roundtable on a Saturday afternoon, or write about it.

We hosted the roundtable as a work of hope. We wanted to take the chance to bring the very important conversation that was being held at the main stage to the ground. Those discussions are the work of resistance and resilience of so many inspiring people who we learn from and look up to. Their work cannot be seen as something that happens in isolation. The experiences that feed into those works of resistance are vivid experiences, real lives that are affected in real institutions that do not embrace their full identities. *Attending [to] Futures* should be more than what fits between [brackets] along three days. It should be the opening to a new education engagement, a new commitment with its community, to embrace decoloniality and antiracism as core values of a design school that seeks liberation, fulfillment, and safety for their students. Without structures that are able to account for change, the work is only half done.

In **PART 2** authors revisit and rethink design **HISTORIES** written from a Euro-Western perspective that universalize an exclusionary set of methods, knowledges, traditions, materials, and tools while neglecting the underlying politics that continue to shape the trajectory of design practices.

2
HISTORIES

POLITICAL ECONOMY PUSHES BACK

How Structures of Power Govern our Design History Narratives

(Bonne Zabolotney)

Design history powerfully governs the design field, regulating how we describe, value, categorize, critique, and uphold design and design practices. This chapter discusses the ways that our design history narratives *precondition* our critique of design, preventing us from shifting towards a more inclusive and diverse design history discourse. These preconditions are symptoms of structural power that guide our understanding and values of design, defining and validating what design is and is not.

As an aspect of the political economy of design, these preconditions disguise themselves as *a priori* principles which push back on the much-needed shifts and changes toward inclusive design history narratives. They are:

1. The depiction of design in its pristine state, as it exists at its point-of-purchase, and the absence of the depiction of design over time or within a flawed state.
2. The fixation on the definition of originality and its conflation with legal terms of ownership and authorship.
3. The promotion of design as though produced by a single author. The commodification of the designer itself factors into this preconception.
4. The exclusion of descriptions of design's ecological impact and labor conditions, excluding this frame of reference to understand design's cultural value and influence.

Drawing from chronically under- and misrepresented Canadian design artifacts, I will illustrate the challenges and possibilities in building an inclusive design history discourse due to these preconditions. These artifacts have been excluded from design history, remaining anonymous and/or misunderstood.

Unpacking the Relationship between Design History and Political Economy

To better understand design history's preconditions, we must first unpack the meaning of political economy and how it influences and underwrites design history. When we examine the political economy of design, we study the structural forces—social, economic, political, and cultural—that guide how we think about and practice design. Following Dominique Bouchet, political economy refers to the "…interactions among social institutions, power relations, representations, structures of meaning, value systems, distribution of roles, rules of conduct, the exchange of goods and ideas, and patterns of production and consumption" (2011, 1101). These structures typically rely on standard business practices, policies, legislation, and socially determined habits to survive, replicate, and forecast future structural arrangements. For designers and design scholars, political economy regulates how we value designers' work and, as a result, influences and directs how we contextualize designers and their designs. Structural power guides historians' and theorists' thinking in determining and developing narratives in design history and pushes back when we attempt to change or divert these narratives to broader or more inclusive versions.

Understanding, theorizing, and historicizing design is also another way to say that design history is invested in the *governing* of design. This governmentality, after Foucault, means "who can govern, who is governed, but also the means by which that shaping of someone else's activities is achieved" (Burchell 1991). What, then, is the practiced state of design government? The political economy of design acknowledges policies/permissions, regulations/limitations, histories, retellings, and adaptations, but in its aim of reproducing itself reinforces practices which do not challenge the existing state of design history. The persistence of these preconditions continues to relegate practices on the periphery to be deemed outsiders, using terms such as "alternative" histories. Interrogating the power structures in design history to remake a broader and more inclusive space begins with the use of language and developing methods in which to reconsider the way we critique and categorize design.

Problematic Preconditions

Precondition one: We depict design as pristine, or how it exists at its point-of-purchase

Design in our history books and in museums is often in its most pristine condition, but why is it important for us to learn from design in this untouched state? Is that what design typically looks like? Does it offer an honest critique? Most design is used, discarded, replaced, or repaired, so what do we really learn from only examining a polished version of it? Design history combats the possibilities of a greater understanding of design production and our "society of producers" (Bauman 2007, 6), negating the creative pathways of reproduction that accompany the culture of repair and adaptation. The heroic depiction of design works at their impeccable point-of-purchase state perpetuates "an approach to understanding design as principally an aesthetic phenomenon ... associated simultaneously with the field's roots in art history and with the fact that it has been dogged by its association with the active and profitable presentation of design in coffee-table, or principally pictorial, books" (Lees-Maffei 2016).

Historians like to know the untouched details of any work to better understand the intentions of the designer. In Canada, access to pristine design works from history is almost impossible[1] because we have not preserved them in museums, nor did we identify important design works in their time. The majority of pristine historical design specimens are often hidden away in private collections, not easily found and accessed by the average design historian or design history student. This leaves Canadian design historians trapped: If pristine versions of design works are necessary to establish a history, what happens to our history if very few works have been kept in that manner or are publicly accessible to researchers? On the other hand, design that is used over

---

1 In 2019, Canada's only design center, the Design Exchange announced it was deaccessioning its collection of Canadian-designed historical artifacts, dividing the collection between the Royal Ontario Museum in Toronto and the Canadian Museum of History in Gatineau, Quebec (Gibson 2019). It is unclear whether any of these artifacts are currently publicly displayed.

time, kept, repurposed, or repaired tells us more about how the design was received and valued by people over time. Canadian design can be found in archives and libraries in various states of condition. In my research of the T. Eaton Catalog,[2] I encountered pages of catalogs that were cut, torn, and written upon. These instances provided evidence of various interactions and corroborated folk stories about the role of this catalog in the daily life of a Western Canadian. In figures 1 and 2, you can see the intentional cut shapes around the catalog figures, an illustration of the many stories of "children [who] loved to cut out pictures for fun, or school projects, [making] cut out dolls with changes of dresses for the girls and suitable clothes for boys" (Comstock et al. n.d.).

[2] The T. Eaton Catalog (also known as Eaton's Catalog) was a mail-order catalog distributed throughout Canada from 1884 until 1976. The mail-order catalog system was a massive nation-wide endeavor, with catalogs produced for four different regions of Canada: Western Canada, Central Canada, Quebec, and the Maritimes. I specifically research the Western catalogs to examine the complicity and impact of consumer culture, colonization, and design.

Fig. 1. T. Eaton Catalogue, Spring/Summer Catalogue, Winnipeg, 1941.

Fig. 2. T. Eaton Catalogue, Spring/Summer Catalogue, Toronto, 1934.

Pristine depictions of design lead us to believe that design is precious and highly valued. But design is almost always commodified. As a commodity, it participates in consumer culture within regimes of value (Appadurai 1986), but we do not examine design's potential cultural, personal, or economic value beyond its point-of-purchase (Heskett 2016). Design depreciates with use, economically speaking. It is a write-off—accountants refer to this term when assets experience reduced value over time. Art, on the other hand, is an investment.
To *avoid* economic depreciation, design mimics art in museums, art auctions, and the kind of coffee-table books that Lees-Maffei refers to. Designers can understand the impact and context of their own designs by learning from design history examples that are worn and used. They see how materials wear down, where structural weaknesses reveal themselves during use and the way people culturally and emotionally value their work. When we *only* document pristine design, we are not encouraging designers to design for longevity, and to value their work over lengths of time. Historians can help designers move away from planned obsolescence and designing for the point-of-purchase by making space for and validating design that has been worn and used on an everyday basis.

Precondition two: Design must be "original" to be historicized, and "originality" directly relates to property and ownership

The fixation on the definition of originality and its conflation with legal terms of ownership and authorship is a barrier in constructing inclusive design histories. The mandate of originality hovers over designers, but most design practices rely on mutual influences, common resources and tools, and the pressures of consumer trends and client expectations. And what does it mean to be original, in any case? Since design history has been published, we have been taught that the European modernists were the pinnacle of originality, demonstrated through graphic abstraction and geometrical purity throughout their design works. In Canada, we uphold Anni Albers's textiles as one representative of modernity alongside other Bauhaus sans serif typography, abstract shapes, and structured compositions. What does this say, then, about the multitude of Coast Salish basket and blanket weaving developed over hundreds, if not thousands, of years prior to the modernists? These weavings display a masterful design language—abstract, geometric, and firmly embedded within west-coast Indigenous culture. Less ancient, but still older than the modernists, is the construction of the Cree syllabics, designed in 1840 in what is now known as the province of Manitoba. Again, these syllabics[3] are geometric and modular[4] in a dynamic and instructive manner that Bauhaus designers would have envied.

Design history narratives generally support the relationship between ownership—intellectual property, copyrights, and patents—and originality. To be original in design is to be viewed as moral or ethical while copying or adapting design is seen as unethical or fraudulent. The correlation between the ethical and moral standing of design copies and their economic value can influence how historians interpret the work. This is a curious exception to the way adaptations and variations of creative works in literature, film, and music are received. In those creative fields, adaptations are celebrated and valued. If design historians could take design adaptations into account rather than merely label them as copies or imitations, our discourse could then center on materials and methods, cultural context, or how economic pressures often shape design. Without discounting the issue of intellectual property/ownership altogether, we can instead set aside our judgements about originality and ownership to work towards deeper reasonings about the design at hand.

The Medalta cup, for example, was meant to replace the post-war Canadian demand for English hotel ware (Figure 3). It is part of a range of hotel ware, utilizing the same white glossy finish and green stripe as English vitrified pottery. This line of pottery is generally referred to as copies as if its white vitrified finish and green stripe are its only designed features. This cup is produced from custom-made equipment, from local clay. Its glazing process underwent extensive material research and testing. It is a cup conceived and built under the conditions of its own political economy—the distinctly Canadian colonial conditions that included competing against cheaper, imported English goods and the social construct that English goods indicated a higher social standing. It is a culturally valued, place-based design adaptation.

[3] The invention and design of the Cree syllabary has been attributed to a Missionary named James Evans. Winona Stevenson, however, asserts that the Cree oral tradition has always held that "a Wood Cree named Badger Call died and returned to life with the gift of writing from the Spirit world" (2000, 20) and that Evans was not fluent enough in Cree to represent the language in such a complex way.

[4] As Stevenson describes, "The Cree syllabary is unique in that it consists of a series of triangles, angles, and hooks of various configurations each of which are mirrored in four directions. Each symbol depicts syllables rather than individual sounds, and to these are added a number of accent characters that represent terminal consonants and vowels" (2000, 22.)

Fig. 3. English Restaurant Ware versus Medalta Potteries Restaurant Ware, ca. 1943–1949.

A second example of Canadian design adaptations can be found in the work of Andrew King, an early twentieth-century printer located in rural Saskatchewan in Western Canada. King's work has been diminished by historians in the past for reusing typography and images (Figure 4), trading illustrations with other poster printers, and producing understated poster designs, often as templates for multiple uses. King's design process and finished posters should be familiar to any working designer today. Contemporary designers rely on specific typefaces and stock imagery, and they collaborate with illustrators for some of their work in the course of their practice. Why would we devalue King's prolific contribution to rural design culture when his methods align with contemporary practices? Further, how do political/economic assertions of originality affect contemporary practices in design and designers' agency to consider adaptations in their work? Property rights, copyright, and legal patents continue to complicate the relationship that designers create for each other and mask the cultural values created by mass-produced everyday objects.

Fig. 4. Andrew King, Enterprise Show Print/King Show Print Template Catalogue, Wilcox, Saskatchewan, ca. 1950s.

Precondition three: Singular authorship and the commodification of the designer

We are in the habit of depicting designers as icons or singular heroes in the making of design in our design history narratives. Designers often commodify themselves in order to elevate their work and resist a kind of personal depreciation. "In the society of consumers, no one can become a subject without first turning into a commodity, and no one can keep his or her subjectness secure without perpetually resuscitating, resurrecting and replenishing the capacities expected and required of a saleable commodity" (Bauman 2007, 12). Histories of design push us to "authorize" our work: to attach a single name to design projects that may have required teams of people to produce over a length of time, overlooking ways of culturally understanding and recognizing anonymous and ordinary works. Disregarding the importance of design because of its anonymous authorship ignores an enormous amount of culturally influential work in favor of the commodification of designers and their star status. The pursuit of iconic status, in fact, often becomes a preoccupation for many designers themselves who are looking for ways to avoid cultural and/or economic depreciation of their work, knowing that "knowledge of technology and experience can appreciate into human capital" (Heskett 2016). Within the political economy's framework of control, design historians continue to assign iconic status to individual designers, recreating design histories that often go unchallenged.

One of the biggest challenges in situating Eaton's catalog within design history is working with a dearth of information about the illustrators and designers whose work blended together to depict the many products depicted in each catalog publication. Limited published information (Nicholson 1970; Davis 1995) about Brigdens Limited—the illustrators, designers, and printers of Eaton's catalogs—tells us that some of their illustrators became well-known Canadian artists. But Brigdens in Winnipeg was known to hire up to sixty or seventy illustrators each year to produce the catalog for over sixty years of catalog production. The identities of this large number of creative staff may never be fully revealed, and yet their work remains a cultural force. Their work is anonymously blended together in each publication. There is much to critique in Figure 5 without needing to identify specific designers in order to value this work. We could consider the entire layout of illustrations and information design as an interdependent body of work. We could place an image, or group of images, within the context of emerging technology for printing or for manufacturing. We could evaluate specific items as unique and only available in this catalog.

Fig. 5. T. Eaton Catalogue, Spring/Summer Catalogue, Winnipeg, 1930.

We precondition our critique of design by valuing authorship before comprehending the design object itself, which forecloses on design narratives that include anonymous and unacknowledged works. In this way, we reject design before we understand its contributions to culture. Even when we do acknowledge authorship, we often confine authorship to a single designer even when we know that the majority of design practices require collaboration and interdisciplinarity. When design historians and theorists fail to acknowledge the many designers involved in a single design project, not to mention programmers, technicians, and manufacturers, they signal a kind of futility of practice to *current* designers: that acknowledgement in history (in other words, fame) requires the kind of leadership that rarely admits to collaboration or the contribution of other intelligence and skills. Singular authorship in design remains a customary narrative in design histories. If design historians begin to acknowledge the complex systems which engage in—and support the process of—design and its collective effort, it's possible that history becomes much more relevant to what designers accomplish daily.

Precondition four: We exclude design's environmental and social impact on this world in our design history narratives

Much of the design represented throughout design histories is presented without an understanding or explanation of its consequences impact over time. As we've discussed, design is typically represented by its point-of-purchase state in design histories, and because of this, the full narrative of its long-term impact is often, if not always, absent.

Historians often rely on the narratives of success and societal solutionism based on the economic/consumer and pop-cultural impact of products, overlooking the social and environmental impacts of designers and their work. Spatialization, "the process of overcoming the constraints of space and time in social life" (Mosco 2009, 157), has been a force rapidly changing design and manufacturing processes (Bohemia and Harman 2010). Design historians, by and large, have not incorporated narratives of global cause-and-effect of design works. Most designers will argue that while changes made by the processes of globalization have benefitted the economic wealth and health of design and have had far-reaching consequences in terms of democratizing design, the impact of the globalization of manufacturing and distribution of designed products is ecologically devastating.

For example, Eaton's catalogs are vague about the details of their mail-order houses (Figure 6). They state that their lumber is high-quality fir, spruce, and cedar from British Columbia, yet it's not until we see an image from a later catalog that reveals their source as old-growth trees. This is not surprising—the lumber industry in Canada at that time would have cleared forests for the very first time and harvested ancient trees dozens of meters in diameter. We don't know the volume of trees that were harvested over time to create these houses or what the overall impact that this flat-packed, DIY house product had on forest ecosystems. Labor and safety conditions also continue to be undervalued as design continues to experience globalization. The social, cultural, and ecologic impact must be accounted for to rewrite notions of success and historical contributions of design. We often refer to well-designed products as value-added but, as Marina Mazzucato states, "by losing our ability to recognize the difference between value creation and value extraction, we have made it easier for some to call themselves value creators and in the process extract value" (2018, 249). Value extraction refers to the siphoning of profit off others through subsidies, tax breaks, or, in the case of ecological impact, neglect.

Fig. 6. T. Eaton Catalogue, Spring/Summer Catalogue, Winnipeg, 1912.

Canada's Challenge in Constructing Its Design History

Canadian design historians will have very little to work with if we accept these preconditions and continue to write design history on the basis of identification and authorship, concepts of originality, and the subjective critique of form and aesthetics. Recorded historical design content in Canada is already scarce, and where scholarly writings mention Canadian Design, they often situate the design work within a framework that marginalizes it as secondary to American or European innovation. This framing doesn't account for the colonizing forces of Canadian culture, the need to indigenize design knowledge, or the conditions in which design practices evolved in various parts of Canada.

Canadian design does not need to be guided by the constraints of any canon, but they do have an opportunity to build a history on their own terms if they are able to recognize the political economy of design as a major influence. The T. Eaton catalog requires an understanding of its cultural and economic power and effect. It is evidence of a designed system of manufacturing, documentation, publication, and distribution which utilized the force of colonialism to achieve success. Their catalog from 1934 (Figure 7) presents itself as a reflection of Canadian patriotism celebrating the "discovery" of Canada. The catalog instilled its customers—the average Canadian consumer—with modernist notions of progress, whereby Indigenous knowledge and culture are replaced with industry, technology, discovery, and confederation. In this image, Eaton's aims to infect their customers with a similar optimistic approach and to conflate consumption with citizenship through modernist imagery and a nostalgic representation of the friendly contact between Europeans and First Nations people. This image, however, is one component of many catalog covers within a designed retail system steeped in the exertion of colonial and consumerist economic power that remains relatively unexamined—as individual design artifacts or a network of designed artifacts and processes—within Canadian design histories.

Fig. 7. T. Eaton Catalogue, Spring/Summer Catalogue, Toronto, 1934.

Fig. 8. Andrew King, Enterprise Show Print/King Show Print, Poster Template and Show Cards, Wilcox, Saskatchewan, ca. 1950s.

Andrew King's work requires a departure from the focus of singular authorship and a deeper understanding of early networks of collaboration. His design and print work reveals a flexible and adaptable proto-design practice (Zabolotney and Derksen 2020) where type and images were sourced and traded with other show printers. Some of his wood-type poster and showcard templates (Figure 8) were created close to one hundred years ago and indicate design practices which mirror contemporary design templates and style guides. Setting aside any preconceived limitations of originality, authorship, or ownership broadens the narratives and terminology we might use to situate his work within Canadian design history.

We can consider Medalta's hotel ware as adaptations of other pottery designs, yet ironically Medalta potteries held a US patent for its unique approach to molding its cup handle (Figure 9.) This conflicts with the narrative of Medalta's so-called lack of originality and offers another complexity in the originality and ownership precondition.

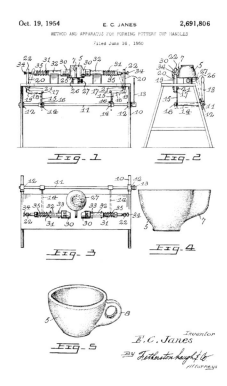

Fig. 9. Medalta technical illustration for US Patent 2691806, 1954.

If histories are created within the constraints and conditions of social structures, what are the conditions in which design histories are expressed or possibly repressed? Where can scholars find opportunities to subvert or challenge these conditions to establish meaningful and inclusive histories of design?

To acknowledge power structures and the constraints of design's political economy, we can begin by asking, where does design history uphold or amplify colonialisms? Where does it constrain or oppress? What are the aesthetic states of design work over time and space? How does a design work acknowledge its ecological footprint? When design depreciates at a rapid rate, at what point is it considered a liability? Design history scholars cannot continue to contribute towards established bodies of knowledge without challenging the power structure which reinforces this body in specific ways of acceptance and expression. Building relevant design culture requires more than expanding our subject matter—it requires practitioners to address structural power to build new and inclusive cultural networks.

BIBLIOGRAPHY

Comstock, E., Manon Guilbert, Ruth Dickson, and Laura Dunford. n.d. "Capturing Customers: Memories of Mail Order." Virtualmuseum.ca. Accessed January 24, 2023. https://www.historymuseum.ca/cmc/exhibitions/cpm/catalog/cat2209e.html.

Appadurai, Arjun. *The Social Life of Things: Commodities in Cultural Perspective.* Cambridge, UK: Cambridge University Press, 1986.

Bauman, Zygmunt. *Consuming Life.* Cambridge: Polity Press, 2007.

Bohemia, Erik, and Kerry Harman. "Globalization and Product Design Education: The Global Studio." *Design Management Journal* 3, no. 2 (2010): 53–68.

Bouchet, Dominique. "Political Economy." In *Encyclopedia of Consumer Culture*, 1102–4. Thousand Oaks, CA: SAGE Publications, 2011.

Nicholson, Edward J.. *Brigdens Limited: The First One Hundred Years.* Toronto: Brigdens Limited, 1970.

Burchell, Graham, Colin Gordon, and Peter Miller. *The Foucault Effect: Studies in Governmental Nationality.* London, UK: Harvester Wheatsheaf, 1991.

Davis, Angela. *Art and Work: A Social History of Labour in the Canadian Graphic Arts Industry to the 1940s.* Toronto, ON: McGill-Queen's University Press, 1995.

Gibson, Eleanor. "Closure of Canada's Only Design Museum Shows 'Lack of Support for Design' Says V&A Curator." Dezeen. Last modified August 29, 2019. Accessed January 24, 2023. https://www.dezeen.com/2019/08/29/design-exchange-museum-deaccession-canada-toronto-brendan-cormier/.

Heskett, John. "Creating Economic Value by Design." Essay. In *A John Heskett Reader: Design, History, Economics.* Edited by Clive Dilnot, 303–29. London, UK: Bloomsbury, 2016.

Janes, Edgar Cecil. *Method and Apparatus for Forming Pottery Cup Handles.* US Patent 2691806 filed June 16, 1950, and issued October 19, 1954.

Lees-Maffei, Grace. "Design History: The State of the Art." CAA Reviews. Last modified November 16, 2016. Accessed January 24, 2023. http://www.caareviews.org/reviews/3152.

Mazzucato, Mariana. *The Value of Everything Making and Taking in the Global Economy.* London, UK: Allen Lane, 2018.

Mosco, Vincent. *The Political Economy of Communication.* Los Angeles, CA: SAGE, 2009.

Stevenson, Winona. "Calling Badger and the Symbols of the Spirit Languages: The Cree Origins of the Syllabic System." *Oral History Forum* 19-20 (2000): 19–24.

Zabolotney, Bonne, and Joel Derksen. "Trading in the Real: Andrew King and Design in the Canadian Prairies." *Devil's Artisan: A Journal of the Printing Arts* 87 (2020).

IMAGES AND ILLUSTRATIONS

Figure 1: T. Eaton Catalogue, Spring/Summer Catalogue, Winnipeg, 1941, Photo: Bonne Zabolotney, 2019.

Figure 2: T. Eaton Catalogue, Spring/Summer Catalogue, Toronto, 1934, Photo: Bonne Zabolotney, 2018.

Figure 3: English Restaurant Ware versus Medalta Potteries Restaurant Ware, ca. 1943–1949. Photo: Bonne Zabolotney, 2022.

Figure 4: Andrew King, Enterprise Show Print/King Show Print Template Catalogue, Wilcox, Saskatchewan, ca. 1950s, Photo: Bonne Zabolotney, 2020.

Figure 5: T. Eaton Catalogue, Spring/Summer Catalogue, Winnipeg, 1930, Photo: Bonne Zabolotney, 2022.

Figure 6: T. Eaton Catalogue, Spring/Summer Catalogue, Winnipeg, 1912, Photo: Bonne Zabolotney, 2022.

Figure 7: T. Eaton Catalogue, Spring/Summer Catalogue, Toronto, 1934, Photo: Bonne Zabolotney, 2018.

Figure 8: Andrew King, Enterprise Show Print/King Show Print, Poster Template and Show Cards, Wilcox, Saskatchewan, ca. 1950s, Photo: Bonne Zabolotney, 2020.

Figure 9: Medalta technical illustration for US Patent 2691806. Janes, Edgar Cecil. Method and Apparatus for Forming Pottery Cup Handles. US Patent 2691806 !led June 16, 1950, and issued October 19, 1954.

DESIGNING THE DESIGNER

Publicity and Immutability as Colonial
and Capitalist Design Imperatives

(Chris Lee)

> The colonist makes history and he knows it. And because he refers constantly to the history of his metropolis, he plainly indicates that here he is the extension of this metropolis. The history he writes is therefore not the history of the country he is despoiling, but the history of his own nation's looting, raping, and starving to death. The immobility to which the colonized subject is condemned can be challenged only if he decides to put an end to the history of colonization and the history of despoliation in order to bring to life the history of the nation, the history of decolonization.
>
> — Frantz Fanon, *Wretched of the Earth,* 2004.

Graphic design education is largely mired in the inertia of a commercial, client-oriented pedagogy. It presupposes an educational telos where the professional motivations and practices of graduates are framed by the concerns of commerce and mass communication. This text explores an alternative to these presuppositions and the recognition of graphic design's historically deep entanglement with colonialism and capitalism. Although the scope of this text is limited to forming this recognition, its aim is to point at the possibility of a praxis oriented towards the cultivation of other forms of knowledge production, memorialization, and transmission counterposed to the ones imposed by state and capital. The work that follows describes a normative publicity-oriented ontology of graphic design as a background against which an alternative immutability-oriented ontology of design might be figured.

Design history as it is narrated in Meggs and others is a historiography that constructs and canonizes the professional figure as singular and original—authorial. My argument is that what such narrations of design omit is the figure of the bureaucracy, dispersed, anonymous, and banal, as an authoritative designing agent. This omission also invalidates the copyist, the forger, the counterfeiter—the unoriginal work and the unattributed author—as a designing subject and presupposition for design school curricula. In other words, design history designs the designer, and the inherited canonical history's implicit function is to delineate the boundaries of who is and is not a designer, and what kinds of objects designing includes and excludes. To be sure, I am not imagining that it is possible to have a substantive discussion about studying and teaching "criminal" activities like forgery, let alone advocating curricular development for cultivating designer-bureaucrats. Rather, I am interested in casting this counterposition as a means for making contingent and contestable that which defines, even hazily, "good design," "qualification," and a "legitimate" practitioner.

Can designs and designers be deemed "good" because they adhere to the discipline's canonical values (or deviate in just the right, legible ways)? Or could they be "good" because they help refugees pass smoothly through violent border spaces by supplying "fake" passports (Keshavarz 2018)? Graphic design education often instills in students the idea that their profession is a problem solving one, and that their value is premised on their capacity to creatively solve problems. But rarely is the question asked: "Whose problems are we talking about?" Our exploration thus begins with the recognition of this unasked question.

Historiography as Ontological Design

Where graphic design history is a formal part of the curriculum, students inherit the horizons and values of the objects and practices recounted. Graphic design education is largely mired in the inertia of a commercial, client-oriented pedagogy. It presupposes an educational telos where the professional motivations and practices of graduates are framed by the concerns of commerce and mass communication. If history is designed—if it is historiography that selects and omits facts to construct a particular narrative (Dilnot 1984)—and design exerts an ontic force (Willis 2006), we can understand the history of graphic design as a delineation of the boundary between what is and what is not graphic design, and as a corollary who is and who is not a designer. Consider for instance, that the canonical history is populated by artifacts like posters, books, brand identities, etc., but not so much money, passports, birth certificates. The design studies scholar Mahmoud Keshavarz challenges us to probe the politics of this boundary. He prompts us to consider passport forgery, for instance, as a genre of graphic design that doesn't get taught in schools. Yet, as design schools increasingly seek moral valorization by promoting policies and programs that foreground political engagement and undertake efforts at shoring up diversity, equity, and inclusion, training design students to help people evade detection by armed border agents with "illegitimate" documents is nevertheless out of the question.

Like borders, such disciplinary boundaries circumscribe a narrowed spectrum of "regulated and regulatable" (Keshavarz 2018, 3) forms of design and foreclose a creative and critical attendance to what the study of design might entail. If we were to rely on the state, corporate, and other institutional/bureaucratic documents that form so much of the archival foundation used to construct official histories, we would know almost nothing about forgers. Of course, their omission from any record is entirely intentional! However, their lack of identity and originality, and their criminality make them illegible (illegal) as constituents of a story designed to shape the professional imagination of the designer who must articulate what they have to offer the market—the designer as an original visionary, a singular artist with a professional capacity to consistently produce masterpieces.

Recent efforts to address a lack of diversity and inclusion in the canon appear as attempts to broaden the scope of the "regulated and regulatable." Resources like Decentering Whiteness in Design History Resources (n.d.), and The People's Graphic Design Archive (n.d.) work towards resolving a lack of diversity and inclusion by casting an ever wider net and acceding entries into the canon through crowd-sourcing from an inexhaustible panoply of perspectives. However, I argue that this misses a more radical problem of design history. Such efforts, while affirmative and laudable, risk making a performative "move to innocence." In their seminal text, "Decolonization is Not a Metaphor," scholars Eve Tuck and K. Wayne Yang call out frequent attempts "to reconcile settler guilt and complicity" (Tuck 2012, 3) through institutional diversity, equity, inclusion initiatives, while evading a more substantive reckoning with decolonization as a dissolution of the settler-colonial nation-state. Though the two examples mentioned above may not necessarily see narration as their role, they risk participating in an impossible quest for a universally inclusive canon while declining the more radical historiographical problem of narration and its ontological consequence.

A story of everyone and everything invests in the liberal politics of representation (Coulthard 2014) and appears ultimately as a disavowal of difference and conflict as constitutive of a disciplinary identity, while attempting to suspend a potentially more radical and destabilizing antagonism. These projects can perhaps be better understood as databases than as stories, because if historiography is to have any consequence, it would be because of how it shapes the imagination of a discipline's pedagogical and practical priorities. I am by no means saying that the value of broadening inclusion and diversity is naught. Rather, I am proposing that the weaponization of canonical design history can pose a challenge to design (and its entanglements with colonialism/capitalism) itself. Suppose that instead of decentering whiteness in design, whiteness were set within the proverbial crosshairs to indict design's entanglement with the quasi-apocalyptic forces that have shaped the so-called modern world. What this means in strictly design historiographical terms is to recast the story of design's "progress" as evidence of design's criminality.

An illustration: the Korean precedent for printing with moveable metal typography precedes Gutenberg's instantiation by two hundred years. However, Confucian ethics prohibited the commercialization of books, so the capital-intensive enterprise of establishing a printing press failed to spawn capitalism as it did in the European context (Burke 2009). As a result, the Asian instantiation's impact on the world (and its place in the historical record) was comparatively diminished. While the Korean precedent is worth acknowledging, aiming at the capitalist phenomenon of job printing—the less glamorous story of the industrialization of traditional scribal labor which was Gutenberg's bread and butter (Steinberg 1955)—makes clearer the genealogical relationship between papal indulgences, stock certificates, and paper money as evidence of design's entanglement with, and role in accelerating the development of capitalism and colonialism.

You may notice from this illustration that papal indulgences, stock certificates, and paper money are not typically cast as elements of canonical design history. The critical historiography of graphic design that I am suggesting accedes the banal documents produced as a matter of course in the administration of the colonial state and the capitalist enterprise. The anthropologist James C. Scott cautions us when engaging the vestigial remains of powerful entities like states because these necessarily privilege the viewpoint of such bureaucratic entities and relegate to oblivion worlds that tend not to produce intentional documental traces. However, following the provocations of thinkers like Ariella Aïsha Azoulay, and eschewing the tendency to affirmatively review history as progressive, the accession of such documents is not meant to array precedents that model best practices of the document (so that the design student might aspire to improve bureaucracy). Rather, a history of the document might be regarded as evidence of crimes against ways of claiming, knowing, and remembering that have been overwritten by such documental regimes. Again, Scott reminds us that "the larger the pile of rubble you leave behind, the larger their place in the historical record" (Scott 2009, 33–34). The subject/object of this story, rather than privileging the author/masterpiece (Drucker 2009)—constitutive of what I'll now refer to as designer1—casts as its anti-hero the bureaucracy/document (Gitelman) as constitutive of designer2. Before developing this further, let us first draw some outlines of the first historiography and its ontological production of designer1 figured by what I call the design imperative to publicity.

The Imperative to Publicity

The imperative to publicity is hegemonic in design education and practice. It guides common understandings of what graphic design is and isn't. It figures the benchmark for what constitutes good design, and delineates the distinction between professional (read: legible, accountable, regulated) practice, and "vernacular" ones (read: illegible, anonymous, unregulated). The pervasiveness of publicity as a logic and an ethic endemic, that is, natural to graphic design, belies its particularity and contingency. Publicity is just one framework for orienting teaching and doing design that privileges the vague mass—the public, the audience category, the consumer, the user—through machineable, that is industrially (re)producible, storable, and transmittable form. It guides students towards outcomes that are legible and affirmative; it privileges simplicity and idealizes the common denominator of consumption as a function of design's interlocutors. In other words, a graphic design student is generally considered successful when they can demonstrate an aptitude for transmitting clear messages to mass publics. This imperative is demonstrably reproduced throughout the world (though, mercifully, not the entire world) through the vehicle of graphic design history.

Historian Clive Dilnot prompts us to ask "to what extent history [can] contribute to what design is and what a designer does[?]" (Dilnot 1984, 5). Theorist Tony Fry has argued that the production of a history invariably bears an agenda that narrows the discursive breadth and disciplinary imagination of practices like graphic design. The canonical history of graphic design shapes the horizon of the disciplinary imaginary, and initiates the learner into a particular "mode of being" (Fry 2015, 29). The de facto accession of Phillip Meggs' History of Graphic Design ([1983] 2012) as the primary textbook demarcating the boundaries of what it means to be a contemporary graphic designer and to do graphic design today, is demonstrative. The book arranges a technoprogressive narrative that aligns cave paintings, the Gutenberg press, and the internet (Drucker 2009). History, for Meggs, "naturalizes sequence as self-evident fact," and "works against [an] analysis of ideological forces" (Drucker 2009, 61). What his story naturalizes is the story of humanity's inevitable emergence from the dark, primitive zero point of the local cave to the high-speed universalism of computational rationality represented by the internet. It suggests teleologically that progress is marked by the *increasing distances and speeds* with which human communication is conveyed, and that we are in this moment at its peak, where designers1 ostensibly command a capacity to reach a global public (imagined as audiences/consumers) anywhere in the world. The story that so many design students are taught about the field into which they are being initiated imbricates (in the alleged apex and hyperobject that is the internet) the values of liberal universalism with the capitalist and colonial imperative to maintain perpetual expansion.

The teleology of Meggs' work suggests that designers1 and the artifacts they create are outside of the social, political, economic, and ideological conditions of their being and making. One of the ontological consequences of this techno-progressive parochialism, argues Johanna Drucker, is the figure of the putatively autonomous designer1—an auteur freely making creative decisions independently from the conditions that constitute their subjectivity. She argues that for Meggs, "Designers are conceived as acted on, not complicit" (Drucker 2009, 64). The heroic, primarily European male Designer1-protagonists of such a history manifest form and style simply as a matter of will, rather than as consequences of economic, political, technological, environmental, social forces (Drucker 2009).

This carries into studio situations. Students will invariably encounter critiques that measure their work against this or that reviewer's conception of clarity, simplicity, and legibility. The essential message in normative design critiques is often something to the effect of: "It should be easily and quickly graspable because it has to inform or sell something to a mass audience." For instance, it would not be unusual for a review panel to comment on the legibility of signage for a new shop concept, while completely avoiding its significance as a sign of gentrification or the extent to which it plays off of racist stereotypes. The plausibility of mechanical reproduction, where the realism of capitalist modes of production and distribution are also deployed as an evaluative measure. In short, the more likely it is that a student's work will move smoothly through the filters that ultimately determine what does and what doesn't exist in the world, using reviewer's best guess as to what would and wouldn't work in a commercial context has a large role in shaping what should and shouldn't be, or can and can't be thought, said, acted upon, and designed.

Perennial debates about the contemporary relevance of Bauhaus education, if not simply its role as the referential mark against which other forms of design pedagogy are cast, attests to the centrality of publicity in graphic design education. The designer and scholar J. Dakota Brown has shown that in spite of the incoherence of the Bauhaus' aesthetic and political commitments, the legacy of the school is commonly thought of as having to do with the valorization of mechanical form and industrial aesthetics as the embodiment of modernist progress, putatively carrying the flag of democracy-contra-fascism (2022). This is narrated as an aspiration to expand access on the part of the mass public to well-designed goods — and the demotion of form that signified an elitist taste for traditional (read: ornamental, labor-intensive, and expensive) craft.

At its worst, this valorization of the Bauhaus echoes the racist and moralizing admonitions of Adolf Loos' "Ornament and Crime" (2002), which would cast as degenerate that which did not adhere to the minimal, utilitarian, and modern (read: democratic) aesthetic of machined form. At its putative best, this evolved into a post-war crusade, echoed in tendencies like the so-called International Typographic Style as a negation of the dangerously irrational expressions of identitarian particularity. Ironically also known as the Swiss Style, this graphical tendency speculated on the dissolution of formal tendencies that were reminiscent of the nationalist schisms that set the continent ablaze during WWII. While filing down the past, its protagonists promoted and defended universalist principles of graphic form in alignment with, and indeed, in service to the ascendant multinational corporations of the Western capitalist countries and the multicultural, albeit precarious, social democracies of NATO (North Atlantic Treaty Organization). Graphic identity programs for countries like Canada, which implemented its Federal Identity Program (1970)—actuating at the scale of a settler colonial nation state the principles of modernist corporate graphic design—abandoned British colonial signifiers and adopted the "neutral" tone of the Swiss Style as part of an effort to resolve the French-English schism that threatened to destabilize the country. The legacy and zenith of modernist graphic design embodied in the work of figures like Massimo Vignelli, Wim Crouwel, Alan Fletcher, Chermayeff & Geismar, and adapted for their corporate multinational patrons remains to this day as the "rule" against which the impact of their being "broken" are measured. As Brown has shown in his chronicling of the Bauhaus' under different political contexts (from the Weimar Republic to the Nazi Reich), and the various shifts of curricular priorities in response to these extra-curricular forces, the principles of form developed at the school were argued variously as being grounded in socialist or fascist agendas. What remains when stripping away the ideological contradictions that inhabited the school is a commitment to design for an increasingly broad, yet potent subject to be interpellated by the industrially produced and commercially distributed design object — the mass public.

The Imperative to Immutability

> There is nothing you can dominate as easily as a flat surface of a few square meters… In politics as in science, when someone is said to "master" a question or to "dominate" a subject, you should normally look for the flat surface that enables mastery (a map, a list, a file, a census, the wall of a gallery, a card-index, a repertory); and you will find it.
>
> —Bruno Latour, "Visualization and cognition: Drawing Things Together", 1986.

A confession: there was some misdirection above in proposing to examine the canon for its crimes. What one seeks in building a case for an indictment of the canon is rather the embarrassment of evidence consisting of the stuff that has been almost entirely disavowed as part of graphic design history. The true target of this investigation is an accomplice to be found hidden in plain sight. I am referring here to the document—a genre of graphical form and practice that has been largely omitted from graphic design's disciplinary imaginary for the reason that it contributes little to the teleological historiography that figures the designer1. Documents range from coinage and contracts to maps and monuments—things that are banal and ubiquitous, but designed to give static, stable form to unstable claims. When it comes to the design of documents, form-making that facilitates mass consumption and universal accessibility are not necessarily prioritized as concerns. Rather, exclusivity, singularity, and security—the design question of how to render an inscription secure and immutable—could be qualities that the design of documents seeks to achieve. Since designer1's opportunities in the field of document design are extremely limited, design school curricula do not prioritize teaching the design of birth certificates, money, or passports. A design historiography that celebrates the singular genius of the creative auteur has little place for the anonymous bureaucratic designer, no matter how elegantly sublime their ability to design a tax form.

But what is a document? Documents give fixed form to fallible memory. They are protected in various architectures of storage, ready to be called up in moments of controversy. They perform what the media historian Lisa Gitelman calls the "know/show" function—they create knowledge and they serve as evidence. Documents move through space and time and retain the integrity of their form as they do so (Latour 1986)—their material and epistemological construction are designed to resist entropy and enmity (Hobart and Schiffman 1998; de Certeau 1992). By contrast, forms of knowledge that are stored, produced, and transmitted through some kind of embodied, often somatic practice work within the realm of what the performance theorist Diana Taylor calls the "performatic." Their instability precludes them from attaining the status of the document. Gitelman has shown us that key to the document's ontology and function as such is that it is not a discrete object, but that it's co-constituted by the bureaucracies within which it circulates—there is no bureaucracy without documents, and documents have no meaning unless they circulate within a knowledge system like a bureaucracy. The document, from the ancient genesis of writing to the present moment, is largely a feature of coercive and hierarchical bureaucratic arrangements (Schmandt-Besserat 1991)—the colonial state and capitalist enterprise are the apotheoses of such entities. Understanding that bureaucratic knowledge, memory, and claims instantiated through inscription are fundamentally contestable, the document's function, ultimately, is to render these immutable—that is, resistant to the entropy of an inscription's movement through time and space, and able to deflect countervalent knowledge, memory, and claims.

Immutability as a praxis becomes discernible through the construction of a historiography that aligns documental artifacts along the lines of the various techniques that bring them into being. These range from the material/technical to the political/epistemological (see below: §2) and even the homicidal (see below: §4). A history of the document is propelled by the dialectical conflict between "legitimate" documental objects and their subversive counterfeits. The subject, or human agent of this history is not the designer1 per se, but the bureaucracy, or, what I will refer to interchangeably with the designation designer2.

The design imperative to immutability is a generic term to begin accounting for the tools and techniques of the document. Seen through this lens, concepts more or less familiar in publicity-oriented design take on a different political charge. Terms like legibility, simplification, standardization, and the rationality of formal notions like the grid, are no longer uncontroversial ideals and mere technical/formal concerns. The anthropologist and agrarian studies scholar James C. Scott shows us that these are also concerns of governance. He elaborates the idea, to paraphrase severely, that the state imposes upon a thick, plural world, onto-epistemological simplifications by figuring its constituents (i.e. countable people and things) in terms of standardized and interchangeable units (i.e. numbers). This way of knowing renders the world legible, reducing things at the scale of the glyph—a form that can be displayed, aligned, compared, and combined on a flat surface the size of a desk, or a screen,

(Latour 1986) in order to make available the things it marks (designates) to managerial command. Take for instance the spreadsheet and its linear, cellular ordering of graphical space. It enables the gathering of signs representing unfathomable multitudes of things onto the same space, ordering it in columns and rows—defining categories of standardized particulars—making possible calculation and policy that are then projected back onto the world (often backed by force!).

Similarly, considered from the perspective of the question: "How to protect a document?" the repeatable action of punching and pressing, ostensibly neutral mechanical actions, actuates a desire for morphological consistency and mechanical objectivity, which at different times served as a means for marking the distinction between valid and invalid (see below: §3); a taste for the modernist notion of truth to material ceases to appear as a sign of technological and ethical progress, but is rather consequential vis-a-vis conflicts around the security and legitimacy of an inscription (see below: §1) .

The techniques of immutability that seek to protect contingent claims implicate graphical objects like documents in the long development of the colonial state and the capitalist enterprise. An historiography of the document is a j'accuse of graphic design. Constructed as a narrative spanning the first known instances of a formal writing system to the development of the blockchain and cryptocurrencies (see below: §5), the document and its designers[2] figure as agents imposing their ever expansive, defuturing (Fry 2015), and apocalyptic claims. Writing emerges in its proto-typical form as a technique for accounting, promise-making, and debt management. It emerges to mitigate the potential violence that might emerge from, say, mis-remembered agreements or fraudulent claims. They serve to limit obligations and avoid the escalation of a dispute to physical violence (Graeber 2011). Though it may be difficult to know the precise sequence of developmental steps, it is plausible that the state emerged as a form of third-party administrative authority to govern, recognize, and adjudicate social conflict through the use of documents (commercial contracts, land claims, tax policies, standards for weights and measures, etc.) so as to manage the eruption of unrest, disorder, and internal conflict (Hobbes [1651] 2002) under its administrative jurisdiction. An ancient Mesopotamian tablet contains the admonishment of a novice land surveyor, illustrating the role of the state as third-party adjudicator and its use of graphics (i.e. the land survey) to facilitate governance:

> Go to divide a plot, and you are not able to divide the plot; go to apportion a field, and you cannot even hold the tape and rod properly. The field pegs you are unable to place; you cannot figure out its shape, so that when wronged men have a quarrel you are not able to bring peace, but you allow brother to attack brother. Among the scribes, you (alone) are unfit for the clay. (Mansfield 2021).

In the following section, I will sketch very briefly some moments of this historiography so as to suggest an array of techniques for actuating immutability. These are identified in the subheaders followed by an ellipses to suggest that further consideration is warranted. This is a preliminary effort. In opposition to the kind of teleological historiography constructed to reify and valorize designer1, a critical historiography of the document eschews progressive linearity and privileges alternative "discursive formations" (Foucault 1972) that postulates the inimical subjectivity and agency of designer2. Although the historiographical sketch below hews roughly to a progressive chronology spanning 5–6,000 years, its linearity is troubled by the recurrence of themes like encryption, and mechanical objectivity, as well as techniques like pressing, and appeals to (coercive) authority, to name just a few, in an effort to dissolve the significance of conventional academic historical periodizations like "the medieval era" endemic to linear-progressive teleological historiographies. The movement from word to word, page to page, is driven less by an inevitable chain of sequences than by the dialectical movement between the creation of legitimate documents and the actants that constitute their subversive counterparts — agents of oblivion (Caffentzis 1989) ranging from forgeries to fire.

1. Clay, categorization, encryption, copying, counter-signing…

The materiality of simple and complex calculi (clay tokens), some of the earliest forms of systematized graphical production enabled a degree of immutability that surpassed the ephemerality and fallibility of verbal agreements. Presumed to represent the quantities of various commodities, the material's plasticity afforded a degree of morphological variety to enable the production of forms with different meanings, and thereby reify as calculable categories anything that could be subjected to administration (Beller 2017). These were sometimes encrypted within clay bullae (spherical clay envelopes) and sealed with a unique signature stamp to function as promissory notes. These were sometimes "countersigned" with a corroborating document to reinforce its validity.

Fig. 1. Bulla with five calculi, late 4th millennium BCE, clay. Musée du Louvre, Paris. Author's reconstruction, 2021.

2. Cuneiform, grids/orthography, standardization, institutional storage…

Cuneiform inscriptions, which in their earliest known instantiations mostly constituted contracts and lists, similarly derive their immutability from the affordances of clay. The morphological repeatability and consistency derived from the technique of pressing into the substrate, then baking it, allows the document to hold its form, evidently, for thousands of years. The advent of a syntactic grid to order semiotic space instantiates an orthographic standard—the correct way to write and read such that misinterpretation and dispute are mitigated. This development of "right writing" is less significant to the development of literary culture and authorship than it is to the development of governance and authority. Grids manifest the earliest known instances of graphical thought, and serve as a technique for mediating between potentially adversarial parties. The extent to which documents are co-constituted as such by their bureaucracies is made evident in the fact that these documents no longer function as, say, contracts, designed to help to order a living society, but exist instead in the generic register of archaeological artifacts, circulating within the undead and rarified discursive formation that is academic archaeology. In other words, the immutability of a document (which lives most of its existence in some kind of protected storage) is partly reinforced by the continued existence of the bureaucracy in which it was filed and circulated as such. David Graeber (2011) highlights the odiousness of the document/bureaucracy matrix when he reminds us that one of the first things that popular uprisings across the world and throughout history have targeted for destruction are the archives of the oppressor!

Fig. 2. Heliog Dujardin, Code de Hammurabi, Recto Col. 9–16, lithograph, published in de Morgan, Jacques and Vincent Schiel. Délégation en Perse 4, 1902, pp. 42–43.

3. Coinage, scarcity, metalworking, die-casting, typography, mechanization...

Coinage, from its earliest instantiations in ancient Lydia, combine die-casting and punching, with the designation of electrum (a rare gold and silver alloy) as the proper process and medium for creating tokens (money created for the purpose of taxation) given to nobles for the provision of goods and services that benefit the state. The morphological consistency afforded by pressing, and its use of a controlled, naturally scarce, mineral substrate reinforces the defense of the tax system—a system of claims the state makes that one "owes" them (Graeber 2011)—by raising graphical and political barriers to foil counterfeiters. The development of coinage, and the various techniques of metalworking (in both the European/West Asian and East Asian contexts) it adapts inform the prerequisite knowledge base for the development of metallic moveable typography.

Fig. 3. Left: Kings of Lydia, AR Stater, Kroisos, ca. 560–546 BCE, electrum. CNG Coins.

Right: Theodore Low De Vinne, Illustration of a punch and matrix, 1876, print, in Theodore Low De Vinne, The Invention of Printing. A Collection of Facts and Opinions Descriptive of Early Prints and Playing Cards, the Block-Books of the Fifteenth Century, the Legends of Lourens Janszoon Coster, of Haarlem, and the Work of John Gutenberg and His Associates. Illustrated with Facsimiles of Early Types and Woodcuts. (New York: Francis Hart & Co., 1876), 55.

Fig. 4. Roman Empire, Emperor Lucius Verus, Bronze sestertius, 163–164 CE, bronze, 3.3 cm. Metropolitan Museum of Art, New York.

Fig. 5. Soho Mint, designed by Conrad Heinrich Küchler, 1 penny "Cartwheel" (reverse), 1797, copper, 3.56 cm.

For thousands of years thereafter, the security vulnerabilities of coinage stemmed largely from the adoption of ever cheaper and common mineral substrates, and an inability to achieve an absolute morphological consistency that enabled commercial players to distinguish authentic from counterfeit coins. This is addressed through various design features (like reeded edges) and largely resolved, ultimately, through the mechanization/industrialization of the minting process, ejecting the fallibility of human manufacture. Rather than seeing this as a progressive development, it harkens back to the process of encrypting clay tokens, and anticipates algorithmic encryption processes like blockchain technology in that each of these techniques seek to remove human/political intervention in the process of designing and creating documents.

4. (Job) printing, typography, coercion, standardization…

The first European instantiations of the moveable metal typography printing press serve as a prerequisite for the emergence of modern capitalism. Rather than valorize Gutenberg's contribution on the basis of its literary significance, an historiography of the document recognizes that the man made his living from job printing: supplying things like calendars and blank-form papal indulgences to commercial and religious clients to help facilitate their various administrative activities (Steinberg 1955). The privileging of the literary over the administrative, erroneously trivializes the role of the printing press in the development of things like paper money and the advent of the printed stock certificate. Printed blank-form certificates expanded exponentially the capacity of an enterprise to raise capital for ever more expansive colonial ventures by spreading risk across a greater public of investors. The development of paper money, public education, national citizenship, modern cartography, double-entry bookkeeping, etc. are corollary to the standardization of national, vernacular languages and the cultivation of national imaginaries that ground the modern nation state (Anderson 2006). The standardization of weights and measures stabilizes the governance of commercial contracts by grounding claims about how much stuff would be made, sold, bought, delivered, and owned (Scott 1998) in increasingly (though, ostensibly) objective definitions. All the while, the ability to extend the jurisdiction of this administration ever expansively as documental production and transmission became faster and more secure (Latour 1986), also figures as the technological scaffolding upon which practices of publicity are premised.

Yet, paper documents, in spite of their power to amplify and project power, were rife with graphical vulnerabilities. Loss, physical damage, illiteracy/misrecognition, counterfeiting, along with a heavy and costly (financially and politically) reliance on coercive enforcement that paper required, were only substantially resolved with contemporary developments like electronic payment and cryptocurrencies. These technologies rely on speed and code (encrypting the creation and transmission of documents in algorithmic processes) to resolve some of the temporal, spatial, and political vulnerabilities of paper.

Fig. 6. Catholic Church, Pope (Nicholas V, 1447–55), Cyprus Indulgence, 31 lines, print on vellum leaf, 21 × 26 cm, printed by Johannes Gutenberg (Mainz), 1455.

5. Digitization, algorithms, blockchain, war...

Cryptocurrencies almost completely evacuate the human/political dimension and the contingency of claims by locating its validation processes and thereby its authority, in the purely technical realm of algorithmic objectivity, effectively threatening to cast in "stone," irrevocably, the media we use to facilitate various scales of sociability—to formalize agreements, to record credits and debts, to create and administer status, and thereby access to privileges and to charge with obligations. The non-negotiability of blockchain inscriptions (Golumbia 2016) echoes the non-negotiability of paper money backed by the state's monopoly of violence. All documents seek immutability—the deflection of doubt, damage, and dispute, through material, political, technical, and homicidal techniques. That's what makes them functionally reliable as such (Hobart and Schiffman 1998).

Documents are made to assert a point of view. They may use paper and ink to articulate colonial claims over Indigenous lands, but are fundamentally legitimized only by long and violent domination; they may order human populations, seeing people along the lines of a gender binary, racial categories, age, nationality, and immigration status, etc., while the bureaucracies that circulate them interpellate human subjects made legible to enforcement arms of administration (claims about who can/can't go where; who can/can't marry whom; who can/can't legally work; own land, legally repel intruders and impose death; and so on). Graeber is quite right when he writes that police are essentially bureaucrats with guns (2015, 73). Documents have worked to make such claims seem natural and inevitable—often deflecting even the thought of contestation. So many of the world's social, political, and economic conflicts have to do with problems generated by designer2's documents and the kinds of claims they make. In a case like the passport, the consequences of the non-possession of the right documents imposed through direct violence, or the denial of protection, puts into relief the relationship between coercion and the document (Graeber 2015; Beller 2017).

These are the markings that figure design as a field of struggle.

To the extent that the design imperative to immutability motivates the design of documents—and to the extent that these facilitate the onto-epistemological violence of the colonial state and the capitalist enterprise—a design praxis that is counterposed antagonistically to it might be figured as one that contests the knowledge, memory, and claims they reify. But what might this entail in terms of praxis? Could we postulate a designer3 whose priorities and ways of being are as distant from designer2 as designer2's are from designer1? What would a pedagogy of designer3 entail? What place is there in an alternative, formal pedagogy and practice for the oblivion of forgery and fire?

Fig. 7. Desktop icon for Satoshi Nakamoto's "Bitcoin: A Peer-to-Peer Electronic Cash System," Bitcoin.org, 2008.

Fig. 8. Stele with Law Code of Hammurabi (detail), c. 1792–1750 BCE, basalt, 225 × 79 × 47 cm.

Coda

Histories help to construct the imaginary figure of a "we." In the case of graphic design, the canonical history and the implicit commitments of design school curricula it supports, figure "us" as agents of publicity and as vehicles of capitalist priorities. An occult, alternative history offers that there is a deeper entanglement of design with capitalism and colonialism that becomes discernible when the narration of design's history centers the document, and its actuation of the imperative to immutability. Each of these imperatives also casts as its protagonist a designing subject, who I have labeled designer1 and designer2. However, the suggestion of the latter as an alternative to the former is not motivated by advocacy. Rather, it is to form a background against which a potential (Azoulay 2019) designer3 might be figured. In sum, if it can be said that what designer1 and designer2 do is give form to ways of being, knowing, remembering, and claiming that serve capitalist/colonial agendas, what would ways of being, knowing, remembering, and claiming look like undertaken by a designer3?

In other words, what would it take to substantively "re-exist" (Mignolo 2017) the names and worlds of the colonized and otherwise subaltern and obliterate the ones imposed by the current forms of hegemonic power? Where designer1 fetishizes technology, and designer2 security, would designer3 be animated by poeisis (poetry)? Perhaps historiography could be about creating history, names, and claims that contest the ones imposed by the colonial state and the capitalist enterprise. Might this involve new kinds of writing, transmission, storage, retrieval, and performance that oppose, obliterate, disrupt, or trivialize the names imposed by these entities? One must also be ready for the possibility that to answer this question, to take it up as a matter of study and praxis, design as such ought to be abandoned, even in the most generous understanding, as a useful category.

I have sketched the subject, object, and motivation of this praxis, but I have not addressed its scalar impact in terms of space and time. Designer1's practice tends to reside in the relatively immediate fiscal cycles of commerce; designer2's impositions seek eternity. Could the significance and impact of an intervention then be apprehended in more immediate timeframes and local registers, or could it be found in the longue durée and the global? These are perhaps the more important questions beyond the scope of this text, but suffice it to say, addressing these questions would be an entirely different project.

BIBLIOGRAPHY

Anderson, Benedict. *Imagined Communities: Reflections on the Origin and Spread of Nationalism.* 2nd ed. London: Verso, 2006.

Azoulay, Ariella Aïsha. *Potential History: Unlearning Imperialism.* London: Verso, 2019.

Beller, Jonathan. *The Message Is Murder: Substrates of Computational Capital.* London: Pluto Press, 2017.

Brown, J. Dakota. "Putting Modernism All Over the Map: The Bauhaus and Weimar Politics" in *After the Bauhaus, Before the Internet,* edited by Geoff Kaplan, 60–73. New York: No Place Press, 2022.

Burke, James. *The Day the Universe Changed.* Boston: Little Brown & Company, 2009. First published 1985.

Caffentzis, Constantine George. *Clipped Coins, Abused Words, and Civil Government: John Locke's Philosophy of Money.* Brooklyn, NY: Autonomedia, 1989.

Coulthard, Glen Sean. *Red Skin, White Masks: Rejecting the Colonial Politics of Recognition.* Minneapolis: University of Minnesota Press, 2014.

Decentering Whiteness in Design History Resources. n.d. Accessed Feb. 5, 2023.
https://docs.google.com/document/d/1KiW2ULDFelm_OuvwhM2lygxwhoNddrEFk5tYl9zbldw.

De Certeau, Michel. *The Writing of History.* Translated by Tom Conley. New York: Columbia University Press, 1992.

Dilnot, Clive. "The State of Design History, Part I: Mapping the Field." *Design Issues* 1, no. 1 (Spring 1984): 4–23.

Drucker, Johanna. "Philip Meggs and Richard Hollis: Models of Graphic Design History." *Design and Culture* 1, no. 1 (2009): 51-77. DOI: 10.2752/175470709787375724.

Fanon, Frantz. *The Wretched of the Earth.* Translated by Richard Philcox. New York: Grove Press, 2004.

Foucault, Michel. *The Archaeology of Knowledge and The Discourse on Language.* Translated by A.M. Sheridan Smith. New York: Pantheon Books, 1972.

Fry, Tony, Clive Dilnot, and Susan Stewart. *Design and the Question of History.* London: Bloomsbury, 2015.

Golumbia, David. *The Politics of Bitcoin: Software as Right-Wing Extremism.* Minneapolis: University of Minnesota Press, 2016.

Graeber, David. *The Utopia of Rules: On Technology, Stupidity, and the Secret Joys of Bureaucracy.* Brooklyn, NY: Melville House, 2015.

———. *Debt: The First 5,000 Years.* Brooklyn, NY: Melville House, 2011.

Hobart, Michael E., and Zachary S. Schiffman. *Information Ages: Literacy, Numeracy, and the Computer Revolution.* Baltimore: Johns Hopkins University Press, 1998.

Hobbes, Thomas. *Leviathan or the Matter, Forme, & Power of a Common-Wealth Ecclesiastical and Civil.* London: Andrew Crooke, 1651. Republished as an eBook on Project Gutenberg, 2002. gutenberg.org/files/3207/3207-h/3207-h.htm.

Keshavarz, Mahmoud. *Design Politics of the Passport: Materiality, Immobility, and Dissent.* London: Bloomsbury, 2018.

Latour, Bruno. "Visualization and cognition: drawing things together." *Knowledge and Society – Studies in the Sociology of Culture Past and Present* 6 (1986): 1–40.

Loos, Adolf. "Ornament and Crime 1908" in *Crime and Ornament: The Arts and Popular Culture in the Shadow of Adolf Loos,* edited by Bernie Miller, Melony Ward. Toronto: YYZ Books, 2002.

Mansfield, Daniel. 2021. "How ancient Babylonian land surveyors developed a unique form of trigonometry—1,000 years before the Greeks." The Conversation. Last modified August 4, 2021. theconversation.com/how-ancient-babylonian-land-surveyors-developed-a-unique-form-of-trigonometry-1-000-years-before-the-greeks-163428.

Meggs, Philip B., and Alston W. Purvis. *Meggs' History of Graphic Design.* 5th edition. Hoboken, NJ: John Wiley & Sons, (1983) 2012.

Mignolo, Walter. "Coloniality Is Far From Over, and So Must be Decoloniality." *Afterall: A Journal of Art and Inquiry* 43 (Spring/Summer 2017): 38–45.

The Peoples' Graphic Design Archive. n.d. Accessed Feb. 5, 2023. https://peoplesgdarchive.org/.

Scott, James C. *Seeing Like a State: How Certain Schemes to Improve the Human Condition Have Failed.* New Haven, CT: Yale University Press, 1998.

———. *The Art of Not Being Governed: An Anarchist History of Upland Southeast Asia.* New Haven, CT: Yale University Press, 2009.

Schmandt-Besserat, Denise. "Two Precursors of Writing: Plain and Complex Tokens" in *The Origins of Writing,* edited by Wayne M. Senner, 27–41. Lincoln: University of Nebraska Press, 1991.

Steinberg, S. H. *Five Hundred Years of Printing.* Harmondsworth, UK: Penguin, 1955.

Tuck, Eve, and K. Wayne Yang. "Decolonization Is Not a Metaphor." *Decolonization: Indigeneity, Education and Society* 1, no. 1 (2012): 1–40.

Willis, Anne-Marie. "Ontological Designing." *Design Philosophy Papers* 4, no. 2 (2006): 69–92.

IMAGES AND ILLUSTRATIONS

Figure 1: Bulla with five calculi, late 4th millennium BCE, clay. Musée du Louvre, Paris. Author's reconstruction, 2021.

Figure 2: Heliog Dujardin, Code de Hammurabi, Recto Col. 9–16, lithograph, published in de Morgan, Jacques and Vincent Schiel. *Délégation en Perse* 4, 1902, pp. 42–43.

Figure 3: Left: Kings of Lydia, AR Stater, Kroisos, ca. 560–546 BCE, electrum. CNG Coins. Wikimedia Commons (CC-BY-SA-3.0-migrated). Right: Theodore Low De Vinne, Illustration of a punch and matrix, 1876, print, in *Theodore Low De Vinne, The Invention of Printing. A Collection of Facts and Opinions Descriptive of Early Prints and Playing Cards, the Block-Books of the Fifteenth Century, the Legends of Lourens Janszoon Coster, of Haarlem, and the Work of John Gutenberg and His Associates. Illustrated with Facsimiles of Early Types and Woodcuts.* (New York: Francis Hart & Co., 1876), 55.

Figure 4: Roman Empire, Emperor Lucius Verus, Bronze sestertius, 163–164 CE, bronze, 3.3 cm. Metropolitan Museum of Art, New York. Accessed May 16, 2023. metmuseum.org/art/collection/search/248045.

Figure 5: Soho Mint, designed by Conrad Heinrich Küchler, 1 penny "Cartwheel" (reverse), 1797, copper, 3.56 cm. Wikimedia Commons (CC-BY-SA-3.0).

Figure 6: Catholic Church, Pope (Nicholas V, 1447–55), Cyprus Indulgence, 31 lines, print on vellum leaf, 21 × 26 cm, printed by Johannes Gutenberg (Mainz), 1455. Princeton University Library. Accessed May 16, 2023. dpul.princeton.edu/catalog/d217qp581.

Figure 7: Desktop icon for Satoshi Nakamoto's "Bitcoin: A Peer-to-Peer Electronic Cash System," Bitcoin.org, 2008.

Figure 8: Stele with Law Code of Hammurabi (detail), c. 1792–1750 BCE, basalt, 225 × 79 × 47 cm. Musée du Louvre, Paris, collections.louvre.fr/en/ark:/53355/cl010174436. Photo: Chris Lee 2017.

Acknowledgements

Acknowledgements and gratitude to Maire Treanor, Edmundo Cuevas, and Juan Valencia Villalobos for sharing their time and expertise with us.

PATIO DESIGN AND CRAFTS

Building Encounters

(Zoë Rush) (Patio International)

How can explorations of the histories and practices of craft challenge the conversation around the future of design?

This workshop is a prototype of an inclusion practice between different ways of seeing and making, and an exploration of how to do future visioning across disciplines. We propose broadening the boundary of design institutions to center collaborations with educators and makers from a diverse array of backgrounds and traditions of making. Drawing from decolonial literature, we attempted a practice of Ahmed Ansari's (2018) proposition to "… reach back to both historical understandings of past being and their changed nature in the present to recover essential ontological features that would point to a new futural state." As the design collective Patio International, we approached artisans to explore the place-based history and personal meaning within their practices, the present states and challenges, as well as the importance of creative making for the future. We transformed these conversations into audio walks, which participants listened to before joining us to discuss how these perspectives could offer a new perspective or vision for the future of making during a workshop.

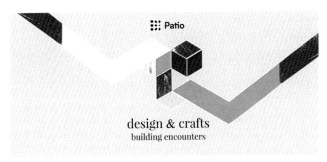

Fig. 1. Patio International branding for *Attending [to] Futures*.

Preparing

As a para-institutional collective of designers from Latin America and Europe, we tell a story about design that does not begin with the industrial revolution. The emergence of design out of the Arts and Craft movement, commonly referred to as the origin story of Western design, needs to be examined with regard to the colonial and patriarchal mechanisms that informed the separation of a discipline from a myriad of similar, related, or comparable phenomena. Canonical design history rendered as "otherwise" precisely those practices that historically are attributed to, e.g., women or indigenous peoples on the basis of a modernist rationale that entitled a specific set of aesthetics and methods to be superior (Buckley 1986). This narrative excludes many from participation in design spaces and limits design's potential to benefit diverse groups of people.

Ahmed Ansari, design scholar and founding member of Decolonising Design platform, proposed that to envision and build futures that break with current systems of oppression, it is necessary to "uncover essential ontological features" by exploring the changes in meaning over time of a historical "thing" (Ansari 2018). This paper kindled our imagination. Exploring the histories and present realities of craft could perhaps uncover values, practices, and concepts from which to act and envision a greater diversity of design futures. Building encounters with artisans was particularly important to us. Craft and design foil one another. In light of their historical overlaps, their different trajectories are stark, particularly when it comes to sustainable practices and narratives of embeddedness in local places and communities. We propose that design has a responsibility to reckon with the heritage and role of craft, and we aim to expose the colonial and patriarchal systems of power that demark the splitting of these entangled disciplines.

Aiming

Our workshop held at the *Attending [to] Futures* conference in November 2021 aimed at building encounters between different forms of making. How could exploring the nature of making from multiple perspectives shape our discussion about the future of design education?

Fig. 2. QR code to The Craft in Conversation series of audiowalks, at www.soundcloud.com/patio-design-jam 2021.

Fig. 3. Themes within The Craft in Conversation series of audiowalks 2021

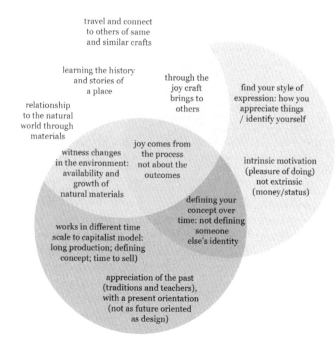

Doing

We began building an aural repository of conversations with makers about their personal relationship to their craft, and the histories and meanings contained within them. We recorded semi-structured interviews with artisans from Ireland and Mexico, underlaid with binaural soundscapes from the places where the conversations took place to create audio walks, a medium in which participants listen to an audio file while walking a route of their choosing. We chose the format of audio walks to create an embodied experience of multiple realities: As our bodies navigate the familiar landscape around us, we simultaneously experience another world through our headphones. In preparation for the online workshop, we sent participants a link to our online archive of audio walks with the collaborating artisans.

Fig. 4. 'What is a question that you still hold about how we can reconstruct our educational systems?', image of questions and voting during the workshop at the *Attending [to] Futures* Conference 2021.

The workshop was structured into three related discussions. We opened the workshop by sharing and discussing our individual responses to questions the audio walk had posed to listeners:

1) What are five words that you consider important for the future of design education?
2) What communities are you connected to? Where do you get your inspiration?
3) What is a question that you hold about how we can reconstruct our educational systems?

The second phase of the workshop used a technique of self-organization called "open space technology".[1] Everyone in the workshop was asked which question regarding reconstructing the educational system they wanted to work on. As we were a small group, everyone preferred to stay as one entity for this discussion and address the question: How to balance the collaboration between different traditions without appropriation or assimilation of either?

1. A method of organizing a meeting or discussion, developed by Harrison Owen, which allows for a participatory design of the agenda. Participants themselves choose what tasks they want to work on in self-organized groups once the general structure has been introduced by organizers (e.g. logistics such as timing). More information can be found at www.openspaceworld.org

Many of us had asked a variation of this question, as seen in Figure 5. Instead of looking for a solution, we asked ourselves what would be suitable methods and criteria to begin addressing this question. We numbered eight participants in total, all having worked or studied within the design field, though three use traditional crafts within their practice. The discussion uncovered deep anxieties in each participant of how to embrace and support knowledge from a multiplicity of sources while being within, and thus supporting, a continuing system of oppression. Participants reflected on personal experiences of privilege and oppression while considering what specific practices and values should be at the foundations of a more integrated education of making.

The final stage of the workshop reflected on perceived barriers and enablers to changing formal design education. We had a distinct impression that we look to individuals to take action to change a system, while we consider institutional barriers at a systematic level.

Fig. 5. 'How could we begin to answer our question? What methods or criteria is important?', 2021, Photo: Patio International, key points from the workshop discussion at the *Attending [to] Futures* Conference 2021.

Learning

The workshop critically engaged with the entrenched power dynamics between design and craft via the establishment of communication channels that considered common futures. As a prototype of an inclusion practice aiming to build relationships between different ways of seeing and making, this project failed to encourage artisans to take part in the workshop, due to language barriers and a significant focus on design institutions. However, the interpersonal relationships between paired designers and artisans gained through the interview process and the sharing of interests and knowledge was a positive experience for both. The workshop participants reported feeling emotionally connected during the audio walk.

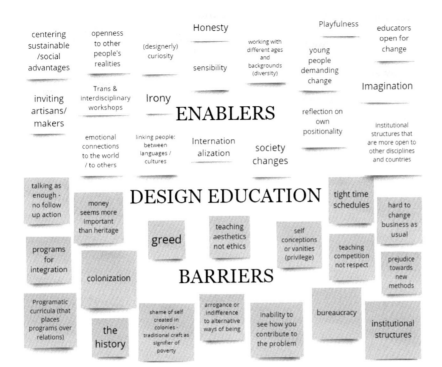

Fig. 6. 'What barriers and enablers exist to changing design edu-cation, especially in light of our discussion?', participant responses from the workshop at the *Attending [to] Futures* Conference 2021.

As an exploration of how to "do" future visioning across disciplines, often we sat uncomfortably with how to achieve our aims while participating in a design-focused conference. The workshop exposed the limits of interdisciplinary thinking and finding common ground in a system in which one is centralized and the other is "other": How to search for common futures for design and craft without commodifying historically marginalized and oppressed knowledge? What can these encounters look like? How can we avoid simply repackaging design knowledge to present ourselves as inclusive? Should we find common futures at all?

BIBLIOGRAPHY

Ansari, Ahmed. 2018. "What a Decolonisation of Design Involves: Two Programmes for Emancipation." Decolonising Design. Last modified March 2018. https://www.decolonisingdesign.com/actions-and-interventions/publications/2018/what-a-decolonisation-of-design-involves-by-ahmed-ansari/.

Alatorre Guzmán, Diego, Zoë Rush, Francisca Lucas Dias, Natalia Grein, Assol Hernández Uribe, and Ibis Lucero Urrutia. "Patio International" in *Exploratory Papers, Workshops, Places, Situated Actions and Doctoral Colloquium*. Vol. 2 of PDC 2022: Embracing Cosmologies: Expanding Worlds of Participatory Design. New York: Association for Computing Machinery, 2022.

Buckley, Cheryl. "Made in Patriarchy: Toward a Feminist Analysis of Women and Design." *Design Issues*, vol. 3, no. 2 (1986): 3–14.

IMAGES AND ILLUSTRATIONS

Figure 1: Branding – Patio International, Patio International Branding for the *Attending [to] Futures* event 2021.

Figure 2: Themes – Patio International, Themes within The Craft in Conversation series of audiowalks 2021.

Figure 3: QR – Patio International, QR code to The Craft in Conversation series of audiowalks, at www.soundcloud.com/patio-design-jam 2021.

Figure 4: Key Words – 'What are five words that you consider important for the future of design education?'. Photo: Patio International, image taken from the workshop Miro board at the *Attending [to] Futures* event 2021.

Figure 5: How to Answer – 'How could we begin to answer our question? What methods or criteria is important?'. Photo: Patio International, key points from the workshop discussion at the *Attending [to] Futures* event 2021.

Figure 6: Barriers and Enablers – 'What barriers and enablers exist to changing design education, especially in light of our discussion?'. Photo: Patio International, participant responses from the workshop at the *Attending [to] Futures* event 2021.

TOWARDS A DEMOCRATIC FUTURE

Art and Education at Black Mountain College

(Ina Scheffler)

Josef and Anni Albers are not the only big names that come to mind when thinking about the Black Mountain College (BMC), founded in 1933 by John Andrew Rice as a liberalist college in a remote and rural area of North Carolina. Named after a small town at the foot of the Blue Ridge Mountains in the Swannanoa Valley, the private school employed many artists and designers that would later become highly influential. Among them are Albers' former colleague at Bauhaus, Xanti Schawinsky, the painters Jacob Lawrence, Robert Motherwell, Franz Kline, Leo Amino and Ben Shahn; photographers Harry Callahan and Aaron Siskind; art critic Clement Greenberg, social critic Paul Goodman and literary critic Alfred Kazin; composer Stefan Wolpe; Bauhaus architect Walter Gropius; designer and futurist Buckminster Fuller, poets Robert Creeley, Robert Duncan and Hilda Morley (who, along with Charles Olson were part of a group of writers known as the Black Mountain Poets); and potters Marguerite Wildenhain, another Bauhaus import, and Shōji Hamada, who, in 1955, was designated a Living National Treasure of Japan. Plenty of students, too, would become famous: Ruth Asawa, Ray Johnson, Kenneth Noland, Robert Rauschenberg, Susan Weil, Cy Twombly, Francine du Plessix Gray, Robert De Niro Sr., Arthur Penn and John Wieners (Duberman 1972, 15 ff.).

The tight-knit community, their shared values and beliefs, and ultimately their artistic productions are among the key aspects examined in a growing body of articles, commentaries, or documentaries about the Black Mountain College. Beyond the legendary tales of student life and the tacit utopianism that still characterize the perception of the school today, this chapter seeks to explain what made it so influential via an analysis of its curricula and pedagogical concepts. Centered around a radical understanding of art as "a province in which one finds all the problems of life reflected" – as Josef Albers put it (quoted in Harris 1987, 243), the curricula of the Black Mountain College prepared students not only to work in the arts, but also to react to and critique the changing world around them as artists as well as citizens.

Exploratory Learning

Not an artist himself, the founder John Andrew Rice, needed a visionary to head the art program. He asked Philip Johnson, curator at the Museum of Modern Art, who suggested Josef Albers. Albers was an abstract artist, a theorist and a popular professor at the Bauhaus in Dessau. The situation at the Bauhaus grew dire in light of the rise of national socialism (Wick 2009, 21). But even before the

Nazi party came to power, the rising nationalist movement increased the political pressure on the institution and its faculty. Ostracized as "degenerate art," Bauhaus productions contradicted the world view of the Nazi regime, with momentous consequences. As the NSDAP pressed to replace existing staff with party members, the faculty of the Bauhaus, which had been relocated to Berlin in 1932, made the radical decision to dissolve the institution in 1933.

Born Annelise Fleischmann, Anni Albers was of Jewish descent. She worked as a textile artist and master weaver and was a former Bauhaus instructor and acting director of the weaving workshop. When a telegram from Black Mountain College arrived and asked the couple to join the faculty, Albers remarked "I don't speak English" and Rice replied "Come anyway" (quoted in Fortini, 2022). Starting in 1933, Josef Albers taught at BMC and became its artistic supervisor and later director. Anni Albers taught as an assistant professor of Weaving from 1939 to 1949.

Albers shaped the Black Mountain College on many levels (Wick 2009, 244, 265). Building on his former teaching experience at Bauhaus, he established the school's preliminary course called the "Vorkurs" and taught drawing, basic design and color theory (Fig. 1). An integral part of the course were uniform assignments and colloquia in which he and the students critiqued works in class together. The preliminary course as taught by Albers promoted action-oriented, discovery-based learning through experience, i.e. the intensive, playful and exploratory examination of materials beyond the typical scope of fine arts, including substances and objects from everyday life. Characteristic of this "learning by doing" approach was the high level of self-efficacy of learners, who were involved in the curriculum design from the very beginning and were encouraged to work in an experimental way instead of passively absorbing a predefined set of course work. Requirements that Josef Albers believed to be false motivators, such as accumulating a certain number of deliverables in class, were deliberately disregarded. Measurements of achievement were to be qualitative, not quantitative.

Fig. 1. An art class meets with Josef Albers on a deck at Black Mountain College, North Carolina, 1945.

Sense of Meeting

The Black Mountain College's curricula and courses accounted for an unprecedented style of education that would inform numerous art and liberal arts schools and art organizations in the U.S. such as the Black Mountain Institute at the University of Nevada, Las Vegas, named in homage to the BMC and with the aspiration to emulate its ethos. In a time characterized by tensions between ambitions to develop more democratic student-teacher relationships versus autocratic modes of organization in university and public-school systems, educational institutions were increasingly controlled by trustees who represented business interests and thus could raise the vast sums of money needed for their programs. The BMC on the other hand was owned and administered by the faculty, who formed a non-stock corporation. Guest faculty, assistant instructors, tutors, and staff, however, were excluded from ownership.

Its founder John Andrew Rice, who in early 1933 was dismissed from his teaching position at Rollins College (Winter Park, Florida) because he was outspoken against the policies of its president, believed in "the freedom to learn in one's own way and according to one's own timetable," as Martin Duberman writes in *Black Mountain: An Exploration in Community* (Duberman 1972, 22). Following the pedagogue and philosopher John Dewey in his conviction that "[...] the remedy is not to have one expert dictating educational methods and subject-matter to a body of passive, recipient teachers, but the adoption of intellectual initiative, discussion, and decision through the entire school corps" (Dewey 1903, 196), there were to be no legal controls from the outside: no trustees, deans, or regents.

Yet, the faculty did have some control over the educational policy and student life. They elected a board of fellows that included students as well as non-teaching members of the faculty (Bowers 1969, 22). As the faculty wanted to avoid the term "president" they elected a rector as the college's official representative. She or he had no real power. Rather than voting on issues, the faculty achieved a "sense of the meeting" (Harris 1987, 7), echoing Quaker ideologies that were foundational to Swarthmore, a liberal arts college in Pennsylvania. A treasurer was in charge of the budget and keeping the books and a secretary handled official correspondence. Eventually, non-faculty staff, including a registrar, dietician, bookkeeper, librarian, farmer, and secretaries, were hired full-time. An Advisory Council of eminent educators, scientists, and artists was appointed to increase the college's credibility to the outside world and offer advice, although it had no legal authorities. Its members included John Dewey, Walter Gropius, Carl Jung, Max Lerner, Walter Locke, John Burchard, Franz Kline, and Albert Einstein (ibid., 6 f.).

The strategic avoidance of being controlled or pressured by outside parties and strong emphasis on self-reliance resulted in distinctly non-autocratic structures and a system of self-directed study, informed by Oxford and Cambridge and the Swarthmore's Honors Program. This means that there were no required courses or regulations that usually guide students through their academic career. Instead each student worked out an individual program of study with an advisor. Although initially no grades were given, they were eventually recorded for the sole purpose of transferring credit – the students, however, remained uninformed of their grades (ibid., 7).

As was the case at Bauhaus, new students first entered a period of general study of usually two years. They had to pass a comprehensive examination covering all teaching areas in order to transition from the junior to the senior division. Consequently, the senior division was designed as a period of specialization that mostly relied on independent studies and tutorials. Studies were concluded by comprehensive written and oral examinations in the student's chosen field of specialization to determine "whether the student knows what he professes to know, and how he can use this knowledge" (Black Mountain College 1933-1934). External examiners such as Jacques Barzun, Marcel Breuer, Marli Ehrmann, Cora Du Bois, Paul Goodman, Bruce Simonds, and Franz Kline were brought in as an extension of the community – a central aspect of the BMC education that transcended the classroom.

At Black Mountain the students were encouraged to study music, drama and fine art, and classes in other subjects were scheduled around them. The arts were seen as equal to the sciences and the synthesis of different knowledge cultures was key for a holistic education that was seen as a preparation for life. "Art was not relegated to the sidelines," says Nicholas Fox Weber, executive director of the Josef and Anni Albers Foundation, "it was the basis of all education" (quoted in Fortini 2022).

Utopian Community

Participation in community life was an integral part of the student's educational experience dissolving the distinctions between artistic activities and everyday practices. In reminiscence of Bauhausian spirit the BMC became a space in which social and artistic interactions were intertwined. Faculty and their families as well as students lived on campus and ate at the common dining hall (Katz 2002, 54). Tales of the humble beginnings of life at the BMC are oftentimes romanticized in historical accounts. Students often performed chores as part of the "work program"; afternoons were left free for activities outdoors, which might have included chopping wood, clearing pasture and planting, tending or harvesting crops. Regular assignments to split wood together, plant seeds, and milk the cows reflects the core ideas of actively giving up established distinctions within the community "between curricular and extracurricular activities, between work done in a classroom and work done outside it" (Duberman 2013, 44). Faculty and students were responsible for general maintenance, such as the serving of meals, except for those jobs that required a specific expertise. Everyone took part in the work program, thus abolishing the "discrimination between students who pay the full fee and those who pay less," the latter generally becoming servants to the former (Black Mountain College 1933-1934.). Considering and explicitly working against classist exclusions also pertained to gender politics. Unlike many other private schools at the time, Black Mountain was coeducational, both women and men studied there and were treated as equals – at least on an organizational level. John Andrew Rice was quick to point out that equality meant "more than the unconsidered association of young men and women in college. Here they should learn to know that their relationship to each other, both while they are in college and afterwards, is to be, in the main, not one of opposites, but of those who live upon the common ground of humanity" (ibid.).

Studying in an environment still in the developing phase required that students learn to make informed, responsible decisions and take initiative when it comes to their education and life. It meant much more than going through an academic process or acquiring a diploma. The study of art taught students that the real struggle lay, in Rice's words, in one's "own ignorance and clumsiness" (quoted in Fortini 2022). At its core, the BMC was not about producing artists or works of art or success on the art market, but thinking citizens capable of making complex choices and participating in a democratic society (Fortini 2022). Democracy and its actualization became the underlying assumption of the college's structure and philosophy. Practiced in daily routines and programmatic in curricula and meetings, democracy was treated as a way of life. In education this meant the opportunity of every person to realize the full development of his or her abilities and, in the context of a political system, the right of every person to have a voice in the decision-making process. The social and political underpinnings of the curriculum as established in 1933 ended up giving rise to a network of artists who would spread its utopian spirit, ideas and vision across the contemporary (art) world (ibid.).

Forgotten Contexts

At a time when many prominent educators, artists, intellectuals, and politicians were looking to totalitarian systems, Black Mountain College reaffirmed the democratic, experimental spirit that had earlier characterized the Progressive Era (Bowers 1969). Black Mountain College was founded at the beginning of a period in which progressive education, against authoritarianism and aimed at the development and emancipation of the individual, was gaining momentum. The demographic, technological and economic transformations in modern industrial societies before and after the First World War triggered rationalization processes that changed the organization, character, and status of work and thus of social life as a whole. As a result, radically new questions and demands were placed on education and curriculum planning and new educational concepts emerged (Buchmann and Kell 2013, 209).

The Black Mountain College also represented a paradigm shift in the field of educational research. It serves as an example of how the lived experience and exploration of aesthetic processes can provide relevant insights for the development of pedagogical theory and educational institutions. Klaus Mollenhauer, a key protagonist in education research, addressed these forgotten aesthetic contexts of education in his 1983 publication *Vergessene Zusammenhänge* (Mollenhauer 1983). He asked to what extent the forms of life expressed in artistic artifacts – such as pictures or texts – enable the shaping of one's own future or rather stand in the way of it. His approach to foundational questions of education represents a modernization approach, which not only recalled the close connection between education, culture and the respective disciplines, but also intended to open up the (often unconscious) regularities, logics, and rules of a lifeworldly educational practice via artistic artifacts (Buchmann 2021, 361).

This approach to artistic practice as a catalyst for social change was foundational to the BMC and still influences contemporary accounts of art and design, just as the pedagogical concepts developed at the BMC still influence educational systems across disciplines.

Model of Society

When the discussion about curricula, goals, academic and artistic management and their evaluation at art colleges was ignited in the first half of the 20th century, it carried with it a positive outlook on the future which – precisely because of its democratic pedagogical approaches – stood at odds with a history of understanding education as the transmission of unchallenged routines and mentalities following hierarchical structures of order. The question of where exactly the curriculum begins and where education ends, or what art and design education has to provide remains vibrant and meaningful in light of ongoing structures of social injustice encoded in educational systems. The Black Mountain College serves as an instructive example and model for what it can mean for art and design schools to develop curricula that are not primarily aimed at producing new artifacts, but at exploring the politics of perception and the social effects associated with the way things are designed, taught, and built. As a place in which new modes of collective living were being explored, the BMC remains a viable case study when questioning the extent to which art and design schools can test or encourage new social models. At a moment when universities are seen as "economic enterprises" the BMC can be a heuristic starting point to critically investigate the histories of the entanglements between design schools, educational programs, and social movements.

BIBLIOGRAPHY

Bowers, C. A. *The Progressive Educator and the Depression: The Radical Years.* Random House, 1969.

Buchmann, Ulrike, and Adolf Kell. "Bildung Architektur Kunst – ein auf(zu)klärender Zusammenhang oder das Bauhaus als Curriculum" in *Subjektentwicklung und Sozialraumgestaltung als Entwicklungsaufgabe: Szenarien einer transdisziplinären Realutopie,* edited by Ulrike Buchmann and Eckhardt Diezemann, 201-216. G.A.F.B., 2013.

Buchmann, Ulrike. "Das Bauhaus – eine Inspiration für die berufliche Bildung?! Oder: über den Blick zurück in die digitale Zukunft" in *bauhaus-paradigmen. künste, design und pädagogik,* edited by Anne Röhl et al., 355-366. De Gruyter, 2021.

Dewey, John. "Democracy in Education." *The Elementary School Teacher* 4/4 (1903): 193–204.

Duberman, Martin. *Black Mountain: An Exploration in Community.* E. P. Dutton, 1972.

———. *The Martin Duberman Reader: The Essential Historical, Biographical, and Autobiographical Writings.* The New Press, 2013.

Fortini, Amanda. 2022. "Why Are We Still Talking About Black Mountain College?" T's 2022 Art Issue – The New York Times. Last modified July 7, 2022. Accessed February 5, 2023. https://www.nytimes.com/2022/07/07/t-magazine/black-mountain-college.html.

Harris, Mary Emma. *The Arts at Black Mountain College.* The MIT Press, 1987.

Katz, Vincent (ed.). *Black Mountain College: Experiment in Art.* The MIT Press, 2002.

Mollenhauer, Klaus. *Vergessene Zusammenhänge. Über Kultur und Erziehung.* Juventa, 1983.

Rainer Wick, Bauhaus. *Kunst und Pädagogik.* Athena, 2009.

Unknown BMC. Black Mountain College, 1933–1934, catalog. Accessed February 5, 2023. https://collection.ashevilleart.org/objects-1/info/6574?sort=0.

IMAGES AND ILLUSTRATIONS

Figure 1: An art class meets with Josef Albers on a deck at Black Mountain College, North Carolina, 1945. Photo: Genevieve Naylor/Corbis via Getty Images.

EMBRACING EQUIVOCATIONS

An Attempt to Attend When Design Has Never Been Modern

(Marius Förster)

> "We have to learn to wonder about what we take for granted, that is to leave the settled, frictionless ground where the question of what is responsible for an eventual misunderstanding matters, while frictionless understanding is taken for granted."
>
> — Isabelle Stengers, *A Constructivist Reading of Process and Reality*, 2008

Haunting Futures

Isn't it telling that within a publication that bears "futures" in its title, the most obvious way to start a chapter, seems to be a list of contemporary crises and global challenges? What drives future-thinking isn't the euphoria of progress but instead the awareness of anthropogenic processes that put life itself at risk.[1] The future becomes a prospect that haunts us because it represents the loss of the most basic conditions of vitality and renders human activity as a planetary-scale threat.

Thinking about design is not excluded from that and influenced simultaneously by the prospect of future paralysis and the sense of necessary transformation. Inevitably, questions arise about the involvement in processes that have brought "us" to this point and the potential of design to change and contribute to preferable futures (for whom). Arguably, design is a paradigmatic practice of anthropogenic geo-physical intervention. Intimately interwoven with the rise of industrial modernity, design has fundamentally contributed to an acceleration of resource extraction, consumption and pollution, global warming, species extinction, and ecological devastation. Its (material) practices reach deep into the social fabric and therefore accompany the enforcement of colonialism, racism, misogyny and so forth.

The question is, what are the underlying ideas that entitle "us" to exploit landscapes, people, and non-human beings? The project of modernity, following Bruno Latour, has been summarized as the cognitive distinction between and separation of nature and culture. Seeing the human as residing outside of nature and nature as a world external to humans allows the appropriation of nature as a resource to be dominated and exploited. Historically, design has been rendered as antithetical to nature as the practice of man-made things and the built environment, in service of the idea of problem-solving or stewardship.[2] The question is, how design—if regarded as a child of modernity—could be capable of transforming futures beyond modern paradigms?

1 In the IPCC Sixth Assessment Report 2022, the calculated risks of the climate crisis center around the irrevocable changes in the planetary ecosystem that will render whole terrains uninhabitable.

2 Maybe most famously put into the metaphor of "spaceship earth" by Buckminster Fuller.

3 Here ruthlessly meant, to imply contesting concepts, such as those of the Chthulucene (Haraway 2016) the Capitalocene (Moore 2015) or Plantationocene (Davis et al. 2019).

Within the Anthropocene discourse[3] human action is rendered as a geomorphic force to the extent that its impact comes to define a geological epoch. This concept contains the conflation of time, material, and agency. While it can be easily read as narcissistic, the conflation contains questions about responsibility towards ecosystems that decenters the human and therefore does not comply with modernist ideas of control. Thus, the concept of the Anthropocene also hints at ways of transforming a lifeworld caught in colonial/capitalist structures through nothing less than a fundamental transformation of western onto-epistemologies.

In order to make haunting futures less paralyzing, let "us" have a look in the mirror. What if design has never been modern? Drawing from Bruno Latour's famous critique that: "we have never been modern" (Latour 2008), this essay investigates the potential of reimagining design beyond its ties to modernity.

We have never been modern

Bruno Latour's famous essay is an attempt of a symmetrical anthropology —an inquiry into modernity capable of integrating all constituent parts (of nature and culture) that always already includes the observing subject as itself an object of observation.

He developed a terminology that well describes the establishment and consolidation of the nature-culture-divide. Rendering the division of nature and culture as a practice with specific actors not only dismantles a once static and stubborn normality, which purports to consist of either natural or social things, but also allows us to work out the specific modern trades of design by activating the concept of hybrids.

By revealing the modern paradoxicality and the working of its ebullition (*Übersprudeln*), his work also contains the image of the setting—a network of agencies—design might be confronted with beyond a modern cosmology. Latour shows how nature and culture are intertwined. His operation combines trajectories of time, material, and agency and through its catchy provocation opens up a discourse that is ultimately concerned with the climate catastrophe and the politics of the Anthropocene.

According to Latour, modernity's main characteristic is the separation between nature and culture, which only becomes an effective and stable paradigm in conjunction with *purification and mediation.*
Purification is the operation of allocating things to the natural or social side and accentuating the difference to its opposite. This way it allows no direct connection between the two spheres. In contrast, mediation is the creation of intermediaries that help to stabilize the paradigm of separation. It is the production of facts that consolidate the division.

Through these parameters, a contradictory constitution is put into operation:
1. Nature is a world external to humans. Its essence is constructed by modern sciences. This facilitates the appropriation of nature as a resource to be dominated and exploited and simultaneously serves as an argument for the "naturalness" of things.

2. Culture is the product of human construction but its essence transcends the possibility of control. This allows for the stabilization of the social order through the naturalization of specific interactions—for example, misogyny, xenophobia and racism is "normal" in a patriarchal imperialist society.
3. God becomes a spiritual force of each individual and an absent God without access to natural and social order. This plays into a hyper-individualism that disproportionately places liability in the personal realm, which has a depoliticizing effect as relations to a common space are cut off.

This schizophrenic triad becomes the system of checks and balances in what Latour calls the "modern constitution" (Latour 2008, 48). However, while the poles are created and fortified (nature and culture), a *middle space* emerges that is indispensable to the modern constitution. This space doesn't comply with either side and becomes their construction site (of purification and mediation). It is populated by hybrids, or quasi-objects, that are at once socially constructed and natural. As hybrid entities, they confront each other as both object and subject (see 70). It is those monsters that do the work of mediation, only to be seized and multiplied by the aim of keeping the middle space small.

The hybrids multiply (mediation) more rapidly the more their existence is argued away (purification). The production of hybrids is a direct consequence of insisting on the dichotomy between natural and social order, because the work of purification and mediation is never considered together (56).

Paradoxically, the modern constitution renders hybrids unthinkable even as it continues to produce them (59). As invisible hands, they enable expansion on all levels, but are carefully ignored. From this contradiction Latour draws the conclusion that we have never been modern, because it is precisely the work of mediation/translation, the creation of quasi-objects, that stabilizes a model of the world in which that practice itself finds no place. Those non-modern monsters are effective and indispensable, even if we don't see them under the bed.

It is precisely the hoarding of hybrids that makes it impossible to keep the gap between the poles "clean" and enables Latour's work to leave the postmodern critique behind. To get an idea of one such hybrid, CO_2 is a good example. Carbon dioxide is a chemical compound playing a tremendous role within the planetary materials cycle. Its increased concentration due to human activities contributes to global warming, climate crisis, and the extinction of species. By accounting for this effect, CO_2 becomes an instrument of economic regulation and politics in the negotiation of consumption limits. Its concentration is an important argument for social movements, enables marketing strategies for "climate neutrality" and ecosystems are valued in relation to their carbon capture capabilities (e.g., swamps, forests). Tracing it helps unveil injustices and the construction of differences (e.g. global north & south). Through contestation new alliances and conflict lines evolve, elections are turned, and so forth. CO_2 thus proves to be an actor that is extremely active as nature as well as a societal phenomenon.

Latour's use of the perfect tense helps see the rewriting of the past as a conciliatory gesture. His anthropology of modernity develops from its

situatedness, a perspective that does not imply a radical break with the past, but a—no less radical—re-evaluation of the network of relationships.
Even as we have never been modern, modernity's specific vision of how things work unfolds continually through various forms of globalization, imperialism, colonialism, xenophobia, racism, denialisms and so forth.

Design has never been modern

At this point we take the entanglement of design and modernity for granted as it evolves to stabilize the relationship between people and their technological expansion. Thus, what follows concentrates on how Latour's terminology can be applied to reorient this relationship towards a point where we can say that design has never been modern.

Design itself has become a profession through the differentiation processes of modernity, a purification effort that creates a specific system of disciplines with ever more distinguished fields of knowledge and dedicated authorities. The growing potentials that arise from specialization are paralleled by tendencies that bundle design competence into a certain space and deny it to others—or to take it from a different angle: certain professions categorically exclude design to be part of their practice.

Parallel to the explosion of the number of things that accompany the expansion of modernity—on its way to becoming a geomorphic force—the importance of design increases, but its position in the modern constitution remains curiously contested or vague. Fortunately, we have never been modern, so a justification of design within a modern wrangling of competencies is not of concern right now. Instead, I follow Latour's invitation of rewriting history by proposing that design has never been modern. However, what has to be endured is the paradox that design appears to be modern and non-modern at once. A closer look at the work of translation, the production of hybrids, will serve to reconcile with this paradox and help turn it into an argument.

As a consequence of the consolidation of the separation between nature and culture, the necessity of purification leaves no place at the table of the modern constitution for the work of mediation—the reconciliation with the technological expansion and the cultural revolution that establish this new conception of the human and the world.

Design comes in handy as an androgynous instance capable of moving in-between, towards the one or the other pole according to necessity. It becomes the specific authority of a schizophrenic bonding, dedicated to the modern project by ignoring the poles and consolidating them at the same time. It sedates the sharp break the moderns instituted towards the past, nature and so forth. Incorporating the logic of separation, it develops concepts, arguments and intentions (such as "form follows function" (Sullivan [1896] 2016) which make it possible to create hybrids and keep them invisible. Design follows modernity's normalization process and drives it forward. It is as much involved in the work of purification as in mediation, and simultaneously a consequence of both operations.

Hybridization requires an agent (design) that is neither wholly on one side nor the other, that is, neither wholly of society nor wholly of nature. Already terminologically, design contains concepts of ideation, craft and object-ness. That is why in the following I consider design as an amalgam or continuation of these traits.

On the one hand: Design is a social practice (ideation and creation) while its outcome embodies things which are clearly denied participation in the social. And yet, quite willingly, the inanimate design object is created for the animation, i.e., to empower certain social practices of the only subject deemed truly animate, the human. The hybrids are not doing their thing by chance, even though they are never controlled.

On the other hand: Design is also not entirely assigned to the sphere of nature. Sooner or later in the design process materials (nature) are set in motion, used, changed, appropriated—the material is enlivened by the intervention, loaded with meaning. It has an effect and therefore can no longer be clearly assigned to nature. Designing a chair, for example, does not mean applying an idea to a passive, receiving material and in the process transferring a wholly natural object into an entirely social one. Rather, it is in dialogue with the agency of the material through which knowledge or *skills* (e.g. Ingold 2018) emerge. This conversation is also attended by the tools or means of production. A wooden chair does not disguise its materiality. On the contrary, materiality may be even emphasized and influence the form (resilience of the material, etc.). At the same time, the chair itself is involved in a discourse about the cultural practice of sitting. The status or meaning of the sitting (in)activity is made visible and negotiated through form and ergonomics. The chair "designs" back. In that sense Design has always been utilized for the design of people—both as an instrument of power and countermovement.

It is precisely this hybridization that subverts the modern paradigm and at the same time becomes constitutive of it. The making visible of the paradox is why we have never been modern. The excluded is present and has an effect. Accordingly, there is a need for operations that "manage" the space between the poles: steady the quasi-objects, their inter-relations and multiplication to remain compatible with the separation. This is the reconciliation work design is tasked with in modernity.

Through this specific constitution, design becomes visible as a knowledge practice that is disciplined during modernity but which isn't solely bound to that paradigm. Much more, we glimpse at an involvement in a relational structure that might operate under different ontological auspices. Design has never been modern.

Mediation & Equivocation

In the following, I am taking a closer look at what is "non-modern" about design by considering the ontological dimension—not how we see things but what can be seen in the first place (Holbraad and Pedersen 2017, 5). In this way, we do not so much break with modernity as we pursue Latour's ambitions of a fundamental re-evaluation of human involvement with-in the world. The assumption is that design, by shaking off its sheep's clothing, might play an important role in the involvement throughout and beyond that self-skinning.

To stay with Latour: If we debunk the modern paradigm, the third space (the middle between the poles) loses its function as an intermediate. (Latour 2008,

[4] The role of quasi-objects and their relation within a network of various entities is an important question throughout Latour's career—most famously developed as actor-network theory in Reassembling the Social as a contribution to science and technology studies. Likewise, the relation with the more-than-human stayed crucial in his engagement with the climate catastrophy (see Facing Gaïa, Critical Zones) and always entailed political questions (Das Terrestrische Manifest).

109) Instead, hybrids become actors who take on an active role as mediators and see themselves officially endowed as being or having agency.[4] While in modernity design enters the world of hybrids as a shape-shifter, it always comes back and closes the curtain behind it. But what if the work of mediation does not produce intermediate links doomed to muteness? What if the mediation takes place through actors with whom communication does not take place secretly, but in all openness? What kind of relations are we talking about then?

Of course, there are many efforts that reconceptualize relations to counter the dualistic imperative—and therefore provincialize the modern constitution despite or because of its global efficacy. The following considerations are influenced in particular by what is subsumed under new materialisms and the ontological turn in anthropology. What connects concepts like assemblage (Benette 2010), entanglement (Barad 2007), network (e.g. Latour 2008) or meshwork (Ingold 2018) is the focus on process: Mutually transforming relations create an ephemeral state of entities, which can only be grasped through these relations. Things do not exist a priori but through a continuous (re)composition of (material) forces.

When the chaotic is understood not as a conflict to be resolved, but as a necessity of ongoing-ness, questions about representation merge into questions about animation, following Anna Tsing (2021, 16). Consequently, the question of human intentionality shifts from exceptionalism to being involved—with the challenge not to humanize the "other." This would be nothing else than narcissism, as it refuses to acknowledge, for example, the specific perspective a virus holds, which is fundamentally different from our encounter with the world. En passant, what it means to be human becomes an important debate (see e.g. Braidotti and Hlavajova 2018: Posthumanism; or for a specific design perspective see Colomina and Wigley 2016).

Questioning very fundamental concepts is what is described by the ontological dimension—not only what we understand by e.g. human or nature, but in what ways these are existing or necessary categories of different cosmologies (world conceptions) and whether they can be presupposed or not. In this sense, it is not about replacing the modern ontology by another one, but to keep the ontological perspective open—multiplication.

[5] Here he points at a key ingredient of the ontological turn: a shift of perspective that does not acknowledge that we perceive the world differently, but that we inhabit other worlds, that is, that the constitution of the world is different. As he quotes Roy Wagner, "their misunderstanding of me was not the same as my misunderstanding them[.]" (Viveiros de Castro 2014, 90).

[6] To categorize "the object of study" as "culture" is already an equivocation.

To bring together fluid ontologies and the presented take on design, I will take a specific look at Viveiros de Castro's concept of *equivocation* in order to outline a possible perspective within non-modern design approaches. Viveiros de Castro sees in anthropology, which has to reflect a heavy colonial heritage, the project of a "permanent decolonization of thought" (Viveiros de Castro 2014, 40) that focuses on "conditions of the ontological self-determination of the collectives" (far from human or not) (43). He proceeds that it is the challenge to conduct an anthropology which "would make multiplicities proliferate [...]. Because it is not at all a question [...] of preaching the abolition of the borders that unite/separate [...] but rather of 'unreducing' [irréduire] (Latour) and undefining them, by bending every line of division into an infinitely complex curve" (45).[5]
It is the recognition of the multiple normalities (or ontologies) between which there is no possibility of understanding.

What in anthropology derives from the attempt to compare different "cultures"[6] can be applied to the work of mediation within a space that is animated by agencies (mediators), e.g. to interact with chairs or CO_2. Of course, the processual is already implied by Viveiros de Castro. According to him, in anthropology—as well as in design, I would like to propose—a core procedure is *translation work* (see 92), i.e., building bridges between incompatible normalities. In order to accomplish this work of mediation, the "constitutive dimension" of equivocation is required (96). Equivocation is the basic condition for the anthropological discourse (comparison and translation), but not by "presuming an original univocality," but by embracing the equivocal to create and occupy a space between incomparable dimensions (89). Equivocation means both ambiguity and misunderstanding (miscommunication)—it is "what founds and impels" the relations (ibid.). The contact surfaces are potentiated, that is the opposite of purification.

Design is now engaged in creating interactions in a network of agencies that form complex collectives. To get along with ongoing processes (reconciliation), design becomes a competency that, from its dependence on constraints, creates opportunities for *ongoing-ness.* Translations emerge from the presence of constraints.[7] The circumstance of (the volition of) involvement creates contact surfaces that do not simply function, but create an equivocal space that multiplies the possibilities of getting along.

[7] Massumi is using the metaphor of walking as controlled falling, which points to how unavoidable constraints (e.g. gravity) make movement possible (Massumi 2010, 35).

The peculiarity of design may now be precisely its ability to slip into other perspectives—we come back to the shape-shifter. This role is equivocal: full of misunderstandings and ambiguities, but allows for relationships that enable stumbling. This navigation is translation work: the reduction of complexity by skillfulness and imagination, the creation of tangible things. It reminds us of the paradox that design is modern and non-modern at once, because translation becomes through equivocation an operation that oscillates between purification and mediation. Thus, the entanglement of the human becomes a "productive" involvement. It is through taking the concept of equivocation seriously that creates sorts of meaningfulness which possibly do not put the vitality of life itself at risk.

Let's summarize: Design has established itself as a term for various knowledge practices that modernity tries to exclude.

What is excluded? It is the continuity or non-definitiveness between nature and culture, i.e. of socio-material space between the ideal and the effective. Design can be described as the putting-into-effect of relationships that exist in principle, but can only be shaped partially. Modernity tries to produce clarity through separation while defining itself as a rupture with the past. The negation of the necessity of hybrids, however, shows the contradictoriness of this paradigm.

The Anthropocene appears as a "reversible figure" (Franke 2013, 12), that defines earth-time as human-time. It points at responsibility as well as the acknowledgement that the history-making of humanity is no less or more important than that of CO_2 and lichens.[8] Through design, purification holds value but becomes intermediary, a temporal necessity bound to a specific perspective, rather than a boundary mark. The process of forming relationships, in the style of a stumbling shapeshifter, always remains blurry. The equivocation is what enables and results from an amalgamation of different dimensions, in the attempt to create continuity in the glitch between the customary and the deviation. It is the utilization and creation of meaningfulness in the process—and it could be called design(ing).

[8] "We are all lichens." Scott Gilbert quoted by Donna Haraway. (Haraway 2016, 82)

Embracing Equivocations

Caught in the middle

The last consideration should be treated here as an outlook and a well-intended loose thread. In focusing on the concept of design, it seems to slip away in the web of relations even more. Though, this is nothing but the consequence of Latour's operation. What if, for a second, we contemplate the claim "We have never been design"—against the backdrop of defining design as a discipline?
In expanding the conception of design, what can be seen is not a growing importance of the design discipline(s), but the importance of the work of translation that is immanent to being human. Design emerges as a promising topos to think about practices of entanglement rather accidentally—but not innocently. And because of the situatedness of the author and readers of this chapter, it is worth a headache. So, looking at design caught between two chairs, we may consider it as a participant of all disciplines or practices—explicitly not as a meta-discipline that is in charge of a transdisciplinary ballet, but as a knot within. The unraveling of the designerly self as an equivocal middle ground might be a possible corrective to disciplining tendencies and an open thread for transdisciplinary processes. To avoid misconception: This does not mean that "design" knows where the design competencies of individual disciplines reside. It is rather a proposition that implies a transformation of all sides—a liquification of poles that multiplies the possibilities of understanding while recognizing the historically grown mechanisms of disciplines, including their necessities and pitfalls.

BIBLIOGRAPHY

Barad, Karen. *Meeting the Universe Halfway*. Duke University Press, 2007.

Braidotti, Rosi, and Maria Hlavajova. *Posthuman Glossary*. Bloomsbury, 2018.

Benette, Jane. *Vibrant Matter: A Political Ecology of Things*. Duke University Press, 2010.

Colomina, Beatriz, and Marc Wigley. *are we human? notes on an archaeology of design*. Lars Müller, 2016.

Davis, Janae, Alex A. Moulton, Levi Van Sant, and Brian Williams. "Anthropocene, Capitalocene, . . . Plantationocene? A Manifesto for Ecological Justice in an Age of Global Crises." *Geography Compass* 13 (5) (2019): e12438.

Franke, Anselm. „Earthrise und das Verschwinden des Außen" in *The Whole Earth. Kalifornien und das Verschwinden des Außen*, edited by Diedrich Diederichsen and Anselm Franke, 12-19. Sternberg Press, 2013.

Haraway, Donna. *Staying with the Trouble. Making Kin in the Chthulucene*. Duke University Press, 2016.

Holbraad, Martin, and Morten Axel Pedersen. *The Ontological Turn: An Anthropological Exposition*. Cambridge University Press, 2017.

Ingold, Tim. "Five questions of skill." *Cultural Geographies* 25 (1) (2018): 159–163.

IPCC Report, Working Group II. 2022. "Climate Change 2022: Impacts, Adaptation and Vulnerability." IPCC. Last modified February 27, 2022. https://www.ipcc.ch/report/sixth-assessment-report-working-group-ii.

Latour, Bruno. *We have never been modern*. Suhrkamp, 2008. Originally published in French in 1991.

Massumi, Brian. "Bewegung navigieren" in: *Ontomacht: Kunst, Affekt und das Ereignis des Politischen*, 25–67. Merve, 2010.

Moore, Jason. *Capitalism in the Web of Life: Ecology and the Accumulation of Capital*. Verso, 2015.

Stengers, Isabelle. "A Constructivist Reading of Process and Reality." *Theory, Culture & Society* 25 (4) (2008): 91–110.

Sullivan, Louis H. "The tall office building artistically considered." *Lippincot's Magazine* (March 1896): 403–409. Digitalized version, Internet Archive, 2016.

Tsing, Anna. "When the things we study respond to each other. Tools for unpacking the 'material.'" in *More than Human*, edited by A. Jacque, M. Otero Verzier, and L. Pietroiusti, 16–26. Het Nieuwe Instituut, 2021.

Viveiros de Castro, Eduardo. *Cannibal Metaphysics*. Univocal, 2014. Originally published in French in 2009.

Acknowledgements

To the Alternatives.

EASTBOUND

A Decolonial Approach to Relocating Vietnamese Design History

(ngọc triệu)

> "Human existence, because it came into being through asking questions, is at the root of change in the world. There is a radical element to existence, which is the radical act of asking questions. … At root human existence involves surprise, questioning and risk. And because of all this, it involves actions and change."
>
> — Paulo Freire, *Learning to Question: A Pedagogy of Liberation*, 1968.

"It's us against the West."

This is probably the only thing that I can remember from all the history classes I used to have in Vietnam. In most cases, the West refers to Europe and the USA. Outside of the classroom and in everyday conversation, I would often hear people discussing, comparing, and playing a game of catch-up, whether it be the rate of economic growth, the quality of the higher education system, or the progression of social policies. For as long as I can remember, xenophilia has been one of the most distinctive traits of Vietnamese consumerism. Growing up, I was acculturated to believe that everything about the West was better than what we had at home.

    In Vietnam, we often talk about how our ancestors fought for independence, against the crime of war, and against the oppression and exploitation by foreign powers. But there has always been so little discussion of the history of colonialism and its lingering manifestation in today's everyday life. What we aren't aware of, or maybe we are but somehow hesitant about addressing collectively and constructively, is that everything has two sides. And the other side of modernity, the darker side of it, has been identified as "coloniality" by Walter D. Mignolo, an Argentine semiotician professor at Duke University, who throughout his work focused on exploring the geopolitics of knowledge, transmodernity, border thinking, and pluriversality. According to Mignolo, the logic of coloniality includes the "constantly named and celebrated" development, progression, innovation, and growth; while addressing poverty, inequalities, corruption, and other "dispensability of human lives" as "problems to be solved" by the above listed social phenomena (Mignolo 2011, 19). He has employed the slash ('/') to indicate the conundrum of "modernity/coloniality," depicting its coexistence as being an "unapologetic response specific to globalization" yet a subtle and concealed one (ibid., 43).

    What we know about design in Vietnam is the product of subjugated knowledge. It is, as Michel Foucault pointed out, the untold histories, the historical contents and knowledge "which were present but disguised" (1980, 81), and as such is constitutive of the colonial matrix of power. It results from a combination of ignorance and a blinded belief that spreads with the perpetuation of the coloniality of knowledge. The ignorance of a design history means an eager acceptance that design arrived with globalization. And much like globalization, design came with a promise to make life better, more innovative, more developed, and more modern—all fit neatly to the description of the rhetoric of modernity and coloniality. It is within the modernity/coloniality of the fast-changing society resulting from the government's political and economic revolution, alias *Đổi Mới* in 1986, and the rise of globalization, including the introduction of the internet in the early 1990s, that the notion of design became recognized (initially as a field of applied arts) in Vietnam. Regardless, the history of design remains ambiguous due to a lack of documentation and a defined development strategy from the state.

As a nation, our desire to move on from the aftermath and further away from poverty by means of economic development and education is constantly exploited, regardless of our approval or awareness. The Vietnamese government is falling prey to the promise of economic development and financial profits that neocolonialism introduces. By promoting an industrial-oriented design education, we are creating a financial incentive that perpetuates the existing system of neocolonialism that operates on intellectual exploitation, power imbalances, and cultural assimilation. Moreover, as an industrial-oriented practice, Vietnamese design is essentially placed within a global economy of making where it is less about knowledge production and more about the manufacturing of creative content.

On the other hand, the cultural discontinuity and socio-political rupture resulting from a prolonged history of wars and colonization render the practice of design without fundamental concepts and theories. Trần Quang Đức, a well-known Vietnamese calligrapher and translator has expressed his concern in the opening of Ngàn năm áo mũ (2013), a thoroughly researched book that focuses on the history of Vietnamese royal attire. In his opinion, the vestige of the Vietnamese traditional culture of design suffered a profound loss when Western cultures were violently imposed on Vietnamese society by the French (Trần 2013, 4). This was followed by constant changes in history and ideology that have prevented us from learning the truth about our past, what our ancestors used to wear, and their way of living, making, and creating (ibid., 4). In essence, it has made us vulnerable and blinded to how the social fabric of how our society works, and how our cultures and perception of values—of who we are—have come to be influenced by neocolonialism and the coloniality of knowledge.

The Decolonial Option

There are three types of critique of modernity as identified by Walter Mignolo in his book *The Darker Side of Western Modernity: Global Futures, Decolonial Options* (2011). To discern which approach would be appropriate to understand certain modernity, one can rely on its point of origin and routes of dispersion. For example, whether it is internal to European history, coming from a Eurocentric perspective such as Marxism, postmodernity, and poststructuralism, or whether it has derived from non-Western histories. The latter, in addition, has two different focuses: the idea of "Western civilization" such as dewesternization, and the concept of "coloniality" such as postcoloniality and decoloniality.

These three categories, however, propose a great conundrum rather than offering convenience to those who seek to understand the hybrid modernity of Vietnam. When postcoloniality fails to suffice, decoloniality proves its capability in offering a new horizon that "opened up beyond capitalism and communism, between the West and the Soviet Union"—spaces that have characterized much of Vietnamese history and present (Mignolo 2011, 31).

From the beginning of its nation-building history, Vietnam suffered from 1000 years of Chinese domination, followed by 87 years under French colonization as part of Indochina and 30 years of war, after which we finally reclaimed our independence from France and the United States. This intricate historical legacy presents a great challenge for those who wish to understand the continuum of changes in Vietnamese society, and for me—to map and comprehend the transformation of activities of everyday life, particularly the nation's various cultural modes of making that characterize the practice of design. Postcolonialism has been proved as a deficient framework to understand colonial and contemporary Vietnam, as Anne Raffin, an associate professor of Sociology at the National University of Singapore, points out in her paper titled "Postcolonial Vietnam: Hybrid Modernity" (2008). Hybrid modernity, as defined by Raffin, is the outcome of the confluence of colonial modernity that has resulted from the history of French colonialism and socialist modernity as a part of the communist dependency coming from China and the USSR (2008, 3). As an elaboration, Raffin's two thorough analyses of medical and therapeutic practices as well as ethnic categorization in Vietnam illustrate how the socialist state of Vietnam conducted its project of modernization. Her study clarifies how Vietnamese medical practice interweaves not only colonial and local traditions but also adopts a precolonial attitude, granting its hybrid status. In other words, not only does Vietnam embrace hybrid modernity, but its communist effort to construct modernity and national-building also resembles that of the colonial states.

This means a country can be both postcolonial and neocolonial. In the case of Vietnam, where its independence has been formally established, the continuation of a neocolonial structure remains dependent on the extent of influence that the nation's varied historical backdrop has on its economy, culture, and everyday practices. The decolonization of Asia indicates an experience expressed by liberation that grows with the independence movements, the retreat of foreign powers, and the creation of several nation-states in the region, as opposed to "emancipation and freedom" (Mignolo and Walsh 2018, 81). This is not necessarily sufficient to depict the full narrative of Vietnam's history, which consists of both the struggles for self-determination and liberation from being a French protectorate, and political independence during the confrontation with capitalism and Western imperialism.

In light of rationality, Mignolo provides an exposition of what would constitute the decoloniality projects—one that is grounded in their aspiration rather than their moments and places in time: "Toward the end of the Cold War, decolonization mutated into decoloniality without losing its historical meaning, to highlight the 'decolonization of knowledge' and to cast Eurocentrism as an epistemic rather than geographical issue" (Mignolo 2011, 53). With neocolonialism, or imperialism without colonies, becoming increasingly prominent by the end of the twentieth century, it is inevitable—and reasonably so—that decoloniality has evolved to be synonymous with epistemic disobedience. It is anchored in coloniality, which aims to disengage and delink from Western epistemology and has thus become an epistemic and political project. As such, Vietnamese design deserves a "decolonial option"—not for its political stance but for its long-lasting encounter with the coloniality of knowledge, which is the central foundation for this endeavor of obtaining an alternative understanding of Vietnamese design.

Eastbound — I am where I think

Born in 1994, eight years after the beginning of Đổi Mới—the country's political and economic reform—and eighteen years after the end of Kháng chiến chống Mỹ (the Resistance War against America, i.e., the Vietnam War as popularized in Western media), I grew up with the nation itself. 1994 marked the discontinuation of ration stamps from the hardships of the subsidy economy and the installment of the first internet-connected computer in Vietnam. It was a time of changes and rapid transformation. Like the nation that looks outward seeking global integration, I too seek to be a global citizen. At age 18, I decided to travel beyond the Vietnamese border to study, first in the Westernized world, then in the West. I wanted to find out whether what they said was true. Most importantly, I wanted to learn from the best. The constant exposure to new knowledge and ideologies has taught me to embrace the unknown(s) and go beyond initial appearances or preoccupations over the years. At the same time, it has encouraged me to start questioning the origin and the border of knowledge, particularly the scope of design in relation to my own culture and background as a Vietnamese design researcher.

Inevitably, the purpose of decolonial thinking and doing is to "delink" from these "epistemic assumptions common to all the areas of knowledge established in the Western world since the European Renaissance and through the European Enlightenment" (Mignolo 2011, 54). However, Mignolo does not provide a step-by-step guide on how to implement a decolonial project. Since there is no single colonial power that exerts itself in the same way across time and space, each project has its own contextual relation to coloniality. Being recently exposed to the discourse of decoloniality, it is my responsibility to consolidate and identify what is essential to the decolonizing of Vietnamese design by proposing two steps that I consider appropriate. First, it is vital to fulfilling the two tasks of revealing and denouncing the hidden colonial matrix of power. Only then is one enabled to "delink" her thought(s), her being(s), and doing(s) from the modern hierarchy of knowledge and obtain a way of making sense of the world in which all knowledge(s) are equally legitimate and important.

By and large, for me to make decolonizing design sensible in this study, I must make recourse to my own positionality. To be „where I think" and to gain an understanding of Vietnamese design discourse, it is important to acknowledge my culture and history without dismissing the bias that comes from an educational background in the West. How is it necessary for me to be engaged and involved in the discourse, yet I can only question it critically and examine it from a decolonial perspective by being far away? As a Vietnamese design researcher, I am more of an observer than a proactive participant. Positionality, therefore, has become my fundamental concern when it comes to determining the locus of enunciation needed for the decolonial project.

Being where one thinks, physically and spiritually, allows the chance of being heard, of being accounted for, and recognized amidst the implications of globalization and modernity. What does it mean to employ a decolonial approach in the hybrid modernity of Vietnam? In the entanglement of the myriad of different histories, navigating Vietnamese design requires one to first understand the historical and contextual differences, and then to look beyond the "hybridized self-other relationship of the colonizer and colonized" (Raffin 2008, 11). This means investigating the various encounters of the Vietnamese design with different cultures, given the country's struggle through precolonial, colonial, and anti-colonial histories, while taking into account the alternatives to modernity during the post-colonial state formation.

Eastbound, then, serves as a guiding light in keeping my thoughts focused on the decolonial strategy. It reminds me of the knowledge system in which this study is embedded. To pursue the daunting task of relocating Vietnamese design history, and through it, revealing the tactics of coloniality, what I need is a critical mind and a relentless curiosity that will strengthen my critiques of the global design narrative and the universal knowledge that I have familiarized myself with during the past five years. Being aware of my positionality allows me to confront my assumption and adopt a stance that acknowledges the multiple layers of history of nation-building and transformation that characterizes Vietnam and its design discourse. To my knowledge, decolonizing is not tracing down one's roots and originality. For instance, if to decolonize meant to erase what was once past and find what was once original, or *thuần Việt* as they say in Vietnamese, then I'd probably have to strip off my family name *Triệu,* for it arguably originated from the Chinese Zhao dynasty when they invaded and governed North Vietnam for over a century, from 257 to 111 BCE. The history of design should never be examined and seen through the lens of binary logic such as West/East, colonized/decolonized, primitive/civilized, et cetera, but rather a process of historicization, of questioning one's history, of figuring out what would be possible to delink from the imperial/colonial legacies including design knowledge. With this in mind, I set out to challenge the current hierarchy of knowledge in Vietnam while acknowledging the significance of the places of being, thinking, and doing that is the lens of decoloniality.

Revealing the Tactics of Coloniality

The history of Vietnam rarely mentioned design but a tradition of nation-building and defense. As an effort to mend this gap, Phan Cẩm Thượng, a leading cultural researcher in Vietnam whose foci include fine arts and folklore of the Vietnamese people, brings attention to the role of design in his "100 years of Vietnamese design" column in *Vietnam Sports and Culture e-Magazine*. In his opinion, design has played an important part in representing the nation's cultural ways of making and is an honest reflection of everyday changes in the lives of the Vietnamese people, especially during the twentieth century (Phan 2014). The practice of everyday life is considered to be the essence of "culture" in Đào Duy Anh's *History of the Annamite Civilization* (original Vietnamese title *Việt Nam Văn Hoá Sử Cương,* published in 1939). As a renowned Vietnamese historian, and linguistic and cultural researcher during the late nineteenth century, Đào (2014) laid the foundation for modern cultural study in Vietnam. He rejects the assumption that culture is only concerned with noble human ideology and academic thought (ibid., 13–14). On the contrary, he indicated that, besides economic, political, and social activities, culture should also address ordinary customs and traditions (ibid.). His simple definition argues for an ostensible fact that if culture is the practice of everyday life, every nation should then have its own culture, regardless of its state of civilization (ibid.). As such, the job of a design researcher should begin with a historical investigation into the transformation of everyday life. That includes common living knowledge about education, languages, literature, arts, and the multiple techniques of making.

The coloniality of knowledge in Vietnamese design expresses itself across different times and spaces as it takes advantage of the country's transitional economy and the complications of a passage through pre-colonial, colonial, and postcolonial histories. It does so through the means of language (categorization, terminology, and selected narrative), interferences with the mind and body (perception, taste, and practice), and the core social fabrics constitutive of the nation's economic framework, educational, and cultural policy. A manifestation of the coloniality of knowledge can be found in Paul Giran's Tâm lý người An Nam (original French title *Psychologie Du Peuple Annamite,* published in 1904 and reprinted in Vietnamese in 2019). It consists of more than three years' worth of research and observation in Annam during the early twentieth century. "Annam" was initially used to indicate the French protectorate encompassing the middle part of Vietnam; however, it is also widely adopted as an alternative term to "Vietnam" as a part of French-colonized Indochina. In his research, Giran (2019) presented an overview of Vietnam's language, literature, arts, science, and technology while attributing race and environment to the formation of the nation's identity. Nevertheless, its ultimate goal was to serve French colonialism in Annam: "… we just do it for the sake of your own interest. We will not take your country, we will transform it. We are not going to make your race go away, but we will definitely improve and enrich [it] under our guidance" (ibid., 14).

As such, to justify their "civilizing mission", it was essential for Giran to write in a condescending tone overflowing with phrases that belittle the history and cultural practices of Vietnam, including design. One of the two colonial tactics used is first and foremost the minimization of Annamite intellectual evolution, most significantly through the analysis of the commercial industry and agriculture: the "not advanced" techniques employed in clothing and housing design, the "less sophisticated" tools and methods which can only afford an "imperfect and raw finished" products, all due to an "inferiority in essence" (ibid., 66).

Regarding design practices, the Annamites are said to be "meticulous craft workers" whose skills are obtained solely through the means of habit as a consequence of their "laziness and shortcomings" (ibid., 74). In the eyes of the colonists, "average" is the essence of the Annamite's innovative spirit—their minds can "recreate images and copy", but never are capable of "actual thought, creativity" or "true art" (ibid., 79). The second tactic is a consistent emphasis on the influence of China at all times and spaces, stripping Vietnamese arts and technology of their origins and progression, combined with an affirmation of the "mediocre" and "primitive" practices of the Annamite, as opposed to the "state-of-art" ways of the European (ibid., 69). The repetition of devaluing word choice and the classification of local craft as different from modern design deem Annamite's modes of making inferior. This is precisely the apparatus through which the coloniality of knowledge exerts its control and perpetuates a relegation of other epistemologies, reducing them to the product of a "barbarian," "primitive past" (Mignolo 2011, 155). Mignolo's concept of modernity/coloniality is clearly exemplified in the way French administration cunningly orchestrated modernity as a guise for their colonialist agenda which was substantially made up of cultural assimilation, economic and labor exploitation, and authority exclusion. Yet at the same time, it also acknowledged the Annamite's way of life as a "joyful mediocre," one that resembles the life of the sage (Giran 2019, 69).

Contrasted to most popular colonialist beliefs and preconceptions that "industry in the Annamite countryside is almost absent or insignificant" (Tessier and Le Failler in Oger 2009, 7), Henri Oger, a young protectorate at the time, provided an early ethnographic study into the material cultures of Vietnam in his *Mechanics and Crafts of the Annamites* (original French title *Technique Du Peuple Annamite*). Oger immersed himself in the daily lives of common people in Hanoi and the neighboring areas for two years. This allowed him to collect and present the richness of Vietnamese artisans' activities and techniques in an extensive collection consisting of two volumes, displaying 4,200 drawings, 3,006 captions written in Vietnamese logographic script (chữ Nôm, see Figure 1), and 4,462 captions in French. With special attention to cultural production in which no instruments were involved but the human body, Oger categorized techniques into three groups of industries closely associated with the everyday life of Annamite people. These include industries that extract raw materials from nature (such as agriculture, hunting, and transportation); industries that process naturally-extracted materials (such as paper, metal, pottery, bamboo, textiles, and silk); and industries that use processed materials (such as sculpture, painting and lacquer, clothing and housing design, and furniture making). Despite an appreciation of the Annamites' techniques, Oger's point of departure, which places material culture in the center of a technological civilization study, eventually leads him to conclude that "the Annamite People must be entered into the class of Semi-Civilized People, who have made considerable but slow progress" (Oger 2009, 124).

Authorship and the marginalization of knowledge in the Mechanics and Crafts of the Annamites have also been topics of discussion. At the 2015 Berkeley Digital Humanities Fair, Cindy Nguyen and Amy Zou introduced a different perspective on Oger's work, highlighting the intellectual contribution of Vietnamese laborers while questioning the marginalization of intellectual knowledge within colonial scholarship in their poster titled Invisible Authorship: New Perspectives on Translation and Colonial Texts. According to Nguyen, who was then a Ph.D. student in History at the University of California, Berkeley, the materiality and methods used during the production of the text are a process that involves a variety of actors, including draftsmen, annotators, woodblock carvers, and printers. Although Oger did enlist the work of Vietnamese labor in the „General Introduction to the Study of the Mechanics of the Annamese People: Essay on the material life, arts and industries of the Annamese People" (1910), his tone signifies a political undertone in which the involvement of Annamites is rather considered as a „local flavor" to add „authenticity" to the work rather than co-authorship contributing to scientific knowledge (Nguyen and Zou 2015). To my knowledge, "Henri Oger" was the only name credited on both the 1909 original publication and the 2009 reprint. This is yet another example that brings to light the implications of the coloniality of knowledge in Vietnamese design: the absence in the history of the "other" as an actor in the production of knowledge.

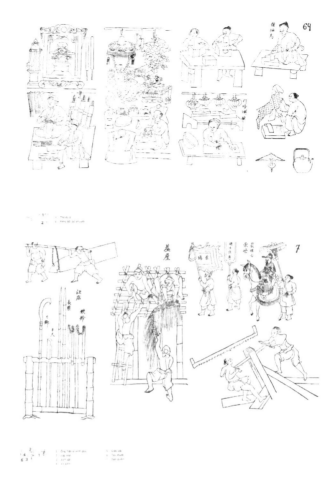

Fig. 1. Drawings depicting the arts and crafts of the Annamites accompanied with captions in Nôm (Source: Oger 2009).

At the same time, colonial authorship poses a challenge for postcolonial and decolonial scholars alike when it comes to classifying cultural heritage. Colonial legacies can be both intangible and tangible. While the intangible takes the form of hybrid cultural practices, such as modern medicine and pharmacy, the tangible is most often seen in urban infrastructure, street planning, and architectural design. Gwendolyn Wright, the author of The Politics of Design in French Colonial Urbanism (1991), describes the experiences of Frenchmen who traveled to Hanoi and Saigon during the late nineteenth century as if they were still at home. Like many ex-colonies struggling with an assimilationist policy, Hanoi was considered a European district in the Far East built with the techniques and hard work of Vietnamese laborers and a „taste for extravagance" that embodied „France's cultural superiority and a strong connection to the prestige of Paris itself" (Wright 1991, 161). As shown in Ab Stokvis's photo taken of Hanoi in 1979, many historic buildings built during the French colonization remain and have become part of Hanoi's identity (see Figure 2). This creates a „sense of place" sentiment for many generations of Vietnamese who inhabit the city.

In Orientalism, Edward Said (1979) revealed that the encounter between the colonized and colonizer not only influenced the identities and cultures of the former, but also transformed that of the latter. The challenge, then, is to distinguish between colonial legacy and cultural heritage—a hybrid production of the colonizer and the colonized. As a result, the relations between local and global are always ambiguous. Thus, determining whether a cultural artifact leans towards one end of the spectrum or the other is an ongoing quest that requires a fair judgment of history from both local authorities and international academic scholars, even if it takes place in spaces of asymmetrical power relations.

Fig. 2. Hanoi 1979–Tràng Tiền Street, Opera House (Source: Stokvis, 1979).

The Decolonial Futures of Vietnamese Design

Rapid technological advancements, where leaps and bounds take place in just a matter of hours, can make the past feel distant. However, it's important to remember that French colonialism ended only roughly 130 years ago, and Vietnam only reclaimed its independence from US imperialism 45 years ago. The legacies and impact of the strong presence of the American military, along with its imported modern culture, are evident in the contemporary lives of most Vietnam citizens. This influence is particularly more noticeable in the South than in the North. Although a strong focus on teaching the history of war and despair in formal education is significant, the fast pace of modern life means that new designs and cultures emerge and dissolve without ever being documented. Therefore, it is only fair that history begins to take into account the transformation of Vietnam's diverse cultural practices as the country transitions to a post-colonial, communist state.

This research began by asking, „What is involved in making the question of decolonizing design sensible in the context of Vietnam, and for whose benefit?" As the process unfolds, there is a need to explore just what that context encompasses before launching a decolonial project. Contemporary Vietnamese design cannot be seen as isolated from the course of history and the many changes that the nation has witnessed. Given the revelation of the colonial tactics in the past and the specific positionality of Vietnam as an ex-colony and a rapidly globalized county, it is more crucial now than ever that the decolonial future(s) is coupled with a national identity by design. It necessitates a full-scale investigation into how capitalism, modernity, Eurocentrism, and the politics and pedagogy of design have contributed to the colonial matrix of power.

Although all of the above approaches and criticisms have originated from very different cultural backgrounds, spreading all across the Global South but also internally to the Global North, they all share something in common. First of all, it is the employment of a variety of theories from both within and outside of the design discipline to form a holistic outlook on the creation of the world and to explore the design disposition within it. Secondly, it is a mutual view and understanding of decolonization/decoloniality—not as another angle to criticize the design discourse and facilitate industrial breakthroughs, but rather as a mandatory prerequisite set out for all future design endeavors. Last but not least is the responsibility to take on the decolonial project fully aware of one's privileges and positionalities. This includes questioning the social milieu between now and the past, as well as acknowledging one's own cultural background and knowledge, and committing to a range of design practices that are more critical, ethical, responsible, collaborative, and open.

Since Vietnamese design is still taking shape and constantly transforming, its study must be placed within the context of the local, regional, and global at once to accurately portray the nation's cultural values and social progress in which it is informed, characterized, and produced. The awareness of how we live, think, and act in the world (or worlds) that we create is integral to the process of designing *Eastbound,* or any decolonial project we might undertake in the future.

 BIBLIOGRAPHY

Foucault, Michel. *Power/Knowledge:* Selected Interviews and Writings, 1972-1977. Edited and translated by Colin Gordon. New York, Brighton: Harvester, 1980.

Giran, Paul. *Tâm lý người An Nam: Tính cách dân tộtc, tiến trình lịch sử, Tri thức, Xã Hội Và Chính trị.* Edited by Văn Văn Nguyễn Tiến. Hà Nội: Nhà xuất bản Hội nhà văn, 2019. First published 1904.

Mignolo, Walter D., and Catherine E. Walsh. *On Decoloniality: Concepts, Analytics, and Praxis.* Durham: Duke University Press, 2018.

Mignolo, Walter. *The Darker Side of Western Modernity: Global Futures, Decolonial Options.* Durham: Duke University Press, 2011.

Nguyen, Cindy, and Amy Zou. "Invisible Authorship: New Perspectives on Translation and Colonial Texts." Poster presented at the 2015 Berkeley Digital Humanities Fair. 2015. https://cindyanguyen.files.wordpress.com/2015/04/dhposterv3.png.

Oger, Henri. *Technique Du Peuple Annamite* (Kỹ Thuật Của Người An Nam An Nam). Edited by Olivier Tessier and Philippe Le Failler. Hà Nội École Française d'Extrême-Orient, 2009.

Oger, Henri. *Introduction générale a L'étude De La Technique Du Peuple Annamite: Essai Sur La Vie matérielle Les Arts Et Industries Du Peuple D'annam.* Vol. 1. 3 vols. Paris: Geuthner Libraire-Editeur, 1910.

Phan, Thượng Cẩm. 2014. "Bài 1: Những Tiền Đề Của Design Việt Nam." Thế Thao Văn Hoá. Last modified September 14, 2014. https://thethaovanhoa.vn/bai-1-nhung-tien-de-cua-design-viet-nam-20140904144832936.htm.

Raffin, Anne. "Postcolonial Vietnam: Hybrid Modernity." Postcolonial Studies 11, no. 3 (2008): 329–44. https://doi.org/10.1080/13688790802226728.

Said, Edward. *Orientalism.* Vintage Books, 1979.

Trần Quang Đức. *Ngàn năm áo mũ.* Hà Nội: Nhã Nam, 2013.

Wright, Gwendolyn. *The Politics of Design in French Colonial Urbanism.* Chicago: The University of Chicago Press, 1991.

Đào Duy Anh. *Việt Nam Văn Hóa Sử Cương.* Hà Nội: Thế Giới Publishing House, 2014. First published 1939.

 IMAGES AND ILLUSTRATIONS

Figure 1. Oger, Henri. Drawings Depicting the Arts and Crafts of the Annamites Accompanied with Captions in Nôm. Internet Archive. n.d. https://archive.org/details/ky-thuat-cua-nguoi-an-nam-2-henri-oger/KyThuatCuaNguoiAnNam1_HenriOger/.

Figure 2. Stokvis, Ab. Hanoi 1979–Tràng Tiền Street, Opera House. December 29, 2009. https://www.flickr.com/photos/13476480@N07/16943644839.

The design **SCENARIOS** described in **PART 3** offer different ways of approaching matters of politics through speculative design futures, fictional worlds, or discursive spaces established via various forms of media from 2D and 3D visualizations, artifacts and films, to interactive games, AR mobile applications, and a speculative online journal.

3
SCENARIOS

Acknowledgements

We thank Laura Popplow and Johanna Mehl for all the support and encouragement in having for the Wicked Problems, Wicked Designs forum at *Attending [to] Futures* conference as well as all of the spect-actors who attended the session either through the conference or through public live streaming.

WICKED RITUALS OF CONTEMPORARY DESIGN THINKING

(Carmem Saito) (Frederick M. C. van Amstel) (Bibiana Oliveira Serpa) (Rafaela Angelon)

> "When a social code does not correspond to the needs and desires of the people addressed by it or when people must perform or not certain acts that do or do not correspond to their desires, we can say that the social code has become a ritual. Thus, a ritual is a code that imprisons, that constrains, that is authoritarian, that is useless or, at worst, that is necessary to convey some form of oppression."
>
> — Augusto Boal, *Theater of the Oppressed*, 2002.

For *Attending [to] Futures* conference held in 2021, we, the authors, a group of non-actors and complicators who coalesce in the Design & Oppression network (Van Amstel et al. 2021), proposed a stage play to explore the theme of oppression. In this insurgence, we were interested in problematizing the wicked problem concept (Buchanan 1992) behind contemporary design thinking practice (Kimbell 2011). The intention was to attest to and denounce its complicity with large systems of oppression such as patriarchy, colonization, and capitalism.

With this in mind, we held a Forum Theater, one of the many methods that Brazilian playwright Augusto Boal introduces in his classic *Theatre of the Oppressed* (Boal 2000). Forum Theater is similar to conventional play but works mainly as a political tool to test and rehearse social emancipation. After every act, theater becomes a forum so the audience can discuss whether what they have seen has anything to do with their reality or just with pure imagination. Breaking the fourth wall, the theater troupe sometimes invites the audience to join the play and improvise alternative courses of action to discover the possibilities of liberating from oppression. Since we could not attend the conference in person due to COVID-19 restrictions, we had to adapt the method for remote interaction (described in detail in Saito et al. 2022).

The play was named *Wicked Problems, Wicked Designs* (2021) after the famous musical Wicked (2003), a prequel to the events in the classic story of *The Wizard of Oz* (Baum 1900). The musical tells the story of the young green-skinned Elphaba and how she later became known as the Wicked Witch of the West. We drew heavily from the musical to construct allegories representing design thinking agents involved in tackling the so-called wicked problems.

In the play, there are three main and one supporting character. The story follows Doris, a Brazilian female designer who is a single mother working on solutions for period poverty. Her character combines the naive girl Dorothy and the Good Witch of the South, Glinda, a well-intentioned character who brushes off her internal ethical conflicts in favor of self-gain and her career goals in Oz.

In the plot, Doris seeks investment from Tom White, a foreign investor who set up a startup accelerator program to support Global-South women in tackling society's wicked problems. Tom is roughly based on the Wizard of Oz, a self-proclaimed all-powerful, knowledgeable, and influential figure that is nothing more than an ordinary man with patriarchal privileges. Thanks to these privileges, Tom White rose as an industry leader and design thinking guru, despite relying on inauthentic magic skills (Kolko 2011) and deceptive coolness.

The third main character is Doris's friend Helena, a feminist activist connected to different social movements who is currently working with awareness raising for period dignity. In the story, Helena is involved in organizing one of seven large demonstrations that protest against the patriarchal policies of the Brazilian government against women. Like Elphaba, she has assumed a wicked position due to her disposition to break social norms and insurge against oppression (Van Amstel et al. 2021). The fourth supporting character is a news anchor named Crystal, who reports on the demonstrations on TV. She does not interact directly with any other characters but provides background information for understanding the basic premises of the second act. We enacted these characters with augmented virtual customs (Figure 1) to explore the aesthetics of the oppressed in the remote forum setup (Saito et al. 2022).

Fig. 1. *Wicked Problems, Wicked Designs* Theatre Forum, Characters Doris (top left), Tom White (top right), Crystal (bottom left), Helena (bottom right), 2021.

There were many diversions from the *Wicked* (2003) plot, the main one being that Helena and Tom White never really meet, which does not afford him to accuse her of being wicked like in the musical. What remains implicit in our story is that Helena embodies authentic design wickedness; in other words, she acts wickedly to fight society's inauthentic wickedness. This intention comes from our critical readings of design thinking discourse that came to the conclusion that design wickedness could be considered a relational quality instead of a system property (Saito et al. 2022).

In this chapter, we wish to perform an interaction analysis (Jordan and Henderson 1995) focused on the rituals and gestures that structure oppression in everyday life and reproduce design wickedness, following the Theatre of the Oppressed hermeneutics of action (Boal 2000; 2005). Augusto Boal claims that Theatre of the Oppressed can depict everyday rituals and gestures that codify oppression, thereby exposing how they become naturalized and normalized. Similarly to how Paulo Freire (1970) codified oppressive situations in picture slides, Theatre of the Oppressed asks the audience to read a theater scene and decodify its underlying oppression. In line with that, we invited the audience to discuss our play at *Attending [to] Futures*, we published the recorded play on YouTube for public discussions,[1] and we performed an interaction analysis on the recordings.

In order to verify and validate how we portrayed the oppressive situation, we triangulated the recordings with the comments left by the audience in the chatbox, our personal experiences with everyday oppression, and the experiences described by other complicators in the Design & Oppression network (Serpa et al. 2022). Through this hermeneutic process, we expected to reveal the social context (Santos 2016) in which the depicted rituals and gestures emerge.

We found eight oppressive situations in our play that could spark further debate on the social context of design thinking—what Freire (1970) would call a generative theme. The themes are: 1) sexism in the design workplace, 2) balancing motherhood and a design career, 3) venture businesses exploiting social gaps in weak states, 4) designers staying apart from social movements, 5) naive problem-solving in design approaches, 6) bamboozling through visual thinking, 7) the colonizing effects of design thinking and 8) the folly of design wickedness. The following sessions describe how these themes appeared in the play, their social context, and how the audience reacted to seeing them expressed this way.

Sexism in the Design Workplace

Sexism is a praxis sustained on beliefs around the fundamental nature of women and men, including their roles in society. Sexist rituals and gestures take the shape of insidious comments, unfounded assumptions, and unequal division of labor. Despite recent legal frameworks set up to prevent discrimination and promote equality, women are still under-represented in decision-making roles, left out of certain sectors of the economy, paid less than men, and disproportionately subject to gender-based violence (EIGE 2020).

The design field is no exception to that. According a report published by the Design Council about the UK design labor market, paid positions are occupied by 77% of people who identify as men and 23% of people who identify as women[2] (Hay, Todd, and Dewfield 2022). Although sexism cannot be determined by such distribution, it is fair to admit that in a male-dominated field, women are more likely to face sexist practices that benefit men.

In our play, we tried to convene this workplace context through several ways. The main character, Doris, is a Latin American woman looking for a great chance to boost her design career. She opens the first act waiting for the arrival of Tom White, a white man from the Global North, in an online meeting room. Doris is anxious but excited about this meeting as she believes she has earned this opportunity. This initial positive feeling about the meeting quickly dissolves due to Tom White's unpleasant behavior. Doris is constantly interrupted by Tom White during her presentation, and he makes various sexist and xenophobic comments and inappropriate jokes. The conversation is interrupted as Doris's baby starts to cry, which immediately puts off Tom White, shocked to find that Doris is a single mother. He doubts her capacity to work in such a fast-paced project (Figure 2) and tells her that he will call her another time.

As the act unfolds, the audience used the conference text chat tool to interact with others and react to the play. Many in the audience recognize

1 The recording is available here: https://www.youtube.com/watch?v=GbAfjbg0Nyk

2 This research lacks information on non-binary people working in the design field.

Fig. 2. Tom White is angry at Doris because she subscribed to the women's acceleration program, not the mother's. He asks her to be more professional next time and points the finger at her while she appeases her child.

Tom White as an archetype of an unpleasant colleague that they have already worked with in the past. Spectators urge Doris to get angry and not let Tom White interrupt her, suggesting she should just give up on the interview because she would never be respected in that organization anyway. The audience chat was populated by sentences like: "Don't let him interrupt you," "Stop this interview," "Don't be so nice," and "Get angry grrrrl."

The oppressive situation was easily recognized by the audience. Doris was unable to present her ideas and suffered recurrent embarrassment throughout the act. However, the oppressor put himself in a position that he cannot be easily avoided. Doris knew that the man who acts abusively towards her is the same who makes the decisions about the investment she needs. Even if Doris felt embarrassed and helpless from Tom White's sudden hang up, she still wanted to take the opportunity.

Motherhood in the Design Career

Doris's situation is not uncommon. Women still shoulder the largest share of care responsibilities towards children and the elderly, having to cope with flexible or inflexible work arrangements (EIGE 2020). As a result, women with children are generally perceived as less competent than women without children, also compared to themselves before becoming a mother (Cikara et al. 2009). Because they are not seen as competent as men to shine in the public sphere, women are pushed to work in the private sphere, where paid and unpaid work accumulates, in larger shares for racialized and working-class women.

Design historian Cheryl Buckley addresses the erasure of the contributions of women in the public sphere of design, pointing to the "selection, classification, and prioritization of types of design, categories of designers, distinct styles and movements, and different modes of production" (Buckley 1986, 3) in which men are at the forefront. Not only are women designers marginalized, but so are design practices associated with feminine affairs reduced to making: crafts, sewing, or knitting, for example—and the associated services of homely routines such as planning meals or organizing care work and parenting duties carried out by women (Buckley 1986; 2020; Scotford 1994). These practices are not recognized as design even if they are based on the same kind of design thinking that male designers employ in the public sphere to empathize, ideate, test, and implement design concepts.

In the play, Doris is a single mother deep into design hustle culture (Julier 2013). She needs the money and will go above and beyond to succeed. Doris's baby starts crying in the middle of their meeting, and Tom White criticizes Doris for being unprofessional while leaving the call to reach out to her crying baby. He adds that the program she applied for was a women's investment fund and not a mother's investment fund, so she should have considered applying for the more fitting program. He feels deceived as she did not disclose that information before and says he does not know how to deal with a caring mother.

Mothers in the audience could relate to the scene where Doris' baby starts crying in the middle of her important call with Tom White. While some shared positive experiences in which they received support from people they were working with, one mother said she went through a similar violent situation while breastfeeding her child in a public space.

Businesses that Exploit the Withdrawal of the State

At the time we performed the play, in October 2021, period poverty was a highly commented topic in Brazil. Brazilian President Jair Bolsonaro had just issued a veto of a bill to distribute free sanitary pads and tampons to people in situations of impoverishment. Instead of framing period poverty and dignity as the result of political choices, we framed it as a wicked problem to examine how design thinking depoliticizes issues and bodies.

Even though Tom White shows little respect for Doris as a woman, he sees feminism and period poverty as great business opportunities. With this, we wanted to bring up a reflection on the design projects taking place where government infrastructure systems are weak or non-existent. While neoliberal ideology praises the benefits of limited government, many nations in the Global South suffer from a withdrawal of the state, lacking the structure, power, and resources to properly regulate a nation-state to deal with several social inequalities and political challenges. Institutions such as venture businesses, NGOs, start-ups, and volunteer organizations exploit these particular dynamics by occupying spaces and taking roles that lack state oversight. This distorted gaze assumes and disseminates the image of countries as weak and needing international help. A neocolonial interventionist approach unfolds, under the guise of development and innovation, like any other design thinking bullshit cover-up strategy (Hernandéz-Ramírez 2018).

In the play, Tom White is very explicit about the fact that he is funding projects in Brazil because it is a cheap investment that will look good in his portfolio. He frames the many social issues in the country as an excellent opportunity for Doris to apply her design skills and make money. In the hopes of taking the opportunity, Doris pitches her idea by putting together a slide presentation she refers to as "visual poetry." She uses images from Russian artist Maria Luneva (a.k.a. Supinatra) and the Chinese-American painter Fong Min Liao. Doris does not really go in-depth on their work during the presentation, implying a lack of care for artists and the appropriation of their work. Yet, she believes the images fit with the aesthetics she wanted—the use of pink and red tones, flowers on clean underwear, and abstract shapes representing menstrual blood.

Even though Doris toned down her visual presentation, Tom White is still shocked and disgusted by the period imagery, saying it is tough for him to stare at such imagery. He terminates her slide presentation before she is finished. Later in the conversation, he remarks about art being something for the elites and elaborates that he knows the reality of Brazilian women living in poverty, claiming Doris's project lacks empathy for them in an awkward attempt at calling out her class privilege. Indeed, third-world girls are one of the typical features of white savior humanitarian imagery, so he pushes Doris to "go and find these people" and connect with them through "empathy" (Figure 3). The audience frames the recommendation as guilt-management: "Seems like empathy in design process is more about reducing a sense of guilt rather than a principle of common good."

The general sense of guilt for the withdrawal of the state normalizes the exploitation of wicked problems as business opportunities. In contrast, feminist movements frame the same issue as period dignity instead of period poverty to emphasize the political opportunity to rethink the social structures that normalize the absence of rights for certain historically vulnerable groups (UNFPA 2022).

Fig. 3. Tom White's gestures for an emphatic attitude point at himself twice.

Designers Staying Apart from Social Movements

Innovation and development programs typically portray target communities as victimized subjects, showing just enough hardship while invisibilizing the structural oppressive relations that give rise to them. They construct users as victims of bad design and designers as heroes of good design (Spinuzzi 2003). Designers who come out of these programs are supposed to master disruption, intervention, and systemic change.

In the play, Doris feel the need to be edgier in her imagery for the second attempt with Tom White. She receives a call from her friend Helena, who tells her she is involved with a social movement organization fighting for period dignity. Helena describes the experiences of people facing period poverty and a community-run project to manufacture reusable pads. She then invites Doris to join them in their next demonstration, suggesting her friend could learn from them (Figure 4). Doris declines the suggestion, assuming she knows enough to represent the movement. The audience reacts with vigor: "Very common behavior from the girl on the left [Doris]… she has not heard anything. She is using feminism for her own interest."

Fig. 4. Helena tries to draw Doris' attention to social movements already working on her issues, but she refuses to join them.

Some days later, after watching TV anchor Crystal reporting on the demonstration, Doris changes her mind. She adds a community-led solution to her project pitch in the next meeting with Tom White; however, the man is unimpressed by it. He is again horrified by her choice of imagery, deemed too political, and he does not even listen to the whole idea. Tom White says that the program is targeted at leveraging women entrepreneurs, not communities. This scene is yet another example of designers committing to a method or a technical solution (Ansari 2019) instead of committing to overcoming oppression by joining social movements and communities that design for themselves (Escobar 2018).

Naive Problem-solving in Design Approaches

Throughout the play, the character Tom White claims his methods are capable of tackling any wicked problems, a typical design thinking bullshit (Hernández-Ramírez 2018). Similar to his archetype Wizard of Oz, Tom White cultivates the magic of design thinking (Kolko 2011), a generic process that can come up with solutions to any wicked problem of the world. It is no coincidence that Wizard of Oz is an actual design method in which a person fakes an interaction with a not-yet functional system (Maulsby et al. 1993).

The problem with magic is that it hides what is going on. In this case, anthropocentrism, capitalism, colonialism, sexism, and whiteness—what Audre Lorde (2021) calls the mythical norm, the universal humans positioned at the centers of power. By hiding what is going on behind wicked problems, design thinking smoothens the reproduction of structural oppression (Saito et al. 2022). Designers aptly learn to use the tools of the oppressors while engrossing the discourse of freedom, effectively reproducing the contradictions of society (Van Amstel et al. 2016).

The contradictory aspect of design work is revealed in two acts. In the first time that Doris and Tom White interact, it seems like she is the oppressed and he is the oppressor. However, in the second act, Doris positions herself at the oppressors' side by trying to co-opt social movements for profit. The ethical basis for solving wicked problems becomes then a problem in itself. In the text chat, a spect-actor proposes that solidarity pushes for the need to be part of the struggle, while empathy implies distance from it (a perspective elaborated on Serpa and Batista 2021). The audience also commented that wicked problems are a tiny part of a larger system of structural oppression, which cannot be tackled by isolated individuals.

Bamboozling through Visual Thinking

Throughout the play, visual thinking appears as the most popular form of design magic. Doris presents her ideas in polished graphic slides to construct a professional image of someone who puts a lot of effort into her work, with the exception of understanding its social context. Doris does not credit the works of artists she adds to her slides and appropriates images from social movements that she doesn't belong to or even support.

In contrast, Tom White's favorite mode of visual thinking is doodling. Unlike Doris, he does not feel the need to present himself professionally. As the Wizard of Oz archetype, he is an almighty free thinker, and conveys his knowledge and power through simple ideas that can fit the back of a napkin. Tom White wants to convey that anyone can draw and think like a designer, or better put, that Doris can think like him if she follows his methods. He plays out pre-recorded doodle videos to mansplain several concepts, including wicked problems, empathy, and mansplaining itself(!). In this way, he bamboozles her with visual thinking several times (Figure 5).

Fig. 5. Mansplaining doodle made by character Tom White (a Global North man) to instruct Doris (a Global South woman) on how it works, as if she did not know it.

Colonizing Effects of Design Thinking

There is a dominating notion of design as a method that can be relevant and useful to people across different genders, races, and nationalities (Ansari 2019). Such a notion presumes a universality which is based on a cis-male, white, Western subject. Despite the criticism of this lack of positionality (Berry et al. 2022; Constanza-Schok 2020; Kimbell 2011), the cannon of design thinking and its methodologies are still widely accepted as universal methods that apply to every context and place (Hanington and Martin 2019).

The fact that the character Tom White is a foreign Global Northern designer sheds light on the colonial and imperialist ways he brings design methods to a project in the Global South, for example, by conducting ethnographic studies in exoticized communities. With a keen eye on that, the audience turned the magic back at its magician: "What if we would come over to his place to do an ethnography of his life? Would he agree to that?" Tom White character embodies the colonialist system of knowledge production that prevails in the Brazilian design academic discourse and industry practices (Angelon and Van Amstel 2021); hence, Doris is always kind enough to take Tom White's demands.

While reflecting on this unequal international relation through Forum Theater, we challenge the notion of the South as inferior and incapable of producing design practice and theory to address our issues on our terms (Gutierrez Borrero 2015). Decolonizing design remains a critical issue for our work (Angelon and van Amstel 2021; Schultz et al. 2018) as it opens up the possibility of recognizing the designs of the oppressed. The audience comments follows keenly: "Sometimes the solution is partially already lying within people, the oppressed ones. You give them an opportunity to speak; possible solutions might arise from this."

The Folly of Design Wickedness

In design research, a wicked problem refers to complex and ill-defined problems, impossible to solve. The term was coined by Horst Rittel at a conference and later published as a paper (Rittel & Webber 1973). According to the German author, wicked problems have no definitive formula, no stopping rule, no immediate solutions, and far-reaching consequences. This type of problem stands in opposition to tame problems—those that can be solved through established objective inquiry and decision-making. This way of thinking is similar to how sexist men believe that they can tame transgressive women or like colonizers believed that they can tame Indigenous people. The choice of the term wicked is related to the malignant, vicious, tricky, or aggressive properties of these problems and the people that originate them.

According to Buchanan (1992), the concept of wicked problems was well accepted by the design community because it formed a "connection between their remarkably diverse and seemingly incommensurate applications of design." Designers working in seemingly unrelated areas and tackling different issues found a point of reference of applicability of their skill set within the concept of wicked problems and that meant they could form a common way of wrapping their heads around them, e.g. design thinking (Brown 2009).

However, by wrapping heads in this way, designers get used to depoliticizing issues, like when Tom White sees period poverty as a business opportunity rather than as a structural social challenge. "If a problem cannot be well defined, it is because it may not even be a problem at all, but rather a person or a group of people who do not admit to being solved" (van Amstel et al. 2022). While framing people as social problems, there is a tendency to ignore the reproduction of anthropocentric, capitalist, colonialist, sexist, and racist tropes that put them into the problematic situation.

To advance the understanding of wickedness in design, we advise seeing how this concept evolved in contemporary culture (Saito et al. 2022). The way wickedness has been dealt with by fantastic literature (Wizard of Oz) or by theater (Wicked, the musical) might refresh how design research frames this aspect of human reality. After reflecting on this generative theme, an audience member writes in the chat that "designers hide behind the term wicked way too often."

Concluding Remarks

The interaction analysis performed on the *Wicked Problems, Wicked Designs* (2021) recorded play has shown how design thinking rituals and gestures reproduce oppressive relations through fake magic and other discursive devices. The analysis turns the magic back upon the magician, asking whether design thinking practice is as wicked as the societal problems it claims to solve.

Through the archetype of the Wizard of Oz, we unveiled a White, cis-male designer from the Global North, who, as a supposedly powerful being, evokes an image of salvation, heroism, and divination (Tom White). As for the Good Witch of the South archetype, we expressed the well-intentioned designer who believes in her capability to do good but lacks critical consciousness to analyze her position in the correlation of power embedded in design practices and the geopolitics of knowledge (Doris). In the musical, the Wizard of Oz persuades the Good Witch of the South to believe in his fake magic. Although she eventually finds out the truth, she chooses to remain in Oz working for the Wizard. Unlike the musical, Doris never questions Tom White's power, and is left inconsolable when he ends their working relationship, blaming herself instead.

With these characters, we aim to acknowledge the complexity of oppressor–oppressed dialectic relation (Freire 1970). In the first act, the audience can relate to Doris and the violence she is suffering as an oppressed woman. In contrast, in the second act, she appears to have a selfish and critical attitude like an oppressor designer (Gonzatto and van Amstel 2022). The activist character Helena is the counterpoint to the establishment as she engages in radical practices, like Elphaba does in the musical, promoting collective engagement as an alternative wicked power (or magic). The forum raised the contradictions that typically emerges in design thinking environments, emphasizing differences in culture, nationality, gender, political view, and readiness for action.

This chapter introduces several generative themes for further design research. The prevalence of sexism in micro-gestures and preparation rituals in the design workplace, the challenge of affording motherhood in a design career, the capitalist exploitation of the social gaps left by weak states, the distance between designers and social movements, the naivete of design problem-solving, the deceptive character of visual thinking gestures, the colonizing effects of design thinking and lastly, but not the least, the folly of design wickedness. We expect these are further explored by design research and artistic practice.

Beyond that, we explored the theme of magic in design thinking and wickedness as a dispute for power. We again denounce that taming wickedness reinforces normativity and reproduces the systems that created these so-called wicked problems in the first place (Saito et al. 2022). We believe that by reframing wickedness as relational quality, we can reclaim it and affirm it authentically. In this way, we recognize the transdisciplinary and transgressive qualities of design wickedness as possibilities for underscoring alternative design practices that explicitly disclose and harness the political nature of design work.

BIBLIOGRAPHY

Angelon, Rafaela, and Frederick M. C. van Amstel. "Monster aesthetics as an expression of decolonizing the design body." *Art, Design & Communication in Higher Education* 20 (1) (2021): 83-102.

Ansari, Ahmed. "Global Methods, Local Designs" in *The Social Design Reader*, edited by Elizabeth Resnick, 417. Bloomsbury, 2019.

Baum, L. Frank. *The wonderful wizard of Oz.* Hill Company, 1900.

Berry, Anne H., Kareem Collie, Penina Acayo Laker, Lesley-Ann Noel, Jennifer Rittner, and Kelly Walters, eds. *The Black Experience in Design: Identity, Expression & Reflection.* Simon and Schuster, 2022.

Boal, Augusto. *Theater of the Oppressed.* 2nd ed. Pluto, 2000.

———. *O arco-íris do desejo: método Boal de teatro e terapia.* Editora Civilização Brasileira, 2002.

———. *Games for actors and non-actors.* Routledge, 2005.

Buchanan, Richard. "Wicked Problems in Design Thinking." *Design Issues* 8, no. 2 (Spring 1992): 5-21. https://doi.org/10.2307/1511637.

Buckley, Cheryl. "Made in patriarchy: Toward a feminist analysis of women and design." *Design Issues* 3, no. 2 (1986): 3-14.

———. "Made in patriarchy II: Researching (or re-searching) women and design." *Design Issues* 36 (1) (2020): 19-29.

European Institute for Gender Equality (EIGE). *Sexism at work: how can we stop it? Handbook for the EU institutions and agencies.* Luxembourg: Publications Office of the European Union, 2020.

Escobar, Arturo. *Designs for the Pluriverse: Radical Interdependence, Autonomy, and the Making of Worlds.* Duke University Press, 2018.

Freire, Paulo. *Pedagogy of the oppressed.* Continuum, 1970.

Fundo de População das Nações Unidas (UNFPA). *Estado da Arte para Promoção da Dignidade Menstrual: Avanços, Desafios e Potencialidades.* Brasília, 2022.

Gonzatto, Rodrigo F. and Frederick M. C. van Amstel. "User oppression in human-computer interaction: a dialectical-existential perspective." *Aslib Journal of Information Management*, 74 (5) (2022): 758-781. https://doi.org/10.1108/AJIM-08-2021-0233.

Gutiérrez Borrero, Alfredo. "Resurgences: south, as designs and other designs." *Nómadas*, no. 43 (2015): 113-129.

Hanington, Bruce, and Bella Martin. *Universal methods of design expanded and revised: 125 Ways to research complex problems, develop innovative ideas, and design effective solutions.* Rockport publishers, 2019.

Hay, Bernard, Jonathan Todd, and Sabina Dewfield. *Design Economy: People, Places and Economic Value.* Design Council, 2022.

Hernández-Ramírez, Rodrigo. "On design thinking, bullshit, and innovation." *Journal of Science and Technology of the Arts* 10 (3) (2018): 45-57.

Jordan, Brigitte, and Austin Henderson. "Interaction analysis: Foundations and practice." *The journal of the learning sciences* 4 (1) (1995): 39-103.

Julier, Guy. *The culture of design.* Sage, 2013.

Kimbell, Lucy. "Rethinking design thinking: Part I." *Design and culture* 3 (3) (2011): 285-306.

Kolko, Jon. *Exposing the Magic of Design: A Practitioner's Guide to the Methods and Theory of Synthesis.* Oxford University Press, 2011.

Lorde, Audre. "Age, race, class, and sex: Women redefining difference" in *Campus Wars*, 191-198. Routledge, 2021.

Maulsby, David, Saul Greenberg, and Richard Mander. "Prototyping an intelligent agent through Wizard of Oz" in *Proceedings of the INTERACT'93 and CHI'93 conference on Human factors in computing systems*, 277-284. Association for Computing Machinery, 1993.

Saito, Carmem, Bibiana O. Serpa, Rafaela Angelon, and Frederick M. C. van Amstel. "Coming to terms with design wickedness: Reflections from a forum theatre on design thinking" in *DRS2022*, edited by D. Lockton, S. Lenzi, P. Hekkert, A. Oak, J. Sádaba, and P. Lloyd. Bilbao: DRS Digital Library, 2022. https://doi.org/10.21606/drs.2022.668.

Scotford, Martha. "Messy history vs. neat history: Toward an expanded view of women in graphic design." *Visible Language* 28 (4) (1994): 367-387.

Schultz, Tristan, Danah Abdulla, Ahmed Ansari, Ece Canlı, Mahmoud Keshavarz, Matthew Kiem, Luiza Prado de O. Martins, and Pedro J. S. Vieira de Oliveira. "What is at stake with decolonizing design? A roundtable." *Design and Culture*, 10 (1) (2018): 81-101.

Santos, Bárbara. *Teatro do Oprimido-Raízes e Asas: Uma teoria da Práxis.* Ibis Libris, 2016.

Serpa, Bibiana O. and Sâmia Batista e Silva. "Solidarity as a principle for antisystemic design processes: two cases of alliance with social struggles in Brazil" in *Pivot 2021: Dismantling/Reassembling*, edited by Renata M. Leitão, Immony Men, Lesley-Ann Noel, Jananda Lima, and Tieni Meninato. Toronto, Canada: DRS Digital Library, 2021. https://doi.org/10.21606/pluriversal.2021.0004.

Serpa, Bibiana O., Frederick M. C. van Amstel, Marco Mazzarotto, Ricardo A. Carvalho, Rodrigo F. Gonzatto, Sâmia Batista e Silva, and Yasmin da Silva Menezes. "Weaving design as a practice of freedom: Critical pedagogy in an insurgent network" in *DRS2022*, edited by D. Lockton, S. Lenzi, P. Hekkert, A. Oak, J. Sádaba, and P. Lloyd. Bilbao: DRS Digital Library, 2022. https://doi.org/10.21606/drs.2022.707.

Spinuzzi, Clay. *Tracing genres through organizations: A sociocultural approach to information design.* MIT Press, 2003.

van Amstel, Frederick M.C., Timo Hartmann, Mascha C. van der Voort, and Geert P.M.R. Dewulf. "The social production of design space." *Design studies* 46 (2016): 199-225.

van Amstel, Frederick M. C., Fernanda Botter, and Cayley Guimarães. "Design Prospectivo: uma agenda de pesquisa para intervenção projetual em sistemas sociotécnicos." *Estudos em Design* 30 (2) (2022).

van Amstel, Frederick M. C., Sâmia Batista e Silva, Bibiana O. Serpa, Marco Mazzarotto, Ricardo A. Carvalho, and Rodrigo F. Gonzatto. "Insurgent Design Coalitions: The history of the Design & Oppression network" in *Pivot 2021: Dismantling/Reassembling*, edited by Renata M. Leitão, Immony Men, Lesley-Ann Noel, Jananda Lima, and Tieni Meninato. Toronto, Canada: DRS Digital Library, 2021. https://doi.org/10.21606/pluriversal.2021.0018.

 IMAGES AND ILLUSTRATIONS

All images are screenshots from the Theatre Forum at the *Attending [to] Futures* conference in November 2021 provided by the authors.

UNIVERSAL SPECIES SUFFRAGE

(Jaione Cerrato) (Jon Halls)

> What if other species could not only vote but were given the dignity that voting entails?

Universal Species Suffrage is a workshop designed and run with the aim of shifting perspectives concerning politics and the environment. Within the climate and biodiversity crises that we face, we have to not only empathize with one another as a species but need acknowledge the plight of other species is on par with our own in order to take sufficient action. In terms of the world's biomass, humans account for only 0.01%. The vast majority of life on this planet is plant life at 82%, and only 0.4% of it is mammalian. However, these percentiles are not reflected in our conceptualization of planetary life; our metrics, legislations and means of production are overwhelmingly focused on benefitting the 0.01%. The species we as humans most empathize and engage with only make up the smallest proportion of the world, therefore finding ways of connecting beyond that is vital for rethinking the environment as its own political actor (Ritchie 2019).

Fig. 1. Universal Species Suffrage, Scenario card, 2020.

The workshop introduces a fictional scenario and invites participants to co-create a new world order in which a global government has enfranchised all species with the right to vote. A consideration of non-human agency provokes questions that reflect back on current geopolitical conditions: How would we utilize fossil fuels when corals could vote against the acidification of the oceans which are dissolving them? How would you pay a tree for the oxygen it produces, the carbon it stores and the biodiversity that it creates, and would it even find money useful? What would be the hierarchy in the global food supply chain when humans and farmed animals have the same right to vote? Would humans have to pay reparations to nature for the historic and current destruction to ecosystems and species extinctions?

The workshop takes on these questions and asks the participants to imagine how they would establish new value systems for the species in this scenario. Through roleplay, participants as their species get a say in this process, voting to best express their characters' needs, worries and wants.

Workshop: Set up and process

The props needed to participate and set up the workshop consist of cards, voting tokens, and a round mat that frames the interaction. The cards allow us to follow a linear narrative and introduce two key elements of the game play: the overarching scenario and the fictional characters' personal storylines as well as thought processes within the scenario.

At each round, the participant reads from two different sets of cards. The "referendum cards" create a shared narrative and structure the workshop, while the "roleplaying cards" enrich the characters' individual stories.

In total there are five characters the participants can speak through:

> Female Human, 45 years old
> Solitary Bee, 2 weeks old
> Coral Polyp, 3 years old
> Sequoia Tree, 2020 years old
> Farmed Chicken, 6 weeks old.

Fig. 2. Universal Species Suffrage, Identity card, 2020.

Representing their species, participants vote on a series of questions on political issues and subsequently elect the first government that best represents the collective votes, enacting their characters at all times. There are five referendums that address key issues of a democratic capitalist society:

| **Civil Rights/Liberties**
How do you define the rights and liberties of species?
| **Resources**
When should a resource be used?
| **Value**
How would you define economic value?
| **Climate Change**
How would you reduce the effects of climate change?
| **Government**
What is the overriding duty of the government?

The referendum questions are accompanied by a range of color-coded responses. In order to vote, participants place a token corresponding to the color of their favored response on a circular mat. The mat works as the focal point during the workshop, where all voting rounds are visualized and over which discussions can occur.

At the end of the voting rounds, we, as hosts, reveal the hidden aspect of the workshop: Each response reflects a particular political ideology represented by a fictional party from the far right to anarcho-leftist. Counting up the tokens we can see which party has won and whether it would need to form a coalition to gain a majority. From here, we open it up to a larger discussion and allow the group to defend their characters' positions and interests to form a global government. Revealing the political parties at the end creates a twist that fundamentally brings the workshop back into our lived realities. The intention is to reflect on the limiting factor of contemporary political debate, where ideas are stifled by party loyalties and agendas. By removing labels, we aim to provide the participants with the space to speculate and let their ideas flow. This often results in surprising advocacy for all kinds of political ideologies and leads to questions about political framing and what values we want to live by.

The value of "props"

We define "props" as tools to frame the workshop and to instigate conversation. The mat, cards, and tokens create an abstract space to interact without

Fig. 3. Universal Species Suffrage, Voting, 2020.

dictating specific outcomes. Given the complexity of the issues and questions raised by the game, the use of props is key to creating an enjoyable gameplay and atmosphere over the course of an hour and a half.

These basic design tools establish a framework for the interaction among players as they mediate and moderate the discussion, ensuring that everybody has an equal opportunity to voice their opinions and thoughts.

The cards are instrumental to this effect and are designed to replace a workshop host. Often, the participants read their story cards out loud, make comments, and establish their characters' storylines with the rest of the group—without mediation. These interactions enable participants to take ownership of the workshop and lead the conversation.

To this effect, participants often spontaneously reach out to one another and try to create commonalities between their species, build alliances, or even rebel against the group, advocating for what was best for their character and their community. In the seven workshops we have held over the course of the past two years, we witnessed that each group had a different focus based on their interests and beliefs.

Reflecting on these workshops, we realized curating a space is important to foster critical conversations. The use of props at different stages of the workshop influenced the conversations and dynamics among participants. While there is always a part of us that views the world through a subjective lens, tools allow us to abstract our day-to-day lives, so we can imagine the possibility of other worlds. Therefore, the creation of props is a valuable asset in itself.

Through the *Universal Species Referendum,* we want to highlight how small acts of world-building can challenge the political narrative of our contemporary world. In this instance, by giving audiences tools to listen to the species that we are impacting through our climate policies, we saw that people would create a radically different world from the one we inhabit.

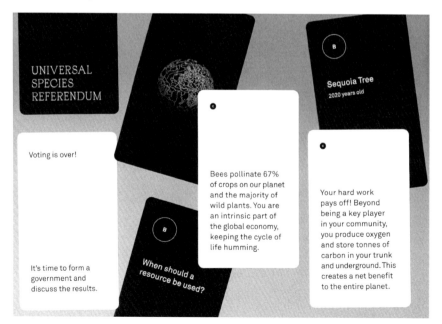

Fig. 4. Universal Species Suffrage, Cards, 2020.

 BIBLIOGRAPHY

Ritchie, Hannah. 2019. "Humans make up just 0.01% of Earth's life – what's the rest?" Our World in Data. Last modified April 24, 2019. https://ourworldindata.org/life-on-earth.

 IMAGES AND ILLUSTRATIONS

Figure 1: Universal Species Suffrage, Scenario card, 2020. Photo: Jaione Cerrato.
Figure 2: Universal Species Suffrage, Identity card, 2020. Photo: Michael Reiner.
Figure 3: Universal Species Suffrage, Voting, 2020. Photo: Michael Reiner.
Figure 4: Universal Species Suffrage, Cards, 2020. Photo: Jaione Cerrato.

Acknowledgements

The bouncy castle was originally designed by Frieder Bohaumilitzky for the project Metapolitisches Hüpfen, and produced by Ursula Klein, schulteswien. We like to thank Steven Lindberg and Alice Lagaay who supported us in translating the manuscript of this contribution.

DESIGN OF UNREST

Right-wing Metapolitics – Paralogy – Knowledge Spaces – Chaos

(Tom Bieling ●) (Frieder Bohaumilitzky ▶) (Anke Haarmann ▲) (Torben Körschkes ◆)

The first starting point for this paper is the idea of an unplanned "bricolage" of fragments of experiences, perceptions and values. Grouped together in a collage-like manner their crumbling edges cannot be puttied with an idea of consistency. The second starting point is a bouncy castle. As a materialized metaphor the bouncy castle brings together our different research perspectives in productive friction. The bouncy castle itself symbolizes the observation that the self-image of a society is increasingly negotiated on the basis of and performed in symbolic spaces. »Bouncing« in this sense can be understood as a breaking out of rigid knowledge productions. The childish bouncing undermines the adult (academic) epistemological seriousness. The bouncy castle can also point to aspects of a chaotic space, that is, to interdependencies, the recognition of complexity and unpredictability, and in this respect also poses the question of how we move in and through spaces of unrest. This also applies to the re/interpretation and staging of symbolic spaces. How can the authoritarian appropriation of the right-wing be countered by design strategies?

▶ Right-wing Metapolitics and Symbolic Spaces

Hambach Castle is a historically symbolic place with contradictory connotations. As the site of the Hambacher Fest of 1832 – where citizens stood up for freedom, free speech, against princely rule, but also for national unity – it is considered the cradle of German democracy. With the Neues Hambacher Fest organized 2018-2020 by Max Otte, chairman of the former WerteUnion and later presidential candidate for the right-wing party Alternative für Deutschland, it has become part of the debate over the political appropriation of history. Otte drew parallels between the complex and contradictory history of the Pre-March era and an alleged present-day dictatorship. In a flag-waving march to the castle, he also performatively imitated historical images of the Hambach Festival, following the lead of the fascist and Alternative für Deutschland politician Björn Höcke. Höcke had called for a turn in the politics of remembrance, intending to put Germans "in contact with the great achievements of our ancestors."[1]

With his Neues Hambacher Fest, Max Otte is pursuing a right-wing metapolitical strategy. The architectural theorist Stephan Trüby (2020, 16) describes this as politics alongside politics and beyond parliaments; it aims to define and change the convictions of civil society and cultural discourse. Right-wing metapolitics is connected to a populist understanding of politics in which political representation is understood as an "imperative mandate." According to political scientist Jan-Werner Müller, the imperative mandate is based on the assumption that the will of a so-called people can be clearly identified and directly

1 Author's translation: Höcke. Dresdner Gespräche mit Björn Höcke, January 17, 2017, Dresden. "mit den großartigen Leistungen der Altvorderen in Berührung."

Design of Unrest

implemented without mediating authorities (J.W. Müller 2016, 130). The "Volk" (the people) is a construct, a right-wing idea of a homogeneous unity with a collective and unified history, traditions, territory, and national character (Reckwitz 2017, 414 ff.). Because the "Volk"[2] does not even exist apart from this essentialist idea, right-wing populists first have to construct and mobilize this imagined entity. Right-wing metapolitics try to do this by employing cultural postulates to construct a hegemony. It works by appropriating and dramatizing symbolic spaces.

[2] In German, the noun „Volk" has the adjective „völkisch", which refers to a fascist ethnic and national dimension of a Volk concept.

● Symbolism and Projection

The castle as a self-enclosed residential and defensive building is closely linked to the feudal form of rule. Since the time of knights and castles, forms of state and political systems have changed, and social forms and formations have diversified. Artifacts conflate a multitude of contradicting cultural and social practices: the castle as a cultural asset and part of the evolved cultural heritage; the castle as a symbol of power and collapse; the castle as a projection for desired continuities of the past. The one is sometimes found in the other, which also means that object-related deconstruction (due to time, weather, or destruction), structural restoration, and even replication seem to culminate in the strategic re-construction of structural and social forms (as an architectural expression of a national romanticism (Y. Müller 2020).

The French Revolution (1789) abolished feudal society. This can be understood as a social, political event in which the abolition of a supposedly natural social order is not only symbolically accompanied by the appropriation of highly symbolic buildings (storming of the Bastille), but the built symbols themselves function as the driving force of an order-related convalescence. "The castle" as a symbol of a patriarchal social order fits into the—national-romantic—narrative of tradition and cultural origin, which to this day serves reactionary and right-wing conservative to right-wing extremist groups as a basis for their argumentation. There is a revisionist form of architectural ideologization in which ideological appropriation occurs: with slogans such as "beauty," "homeland," "tradition," "identity," "soul" (Trüby 2020, 28) or also with legendary, glorifying constructions of heroic ethos and knighthood. The latter have been used throughout history to idealize, legitimize, and consolidate social order.

These are the expressions of an essentialization, i.e., an attempt to define "the other" in terms of otherness or the self in terms of a supposed original essence. This is sometimes a defense strategy against the influence of a globally networked, diversely structured modernism and is formulated in a romanticized, escapist, retropia (Bauman 2017) pitched against a pluriversal society. It is backward-looking—and thus, in a revisionist sense, forward-looking—as a practice of historical misrepresentation.

● Material Power Dynamics

Architectural spaces, as well as the designed things they contain, the institutions they harbor, and the symbolism they embody are shaped by the power dynamics they in turn perpetuate. Racism, sexism, ableism, classism, ageism … these are all aspects that are not only closely connected to the way we shape the world, they also ignite their own dynamics in their interrelationships. The fact that forms and experiences of power and powerlessness do not occur in isolation from each other, but are interdependent, calls for an intersectional approach.

Design and architecture are massively involved in all of this. Our entire everyday life is permeated by design. Everywhere and all the time, artifacts interfere with our cultural and social practices. Our knowledge of the world and our ways of interpreting it are thus always linked to the things that surround us. And conversely: how we shape things allows us to draw conclusions about our value system.

It is important to look at this with a critical eye. What exclusion parameters are we dealing with in design? How can we identify them? What are ableist things, white spaces, misogynous products? This also includes the duty to critically question one's own perspectives. Because this also becomes clear: what we do in the castle and what the castle does with us has to do with each other. We bounce. But also: we are being bounced. By shaping, we are being shaped. The thing (the castle) has a material agency, an inherent power dynamic. Consequently, we can only partially control what happens to us in the castle.

▲ Bouncing

NASA has trained for weightlessness in space travel with trampoline bouncing. So, when jumping are we training ourselves to think and act in leaps beyond the laws of gravity? I bounce, therefore I recognize in a different way—in a mental leap.

Childish bouncing leaps over the adult seriousness of thinking. Thought takes off, gets out of its usual equilibrium, floats in the open—and when it comes down again, it is somewhere else than before. At the same time, this landing and remaining somewhere else other than in a straight line are motivated by transcending forces that do not simply correspond to the jumping intentions of the leaping subject. Crosswinds – the collision of the familiar and unfamiliar – lift us up, let us leap, sometimes clumsy, sometimes awkward. Nevertheless, leaping thought always moves in high-flying weightlessness. It momentarily escapes the laws of gravity. The gravity of the world is one thing; the dance of free imaginative forces is another. The German term Hüpfen (hopping, jumping) derives from a Middle High German word meaning "to bend in dance." By bouncing are we moving in a bendy dance-like way of thinking? However, leaping only becomes a critical practice—by means of its pliability and its restless flexibility—when it understands itself as a way of knowing—methodos—that is not only asserted but done, that not only progresses but reaches its goal by leaps and bounds. One should not only speculate about leaping thinking as a mental practice; one must also do it, trying it out as an alternative to other ways of knowing: Leaping wants to be practiced as paralogos, as a crazy, inspiring logos against the heavy logos of progress—that is, against the idea of successive steps of knowledge (Fig 1). The paralogical practice is paratyping and accordingly one can speak of a crazy production of knowledge as paralogy.

◆ Navigating and Chaos

Navigation is essential to seafaring: The wild, restlessly bouncing and unmanageable sea requires constantly comparing a calculated route to one's actual position. The art of the helmsman could also be described as mediation between

Fig. 1. "Design of Unrest" video still, Anke Haarmann

deliberate and surprising events (Reed 2019) with the help of different tools or navigation devices. In some creation myths, the sea stands symbolically for chaos. The interpretation of the term chaos has taken a few leaps over the years. It has been defined differently by philosophers, physicists, and in everyday language. Chaos could be summarized for the time being as arrangements which the human being can neither comprehend nor predict. Chaos is a restless space.

The relationship between chaos and navigation shapes our social reality, just as our social reality shapes this relationship (Fig. 02). Technological possibilities as well as political ideas are starting points for conceiving this relationship. The dynamic storage used in modern warehouses and the organization of the shelfs in the art library Sitterwerk will serve as two examples that show the extent to which the tools or navigation devices available for faring this chaos can open up or limit possibilities, actions, and relationships. The negotiation of navigating and being navigated decides how we want to deal with the complexity of the world (1) without getting lost in it; (2) without (re)producing social relations of oppression; (3) without breaking them down and provoking totalitarian encrustations.

Fig. 2. Design of Unrest" video still, Torben Körschkes

◆ Relational Arrangements

According to sociologist Martina Löw (2001), space is constituted by the arrangement of social goods or people and the synthesis of these social goods or people into spaces, i.e., the ability to recognize and combine arrangements. In German, Löw writes of "(An)Ordnungen," implying both the act of arranging and the arrangement as order or structure. Orientation presupposes spatial perceptions and spatial knowledge: We need reference points and systems that we bring together cognitively in order to be able to act independently (Schranz 2019). In chaos, social goods or people are also arranged and combined into spaces, but humans can neither comprehend nor predict these arrangements.

▶ Appropriation of the Dramatic Quality of Historic Things

The self-conception of societies is increasingly negotiated and rehearsed in symbolic places. This observation can be linked to the idea of a metapolitics alongside politics and beyond parliaments. But the metapolitics that occur beyond framing institutional formal conditions has institutionally historical role models. This can be shown using the example of the "thing." The design scholar Pelle Ehn (2013, 79 f.) explains that things were places in pre-Christian Nordic and Germanic societies where governing assemblies met, conflicts were resolved, and political decisions were made. The thing was thus not just a spatial setting but also entailed inherent methods for resolving conflicts and making decisions. The National Socialists appropriated the dramatic quality of historic things and reinterpreted them for their propaganda. In their propaganda, so-called thing "Thingplätze" or "Thingstätte" (thing places/sites) served to dramatize an Aryan "Volksgemeinschaft" (community of the people) and imagine a shared German history (Bosse 2020, 6). The photographer Katharina Bosse studied many open-air theatres built between 1933 and 1936 and their ideological motivation. She explains that the National Socialist Thingstätte refers to historic German things but did not correspond to them in their geography or meaning. The theme of the thing-plays performed there was German history, but they were also used as for National Socialist announcements and celebrations and served to dramatize the Volksgemeinschaft. The name Thingstätte was therefore a politically motivated appropriation intended to produce "instant historicity" (ibid.)

▲ Paralogos — Crazy Logos

Paralogy derives from the Greek parà "next to" and logos "word/reasoning." In linguistics, paralogy refers to the deviant use of words as a preliminary stage to a change in meaning. The deviant attribution slowly becomes the new core of the term.

In psychology, paralogy names a disorder of grammatical language structure triggered by psychosis that can lead to confabulation. Confabulation is the production of false statements or narratives. These are based on perceptions that are not shared by the rest of the world or on a function of memory understood as pathological, like when someone tries to retrieve more information from their memory than is stored there. Interestingly, in the practice of speculative thinking/creating, philosophers, inventors, designers, artists do just that: They confabulate! They pull new ideas or previously unthought information out of themselves and tell tales or paratype for the world.

For philosopher Jean-François Lyotard, paralogy denotes a science understood in a new way. Paralogical science produces "not the known, but the unknown. And it suggests a model of legitimation that has nothing to do with maximized performance, but has as its basis difference understood as paralogy" (Lyotard 1986). The usefulness of this science or critical practice is that

Design of Unrest

it gives rise to new ideas. Its value is that of being rich in ideas and producing new statements—statements that are not to be found exactly where one jumped off on the way to look for them.

◆ **Chaotic Storage**

In logistics, the principle of chaotic storage has existed for several years. Goods are stored where there is space at the moment. They do not have a fixed, previously assigned shelf, but are always placed where another product last left the warehouse. This is also known as dynamic storage. Chaotic storage systems save enormous storage capacity, and many more goods can be stored in much smaller warehouses, because the occupancy rate does not depend on the quantity of a single product.

In these warehouses, each location and each product are marked. Special software is required to register all steps and instruct the logical next steps. If data were to be lost or hacked here, the consequences would be catastrophic because no one but the software knows where any given product is located.

Amazon also uses this principle in their warehouses. They have optimized the software so that products that are frequently ordered together are also stored in close proximity. When an order comes in, the workers are navigated through the warehouse on a route optimized by the software. For this purpose, all workers are equipped with a GPS navigation device with which they can also scan the respective goods and thus report back to the software.[3]

◆ **Sitterwerk**

In St. Gallen, an art library was set up in an old industrial site. The bookshelf of the Sitterwerk library extends over 20 meters on two levels. The publications do not follow any predefined order, but are placed on the shelf at random. Those who work there return the books they have taken out to any free space. All books are equipped with a small RFID chip. Every night, a robotic arm moves along the bookshelf and scans all the titles. The next morning, if you search the database for a particular book, the system shows you its exact position.

◆ **People after Machines**

On a technical level, both systems function more or less alike. Both bookshelf and Amazon warehouse can be described as chaotic: Both arrangements are neither comprehensible nor predictable for humans; they are dynamic and subject to constant change. In both systems, this chaos is neither a political failure nor a natural event, but actively designed. Both systems "work" only through the human/software interface; both "work" only because the technical tools, the navigation devices, have been designed accordingly to order certain parts of the system in a certain relationship to other parts of the system. At the same time, the relationship between chaos and navigation is designed very differently in both cases, and very different actions, possibilities and relationships result from this design.

At Amazon, products and workers are tracked, and the navigation device is also a monitoring tool: If two devices/workers stand together for an

---

3 For more information on how Amazon's warehouses work, see for example Bridle 2019, 116, or Vijai 2016.

unusually long time, this is registered and reported. If a device/worker is on the toilet for a longer period of time, this is registered and reported. The combination of chaotic storage and navigation by software and GPS also means that the workers need absolutely no qualifications or even to speak the local language or each other's language. This may be advantageous for starting the job, but it (1) gives the company no incentive to promote its employees and (2) makes them extremely interchangeable. Artist James Bridle (2019, 40) describes this type of computer-based process as a combination of "opacity and complexity."

◆ Machines after People

In contrast to the dynamic storage of Amazon's warehouse, in the Sitterwerk library only one area is connected to software and tracking: the publications. Visitors can use the software to search for specific titles, but the software cannot track which visitor has searched for what and also does not know whether a visitor ultimately takes the book they were looking for from the shelf. So what are the actions and relations that emerge from this? While Amazon's calculations are aimed at absolute optimization and human actions are limited to running behind, in the Sitterwerk library running behind is the action of the robot. This provides a large room for (spontaneous) action on the part of the human visitor. The system of the Sitterwerk library puts this large room for (spontaneous) action in the foreground. While the entrenched systems of reference and order, categorizations and ideas of seclusion are negated in the Sitterwerk library, it still offers the possibility of purposeful, technology-optimized and data-supported navigation through the database. But the interface between physical space and digital data processing is designed in a way, that humans are empowered to engage with the neither comprehensible nor predictable chaotic arrangement. This is possible because 1) the human visitor can access the books also without interacting with the machine. They can bypass the technical apparatus. 2) The robot/computer at Sitterwerk library does not optimize and does not dictate. It does not make the order more valid, correct or final. It has very little agency. Connected with this is 3) The database is simply a digital copy of the bookshelf, which – as every copy – runs always late. The robot at Sitterwerk cleans up without cleaning up: it does not change anything physically, the material structure stays untouched. At the same time, however, the database/digital copy enables targeted access to specific titles. This is a system with multiple access points.

Consequently, an encounter with chaos is designed without putting that chaos in order and without turning the navigator into the navigated. It is not possible for the human visitor to find a comprehensible order in the Sitterwerk library, but they can make an unlimited number of links, interventions and leaps, all unpredictable. The order of the Sitterwerk library thus always remains restless. Maybe even the robot sometimes gets surprised at night when it copies the unrest of the day to the database.

▲ Leaps of Thought

So, when do thoughts become critical practice? How do we model the context of our thinking so that leaps become possible? Leaps of thought that wager on changing insight like a gambler who bets on winning by chance. To jump means to leap up and move through the air for a short distance. Jumping thinking allows gravity, dilettantism, and crosswind to influence the course of thought. The crosswind is perhaps the bricolage with which Claude Lévi-Strauss tried to characterize what he called 'savage thinking' (1962). It is the idea of an unplanned "bricolage" of fragments of experiences, perceptions, values, grouped together in a collage-like manner and whose crumbling edges cannot be puttied with an idea of consistency. Models of this construction would be a compromise of event and foreknowledge, so that the truth in them is continuously shifted.

● Spaces as Spaces of Knowledge and Negotiation

Those who think about pasts and also presents or futures like to imagine them as temporalities, as moments in time. The attempt to imagine them as spaces is perhaps more revealing. Spaces of knowledge or spaces for dialogue, negotiation, expression (such as of feelings, hopes, fears, desires, or losses). Just like physical or virtual spaces, these are also permeated and determined by design.

Design itself functions as a space of knowledge and negotiation. As a space in which (or out of which) knowledge is created and negotiated. Or as a space about which we believe we know something and realize that this knowledge is situated and linked to different attributions of meaning, determined by normative settings.

To gain an understanding of the normative power of design is to develop an understanding of places as places of knowledge, of spaces as spaces of negotiation, of things as things of meaning (Bieling 2019). Be it a particular space (a square, public building, or castle), an indefinite place (the academy, the institution of science) or a thing (as a designed artefact), these do not generate their meaning out of themselves; they are charged with meaning (e.g., through use, through convention, as the provisional outcome of a negotiated matter). Consequently, they are not fixed, but tend to be open, interpretable, variable, flexible. But this flexibility does not preclude the meaning inscribed in them and consequently communicated through them. In fact, it is sometimes difficult to determine who actually has the sovereignty of interpretation over the respective attributions of meaning.

Just as Hambach Castle is read differently by different groups and instrumentalized for their own purposes (e.g., as a symbol of European unification, as a symbol of the ideals and history of Europe, as a national monument and symbol of freedom and brotherhood, etc.), this in turn results in certain codes of belonging or exclusion. This sometimes leads to overlapping meanings that can reinforce but also contradict each other, which in turn leads to processes of interpretation and negotiation that are inevitably ideological and carried out on different levels. In this context, one could argue with Silvia Lindtner and Paul Dourish, who point to the cultural context as fundamental for the interpretation of things: appropriation is always related to corresponding aspects of value (Lindtner, Anderson, and Dourish 2012, 77ff; Vertesi/Dourish 2011).

▶ Complex Assemblies of Contradictory Issues

The thing is discussed repeatedly in design theory as well. The point is usually to trace things—the word "thing"—back etymologically in order to argue that whatever it is should be understood materially and socially. Its quality of conflict or practice of negotiation is often emphasized. For example, Bruno Latour (2009, 4) says that in the thing, artefacts become conceivable "as complex assemblies of contradictory issues." Perhaps it makes sense to understand Hambach Castle, with its various connotations, as a complex assembly of contradictory issues and to make it clear that specifically German and perhaps problematic self-images are articulated there. The castle itself has a dual function in this negotiation: As a thing, it is at once the imaginary object and the place for playing out a meta-politics of revisionist history. Gustav Rossler (2020, 36) has emphasized that "thing politics" always means both: Things being debated and thing-like media and infrastructures in which and with which debates are held.

Both articulations—the narrative of a cradle of German democracy and the assertion of a parallel between the Pre-March and an alleged present-day dictatorship—aim to construct self-contained identities. At the same time, they bracket out Germany's National Socialist past. The Hambach Festival cannot be interpreted solely as evidence of a striving for civil rights and a state based on the rule of law, but also as evidence of patriotism and the desire for national unity. For example, the Alternative für Deutschland party recently commissioned seven drawings of German history for its party chamber in the "Bundestag" (Parliament of the Federal Republic of Germany). Although the founding of the Federal Republic was not pictured—supposedly because only part of the "Volk" was represented there (cf. monopol 2019)—, the Hambach Festival is featured quite prominently. This shows how the historical Hambach Festival can be appropriated for a nationalist historiography.

▶ Interaction and Delegation

In the context of design and right-wing metapolitics, it is worth considering the question of the agency of things and, following Gustav Rossler, differentiate between two possible social mechanisms: interaction and delegation. Rossler (2020, 38) sums up the latter with a formulation from Bruno Latour for mediated social action: "faire faire" (make someone do something). Analogously, Anne-Marie Willis (2006, 77 f.) speaks of "design design" or "designed to design". She thus declares a design of the space and artefacts of the path of life to be a fundamental cultural and design activity. By contrast, Pelle Ehn (2013, 80 f.) advocates interactions and speaks of a "design after design," which he connects to a participatory concern. He is thinking of infrastructure that remains open to contradiction. With an eye to a right-wing metapolitics that seek to define the convictions of civil society and cultural discourses and change them in accordance with its own ideas, delegation is clearly well suited for this purpose.

⬢ Ontological and Pluriversal Design

Design creates worlds, be it on the micro-level in the form of everyday things (tables, plates, smartphones) or on a larger scale (cities, systems, science, knowledge/culture). It introduces premises into our world, to which we are then subordinated. Designers create ways of being, thinking and acting. In designing, we are being designed (Fig. 03). Perhaps this mechanism has never been more evident than in the era of modernity, which may be reaching its limits for this reason. Design in the mirror of modernity, and with it the principles of progress, science, truth, values, markets and capitalism itself have brought to light a mechanism strongly oriented towards binaries: nature and culture, ugliness and beauty, right and wrong, etc. But what if life is actually based on a pluriversal principle rather than a universal one? ("The world where many worlds fit"—Arturo Escobar). The central task of design would then be to "become mindful and effective weavers of the mesh of life" (Escobar 2018). The pluriverse of worlds and forms that modernity has torpedoed with universalizing structures… What could it look like? And what might bouncing have to do with this? Perhaps as a subversive practice of (civil) disobedience? Because the question of who is weaving and who is being weaved here relates to how we understand this mesh as an infrastructure. Especially since infrastructure tends to evoke images of associations with drawing boards, concepts and structures. The weave of life, however, is often unstructured, unconceptualized and runs along beaten paths. So, the question might be whether design intervention necessarily has to do with (infra)structuring (not only in Pelle Ehn's sense), or whether there is another, less strategic kind of design intervention. And how effective and mindful this would be. In any case: do "mindful" and "effective" perhaps get in each other's way or are they the key to each other?

Fig. 3. "Design of Unrest" video still, Tom Bieling

▲ Paratypes Not Prototypes

Paratypes are derived from the Greek parà "next to" and typus "pattern." A paratype lands next to the pattern piece. Essential aspects of paratypes are their unexpected implementations—i.e., crosswinds. Paratypes are patterns or models that are not finished, but drift unpredictably to the side in the process of being created. Carolin Höfler proposes to understand models in terms of their unpredictable and surprising effects—in other words, to understand them as paratypes. She says: "This perspective is linked to the intention of making models productive as agents of change and transformation for the shaping of public affairs and interests." (2018, 385)

Paratypes, then, do not just produce f-acts, that is, things that are acts, as in deeds, or deeds that are things. They are also playful agents of negotiation with other expectations, unexpected realities, objects and practices. But this means that paratypes have to be realized continuously in order to "put into action" this playful negotiation of imagination and reality. With the bouncy castle, for example, it is above all about the paratyping of leaps of thought as critical practice in action.

Paratypes are both a concept (idea) and an object (shape). They are real models and models of thought (like drafts). Against this background, paratyping can be understood as a restless process of (object-like) production of questions and ideas. Paratypes realise the questions inherent in things because they are small and yet real or real and yet somehow inflated – like the bouncy castle with which we can think as and in design practice. Our critical thinking is thereby held together and at the same time unbalanced in its small model-like fragmentedness by the bouncy castle as the place of thinking. As a paratype – not a prototype – the bouncy castle does not stand for a generalisable, but a model-like, situational, negotiable, unstable, displaced thing and thinking.

▶ Keeping Societal Self-images in a State of Unrest

Metapolitics was originally a leftist theoretical concept and was intended to help create a civil society that is as strong as possible. When right-wing metapolitics misuses things as delegations, it is perhaps time to seek interaction with things (Fig. 04). Like things, social self-understandings must remain negotiable. Chantal Mouffe (2018, 62) for example, understands the "Volk" not as an empirical reference but rather as a discursive political construction: "It does not exist previously to its performative articulation." The word "Volk" should be replaced with the word "society." The goal must be to keep societal self-understandings open to contradictions. This means keeping self-images in a state of unrest so that they do not solidify into an essentialist idea of "Volk". An antifascist and democratic society needs more than formally intact institutions and procedures; it also needs an active antifascist and democratic culture.

Fig. 4. "Design of Unrest" video still, Frieder Bohaumilitzky

This text is based on the film "Design of Unrest: Right-wing Metapolitics – Paralogy –Knowledge Spaces – Chaos" that was produced originally for the conference *Attending [to] Futures* (2021) by the authors, together with Stephan Kraus and Tamara Hildebrand.

# BIBLIOGRAPHY

Bauman, Zygmunt. *Retropia*. Edition Suhrkamp, 2017.

Bieling, Tom. *Inklusion als Entwurf*. Teilhabe orientierte Forschung über, für und durch Design. BIRD Board of International Research in Design. Birkhäuser/DeGruyter, 2019.

Bosse, Katharina. „Thingstätten" in *Thingstätten. Von der Bedeutung der Vergangenheit für die Gegenwart*, edited by Katharina Bosse. Kerber, 2020.

Bridle, James. *New Dark Age. Technology and the End of the Future*. Verso, 2019.

Ehn, Pelle. "Partizipation an Dingen des Designs" in *Wer gestaltet die Gestaltung? Praxis, Theorie und Geschichte des partizipatorischen Designs*, edited by Claudia Mareis, Matthias Held and Gesche Joost. Transcript, 2013.

Escobar, Arturo. *Designs for the Pluriverse. Radical Interdependence, Autonomy, and the Making of Worlds*. Duke University Press, 2018.

Höfler, Carolin. „Modelloperationen: Zur Formierung gesellschaftlicher Wirklichkeiten" in *Was ist Public Interest Design*, edited by Christoph Rodatz, Pierre Smolarski. Transcript, 2018.

Lara, Fernando Luiz. "Design and Activism in the Americas" in *Design (&) Activism. Perspectives on Design as Activism and Activism as Design*, edited by Tom Bieling. Design Meanings / Mimesis, 2019.

Latour, Bruno. "A Cautious Prometheus? A Few Steps Toward a Philosophy of Design (With Special Attention to Peter Sloterdijk)," in *Proceedings of the 2008 Annual International Conference of the Design History Society (UK)*, edited by Fiona Hackney, Jonathan Glynne and Viv Minto. Boca Raton, 2009.

Lévi-Strauss, Claude. *Das wilde Denken*. Suhrkamp, 1973. Originally published in French in 1962.

Lyotard, Jean Francois. *Das postmoderne Wissen*. Passagen, 1986. Originally published in French in 1979.

Lindtner, Silvia, Ken Anderson, and Paul Dourish. *Cultural appropriation: Information technologies as sites of transnational imagination*. ACM, 2012.

Löw, Martina. *Raumsoziologie*. Suhrkamp, 2001.

Mouffe, Chantal. *For a Left Populism*. Verso, 2018.

monopol. 2019. "Bundestag. Ist die Kunst im AfD-Fraktionssaal Ausdruck einer 'erinnerungspolitischen Wende'?" monopol. Last modified September 12, 2019. Accessed June 20, 2022. https://www.monopol-magazin.de/kritik-fraktionssaal-kunst-der-afd.

Müller, Jan-Werner. *Was ist Populismus? Ein Essay*. Suhrkamp, 2016.

Müller, Yves. 2020. "Ein Volksschloss sicher nicht." taz. Last modified August 31, 2020. https://taz.de/Debatte-um-das-Berliner-Stadtschloss/!5707717/.

Reckwitz, Andreas. *Die Gesellschaft der Singularitäten*. Suhrkamp, 2017.

Reed, Patricia. 2019. "Orientation in a Big World: On the Necessity of Horizonless Perspectives." e-flux Journal. Last modified June, 2019. https://www.e-flux.com/journal/101/273343/orientation-in-a-big-world-on-the-necessity-of-horizonless-perspectives/.

Roßler, Gustav. "Dingpolitik" in *Zurück zu den Dingen! Politische Bildungen im Medium gesellschaftlicher Materialität*, edited by Werner Friedrichs and Sebastian Hamm. Votum, Beiträge zur politischen Bildung und Politikwissenschaft, Bd. 6, 2020.

Schranz, Christine. *Augmented Spaces and Maps: Das Design von kartenbasierten Interfaces*. Birkhäuser, 2019.

Trüby, Stephan. *Rechte Räume. Politische Essays und Gespräche*. Bauwelt Fundamente / Birkhäuser, 2020.

Vertesi, Janet and Paul Dourish. "The Value of Data: Considering the Context of Production in Data Economies" in *Proceedings of the ACM*. Association for Computing Machinery, 2011.

Vijai, J. Prince. *Inside Amazon: Chaotic Storage System*. IBS Center for Management Research, 2016.

Willis, Anne-Marie. "Ontological Designing." *Design Philosophy Papers* 4, no. 2 (2006): 69-92.

IMAGES AND ILLUSTRATIONS

Figure 1: "Design of Unrest" video still, Anke Haarmann 2021.

Figure 2: "Design of Unrest" video still, Torben Körschkes 2021.

Figure 3: "Design of Unrest" video still, Tom Bieling 2021.

Figure 4: "Design of Unrest" video still, Frieder Bohaumilitzky 2021.

Acknowledgements

First, I want to express my gratitude to the Detroiters who participated in workshops that informed and critiqued this work during the summer of 2021; fabricators Nayomi Cawthorne, Logan Merry, and Sarah Wondrack, who helped realize the spatial dimensions of the installation; artists saylem celeste, Glenn Miles, Alexis Shotwell, Monique Thompson-Curtis and Seti Iyi, who contributed to the artifacts and soundscapes in the installation; and the countless friends who shared time, energy, and advice throughout the course of this project. This work was made possible by support from the Detroit Justice Center's (DJC) inaugural Artist-in-Residence program. I'm grateful to DJC's Casey Rocheteau for their vision for this offering and their support throughout the project. Thank you to Red Bull Arts for the space and support to mount this show as a part of *Monolith*.

Portions of this article were previously published on Futuress.org in 2021: https://futuress.org/stories/making-room/

MAKING ROOM FOR ABOLITION

(Lauren Williams)

Fig. 1. Making Room for Abolition, Red Bull Arts Detroit, 2021.

We struggle to imagine a world without police, prisons, or capitalism, myself included. We're beholden to a crisis of imagination which is, in many ways, symptomatic of the "disaster capitalism" of which Naomi Klein (2008) writes: Catastrophic (often humanmade) moments in which "we are hurled further apart, when we lurch into a radically segregated future where some of us will fall off the map and others ascend to a parallel privatized state." Detroit, Michigan—where I live—is a city defined by manufactured disasters and disasters of manufacturing: The abandonment by the auto industry and the subsequent mismanagement by the apparatus of the city itself decades later have unmistakably shaped life in Detroit. The fallout of these crises left behind thousands of stranded workers, literal industrial and residential ruin, structural decay, streets in disrepair, gutted houses and gutted homes and gutted neighborhoods, disinvestment in people and place, a tragedy and a "beautiful wasteland" as described by Rebecca Kinney (2016) in *Beautiful Wasteland: The Rise of Detroit as a Post-Industrial Frontier.* The "New Detroit"—the shiny, saccharine, "revitalized" downtown—is the parallel privatized state that Klein referenced. It is the prize of catastrophe awarded those who stand to benefit from this radically segregated future.

In The Future as Cultural Fact, Arjun Appadurai (2013) writes that the future has "been more or less completely handed over to economics." We are convinced en masse that the capacity to "speculate," to construct futures, is the exclusive domain of those who've mastered speculation in a neoliberal sense. Only through the specialized techniques of contrived calculations, computational sciences, and statistics can we model and predict the future. Speculation has become the purview, exclusively, of those who command enough capital to make new worlds appear out of ruins or thin air. "To most ordinary people—and certainly to those who lead lives in conditions of poverty, exclusion, displacement, violence, and repression—the future often presents itself as a luxury, a nightmare, a doubt, or a shrinking possibility" (ibid.).

To borrow from Appadurai, what's needed, in a space where the capacity to speculate is denied, is a politics of hope which depends on our capacity to "convert uncertainty into risk" by—in my estimation—collaborating to imagine a world that the calculations of neoliberal financial speculation tells us is impossible.

What if we could imagine a world without police and prisons and capitalism? Not just think, talk, or write about it, but truly see, feel, hold, and sit in it?

On display from October 8 to November 5, 2021, at Red Bull Arts Gallery in Detroit, MI, "Making Room for Abolition" is an installation of a living room that evokes critical conversations around what stands between us and a world without police and prisons. Situated in a domestic space, this installation draws attention to our home's most quotidian objects and sounds. It acknowledges how our homes and belongings reflect the world outside, especially in a city so deeply shaped by over-policing and carceral politics as Detroit. This experience is a provocation, not a vision, intending to posit possible futures; hint at how abolition demands that we evolve through time; and pose questions about an abolitionist world through the lens of a home.

That this imagined world takes place in a living room is an acknowledgment that our homes are microcosms of our wider worlds. The artifacts that populate our homes express, articulate, embody, and reflect the social relations and systems that govern our lives outside of them. They contain histories and forecast futures: The bills that pile up on our tabletops; the artwork that decorates our walls; the TV shows we stream; the songs we listen to; the heirlooms we cherish and the ones that collect dust. They tell stories about who we were, where we came from, the worlds that shape us, the rules we follow and break, the environments we inherit, the ways we survive, the worlds we presently inhabit, the things we fear and protect, and the worlds we hope to shape.

Fig. 2. Scene with *The Rise and Fall of Policing*.

Fig. 3. Scene with sewing machine and ginger beer.

Each artifact in the room poses a set of questions to visitors as they navigate through a living room set in a world without police and prisons. The primary operating assumption behind every object in the room is that in order for this world to exist, nearly every system we know must change: systems of governance, markets, food, media, environment, and more. Secondly, each artifact posits that the primary shifts those systems must make is in how we relate with one another: How we extend trust, regard nature, tell stories, value our ancestors, and more.

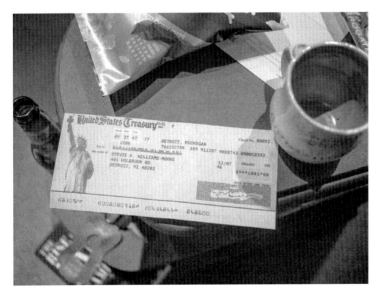

Fig. 4. Scene with guaranteed income check.

A side table littered with various forms of currencies asks: How would our economic system change? What would constitute economic value? How would we navigate in a world where the American dollar doesn't dominate? A bag of chips and a ginger beer question: How would our food systems change?

Making Room for Abolition 185

A guaranteed income check asks: What would labor look like? How would we make a living? A graphic novel called "Chrysanthemum City" designed by Glenn Miles wonders: How would popular media shape our kids' imaginations? What might replace copaganda?[1] A messy workstation where a mother studies for a "water steward" certification exam ponders: What would our relationship to the environment, specifically water, be like? What kind of labor might support our environment, instead of degrading it? A mug featuring notes about Assata Shakur questions who we might venerate and what heirlooms we might hold onto? While extensive backstories are embedded in the construction and details of each artifact, those narratives were not otherwise externalized for visitors to the installation. Visitors were invited, instead, to piece together stories of their own as they paced through the living room, picked up artifacts, and listened to the conversations taking place around them.

1 Copaganda is a portmanteau of „cop" and „propaganda," usually referring to media that makes police seem like friendly, helpful, harmless, silly characters and helps to sway public opinion in favor of policing. In this case, we were thinking of buddy cop movies, kids' TV shows, popular dramas, etc.

Fig. 5. Scene with Chrysanthemum City graphic novel.

Fig. 6. Water steward study scene with notes.

Fig. 7. Water steward study scene with maps, textbook and water samples.

This was intentional. In ongoing instantiations of this body of work, I have invited Detroit organizers into conversation with the room and each other to expose the stories they constructed and the ones I intended. Moving forward, I am building out more mechanisms for sharing and expounding on this work as a "distributed," non-linear story, wherein those who see it can engage with the backstories of each artifact and scenes in a way that allows for a more robust and informed space of contention around the worlds they suggest.

This work intends to immersively propose possible worlds through domestic artifacts for the sake of contestation. I find a tendency among much speculative design work to err toward techno-utopianism or -solutionism, or to rely so heavily on technology as a point of departure for speculation that it fails to consider the shifts in social relations and mundane elements of daily life that would necessarily evolve before, alongside or as a result of drastic technological transformations. Instead, I hope, the artifacts in this room contend first with our values, our relations with one another and the environment, and the attendant shifts away from neoliberal imaginaries around race, carcerality, capital, and nature that I believe to be necessary in order for us to move toward abolition. This installation struggles against and with time, contends with the ways our institutions evolve, and posits earnest questions about how our lives might shift to make space for the work of abolition through the lens of a home.

 BIBLIOGRAPHY

Appadurai, Arjun. *The Future as Cultural Fact: Essays on the Global Condition.* New York, NY: Verso Books, 2013.

Kinney, Rebecca. *Beautiful Wasteland: The Rise of Detroit As America's Postindustrial Frontier.* Minneapolis, MN: University of Minnesota Press, 2016.

Klein, Naomi. *The Shock Doctrine.* Harlow, England: Penguin Books, 2008.

IMAGES AND ILLUSTRATIONS

Figure 1: Lauren Williams, Making Room for Abolition, Red Bull Arts Detroit, 2021, Photo: Clare Gatto, View of Making Room for Abolition in Monolith at Red Bull Arts Detroit, 2021.

Figure 2: Lauren Williams, scene with The Rise and Fall of Policing in America featured in Making Room for Abolition, Red Bull Arts Detroit, 2021, Photo: Giizhigad Bieber, View of Making Room for Abolition in Monolith at Red Bull Arts Detroit, 2021.

Figure 3: Lauren Williams and Saylem Celeste, scene with sewing machine and ginger beer featured in Making Room for Abolition, Red Bull Arts Detroit, 2021, Photo: Giizhigad Bieber, View of Making Room for Abolition in Monolith at Red Bull Arts Detroit, 2021.

Figure 4: Lauren Williams, scene with guaranteed income check featured in Making Room for Abolition, Red Bull Arts Detroit, 2021, Photo: Giizhigad Bieber, View of Making Room for Abolition in Monolith at Red Bull Arts Detroit, 2021.

Figure 5: Lauren Williams and Glenn Miles, scene with Chrysanthemum City graphic novel featured in Making Room for Abolition, Red Bull Arts Detroit, 2021, Photo: Giizhigad Bieber, View of Making Room for Abolition in Monolith at Red Bull Arts Detroit, 2021.

Figure 6: Lauren Williams, water steward study scene with notes featured in Making Room for Abolition, Red Bull Arts Detroit, 2021, Photo: Giizhigad Bieber, View of Making Room for Abolition in Monolith at Red Bull Arts Detroit, 2021.

Figure 7: Lauren Williams, water steward study scene with maps, textbook and water samples featured in Making Room for Abolition, Red Bull Arts Detroit, 2021, Photo: Giizhigad Bieber, View of Making Room for Abolition in Monolith at Red Bull Arts Detroit, 2021.

Acknowledgements

My gratitude goes to all the amazing contributors of *Out of Stock*'s first and only issue, to Ana Labudović who graphically envisioned this idea, to the transnational collective Heckler and my dear friends, artists Flaviu Rogojan and Tăietzel Ticălos for their continuous support.

The project has been presented within the context of Akademie Schloss Solitude.

OUT OF STOCK

Notations on a Speculative Journal for Fashion and Design

(Edith Lázár)

As any dreamer knows, dreams are worlds of their own, growing bizarre architectures that refuse control. Their logic is not an error, but another form of thinking that falls out of the structures of the everyday. They allow scenarios and depths of emotions that follow us in our waking life. Dreams, as psychologist James Hillman (1979) pointed out, are how we recover the complexities of the world and the whole of our being. They constitute the inner place where we resituate ourselves in relationship with life and experiences. It is not bodies that dissolve here, but those divisive learnt constructs. Thus, dreams make for an escape that doesn't slip into an elsewhere, but rather engages further with the world as to see with new eyes.

Against the neoliberalist instrumentalization of dreams and desires to consumerist ends, attending to the wildness of dreams has the potential to incite stories that disturb already given narratives. Because "[i]t matters what stories make world, what worlds make stories" – as Donna Haraway (2016) beautifully states in one of the emblematic phrases that have infused processes of thinking—with others, human and non-human alike. To *matter* is to acknowledge that something materializes, that is meaningful, unfettering relationships unaccounted for. Think of the bodies silenced and belittled, finding ways to dream other world-realities for themselves: resituating, recovering, alleviating. And so it matters what dreams dream the dreams of future, for many kinships and political times to come are entangled in them.

Can thinking with fashion and design contribute to such a process of resituating, when they've been complicity entangled with capitalist production? What could be different? What other set-ups or world-dimensions can they enliven out of the fabric of dreams? Or have we run out of stock?

Confronting the Empire of Stuff

I initiated *Out of Stock* back in 2020 together with graphic designer Ana Labudović. Posing as a onetime journal, the project aimed to tackle fashion and design in their ability for imagining (future or speculative) scenarios through Eastern-European perspectives and sensibilities. Its first and only issue appeared on the backdrop of an escalating pandemic, and asked how we might think with shortages and scarcity in order to reframe everyday experiences and find empowering imaginaries for equitable futures. The contributions probed scarcity in connection to identity, unseen forms of labor, mismanaged distribution of resources, or traumatic memory. From visions of queering design, to modular garments and upcycled items, second-skins, soundscapes, and practices of healing, *Out of Stock* lays out Eastern-European rehearsals for dressing the future as otherwise.

With the many deficits COVID-19 made visible (from infrastructures to vaccines), the topic of shortages, however, was equally rooted in accumulated feelings of exhaustion, of weariness towards the Western European practice of associating certain bodies—mine included—with shortages, of lacking and lagging. Furthermore, a dissatisfaction became apparent with our always switched-on world and its extractive culture of overproduction wedging narratives between economical fear and the looming climate crisis. In this sense, *Out of Stock* began as an attempt to rehearse imagination for a something else, in order to address design and fashion by dint of dreams beyond capitalist heteropatriarchy and its seemingly blindness to shortages.

As theorist and designer Marjanne van Helvert noted, we have trouble imagining shorts of supply, or an end of resources:

> The idea of shortages stands in sharp contrast with much of our lived experience amid the abundance of stuff we have created, among masses of cheap products that are offered to us on a daily basis. It seems we can purchase a limitless amount of gadgets and clothes, take unlimited air trips, and forever eat the last pieces of tuna (van Helvert 2016, 91).

Within the system van Helvert describes, we find ourselves unable to imagine the much-needed waste reduction that could mitigate the spread of (toxic) excess infiltrating lands and bodies. Even areas that haven't been associated with the abundance of Western markets, like the sub-Saharan Africa, end up flooded with goods (ibid.). This is, however, a devious abundance made out of second-hand leftovers and discarded used goods. Ironically, the same places for outsourcing waste—and pollution—are the ones providing cheap labor to produce brand new commodities for the same Western markets. How shortages manifest, and who stocks up, are thus embedded in geopolitical conditions. Considering shortages as everyday experiences that affect people in a visceral way, yet bound to economic and political policies, makes one apprehend the failures of the infrastructures and the nodal power points at play.

In *Staying with the Trouble*, Donna Haraway notes that: "Nobody lives everywhere. Everyone lives somewhere. Nothing is connected to everything. Everything is connected to something" (2016, 31). And so, I live in my body, carrying around pieces of the place from where it sprung. It is from the Eastern parts of Europe, from Romania, that I speak, attempting to navigate this networked world—the Eastern parts that the Eurocentric discourse casts as the peripheral or the developing other[1] (Kiossev 2011). These Eastern parts are from where I respond with an ironic "here's your business as usual" when Romanian workers turned out still to be the most convenient labor resource—despite fierce COVID-19 movement restrictions—to be dispatched to Germany in order to make sure the asparagus made it from German fields to German plates in the infamous *"Spargelbrücke"* invoking the desperation of the Cold War "Air Bridge".[2] In the words of political scientist Nikita Dhawan (2018), in face of crises "though we might all be facing the same storm, we are not all in the same boat," for where do you come from does indeed matter and has continued to establish veiled hierarchies.

Rewriting this text now, with a war at the borders, Dhawan's words run deep. But just like then, when the pandemic was shifting our perspectives, I feel

---

1 In the *Self-Colonizing Metaphor*, Bulgarian scholar Alexander Kiossev explains that processes of colonization extend beyond colonial rules; they include areas which succumbed to the economic and cultural power of Western Europe that keeps ranking people and geographical spaces between superior and inferior or, nowadays, developed and developing (2011, Atlas of Transformation).

2 The exceptional borders-crossing reflected the effects of unequitable economic agreements, even more so as Romanian workers in Germany were met with poor housing conditions and disregard for health measures. The pressure to accept such agreements builds on the hope that Romania, though part of European Union since 2007, will be included in Schengen Area and benefit from less taxing economic measures.

the questions are hanging in the air, though I wish once again they were less burdened by the heaviness of current circumstances.

Yet, could thinking with shortages and in "out of stock" terms lend itself to an in-between space for dreaming? What is already at hand, and what could be invented?

Fashion and design are at the core of these needed exercises of imagining. Manners of doing and shaping, they have for a long time waved the vast fabric of our everyday life, from images to materiality, to technologies and habits, to our own body matters in which they—literally—infiltrate with every single touch. What we wear and surround ourselves with is not only political and shapes our lives but extends bodies (human and non-human alike) beyond the limits they've been confined to. Complicit threads in oppressive structures—or means of hidden violence—design and fashion are nevertheless ambivalent surfaces, agents of meaningful change. Consider how easily fashion becomes part of the shifts between and within social realms, making bodies visible through the way they are clothed, realer bodies or prior unaccounted for—like racialized or disabled ones. But this simultaneously points to the former restrictive rules, caught in designed cuts and fabrics, like so the obstinate gender divisions and clothing measurements, confining people to certain roles and body movements. Or the clothes obscured production and pollutant colors whose toxicity affects both the workers and the wearers as they affect landscapes—how designers have urgently called for sustainability in the larger discussion about climate catastrophes.

Fig. 1-3. Tăietzel Ticălos, Techno-Vision Deck, digital tarot cards, 2020 (featured: The Chariot, The Empress, The Star). Courtesy of the artist.

In this sense, fashion and design are making and unmaking realities. And so, it matters who are the ones envisioning or dreaming them, and how matter manifests with the unruly magic of sensitivity.

On Falling Short under Projections

Thinking with shortages hits differently in Eastern Europe. In the collective memory, the area has been shaped as "the societies of shortages and need" (Crowley & Reid 2010, 9–11), as if pleasure, desire, and style couldn't find a proper place here. The socialist or communist pasts remain haunted by insufficiencies: either of everyday goods or freedoms that kept running out, cutback by state control. The Great Transition during the '90s, which all post-socialist countries experienced, might have raised hopes and bodies of freedom, but did so only to crush them under capitalist markets' invasive rule. Political observer Naomi Klein called out these brutal free-market reforms as shock-therapy doctrine: the neoliberal reengineering of societies by exploiting moments of profound collective distress to push a corporate agenda.[3] For the disintegrating Soviet Union, the doctrine meant to align the "lagging East" with the policies of the West in the shortest time possible, urging everyone to abide by the liberal system so as to avoid economic collapse. This tactic soon produced what today we recognize as the frightening swamp of privatization, loans, and debt—strategies for veiling the reality of shortages—creating even wider social gaps and inequality (see Klein 2007). No wonder that the promises of well-being carried by dreams of new democracies couldn't but shatter amidst economic drawbacks and poor life conditions. Unable to fully grasp the so-called wonders of Western dreams, the region got trapped in the geographically elusive construct of the former East and a stereotype of always lacking something. This condition still manifests within an internalized inferiority complex.

In the wake of these shattered dreams, as cultural critic Agata Pyzik (2014) weighs, some areas—like Poland or Russia—have steadily become the mirage of poor-but-sexy, fashioning themselves to accommodate the others' dreams. The same myth-making model that post-Wall Berlin relied on when advertising itself as cheap and attractive, yet endowed with cultural and historical capital (clinging to an anarchic spirit and hopes for future) became a strategy to assure foreign investments. Not that it has always worked out, but in a clap-back to the stereotype of an Eastern-Europe artistically sterile and dressed in gray drab, most areas compensated through creativity, (cultural) work mobility, and a certain feeling of authenticity (Pyzik 2014).

After the 2008 economic crash and its persistent series of recessions and consequent sets of austerity measures and policies, societies have seen another surge of inequality. Searching for possible survival kits, design and fashion practitioners stirred once more the dust of the socialist past and revisited its alternative life models. Among them, values of recycling, everyday creativity, and models of non-hierarchical distribution became chants for what-to-do-next discourses, as did the idea of a new commonism.[4] But it's hard to shun the capitalist gambit most of these practices succumb to: of a right way of consumption which champions sustainability as the new favorite child in the production/consumption scheme.

Fashion writer Anastasiia Fedorova fittingly notes that, as the social gap keeps widening, there are of course reasons for:

> looking to those who grew up in the ruins of a collapsed system hoping to get some useful lessons for the future. We are all, to some extent, in the same position as kids by the Wall. We are poor. But cool. (2015)

Fashion, of course, has lots to reflect on the matter, as it became a catalyst for this redeemed creativity, with poor-but-cool clenching like a label to designers emerging from Eastern-European countries, regardless of their

---

3 In *Shock Doctrine: The Rise of Disaster Capitalism*, Naomi Klein analyzes the aftermaths of Chile's '70s political coup, the collapse of Soviet Union, or, more recently, Hurricane Katrina's devastations, arguing that current hyper-capitalism feeds on crisis, often giving hidden power to multinationals using crisis as a terra nova for speculative opportunities—which make up the free market. Klein has been criticized for an emphatic, alarmist tone, yet my lived experience of growing up in the aftermath of the neoliberal opening of post-communist Romania finds similar notes.

4 Introducing *Commonism: a New Aesthetics of the Real*, editors Nico Dockx and Pascal Gielen differentiate commonism (coined by Canadian Marxist Nick Dyer-Witheford in 2007) from communism, insisting that this is a new political belief, concerned with ways of sharing (intellectual) ownership, other forms of economy and implementing social co-operations, closer to contemporary ecological and social realities (2018).

wishes. This visibility revealed how easily what used to be frowned upon as kitsch, cheap, or the (Eastern) misappropriation of Western styles can end up hyped by designers and a media capitalizing on nostalgia and the exotic other. For one, the elusive term of 'post-Soviet aesthetics' (Fedorova 2015) which has rekindled second-hand practices, the working-class attire, and taste—reflected in the '90s cultural clash between Western clothing and the locally produced one, and worked-up a heavy socialist concrete atmosphere peppered with trashy post-industrial sites. More recently, designers like Demna Gvasalia and the former collective Vetements have drawn Western media's attention to the creative potential of the area by starting a conversation about the past and the present, isolating elements from day-to-day life clothing like workwear, counterfeit culture, or sportswear. Yet they did so by wrapping these new assemblages in the narrative of cool and edgy.

Many designers from Eastern Europe sensed this renewed interest and the overuse of everyday people's ways of dressing a certain class-tourism and another raid of the cultural periphery. Such visibility—of unaccounted people and the creative validation—appeared on the fine line between everyday empowerment and what Michelle Millar Fisher (n.d.) calls "flirting with the aesthetics … without experiencing the drawbacks of the lived lifestyle." The aesthetics of rawness, unkempt, or unprocessed past, which linger in Western representations, don't talk about a place but of a repository of images and imaginaries, attractive in their contrast to the West's sanitized wishful images. These patterns of looking affect even those representations which act as witnesses of the present and account for the geopolitical history of the everyday. Reflecting one's surroundings can still fall into this fictitious trope (see Fedorova 2018). Not just once, I too have felt torn between expressing my cultural background and the image inflicted from the outside.

The question remains: How can counter-histories and local concerns be invoked without fetishizing the past and crediting the inventory of illusive images? *Which East?* remains relevant in the process of demystifying assigned identities. Academic approaches have grappled with the Western-centric perspectives in reframing socio-cultural and political repercussions of the events of 1989. Shifting terminologies might carry us through *the former East/new West,* or what I playfully have come to address as the *new east(thetics)*[5] that infiltrated fashion.

But, as we still have to live with the ongoing specter of the Eastern condition, confronting stereotypes is also about disentangling the inherent threads that design the duality of the region, and how often they're part of an extractive culture of materials, bodies, and spaces. Take example MADE IN EU, i.e., fashion production with garments mostly manufactured in countries like Romania, Moldavia, and Bulgaria. Since the '90s, they have been working in lohn-production, a term designating the "sale of intensive labor operations: (of workforce done mainly by women) for the production of clothing pieces or components." Subcontracted for re-exportation by international companies, they provide cheap labor for brands like Lacoste, Hugo Boss, Prada, or Inditex retailers profiting from economic inequality. Not only has investigative journalism revealed poor working conditions; retailers often move factories further to the Eastern borders of Europe where the high unemployment rates mean wages can stay low (see Petcu 2004, 30; Ștefănuț 2016). MADE IN EU doesn't mean sweatshop free—as many seamstresses in my family attest. Likewise, just

5 Building on Anastasiia Fedorova's attention to the visual cues involved the new east aesthetics, I take *new east(thetics)* as both the political reclaiming of Eastern Europe in its presentness, and what philosopher Jacques Rancière calls aesthetic regime—the process of breaking down hierarchies in what is seen and said in a society when creating social and economic spaces. In other words, aesthetics becomes a means to create new fictions for imagined communities; to bring together artistic, creative, economic and everyday practices in new narratives (see Rancière 2004).

see how big retailers claim to recycle while dumping unprocessed clothes and garments in the same countries, since these have fewer waste regulations. And so, second-hand culture thrives in the region.

Unraveling the Threads to Make'em Anew

Ex-centric or eccentric: what else is there to wear? And how to place oneself differently?

Reflections on daily experiences, joy, stories, or fictions reconsidering the relationships and connections we make all prove to be transformational tools. It is how we redistribute meaning, similar to the sequenced fabric of dreams. As to let futures slide under the surface of the present, of the everyday, in the shadowy edges.

The contributions which composed the *Out of Stock* publication move through the complex entangled threads our lives are embedded in, and the vitality of their materiality in ways that seem chaotic and unbound. In the opening essay, *Thoughts on Porous Skin: A Matter of Design,* writer Ana Maria Deliu (2020) suggests that allowing oneself to look at things with new eyes exceeds patterns of seeing. By acknowledging the many exchanges that intrude the senses, acting as bonds to an environment and to the others, the porosity of our being recalls the notion of a shared body. Though perhaps unsettling, this is a site for pleasant reimagining, attuned to social and ecological relationalities, from where another understanding of fashion and could emerge.

Throughout the journal, this feeling creates different convolutions. *Past Pieces Merging With What I Call Now,* the performative video-work of artist Monika Dorniak (2020), composes a poetic choreography, tracing the memories and impressions of our ancestors stored in the body. The clothing pieces of the performer, tailored by the artist herself, lend their pink hues in reference to flesh and skin itself as a loose boundary that writes emotional cartographies. Grounding this understanding in the emotional and psychological scars political regimes have left on people and landscapes, on nations, her essay entangles biographical stances. Passages of memories for the Polish context are mapped through the tailoring work of her Lithuanian-Polish grandfather and his attention to materials and body differences in cloth-making. The remnants of war overgrown by vegetation, the uniformity brought by the soviet occupation enacting the so-called dream of equality, or the prepackaged abundance of capitalism numbing past scarcity—are as many aggressive

Fig. 4. Monika Gabriela Dorniak, Past Pieces Merging with what I Call Now (video still), 2020.

alterations of bodies, dismissing specific needs. Dorniak references philosopher Isabelle Stengers's Reclaiming Animism (2012) where to reclaim—as a political act—means to recover, both as a process of healing and honoring being in-difference that can nurture new gestures beyond the human-centered views. And so: "before we tailor clothes for the future, we need to take off layers of corsets from the past" (Dorniak 2020), unfold the self as in-becoming, able to trace itself with new alliances, inhabit new communities.

Meanwhile, Laura Naum and Petrică Mogoș (KAJET Journal) call back the sensate body as the entanglement of material assemblages and representational tropes. In their essay, Queer Bodie, Queer Futures – XXX (Naum & Mogoș 2020), the debut collection of the Romanian fashion designer Lucian Varvaroi, lays the groundwork for discussing the conflicting position of the Eastern-European male body. Lucian Varvaroi's practice tackles the trope of hypermasculinity by queering the local familiar image of the macho man within deconstructed futurist pieces of clothing, exalting the brazen muscles, tribal tattoos, and free-nipples. Naum and Mogoș point to the regional post-communist past as a conflation of masculinity with a lingering nationalist hubris or what queer and feminist observers have called "democracy with male face": poignantly heteronormative, homophobic, and in many ways regressive, within surges of religious values (Pejić 2010). They inlay the present "body-work" promoted by the new logic of performative capitalism.

Fig. 5. Lucian Varvaroi, XXX fashion collection, 2019. Visual concept and ph.: Carnation Studio (Raya al Souliman and Horațiu Șovăială).

Varvaroi's assemblages, however, serve not as provocateurs but as reflections rooted in the designer's queer counter-history, as a retro-future where the '90s imagining of Western culture is twisted into a pop-aesthetic with futurist elements. A future that could have been, perhaps still open, translates into a process of recovery counting erased histories and imaginaries, and the materiality of garments themselves. Pre-worn garments and debris—the periphery of the materiality—get upcycled, with even sneakers incorporated into jackets and turned back into wearable items. At play is fashion's possibility of being a regenerative practice not only by repositioning (the queer) identity but in terms of production as well.

Fashion designer and caretaker Anne-Kristin Winzer (2020) openly reflects that in shifting perception it does matter who are the ones designing design. In her *working_lass_hero_ine,* personal experience, influences from literary scholar bell hooks, and sociological investigations probe the scarce possibilities for working-class children within the German educational system. Access and affordances are not only an economic issue, but moreover one of navigation where habits, jargon, and institutions modalities (like applications) appear unfamiliar. This unease often weighs heavily in class-related exclusion from the design field, how working-class children are perceived, but equally how, by self-exclusion, they perceive themselves. Under the surface of the present, echoes the troubled history of the soviet socialism in East Germany, which affected not only the contemporary economic status of the lands occupied but had real consequences afterwards on the working-classes' mindsets. To break the ceiling, as the fashion designer follows sociologist Andreas Kemper, children of the working-classes need to see themselves as in-possibility-being not just according to possibility.

Fig. 6. Ann Kristin Winzer, working_lass_heroine (video still), 2020.

The correlated fashion video is a playful play of these hierarchical dynamics, with performers engaged in a funny pole dance routine, clothing pieces so designed that barely hold together, while a familiar Eurodance song is blasting, further hinting at the '90s migrant mobility. The "working class heroine" is excelling, worked out, performed until exhaustion, hyper-aware. But the warm laugh shared at the end of the frantic choreography calls back a sense of togetherness, weaving that needed network of in-support-of-each-other.

As laughter does, sound reverberates through matter, through bodies as it envelops them, creating shared spaces in acts of listening. Queer artist and DJ Chlorys renders the possibilities of becoming hidden in the porosity of the sensate body through the mix-set Fungoid Horror and the Creep of Life (Winzer 2020). Decay and decompositions, slimes, oozes, fungi, or the verminous life—viscerally described by horror writers Thomas Ligotti and Clark Ashton Smith—slowly transform into a celebration of life's bubbling force. Like the unruly logic of dreams, the shadows and the underworld of these beings hint at the illusion of human control, whether for taming landscapes or people and non-human beings. An unfamiliar, but not unpleasant becoming.

Fig. 7. Chlorys (Mihaela Vasiliu), Fungoid Horror and the Creep of Life (cover for music set), 2020.

Listening, I recalled philosopher Sèverine Janssen's note that sound, like the skin, makes a juncture between the interior and the exterior, stitching rifts in time where "what is gone reappears, what is dead comes to life, and what was far away, approaches us once again" (see Janssen 2019, 26–27). Thinking about what comes next feels similar—a mesh where past, present, and future merge. Spreading out Tarot's major Arcanas in her TechnoVisions Deck, artist Tăietzel Ticălos reiterated that these scenarios are not unambiguously kind or desirable, but—I would add—they are sensitive.

Where we come from does indeed matter. And if matter is composed of living flows, vibrations across distances, then like the dreamers that connect to each-other in their dreams, an Eastern-Europeanness can be made of these magnetic sensibilities. It exceeds borders and limitations, stereotyped images, or the label itself: of Eastern Europe.

Afterthought

Patching wandering thoughts for the journal, I wanted to bend the notion of scarcity into a practice that could address shortages in both local and larger contexts. One of the reasons for addressing scarcity was that—as a real everyday issue—it touches upon the idea of artificially constructed shortages and the inescapable condition of depletion; thus, it can also ask "what, if instead of adding, one redistributed what is already there?" (Till 2014, 10), trumping growth as continuous accumulation. Many practices of making do, mending, and design by means of improvisation, otherwise common in the everyday practices of former socialist/communist countries, were indeed addressing shortages by creating with less and by sharing (admittedly in the struggle of necessity), beyond the authoritative socialist design-for-the-many. These forms of navigating the world (seemed to me to) function like a refusal to be defined by scarcities and the system implementing them.

This attempt at re-positioning scarcity sounds perhaps naïve and effusive, because we do live in a netted world, where market evaluations are manipulating scarcity with different economic stakes, whether in consumer culture, slick interface design, or industry productions, but more painfully in vital resources (like water and crops), housing, food, and war. We do need tools to think with, and yes, practices emerge from hacking and bending dispositions in local contexts, rewriting their history. To think with an out of stock, however, might mean to drop the old ideology of desired resources, and think with embodied co-relations and the many those which are not us. Perhaps, another word would be dignity.

BIBLIOGRAPHY

Chlorys. n.d. "Fungoid Horror and the Creep of Life." Out of Stock. Accessed November 27, 2020. https://outofstock.xyz/contributions/chlorys-fungoid-horror-and-the-creep-of-life-backup.html.

Crowley, David, and Susan E. Reid, eds. "Introduction: Pleasure in Socialism?" in *Pleasure in Socialism. Leisure and Luxury in the Eastern Bloc*. Northwestern University Press, 2010.

Deliu, Ana Maria. n.d. "Thoughts on Porous Skins: A Matter of Design." Out of Stock. Accessed November 27, 2020. https://outofstock.xyz/contributions/ana-maria-deliu-thoughts-on-porous-skins-a-matter-of-design.html.

Dhawan, Nikita. "Decolonizing Enlightenment. Transnational Justice in a Postcolonial World." Lecture, part of Dictionary of Now #11 – Justice. April 19, 2018. HKW Berlin. Accessed February 21, 2019. https://www.hkw.de/en/app/mediathek/video/63347.

Dockx, Nico, and Pascal Gielen. *Commonism: a New Aesthetics of the Real*. Valiz & Antennae Series, 2018.

Dorniak, Monika G. 2020. "Past Pieces Merging With What I Call Now." Out of Stock. Last modified 2020. https://outofstock.xyz/contributions/monika-gabriela-dorniak-past-pieces-merging-with-what-i-call-now.html.

Fedorova, Anastasiia. 2018. "Post-Soviet fashion: identity, history and the trend that changed the industry." The Calvert Journal. Last modified February 23, 2018. https://www.calvertjournal.com/features/show/9685/post-soviet-visions-fashion-aesthetics-gosha-demna-lotta-vetements.

———. 2015. "Poor but Cool: how has the Cold War become a defining system for modern fashion?" The Calvert Journal. Last modified May 19, 2015. http://www.calvertjournal.com/features/show/4134.

Fisher, Michelle Millar. n.d. "Acting as If. On Trench Coats, Tracksuits and the Counterfeit Self."Vestoj. Accessed February 24, 2019. http://vestoj.com/acting-as-if.

Haraway, Donna. *Staying with the Trouble: Making Kin in the Chthulucene*. Duke University Press, 2016.

Hillman, James. *The Dreams and the Underworld*. Harper & Row, 1979.

Janssen, Sèverine. "Sonic Harbour"in *Sound as Interstice: The Middle Matter*. Translated by Deborah Birch, edited by Caroline Profanter, Henry Andresen, Julia Eckhardt. Umland, 2019.

Kiossev, Alexander. 2011. "The Self-Colonizing Metaphor." Atlas of Transformation. Last modified 2011. http://monumenttotransformation.org/atlas-of-transformation/html/s/self-colonization/the-self-colonizing-metaphor-alexander-kiossev.html.

Klein, Naomi. *Doctrine Shock Therapy: The Rise of Disaster Capitalism*. Metropolitan, 2007.

Naum, Laura, and Petrică Mogoș. 2020. "XXX—Queer Bodies, Queer Futures." Out of Stock. https://outofstock.xyz/contributions/laura-naum-petrica-mogos-xxx-queer-bodies-queer-futures.html.

Pejić, Bojana. *Gender Check: A Reader. Art and Gender in Eastern Europe Since the 1960s*. Buchhandlung Walther König, 2010.

Petcu, Mariana. "New Initiative for Social Standards in Romania", in *Made in Eastern Europe. The new fashion colonies*. Edited by Bettina Musiolek. Clean Clothing Campaign, 2004.

Pyzik, Agata. *Poor but Sexy. Culture Clashes in Europe East and West*. Zero Books, 2014.

Rancière, Jacques. *The Politics of Aesthetics: The Distribution of the Sensible*. New York/London: Continuum, 2004.

Stengers, Isabelle. 2012. "Reclaiming Animism." e-flux Journal. Last modified July 2012. https://www.e-flux.com/journal/36/61245/reclaiming-animism.

Ștefănuț, Laura. 2016. "Fabricat în Europa (Made in Europe)" Casa Jurnalistului (investigative journalism platform). Last modified February 9, 2016. Accessed May 6, 2017. https://casajurnalistului.ro/fabricat-in-europa.

Till, Jeremy. "Scarcity and Agency" in *Journal of Architectural Education* 68:1 (2014): 9-11.

van Helvert, Marjanne. "Good Design for Everyone. Scarcity, Equality, and Utility in the Second World War" in *The Responsible object. A history of Design Ideology for the Future*, edited by Marjanne van Helvert. Valiz, 2016.

Winzer, Anne-Kristin. "working_lass_hero_ine." Out of Stock. Accessed November 27, 2020. https://outofstock.xyz/contributions/anne-kristin-winzer-working-lass-hero-ine.html.

 ## IMAGES AND ILLUSTRATIONS

Figure 1, 2, 3: Tăietzel Ticălos, TechnoVision Deck, digital tarot cards, 2020 (featured: The Chariot, The Empress, The Star). Courtesy of the artist.

Figure 4: Monika Gabriela Dorniak, Past Pieces Merging with what I Call Now (video still), 2020, performer: Jäckie Rydz. Courtesy of the artist.

Figure 5: Lucian Varvaroi, XXX fashion collection, 2019. Visual concept and ph.: Carnation Studio (Raya al Souliman and Horațiu Șovăială). Courtesy of Carnation Studio.

Figure 6: Anne Kristin Winzer, working_lass_heroine (video still), 2020. Courtesy of the artist.

Figure 7: Chlorys (Mihaela Vasiliu), Fungoid Horror and the Creep of Life (cover for music set), 2020. Make-up: Ada Mușat; Claws: Dana Bordea. Courtesy of the artist.

MEXICO 44
AND LATINOFUTURISMO

(César Neri)

Mexico 2044 is a piece of speculative design investigating issues of sociocultural identity through the lens of the Zapatista Movement. The project takes the form of a national rebranding campaign that examines the identitarian fiction of the Mexican state and the ongoing violence against native people within its borders.

The various images and artifacts of the project illustrate a future of mass-commodified Indigenous identity in the face of a fully Westernized and hyper-capitalist State. Mexico 44 facilitates the integration of Indigenous land into global cities in the Global North as a means to monetize the public's fetishization of the autochthonous. The extrapolation of the idea of people and land as cultural exports intentionally touches on the ridiculous as to border satire.

Fig. 1. Mexico 44 Logo, Vector Artwork.

The timeline is set in the year 2044—commemorating the 50-year anniversary of the passing of the North American Free Trade Agreement. At this point, the Mexican State has achieved the first-world-nation status it has been after for centuries. In the meantime, the historically isolated pockets of Indigenous culture in the southernmost region of the country are facing their imminent extinction. Seeing an opportunity to monetize, the Federal Cultural Preservation Bureau decides to save these communities for the sake of mass consumption. Their ontologies and traditions serve as exquisite anthropological artifacts, a reminder of the civilizations that had to rise and decay to give way to our great modernity.

The extensive international marketing campaign of Mexico 44 promises to make deteriorating, globalized neighborhoods around the globe flourish again by offering a unique, autochthonous character. By implanting a piece of Indigenous land, these unadulterated specimens are capable of revitalizing the cultural production of homogenized urban centers under a comprehensive 20-year plan.

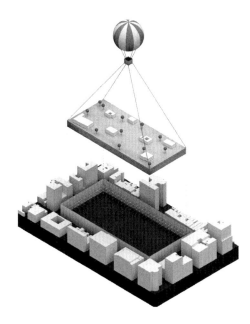

Fig. 2. Diagram of Transplant Installation, 3D Render.

The following images capture the potential of the urban revitalization program by showcasing three existing transplants: in Paris, New York and Tokyo. The emerging conditions and artifacts from each of these are to serve as marketing material for other over-globalized localities around the globe.

Fig. 3. San Juan Chamula, France Postage Stamp, Digital Collage.

Fig. 4. San Cristobal de las Casas, USA Postage Stamp, Digital Collage.

Fig. 5. Zinacantán, Japan Postage Stamp, Digital Collage.

Fig. 6. San Juan Chamula, France Site Plan, Architectural Drawing.

Fig. 7. San Cristobal de las Casas, USA Site Plan, Architectural Drawing.

Fig. 8. Zinacantán, Japan Site Plan, Architectural Drawing.

Fig. 9. Life in San Juan Chamula, France, Digital Collage.

Fig. 10. Life in San Cristobal de las Casas, USA, Digital Collage.

Fig. 11. Life in Zinacantán, Japan, Digital Collage.

Fig. 12. Man Waiting for the Metro, 3D Render, Collage.

Design pieces such as Mexico 44 fall under the moniker of Latinofuturismo—a cultural aesthetic that attempts to dispel the myth of Western universality in the Latinamerican region. To design towards a decolonized Latin America is to acknowledge the contradictions of dealing with a geography that is grouped specifically by its colonial past, as well as a set of people that embody both the colonized and the colonizer. Most importantly, Latinofuturismo centers stories of indigenous resistance and survival, stories that emphasize the existence of its people across multiple temporalities, and rekindles ancestral knowledge that has been lost to modernity.

My personal practice within the discipline is situated in the Mexican context and rooted in Zapatista ideals of emancipation through multiplicity. I believe that we're tricked into thinking that we need to tackle the fallacy of Western universality with an equally single-handed solution. In fact, it's because of this misconception that many decolonial projects often end up replicating the same patterns of invasion they try to address. This is why we must return to situated solutions that address the intersectionality of worlds we cohabit. Decolonization starts with the self, and is therefore different for every person and every community. As the Zapatistas remarked, in order to survive neoliberal capitalism, we must build "a world where many worlds fit" (Shenker 2012, 432).

Chicanafuturism is an example Latinofuturismo that is situated within its own microcosm of layered conditions. It examines issues of identity, self-determination, and assimilation of female Mexican immigrants in the United States. Chicana writer and scholar Gloria Azaldúa, for example, recounts her experience as a queer woman fighting against heteronormativity, racism, the patriarchy, and the many invisible borders that enable them (see Anzaldúa 2010). Her explorations around the dualism of her identity point towards a solution that is tailored to her specific set of experiences, however, her resolution to embrace the liminal space created at the tension between two seemingly opposite forces is one that speaks to the core of the mestizo identity, and therefore enriches the overarching narrative towards decolonial futures in Latin America.

Additional examples include Fernando Palma's Indigenous cyborgs—half organic half mechanical robotic sculptures that embody Nahuatl cosmologies via transistors. Contemporary vernacular architecture, and similarly "lowbrow" forms of art, showcase an act of rebellion against an industrial and capitalist society that constantly aims to dominate and homogenize. My current personal favorite instance of Latinofuturism is a 2011 music video to Tribal Guarachero called "Inténtalo" by 3BallMTY. The visuals are akin to cowboys in space, except people are dancing to a mix of electronic and cumbia music at a club, all while wearing boots pointy enough to reach knee-height along with Star Trek style visors.

Design counterculture succeeds when it sheds light on that which otherwise seems invisible to the dominant culture. To expect the design discipline alone to dismantle centuries worth of colonial structures across a whole subcontinent is both impossible and incredibly unproductive. However, to reframe our conceptions of the world as designers, if only little by little, could result in a new generation of practitioners that enable true social transformation via their work.

BIBLIOGRAPHY

Anzaldúa, Gloria, and Ana Louise Keating. "On the Process of Writing Borderlands / La Frontera" in *The Gloria anzaldúa Reader*, 187–197. Durham, NC: Duke University Press, 2010.

Shenker, Sarah Dee. "Towards a world in which many worlds fit?: Zapatista autonomous education as an alternative means of development." *International Journal of Educational Development* 32, no. 3 (2012): 432-443.

IMAGES AND ILLUSTRATIONS

All images are part of *Mexico 44*. They were created by the author and exhibited at the Miller Institute of Contemporary Art in Pittsburgh from April 19 - 25 of 2018.

Figure 1: Mexico 44 Logo, Vector Artwork. Cesár Neri, *Mexico 2044*. Miller Institute of Contemporary Art in Pittsburgh, PA, 2018.

Figure 2: Diagram of Transplant Installation, 3D Render. Cesár Neri, *Mexico 2044*. Miller Institute of Contemporary Art in Pittsburgh, PA, 2018.

Figure 3: San Juan Chamula, France Postage Stamp, Digital Collage. Cesár Neri, *Mexico 2044*. Miller Institute of Contemporary Art in Pittsburgh, PA, 2018.

Figure 4: San Cristobal de las Casas, USA Postage Stamp, Digital Collage. Cesár Neri, *Mexico 2044*. Miller Institute of Contemporary Art in Pittsburgh, PA, 2018.

Figure 5: Zinacantán, Japan Postage Stamp, Digital Collage. Cesár Neri, *Mexico 2044*. Miller Institute of Contemporary Art in Pittsburgh, PA, 2018.

Figure 6: San Juan Chamula, France Site Plan, Architectural Drawing. Cesár Neri, *Mexico 2044*. Miller Institute of Contemporary Art in Pittsburgh, PA, 2018.

Figure 7: San Cristobal de las Casas, USA Site Plan, Architectural Drawing. Cesár Neri, *Mexico 2044*. Miller Institute of Contemporary Art in Pittsburgh, PA, 2018.

Figure 8: Zinacantán, Japan Site Plan, Architectural Drawing. Cesár Neri, *Mexico 2044*. Miller Institute of Contemporary Art in Pittsburgh, PA, 2018.

Figure 9: Life in San Juan Chamula, France, Digital Collage. Cesár Neri, *Mexico 2044*. Miller Institute of Contemporary Art in Pittsburgh, PA, 2018.

Figure 10: Life in San Cristobal de las Casas, USA, Digital Collage. Cesár Neri, *Mexico 2044*. Miller Institute of Contemporary Art in Pittsburgh, PA, 2018.

Figure 11: Life in Zinacantán, Japan, Digital Collage. Cesár Neri, *Mexico 2044*. Miller Institute of Contemporary Art in Pittsburgh, PA, 2018.

Figure 12: Man Waiting for the Metro, 3D Render, Collage. Cesár Neri, *Mexico 2044*. Miller Institute of Contemporary Art in Pittsburgh, PA, 2018.

Acknowledgements

Creative Director, Tech Activist Heather Snyder Quinn
Creative Director, Overdose Activist Adam DelMarcelle
Film Producers, Westfield Production Co. and Joe Gietl
3D Type Designer, Zishou Wang
Web Designer, Valerie Shur
Designer, Leslie Ramirez
Animator, Les Garcia
Developer, Jake Juraka
Designer and App Developers, Flor Salatino and Luis Colaco

Rhonda Lotti, Lizzy Schlichtingg, Brian Wassom Esq., Joe Quinn Esq., Dan Wong and his partner Jay, Jane Quinn, DePaul University (University Research Competitive Grant, Wicklander Ethics Fellowship Funding, University Research Assistance Program, Jarvis College of Computing and Digital Media), Washington University in St Louis (various funding), Sam Fox School of Design and Visual Arts at Washington University in St Louis (various funding), Letterform Archive.

MARIAH

Acts Of Resistance, Legally "Trespassing" in The Metaverse

(Adam DelMarcelle) (Heather Snyder Quinn)

Fig. 1. "Funded by Loss: Death in Real-Time" is a geolocative augmented reality installation at the Pyramide du Louvre, Paris, France (Sackler funded) that is viewable on the Mariah app via a smartphone. The installation is a large-scale, 3-dimensional number that increases every 5 minutes to represent real-time opioid fatalities. More locations across the globe are forthcoming.

Mariah: Acts of Resistance is a new form of digital protest that arose from the collaboration and co-creation of artists Adam DelMarcelle and Heather Snyder Quinn. Both artists were pursuing their MFA's at a progressive low-residency graduate school in Vermont and were motivated to challenge societal systems of power, including capitalist, technocratic, and legal.

Adam DelMarcelle's journey began with a personal tragedy, the loss of his brother to a fentanyl overdose. This event led him to investigate the American war on drugs and the power structures responsible for the overdose epidemic. He used various forms of revolutionary art, including poster bombing and building projections, to raise awareness and encourage the public to reflect on their role in the current state of drug use in America. One notable projection was onto the headquarters of Purdue Pharma, the makers of OxyContin, which is responsible for over 600,000 overdose deaths.

Heather Snyder Quinn, a former designer turned hacker, uses technology as a means of resistance and exposes vulnerabilities in big tech companies. She reflects on the negative impacts of technology on mental health and the immense power of big tech companies, who hoard control of technology for profit and growth with little regard for humanity. Heather's work includes speculative narratives told through design fiction, hidden messages, and photographic protest.

The artists' works challenge systems of power and provide crucial information to the public. Through their collaborative effort, *Mariah: Acts of Resistance* highlights the importance of reflecting on our role in society and the impact of technology on our lives.

Fig. 2. Screen-Capture—Renaming of the Dendur Wing—Mariah Lotti's virtual memorial, MET Museum is a ground/plane augmented reality installation placed by the viewer.

> "Not everything that is faced can be changed, but nothing can be changed until it is faced."
>
> —James Baldwin, *No Name in the Street,* 1972

Background

Collaboration and co-creation are often the result of accidental encounters, fortuitous timing, chance experiences, and powerful intentions that manifest through the creation of art. *Mariah: Acts of Resistance,* a new form of digital protest, is an example of this serendipity. In 2016 artist Adam DelMarcelle and Heather Snyder Quinn were both amidst career pivots into higher education, and, as a result, met at a progressive low-residency graduate school in Vermont to pursue their MFA's. Although their paths were quite different, both Adam and Heather were motivated to challenge the status quo and confront societal systems of power—be it capitalist, technocratic, or legal.

Tragedy has the potential to forge purpose, and Adam DelMarcelle's journey began during tumultuous times. He had recently lost his brother, Joey, to a Fentanyl overdose, shattering his family and sending him searching for answers and purpose. The trauma of losing his brother sparked many things in him—among them, an intense desire to learn more, do more, to dig deeper into the landscape of American addiction and the exploding overdose epidemic that is intensifying with each passing day. In 2021, 107,000 people died of overdose in the United States. That equates to one death every 5.6 minutes.

Adam began to take aim at the power structures responsible for the current state of the American war on drugs with his work focused on documenting the unseen, giving voice to the countless lost, and above all encouraging his community to ask difficult questions about their own responsibility in the current state of drug use in America. He used traditional means of revolutionary art action and resistance, including poster bombing communities with screen-printed materials. When police destroyed this work, he turned to large-scale building projections, casting 80-foot-tall images onto the sides of buildings in his hometown. In 2018, he projected onto the headquarters of Purdue Pharma, the makers of OxyContin. The projector beamed from a terrace across the street—scrolling white text onto the front entrance of Purdue's building at 201 Tresser Blvd., "where those responsible for the opioid epidemic hide inside."

The projector's message also said the company was an "American cartel" and a "criminal organization," which had started a "chain reaction" responsible for the deaths of 300,000 people and made billions of dollars in profits "off their suffering and death." To date, Purdue Pharma is responsible for over 600,000 overdose deaths.

Big Pharma became an area of interest as it would become clear that the many dead and dying began their substance use disorders from prescription medications given to them by their trusted physicians. Medications, such as OxyContin, were marketed as safe, with little or no chance of forming addiction. In many cases, the prescribed substances were responsible for both overdose and the seeking out of drugs like heroin once the individual could no longer afford prescriptions or their physicians cut them off. Through false and skewed marketing techniques, companies like Purdue Pharma were able to get hyper-potent pain medications to the masses. As early as 1996, the practice of crushing these oral medications for recreational abuse and snorting the resulting powder came to light, a fact that the executives of Purdue Pharma denied and purposely buried from public view. Richard Sackler[1], the head of the privately-owned Purdue Pharma, said at OxyContin's release, "the launch of OxyContin tablets will be followed by a blizzard of prescriptions that will bury the competition. The prescription blizzard will be so deep, dense, and white..."

The prescriptions did more than bury the competition—they buried 600,000 American bodies, creating generations of loss and suffering. The blizzard of prescriptions started an avalanche of illicit Fentanyl, a cheap and easily produced alternative to OxyContin, that has now entered the bloodstream of the heroin market. The effects of this have forever changed the landscape of drug sale and use worldwide.

Adam's work blatantly challenges systems of power while simultaneously providing crucial and often invisible information to the public. Additionally, in the case of the building projections, he augments the physical landscape with digital protest; and these works led to the connection with Heather's more subversive acts of digital protest, particularly those using augmented reality—a technology that superimposes a computer-generated image on a user's view of the real world, thus providing a composite view.

Heather uses technology as a means of resistance—allowing the oppressed to challenge the oppressor with their own tools. Often creatively breaking machine learning, she exposes vulnerabilities in seemingly unbreakable corporate technologies in quiet, subtle, and sometimes humorous ways.

1 The Sackler Family founded and owned the pharmaceutical company Purdue Pharma and has faced lawsuits regarding the over-prescription of addictive pharmaceutical drugs, including OxyContin.

Fig. 3. Photo—Legally trespassing—augmented reality installation—MET Museum, NYC.

2 FAAMG (also known as *The Big 5*) include Facebook, Apple, Amazon, Microsoft, and Google (Alphabet).

Having witnessed the negative impacts of technology on her two daughters' mental health, Heather had left a 20-year career in big tech for a professorship which would allow her to teach and research the ethics of emerging technologies. Utilizing her internal knowledge and harnessing her experience in the field allows her to dig deep into the global, political, and economic power of the big 5 (also known as FAAMG[2]). Collectively more powerful than most governments, these elite companies hoard control of technology from start to finish, including creation, access, distribution, and privacy, with little consideration for future implications of humanity—beyond profit and growth. Technology moves faster than the law, making it essentially above the law.

Themes of massive corporate power are ever-present in Heather's work including speculative narratives told through imagined fictional nations—dystopian tales—including "Google.Gov" and "Primeland: The Nation of Fulfillment." The provocative power inherent in design fiction serve as critical pillars in Heather's work; fostering the idea that designers possess the creative foresight to challenge big tech (and other systems of power) and speculate possible futures before they are our unforeseen reality.

In other more serious work foundational to *Project Mariah,* Heather places hidden messages, scavenger hunts, and photographic protest in unexpected places—such as Amazon and Yelp reviews; and, in more significant acts of photographic protest on Google Street View—using typographic obfuscation to fake out Google's algorithm. Her augmented reality work, however, began more playfully—hacking into her friends' apartments and placing secret messages using public photos found on social media as trigger images. What began as a scavenger hunt led to the discovery of something much more serious—the implications of our human rights in the metaverse—a virtual realm which had not yet come to fruition, but was a real possibility looming on the horizon. The implications are problematic—imagine a future where your property (interior/exterior of your home or your face/body) can be easily augmented with ads, slander, or personal credit ratings, among other horrors. It's as simple as accessing photos from a real estate website, Google Earth, or a profile picture. Currently, AR can only be viewed via specific apps. Still, the fight for power over the metaverse could lead to one centralized authority, and many believe the metaverse could become the most important software infrastructure in the history of computing.

4 The First Amendment protects the right to express opinions without censorship or restraint in the United States.

"Of particular concern is how AR will challenge traditional property rights and stretch interpretations of free speech" (McEvoy 2018). According to lawyer Brian Wassom, AR content is an expression akin to digital speech and is protected by the First Amendment of the U.S. Constitution.[4] If so, this has massive implications for any digital space, place, or surface with a GPS coordinate—including possibly even inside your property—in essence, free real estate for those with the power and ability to augment.

Tech legal policy is primarily created *after the fact* and with corporate power and profit at the forefront (ad placement, user data, algorithmic user behavior prediction), not so much for the purpose of privacy and human well-being. These findings were significant, and Heather wondered if design could be used to provide a lens proactively into the future to ask and answer these big questions. Who owns our virtual space, and what can be placed there? Can we raise awareness for these ethical concerns by challenging the systems that exist? Can we unsettle the future by hacking this space for our own means?

Our original hypothesis

Adam's work in opioid activism and Heather's work in tech activism sparked many conversations. In 2017 they first discussed the idea of a collaboration, and in 2019 they began work on *Project Mariah*. Specifically they wanted to see if they could hack a public space with augmented reality (AR) as a means of protest. Would it work technically? Could they create a rogue app and, if not, would the app store pass it? Was this work considered free speech, or was it trespassing? Were there any laws governing this space at all? Were their augmentations (il)legal? Could they take back power and give agency to those who had suffered? *Mariah* would bring these questions to light.

The Project

Fig. 4. Images of the Mariah app.

After building several prototypes, *Mariah* was built in full and successfully launched on the app store in September of 2020—a virtual takeover of "high capitalist real estate" and a collaborative initiative that challenges societal power systems, including big tech and big pharma, by "hacking the metaverse" as an act of protest. Most notably, *Mariah* was built entirely remotely (during the pandemic) using publicly available images. Specifically, Adam and Heather virtually hacked into the New York City MET Museum using augmented reality to replace Sackler donated art and signage with names, audio, and video from victims of the opioid epidemic—creating virtual memorials for those who had perished for capitalist greed projected upon the cultural goods bought with overdose windfall. AR served as a multilayered narrative to subvert 'reality' and replace what we see with the underlying truth. Named after Mariah Lotti, who lost her life to opioids at 19 years of age, and with support from her mother, the app enables viewers to "legally trespass" at significant locations across the globe (with more locations forthcoming).

Initiated in 2020 in NYC on a bootstrap budget, the app originally transformed the Met's Sackler wing into a virtual memorial for Mariah and others who have lost their lives to the opioid epidemic. Exploring AR's potential to revise historical narratives and its ethical implications, the app augments Sackler donated art with audio and video of the lives of opioid victims. Exploring a more global reach in 2021, *Mariah* expanded to The Pyramid du Louvre in Paris, France (also Sackler funded) with a geolocative installation. Titled "Funded by Loss: Death in Real-Time," the installation is a large-scale, 3-dimensional number that increases every 5 minutes to represent real-time opioid fatalities. In later experiments, the typography becomes sculptural and reflective of its environment and allows the viewer to walk around it. The project has since expanded into a documentary short film titled *Mariah: Acts of Resistance.*

Collectively, the work serves to raise awareness for the opioid epidemic and the future implications of our human freedoms in the metaverse, including interpretations of free speech and property rights by asking who owns our virtual space and what can be placed there? Can we raise awareness of these ethical concerns? Can we challenge systems and re-imagine the future by augmenting the space for our own means?

The work remains ongoing, and *Project Mariah* continues to serve as a provocation—challenging the status quo and making the invisible visible. In 2023, both artists are moving forward into new territory—using art to inform various aspects of policymaking. Mariah's presence is a powerful statement about curiosity, power, and giving agency back to "we the people"[5] to cultivate futures for all.

5 "We the people" is the preamble to the United States Constitution.

Project: Mariah App (The Apple Store, US and Europe only)
Location: MET Museum, NY (more locations forthcoming)
Artists: Heather Snyder Quinn & Adam DelMarcelle
Date: September 30, 2020 (launched)
Land: USA
App store link: https://apps.apple.com/us/app/mariah/id1528779172
Description: Mariah is an augmented reality experience that narrates stories of historical injustice through the backdrop of significant cultural institutions and the funding that has allowed them to exist.
URL: https://www.mariahonview.com/

BIBLIOGRAPHY

McEvoy, Fiona J. 2018. "What Are Your Augmented Reality Property Rights?" Slate. Last modified June 4, 2018. https://slate.com/technology/2018/06/can-you-prevent-augmented-reality-ads-from-appearing-on-your-house.html.

IMAGES AND ILLUSTRATIONS

Figure 1: Funded by Loss: Death in Real Time. Heather Snyder Quinn and Adam DelMarcelle, Mariah App, Paris, France, May 10, 2023, Screenshot of augmented reality installation: Heather Snyder Quinn.

Figure 2: Mariah Lotti Memorial Gallery. Heather Snyder Quinn and Adam DelMarcelle, Mariah App, NY, NY, July 9, 2021, Screenshot of augmented reality installation: Heather Snyder Quinn.

Figure 3: Augmented Slab. Heather Snyder Quinn and Adam DelMarcelle, Mariah App, Met Museum, NY, NY, September 2020, Screenshot of augmented reality installation: Adam DelMarcelle.

Figure 4: Screenshots. Heather Snyder Quinn and Adam DelMarcelle, Mariah App, Various Locations, 2020-23, App Store MockUps: Heather Snyder Quinn and Adam DelMarcelle.

PART 4 is about the disruption of stereotypical and discriminatory **NARRATIVES** about forms of embodiment, identity, and sexuality through design.

4

NARRATIVES

DESIGN NARRATIVES AND THE WHITE SPATIAL IMAGINARY

Becky Nasadowski

Graphic designers are ideological storytellers, often creating signs and symbols that help reproduce the material and affective economies of neoliberalism. Recently, scholars across varying fields have shown an interest in the aesthetic components of gentrification, but the role of the graphic designer has yet to be explored in depth. I argue graphic design not only plays a role but is a *logical* contributor to gentrification in the US, helping to reproduce what George Lipsitz (2011) refers to as the *white spatial imaginary.*

To frame the designer's complicity in the violence of gentrification, I will begin by exploring professional design culture's embrace of diversity as a commodity and its enthusiasm for entrepreneurialism.[1] Then, with two case studies of gentrified US neighborhoods—the East Austin neighborhood in Austin, Texas, and the Logan Square neighborhood in Chicago, Illinois—I will examine verbal and visual rhetoric produced and deployed by designers that helps (re)define racialized boundaries. Studying both professional design discourse and design in situ enables us to more clearly see how designers exploit ideological narratives as a public pedagogy to, consciously or unconsciously, participate in the rationalization, justification, and perpetuation of the white spatial imaginary.

Diversity as Amenity / Designer as Business

In a 2013 LoganSquarist blog post, Rich Cohen, the owner of a Chicago-based eco-friendly packaging and design company, articulates the top five reasons to open a business in Logan Square: (1) rapid growth, (2) supportive business community, (3) progressive spirit, (4) artisan focus, (5) inspiration. Cohen's language is useful as it describes the way entrepreneurial strategies and visions for regeneration might be weaponized as design decisions. He praises the growth in terms of "the number of strollers and families in the neighborhood" and "premium artisan restaurants and retail stores," and he calls the neighborhood's entrepreneurs "radical, progressive, and innovative" as they are "defining the edge" and "leading the trends." He identifies the area as a good match for consumers interested in "alternative" cultural tastes, further illustrating how gentrification is often conflated with the apparent aesthetic progressivism of entrepreneurialism, and assures businesses they will find inspiration through "Logan Square's exciting and seemingly endless flow of revolutionary ideas and new concepts." Elsewhere, Christian Diaz, Lead Housing Organizer for the Logan Square Neighborhood Association, says of the neighborhood's growth: "Overwhelmingly, we feel that that does not include us, it does not include people of color, it does not include families" (Moore and Yousef 2018). Two years later Diaz

1 I use "professional design culture," in short, to mean any design practice, research, or education that embraces capitalist ideologies and is subservient to its demands.

asks in another interview: "Who [gets] to live in a safe, desirable, and walkable neighborhood? It's white people and people with money" (Zegeye 2020). As will become clear, part of a gentrifying neighborhood's constructed self-image requires mythologizing the residue of its former residents—poor, working class, and/or non-white populations—and connecting it to *the image* of progressivism and/or "edginess." Like walkability and nightlife, (proximity to) the image of economic and racial diversity become amenities as gentrifying neighborhoods write new stories to romanticize their once diverse cultures, enabling an alternative lifestyle from that of the suburbs and mainstream consumer culture (see, e.g., Cabrera 2019; Summers 2019; Zukin 2008). It is in this manufacturing of the *image* of diversity that designers are often most culpable, producing mythologies of the gentrified city that obfuscate histories of violence inherent in the neoliberal project.

Geographer Brandi Thompson Summers' (2019) scholarship is useful to highlight professional design culture's embrace of neoliberalism—in particular, viewing diversity-as-commodity. Summers theorizes *black aesthetic emplacement* to describe a "mode of representing blackness in urban capitalist simulacra, which exposes how blackness accrues a value that is not necessarily extended to Black bodies" (ibid., 3). She cites feminist and queer theorist Sara Ahmed (2012, 53) who argues that "diversity becomes an aesthetic style or way of 'rebranding' a particular space, institution or organization." It is this "aesthetic approach to equality" (Summers 2019, 23) that creates a "palatable and consumable" (ibid., 66–67) version of blackness presented as a lifestyle amenity for new residents in gentrifying spaces *and* a marketable amenity for the designer/entrepreneur to exploit under the guise of progressivism, revolutionary ideas, and alternative tastes. This marketability is visible in Cohen's pro-entrepreneur blog post, with language that facilitates the free circulation of some bodies and the restriction of others, typically falling along racial and economic lines.

As a professional field that accounts for a particularly large number of freelancers, design is especially indulgent in myths of entrepreneurialism, here understood as a life of creative freedom via embodied capitalism. This desire for freedom, or individualist escape from the worst drudgery of the poor and working class, finds a natural affinity in the gentrifying neighborhood and its retreat from the monotony of the suburbs. This is demonstrated in AIGA's 2021 report, *Design POV: An In-Depth Look at the Design Industry Now,* which makes for compelling insight into contemporary professional discourse with representation of more than 5,000 participants from 100 countries.[2] In several instances that ooze a neoliberal mindset, the report directly connects the myths of entrepreneurialism with diversity-as-commodity and supposed progressive politics weakly defined as "doing good." For example, when sharing respondents' feedback on what it means to be a designer, one of AIGA's primary lenses for categorizing responses is "Impactset," which they define as a "force for change, progress, and good" with no context of what positive change or progress might constitute (2021a, 60–62). Select quotes from respondents at the end of the report briefly note the need for designers to recognize the social, technological, and environmental impact(s) of their work. AIGA flattens these concerns with their closing statement: "The Design community has a unique opportunity to show leadership, to do good, and to inspire" (ibid., 112). Although never clearly defined, we might speculate "doing good" includes promoting greater

---

[2] AIGA (formerly the American Institute of Graphic Arts) was founded in 1914 and is now "the profession's oldest and largest professional membership organization for design" with over 15,000 members (AIGA 2021b).

representation in the field as a lucrative feature of the design process, particularly due to their section that discusses "advancing diversity, equity, inclusion, and accessibility" (ibid., 10). Here an excerpted quote from art director Carlos Estrada reads: "How do we make people feel welcome and how do we get their perspective; because it is valuable and it will make us more creative, it can help a company be more profitable." Leadership, on the other hand, is positioned as inherent to the designer's very essence. In a section titled "Market Intelligence," the first line reads: "Every designer is a potential business" and a highlighted takeaway states: "Contrary to many other professions, your professional craft has an intrinsic value" (ibid., 11). These excerpts illustrate commonplace thinking regarding diversity and entrepreneurialism: diversity can be considered a commodity, and designers not only produce commodities of "intrinsic value" but are embodied businesses in wait. This embodied entrepreneurialism makes design a de facto vanguard in our neoliberal world that so prizes both individualism and capitalism. It also makes the designer a natural friend to the gentrifying city.

It is no surprise that a professional culture so cynical about diversity and confident in its (capitalist) value would produce armies of designers integral to gentrification's aestheticization of displacement, where embodied and multicultural capitalism might signify a "force for change, progress, and good" (ibid., 60). Like the gentrifying city, the design industry views diversity and good deeds as tethered to capitalism and the implicit answer to structural inequities. In this way, designers become a logical cog in what scholars have described as the entrepreneurial turn in urban planning, with contributions that build upon a long history of racist housing discrimination, segregation, and displacement efforts alongside new tax and zoning policies that continue to reward whiteness and intensify uneven geographies (see, e.g., Barnes et al 2006, 337; Lipsitz 2011, 28; Summers 2019, 73–74). Thus, I want to implicate not individual designers but the professional discipline of design as a contributor to the violence of the gentrifying city, a contribution perhaps most visible through design's assistance to reproduce the white spatial imaginary.

The White Spatial Imaginary: East Austin and Logan Square

The White Spatial Imaginary
The state has historically sanctioned the displacement of multiple communities of color. While scholar George Lipsitz is quick to point this out in his book *How Racism Takes Place*, he notes over 75% of those displaced during the first eight years of federally funded urban renewal projects in the mid-twentieth century were Black or Latino (2011, 12). Decades later, these same demographics are losing a significant percentage of their communities in the East Austin neighborhood of Austin, Texas and the Logan Square neighborhood in Chicago, Illinois. Following Lipsitz, this is direct evidence of the ways in which "race is produced by space" (ibid., 5), supported by the structuring logic of what he calls the *white spatial imaginary*:

> The white spatial imaginary has cultural as well as social consequences. It structures feelings as well as social institutions. The white spatial imaginary idealizes "pure" and homogeneous spaces, controlled environments, and predictable patterns of design and behavior. It seeks to

> hide social problems rather than solve them. The white spatial imaginary promotes the quest for individual escape rather than encouraging democratic deliberations about the social problems and contradictory social relations that affect us all. (Ibid., 29)

By employing narratives of up-and-coming neighborhoods, graphic design helps to sustain the cultural commitments of the white spatial imaginary. Before further examining the mechanics of the verbal and visual storytelling in these neighborhoods that comprise "predictable patterns of design and behavior" (ibid.), some brief context for each city will help to underscore the impacts gentrification—and design strategies by extension—have had on these communities.

Austin, Texas

According to census data, Austin's population *grew* by 20.4% from 2000 to 2010, but critically, its Black population dropped by 5.4%. Austin was the only major growing US city at that time that saw an absolute numerical decline in its Black population (Falola, West Ohueri, and Tang n.d.). In 1928, the city created a "Negro district" on the east side of downtown, starkly demarcated by the interstate, that limited access to schools and other public services for Black residents to these boundaries. The city reinforced this segregation in the decades to follow, and its effects felt for much longer, through such redlining policies and practices as the Home Owners Loan Corporation refusing loans to this area (Zehr 2015). By 2010, many established community members on the east side were priced out due to gentrification when families sold their homes to wealthy newcomers and subsequently moved outside Austin's city limits. In the past decade, from 2010–19, census data shows Austin's estimated growth remained high at 22.1%. In 2020, the average rent for a one-bedroom apartment in East Austin was $1,825 a month (Vega 2020). In one notable example of ongoing pressure for current residents to relocate, developers first offered Brian Mays, long-time owner of Sam's Bar-B-Que—a neighborhood shop on the east side since 1974—three million dollars, then later five million dollars, to purchase his business. Mays refused, citing a commitment to the community over financial rewards (Rodriguez 2019).

Chicago, Illinois

Logan Square is on the northwest side of Chicago and just a train stop away from the Wicker Park neighborhood, infamously gentrified throughout the 1990s–2000s (Lloyd 2006). According to The Institute for Housing Studies at DePaul University, Logan Square is currently one of the neighborhoods with the highest displacement pressure in Chicago. Between 2000 and 2014, the Marguerite Casey Foundation noted a 35.6% loss of the Latino population (over 19,000 residents) and an 8.2% loss of Black residents. The white population, however, has increased by over 12,000 residents during that time and is now the majority in the neighborhood—a switch from the Latino majority of the 1980s (Zamudio 2018). In 2017, the number of demolition permits in Logan Square surpassed other Chicago neighborhoods with 109 issued (Zamudio 2018; LSNA and LISC 2018), and a surge in development led to building 1,000 "luxury" housing units that same year (Carmona 2019). From 2017 to 2018, longtime residents felt even more obliged to sell when Logan Square's property taxes increased by 24.09%, significantly more than the citywide average of 2.15% (Bloom 2019). Meanwhile, Chicago neighborhood news source, DNAinfo, hailed the Logan Square neighborhood as the new "Cocktail Bar Capital of Chicago" (Bloom 2017).

The Designed Objects and Spaces: Stabilizing Meaning through Use

Edgy Artisanal Histories

The linguistic patterns—from the city to the consumer—across gentrified spaces are salient. In Chicago, Joe Moreno, alderman from 2011–19 of the 1st Ward (where Logan Square is situated), expressed his enthusiasm for the Logan Square cocktail boom: "I like the fact that it's more craft than just opening up a sports and beer place. It brings eccentric, craftness to the area" (Bloom 2017). Cohen's support of the neighborhood's "artisan focus" mirrors this, and Cohen's description of the area's entrepreneurs as "radical, progressive and innovative" is also reflected in geographer Oli Mould's critique of the "veneer of 'edginess'" required for the creative city to "appeal to hipsters and maintain a radical, progressive and perhaps even anti-capitalist aesthetic" (2018, 159). One especially blatant illustration of these points is in Logan Square with Illinois' largest independent craft brewery. The logo of Revolution Brewing depicts a red and black illustration of hops gripped tightly in a raised fist demonstrating resistance and desire to be liberated from something undetectable. Once inside the brewpub, visitors can see the bar is being supported by these same fists carved out of mahogany, each about two feet high, along with a series of raised fists as the taps.[3] Here, you can order beers such as the Rise American Stout, the Anti-Hero IPA, or the Working Woman Brown Ale, while ordering an entrée at the average cost of fourteen dollars. Supporting and shaping "alternative" consumption practices and desires of course does not mean an absence of commodification. With Revolution, visitors get the appeal and ability to consume protest and faux working-class aesthetics without having to actually protest or be working class. Meanwhile, Yelp reviewers describe Revolution's decor as "beautiful, modern, industrial" (Laura V. 2011) and "mega-urban in appearance" (Bryan M. 2010), identifying what seems to be an "interesting story behind every design choice" (Laura V. 2011). One person ends their review by exclaiming "*Viva la revolucion* [sic]!" (Tim J. 2011). In addition to consumers, the design industry also embraces this "edgy" language, evidenced in the 2020 PRINT Awards' Best in Show, awarded to a DC-based studio for campaign work on behalf of luxury eyewear (Deseo 2020).[4] In a video spot titled "Eyes Say More Than Words," a voiceover declares: "Silent revolutions are planned with revolutionary eyewear and radical style." Ironically, words indeed continue to play a critical role in popular design culture: antagonistic political language is commonly stripped of its teeth in favor of style and is rewarded for doing so.

Another version of apparent progressivism can be found in the form of businesses producing artisanal goods, with perhaps the most visible example of the artisan being the cafe. Just a block from Revolution Brewery you can purchase coffee from Gaslight Coffee Roasters who carefully package beans harvested in Ethiopia and Brazil with an elegant wax stamp and ribbon. Streetside, the cafe's name spans the length of the building and is evocative of mid-twentieth century sign painting, featuring a bold white sans-serif with a subtle yellow

3 Brandi Thompson Summers (2019) introduces her book with an example of a remarkably similar logo—stylized in red—for DC's now closed Chocolate City Beer. On page 1, she notes "the absence of an actual black fist allows the red fist to operate in aesthetic proximity to blackness."

4 In the video spot by Design Army for Georgetown Optician, an overzealous librarian sits in a lifeguard's chair aggressively monitoring and punishing bespectacled patrons—with styling inspired by 1970s yearbooks—for any trace of noise. The library visitors use the catalog to locate "Revolution" to strategize how to topple the tyrant.

drop shade contrasted against the painted black exterior. Inside, hanging on the wall, and visible in a photograph on *Bon Appétit*'s online review (n.d.), is a reclaimed barbershop letter board offering weaves and relaxers, services for a demographic of clientele that is curiously represented here on behalf of two white owners in a neighborhood with a Black population of about 5%—a design decision that aligns with Summers' theorization of black aesthetic emplacement. The exterior lettering, baroque wallpaper, and, more critically, this reclamation of the letter board instrumentalize history in the name of nostalgia but ignores recent displacement histories of this neighborhood. This "deracialized nostalgia" can be seen as "a mode of remaking history, without memory" (Bond and Browder 2019, 211), as well as a strategic manipulation of racial dynamics to signal "legitimacy" in urban development (Mele 2019, 28). At Gaslight, the letter board is not actually a historical reference, but a cultural marker in service of the market. A few blocks away, Bang Bang Pie & Biscuits' handcrafted aesthetic is reflected in the large, reclaimed vintage letters spelling out P-I-E on their exposed brick interior wall, and we see the return of more letter boards, hand lettering, stamping techniques, and brown kraft paper across their brand. Doing a Pinterest search for "Artisan Coffee Roaster" gives me a board full of this same style, gesturing to a fantasy of production techniques and styles of years past—more models of remaking history without, or at least with selective, memory.

Moving back to East Austin, Wright Bros. Brew & Brew boasts 38 craft taps, coffee, and food. They fashion their interior with wood, metal, and concrete for "stylish industrial digs," according to one of Google's editorial summaries.[5] The generous letter spacing of the all-caps sans-serif centers the trendy "&" as a signpost for their business. One Yelp reviewer describes the cafe's clientele as "the fraction of the Austin population that can afford to pay the highest rents and condo fees. They are hip. They are cool. They are well-upholstered" (Samuel C. 2019). It is difficult to discern whether this latter description is about the individuals or the space, and the reviewer's collapse of the two is telling. This merging of identities is really all the same, as these businesses create a collective (sometimes aspirational) identity based on their design and use, reflecting Cultural Studies theorist Stuart Hall's insistence that the images we make also construct us and our "fantasy relationship" to them (1997, 40:07). Just as every designer is a business, every well-upholstered customer is a commodity that constellates the white spatial imaginary of the gentrified neighborhood. Whether it is via revolutionary brews or "deracialized nostalgia" in the form of reclaimed barbershop letter boards, the designer and the well-upholstered customer are implicated in these meanings that prefer their diversity in the form of aestheticized storytelling, making gentrification's ideology visible on cafe, bar, and restaurant walls.

Narrativizing (in) Place

The designer-as-storyteller narrative is reinforced from multiple directions. Book titles assert that *Design is Storytelling* (Lupton 2017); articles in trade magazines declare that "experiences will never be more than the narratives with which they come" while encouraging designers to manufacture desire through stories and presentation (Liedgren 2016); instructional websites advise design students to study storytelling strategies in order to "get insight into users, build empathy and reach them emotionally" (Interaction Design

---

5 Google's editorial descriptions are the short one-liners about a business that show up within the map view following a Google search. Critically, these are not supplied by the owner of the business but by Google copywriters; owners can edit their lengthier business descriptions but not these. The *Google My Business* Help page specifies they will only accept edits to "services the business doesn't offer."

Foundation n.d.); and design agencies tell potential clients: "Because design strategy is fundamentally user-centered, this means that we are giving the very people in our stories a voice, acting as their proxy to fulfill their wants, needs, and desires" (Kolko n.d.).

Graphic design requires a process of translation that reifies ideas, values, and language, reliant on a semiotic understanding of how to codify intended associations with a particular audience. In addition to Hall's articulation of images constructing us, I would add spaces, artifacts, and experiences, all hold personal and social meaning through their representation and use, helping individuals both see their present and aspirational selves in their surroundings. Graphic designers build their practices around what is commonly described as the "look and feel" of spaces, artifacts, and experiences, where the *look* refers to convening an intended audience through formal decisions (e.g., typography, color palette, imagery, materials, and organization) while the *feel* refers to the experience informed by those aesthetic decisions (e.g., the way a user interacts with and processes information on a website, how one is guided through a physical space, and whether one "feels" or interprets the designed experience as nostalgic/upscale/edgy/etc.). To study these translations and their socio-political impacts, their deployment can be seen as part of a lineage of well-crafted, generative processes that help to enable and mobilize some bodies and constrain or isolate others.

One might recognize black aesthetic emplacement along a continuum of exclusionary aesthetic practices. For example, mid-century US suburban homeownership came to symbolize meritocratic success, though discriminatory mortgages only enabled white success. Just as government policy enacted popular white supremacist narratives of belonging, contemporary gentrified cities materially whiten the city while aestheticizing a diversity that once was. When Lipsitz says racism "takes place," he not only refers to isolated events but how structured "social relations take on their full force and meaning when they are enacted physically in actual places" (5). It is through this concrete spatial unfolding of racialized social relations that he articulates a "fatal coupling of race and place" (ibid.).

Taking place is supported by two key components of the design process—storytelling and visual articulation—that are often framed by a creative brief, a document introduced at the formal start of a client-designer relationship. Part of every commercial design process is asking who the intended audience is to ensure the formal and conceptual strategies align with the client's values and the audience's needs and desires. Documenting this in a brief facilitates the designer's use of language as a blueprint to then translate into visual and physical form. They commonly include notes on taste (that of the client and/or audience) and the "cultural position and aspirational values of the brand" (Dorland 2009), making space for—as noted by the design agency above—the designer to function as a proxy for the audience "to fulfill their wants, needs, and desires" (Kolko n.d.). The brief serves as a guide throughout the design process: Does the work adhere to the technical specs and the prescribed "look and feel"? Does it align with project objectives and short-/long-term measures for success—e.g., are our tactics clearly inviting x and y groups to this space/brand? In catering to areas of gentrification, the initial discovery stage of the design process allows those in control of the urban renewal narrative—those with the appropriate forms of capital—to assist designers in defining a hierarchy of belonging. We then see the design brief reanimated in venues like the aforementioned Yelp reviews, proof of the designer's success (or failure), in the form of a review by consumers for consumers. For new businesses in these areas, the prioritized audience has proven to be the profitable newcomers who, predictably, reinforce Lipsitz's white spatial imaginary.

Entrepreneurial Paradigms and Public Pedagogy
A number of online parody "hipster generators" elucidate how designers reproduce recognizable forms to signal to a particular audience. For example, the Hipster Business Name generator (n.d.) cycles through an assortment of names such as Pearl & Coffin, Death & Sandstone, Hobby & Peach, or Leopard & Frog with an accompanying simplified mark. In East Austin and Logan Square, we find a similar rhetorical convention used by small- to medium-scale entrepreneurial businesses. In addition to East Austin's *Brew & Brew*, other examples include Logan Square's *Table, Donkey and Stick* (their website expresses the proprietor's desire to "reflect the convivial spirit of the mountain inns [he] has visited on trips to the Alps" [n.d.]) and *Longman & Eagle* ("providing urban 'travelers' a refuge that appeals to a variety of senses—be they aesthetic, consumptive, culinary or restorative" [n.d.]). Bay-area brand strategist Ben Weis (2014) connects this trend to histories of family partnerships and notes "21st-century versions of these names harness associations of craftsmanship and self-ownership while replacing last names with nouns that outline their focus." Arched typography, distressed textures, script lettering, "blank & blank" names, stories of escape: these are all demonstrative of formal conventions congealed into a paradigm of representation that caters to, and produces space for, middle-class consumers and entrepreneurs.

The parodies are amusing but also demonstrate how clearly these identities reflect a set of social conditions and uninterrogated design practices, namely a shifting neoliberal landscape of cities rebranding themselves through deceptively homogeneous aesthetics and narratives that reproduce the white spatial imaginary. Branding is intended to both distinguish and speak to a particular audience. It can be emulated and reproduced to reinforce a particular community and ideology; the pattern is created, and it creates. Digital archives—from Google to Pinterest to Instagram—work as collections to be referenced; stock logo packs and generators use the environment and these archives to sustain and feed patterns. This style communicates with its intended audience, utilizing as Mould says, the stabilized aesthetics of the "edgy" creative city with very real consequences for those who are not invited.

These instances of visual culture in everyday life help create our worlds. These do not act outside of policies, laws, customs, and regulations (and their enforcement), but instead reflect, articulate, and sometimes produce them. Designers participate in a public pedagogy, manufacturing desire through storytelling and linking signs and symbols to a shared cultural understanding of exclusionary belonging, often as a routine part of their jobs. Lipsitz (2011) notes "[t]he white spatial imaginary often relies on misdirection, on creating spectacles that attract attention—yet detract our gaze from the links that connect urban place and race" (13). This misdirection is exemplified, for example, in pronouncing Logan Square the "Cocktail Bar Capital of Chicago" despite its devastating displacement rates.

As a form of storytelling, misdirection is a comfortable weapon in a designer's arsenal. Design, as with all translation, is always political (Keshavarz 2019, 21). The affective dimension of language, images, and places grounds designers in the drive to create connections between certain people and certain businesses. These connections help to pull some to a place but also push others from it. In the urban revitalization project, colorblind narratives—seen on Austin and Logan Square's tourism websites à la "eclecticism" (Visit Austin n.d.) and "urban vibes" (Choose Chicago n.d.)—can script the city as welcoming, livable, and cosmopolitan while masking structural inequalities. These narratives promote a version of social and cultural diversity that is safe and comfortable for (white) visitors, consumers, and potential newcomers, while simultaneously justifying increased surveillance and policing against racialized residents (see, e.g., Julier 2005; Mele 2013, 2019; Alvaré 2017; Bond and Browder 2019; Gregory 2019; Stein 2019).

Conclusion

Marketing rhetoric, design culture, and visual design join with developers, city officials, the police, and others to produce and uphold "order" by narrativizing violent displacement as economic progress. These stories and spaces—both verbal and visual, digital and physical—fold and collapse into each other, immersing new residents and neighborhood tourists in a white spatial imaginary that encourages individual escape toward fantasies of righteous activism, multiculturalism, and phantom memories of the corner print shop.
The newly gentrified spaces are not on the margins living against official culture but have exploited and subsumed the margins. Following Lipsitz, individual escape is possible here in a controlled, predictable environment where gentrification seeks to obscure social problems. Stories and style in these instances create an index to selective histories and to neoliberal acts of violence, contributing to a project that helps to bolster racist and classist policies, facilitate actions on behalf of urban renewal, and legitimize harm whether the designer intends to or not.

BIBLIOGRAPHY

Ahmed, Sara. *On Being Included: Racism and Diversity in Institutional Life*. Duke University Press, 2012.

AIGA. *Design POV: An In-Depth Look at the Design Industry Now, Full Report*. AIGA, Design Point of View Research Initiative, 2021a. https://www.aiga.org/design/design-research-insights.

AIGA. 2021b. "Our Story | AIGA." Accessed September 1, 2021. https://www.aiga.org/our-story.

Alvaré, Melissa Archer. "Gentrification and Resistance: Racial Projects in the Neoliberal Order." *Social Justice* 44 (2/3) (2017): 113–136. https://www.jstor.org/stable/26538384.

Barnes, Kendall, Gordon R. Waitt, Nicholas J. Gill, and Christopher R. Gibson. "Community and Nostalgia in Urban Revitalisation: A Critique of Urban Village and Creative Class Strategies as Remedies for Social 'Problems.'" *Australian Geographer* 37 (3) (2006): 335–54. doi:10.1080/00049180600954773.

Bloom, Mina. 2017. "Logan Square Now Cocktail Bar Capital Of Chicago, But Has It Gone Too Far?" DNAinfo. Last modified March 15, 2017. https://www.dnainfo.com/chicago/20170315/logan-square/is-logan-squares-booming-cocktail-bar-scene-sustainable/.

———. 2019. "Logan Square Saw Highest Property Tax Hike of Any Neighborhood in the City, Ald. Ramirez-Rosa Says." Block Club Chicago. Last modified July 24, 2019. https://blockclubchicago.org/2019/07/24/logan-square-saw-highest-property-tax-hike-of-any-neighborhood-in-the-city-ald-ramirez-rosa-finds.

Bon Appétit. n.d. "Gaslight Coffee Roasters Review | Bon Appetit." Accessed November 20, 2019. https://www.bonappetit.com/city-guides/chicago/venue/gaslight-coffee-roasters.

Bond, Patrick, and Laura Browder. "Deracialized Nostalgia, Reracialized Community, and Truncated Gentrification: Capital and Cultural Flows in Richmond, Virginia and Durban, South Africa." *Journal of Cultural Geography* 36 (2) (2019): 211–245. doi:10.1080/08873631.2019.1595914.

Cabrera, Sergio A. "When Bourgeois Utopias Meet Gentrification: Community and Diversity in a New Urbanist Neighborhood," *Sociological Spectrum* 39 (3) (2019): 194–213. doi:10.1080/02732173.2019.1645065.

Carmona, Armando. 2019. "Una Respuesta Comunitaria Contra la Gentrificación en Chicago" [A Community Response Against Gentrification in Chicago]. La Raza. July 31, 2019. https://laraza.com/2019/07/31/una-respuesta-comunitaria-contra-de-la-gentrificacion-en-chicago.

Choose Chicago. n.d. "Logan Square - Chicago Neighborhoods | Choose Chicago." Accessed September 1, 2021. https://www.choosechicago.com/neighborhoods/logan-square.

Cohen, Rich. 2013. "Top 5 Reasons to Start a Business in Logan Square." LoganSquarist. Last modified August 27, 2013. https://logansquarist.com/2013/08/27/start-business-logan-square.

Deseo, Jessica. 2020. "The Best Graphic Design of the Year: Announcing the Winners of the PRINT Awards," *PRINT*. Last modified December 17, 2020. https://www.printmag.com/advertising/the-best-graphic-design-of-the-year-announcing-the-winners-of-the-print-awards.

Dorland, AnneMarie. "Routinized Labour in the Graphic Design Studio." In *Design and Creativity: Policy, Management and Practice*, edited by Guy Julier and Liz Moor, 105–121. Bloomsbury Design Library, 2009. http://dx.doi.org/10.5040/9781474293693.ch-006.

Falola, Bisola, Chelsi West Ohueri, and Eric Tang. n.d. "About." About—East Avenue. Accessed January 5, 2019. http://www.segregatedaustin.org/about

Google Maps. 2018. "Review of Wright Bros. Brew and Brew by Marc Williams." https://goo.gl/maps/7AYEPSQ9K2YZAYuS8.

Gregory, Siobhan. "Authenticity and Luxury Branding in a Renewing Detroit Landscape." *Journal of Cultural Geography* 36 (2) (2019): 182–210. doi:10.1080/08873631.2019.1595913.

Hall, Stuart. "Representation & the Media." Video, 55:00. Northampton: Media Education Foundation, 1997. https://www.kanopy.com/product/stuart-hall-representation-media.

Hipster Business Name Generator. n.d. Accessed November 20, 2019. http://www.hipsterbusiness.name.

Interaction Design Foundation. n.d. "What is Storytelling?" Accessed July 20, 2021. https://www.interaction-design.org/literature/topics/storytelling.

Julier, Guy. "Urban Designscapes and the Production of Aesthetic Consent." *Urban Studies* 42 (5/6) (2005): 869–887. doi:10.1080/00420980500107474.

Keshavarz, Mahmoud. "Sketch For a Theory of Design Politics." In *Para-Platforms: On the Spatial Politics of the Right-Wing Populism*, edited by Markus Miessen and Zoë Ritts. Sternberg Press, 2019.

Kolko, Jon. n.d. "Stories: The Way to Our Hearts and the Key to Design Strategy." Modernist Studio. Accessed September 25, 2021. https://www.modernistudio.com/service-design-stories-the-way-to-our-heart-and-the-key-to-design-strategy.

Liedgren, Johan. 2016. "On the Narrative Structure of Creating Desire." *PRINT*. Last modified August 18, 2016. https://www.printmag.com/featured-design-inspiration/on-the-narrative-structure-of-creating-desire.

Lipsitz, George. *How Racism Takes Place*. Temple University Press, 2011.

Lloyd, Richard. *Neo-Bohemia: Art and Commerce in the Postindustrial City.* Routledge, 2006.

Longman & Eagle. n.d. "About Longman & Eagle." Accessed September 4, 2022. https://www.longmanandeagle.com/about.

LSNA (Logan Square Neighborhood Association) and LISC (Local Initiatives Support Corporation) Chicago New Communities Network. *Hermosa and Logan Square West: Here to Stay. Quality-of-Life Plan Executive Summary.* LSNA and LISC, 2018. https://www.lisc.org/media/filer_public/18/6b/186bb965-a013-40ca-a7e1-5759a406a55b/120318_chicago_qol_hermosa_2018_summary.pdf.

Lupton, Ellen. *Design is Storytelling.* Cooper Hewitt, Smithsonian Design Museum, 2017.

Mele, Christopher. "Neoliberalism, Race and the Redefining of Urban Redevelopment." *International Journal of Urban and Regional Research* 37 (2) (2013): 598–617. doi:10.1111/j.1468-2427.2012.01144.

———. "The Strategic Uses of Race to Legitimize 'Social Mix' Urban Redevelopment. *Social Identities* 25 (1) (2019): 7–40. doi:10.1080/13504630.2017.1418603.

Moore, Natalie and Odette Yousef. 2018. "Chicago Has a Plan to Build Near CTA Trains. But Who Does it Help?" WBEZ Chicago. Last modified November 26, 2018. https://www.wbez.org/stories/chicago-has-a-plan-to-build-near-cta-trains-but-who-does-it-help/e967316b-2d98-4d1b-b2f3-2ba1eb066929.

Mould, Oli. *Against Creativity.* Verso, 2018.

Rodriguez, Candy. 2019. "Sam's BBQ Owner Names a Price at Which He Will Sell to Developers." KEXP. Last modified March 2, 2019. https://www.kxan.com/news/local/austin/sams-bbq-owner-names-a-price-at-which-he-will-sell-to-developers.

Stein, Samuel. *Capital City: Gentrification and the Real Estate State.* Verso, 2019.

Summers, Brandi Thompson. *Black in Place: The Spatial Aesthetics of Race in a Post-Chocolate City.* University of North Carolina Press, 2019.

Table, Donkey and Stick. n.d. "Table, Donkey and Stick | People." Accessed September 4, 2022. http://www.tabledonkeystick.com/people.

Vega, Muriel. 2020. "Austin Neighborhoods by Average Rent Prices." Apartment Guide. Last modified July 27, 2020. https://www.apartmentguide.com/blog/austin-neighborhoods-by-average-rent.

Visit Austin. n.d. "East Austin | Visit Austin, TX Entertainment Districts." Accessed September 1, 2021. https://www.austintexas.org/things-to-do/entertainment-districts/east-austin.

Weis, Ben. 2014. "The Rise of the Blank and Blank Restaurant Naming Trend." A Hundred Monkeys. Last modified March 4, 2014. https://www.ahundredmonkeys.com/resources/restaurant-naming-trend.

Yelp. 2010. "Bryan M.'s Reviews | Chicago - Yelp." October 15, 2010. https://www.yelp.com/biz/revolution-brewing-chicago?hrid=MRBUb6Uw1qIWXUK_8hJwsw&utm_campaign=www_review_share_popup&utm_medium=copy_link&utm_source=(direct).

Yelp. 2011. "Laura V.'s Reviews | Oconomowoc - Yelp." March 22, 2011. https://www.yelp.com/biz/revolution-brewing-chicago?hrid=szNPFiA_0gz7yIO2I1R-0w&utm_campaign=www_review_share_popup&utm_medium=copy_link&utm_source=(direct).

Yelp. 2019. "Samuel C.'s Reviews | Austin - Yelp." March 29, 2019. https://www.yelp.com/biz/wright-bros-brew-and-brew-austin?hrid=fn_n74zSS1gDJZ5XjW8Ahg&utm_campaign=www_review_share_popup&utm_medium=copy_link&utm_source=(direct).

Yelp. 2011. "Tim J's Reviews | Chicago - Yelp." February 26, 2011. https://www.yelp.com/biz/revolution-brewing-chicago?hrid=jkCxXiefIW9xJMsAZ8mbqw&utm_campaign=www_review_share_popup&utm_medium=copy_link&utm_source=(direct).

Zamudio, Maria Ines. 2018. "As Logan Square's White Population Surpasses Latinos, the Reverse Happens in Other Communities." Block Club Chicago with WBEZ Chicago. Last modified December 11, 2018. https://blockclubchicago.org/2018/12/11/after-decades-as-a-hispanic-enclave-white-population-surpasses-latinos-in-logan-square.

Zegeye, David. 2020. "How Chicago's Legacy of Segregation has Pushed Black People into Transit, Job Deserts." Streetsblog Chicago, Chicagoland Streets Project. Last modified January 21, 2020. https://chi.streetsblog.org/2020/01/21/how-chicagos-legacy-of-segregation-has-pushed-black-people-into-transit-and-job-deserts.

Zehr, Dan. 2015. "Inheriting Inequality." *Austin American-Statesman*, January 18, 2015. https://projects.statesman.com/news/economic-mobility.

Zukin, Sharon. "CONSUMING AUTHENTICITY: From Outposts of Difference to Means of Exclusion." *Cultural Studies* 22 (5) (2008): 724–748. doi:10.1080/09502380802245985.

Acknowledgements

A collective work, we acknowledge all those seen and unseen who have contributed to this work, including those who have mentored us as educators, designers, mothers, caregivers, and radical thinkers. Below we'd like to credit specific contributors who served as designers, researchers, or participated in our workshops.

Contributors
Aaliya Jamal Zaidi, Cynthia Lu, Lucinda Bliss, Karol Martinez-Doane, Kathleen Grevers, Laura Kozak, Emily Hanako Momohara, Martha Rettig, Caroline Schlegel, Sally Sutherland, Vanessa, Mafalda Castro Moreira, Ali Place, Cara Bremen, Sophie "Fi" Engel, Laura Rossi Garcia, Claire Rosas, Aasawari Kulkarni

Support
AICAD (the Association of Independent Colleges of Art & Design), *Attending [to] Futures* conference team, DePaul University, Jarvis College of Computing and Digital Media (research support and funding), Washington University in St. Louis (research support and funding), Rhode Island School of Design (research support and funding), Ali Place for our dialogue in her forthcoming book titled Feminist Designer, and Binch Press for risograph printing of our workbook.

MATRIARCHAL DESIGN FUTURES

A Collective Work in Progress

(Heather Snyder Quinn)   (Ayako Takase)

Breaking Barriers and Imagining New Futures

Matriarchal Design Futures is a pedagogical framework that centers practices and values of caregiving and nurturing, which holds for all identities: for caregivers, mothers, those who are not mothers, women, men, and non-binary alike as similarly defined by HAGIA—the International Academy for Matriarchal Studies and Spirituality. While the term "matriarchal" is presumably interrupted as a binary language in opposition to "patriarchal" and "ruled by women," or that it is only for mothers in the traditional sense, this work includes anyone who shares care-centered values. We intentionally use and self-define "matriarchal" (see the next section for Matriarchal Guiding Principles) as a value-guided framework and "futures" as plural possibilities that result from practicing a matriarchal framework. It is a collective work in progress—a set of holistic guiding principles and aspirations. We mean to validate and empower the invisible work to be visible and to collectively move towards care-centered futures in design education and practice.

    The foundation of this work began as a dialogue between two friends (who also identified as women, caregivers, industry practitioners, and educators) as a support system of shared thoughts, ideas, emails, and text messages. This dialogue served as a lifeline of encouragement and empowerment as we navigated the old guard and legacy rules of academia and industry. Through our approach, we were slowly changing the rules, unlearning the systems and structures under which we had been trained. Small changes can be radical, and according to Allan G. Johnson in *The Gender Knot,* "It's important to note how rarely it occurs to people to simply change the rules. The relationship, terms, and goals that organize the game aren't presented to us as ours to judge or alter. The more attached we feel to the game and the more closely we identify ourselves as players, the more likely we are to feel helpless in relation to it" (2007, 35).

    Our dialogue continued to grow and, in 2020, manifested into a public conversation at AICAD (the Association of Independent Colleges of Art & Design). AICAD provided a solid base to test these ideas and develop the work further into a framework reflecting our uncommon (matriarchal) pedagogy and practices—with realizations that matriarchal framework and values have not been discussed or shared enough in design education or industry. Incentivized to gain more international perspectives, we explored the ideas in a workshop at the *Attending [to] Futures* conference in November of 2021 at the Köln International School of Design, Germany. Here, we learned that although there were occasional nomenclature differences among participants, we all shared similar struggles and desires for change.

It is essential to note some fundamental principles and threads in this matriarchal work, which centers around "care" and embracing the "incomplete" and the "imperfect." In the spirit of our words, we tread carefully and lightly, harkening back to those that paved the way before us. While we draw connections to the scholarly works of matriarchal studies (Goettner-Abendroth), feminist pedagogy (Shrewsbury), engaged pedagogy, and Black feminism (hooks), our main inspirations are non-academic. We acknowledge and respect that matriarchal concepts date far back in Indigenous cultures. Care-centered communities have always existed and are practiced by BIPOC women, LGBTQ folks, and marginalized lives as means of survival. We are not reinventing or claiming ownership of the idea; rather, we wish to provide space for support, dialogue, learning, unlearning, and growth. We keep an open mind and remember that this is just the beginning—we may begin again and again, and we hope the work will evolve and grow collectively through the contributions of many. Because the work is never done, we call it a WIP (work in progress)—which is also how we see ourselves—evolving together now and as we attend to our future(s).

Matriarchal Guiding Principles

In evaluating the present and looking to the future, we found our language problematic and limiting—words could not define what we sought to evoke. As such, we began to collect key terms and redefine them. Like all of our work, we see them as fluid, evolving—a starting point for critical thought and dialogue.

Matriarchal
A way of being that centers the practices and values of caregiving and nurturing, which holds for everybody: for mothers and those who are not mothers, for women, men, and non-binary folks alike (HAGIA 2022). Matriarchal opposes patriarchal traits of white supremacist, colonial, racist, homophobic, and xenophobic concepts; however, it does not mean being ruled by women in a place of power.

Anti-exceptional
To actively counter traditional, white supremacist, and capitalistic measures of exceptionalism and success in education, including obedience, over-working, perfectionism, checking off boxes, and working to "please the professor." Our anti-traditional academic metrics encourage the development of self-awareness, embracing personal strengths and passions, self-care, and self-love.

WIP (Work in progress)
Inspired by the Work in Progress book series by The Wellesley Centers for Women, we embrace the idea that "it is important to exchange ideas while they are being developed" and acknowledge our work is always WIP. This approach invites a "letting go" of academic perfectionism and expectations and serves as an invitation to collective evolution based on continuous dialogue, reflection, and iteration.

Engaged Pedagogy
As explained by bell hooks, engaged pedagogy (hooks 1994) centers on a mutual, nurturing relationship between teacher and student—intending to create trust, commitment, and empowerment for a more engaged and meaningful learning environment.

Guiding Principles
The collaborative creation of core values intended to guide motivations and actions. These principles are not a top-down manifesto; rather, they intentionally rely on individual interpretations and lived experiences.

Collective/Collectively
Both a noun and an adverb, the collective is a method of organizing and working that removes hierarchy, authority, and individualism to make a broader impact. Embracing the idea that it is critical to hear more voices and amplify those voices louder and louder to move beyond homogeneity and normalize diverse perspectives.

Circular Classroom
A democratic classroom that fosters participation, collaboration, mutual learning, and respect. Non-hierarchical in structure, it creates an equitable learning environment that removes the top-down, podium-style teaching and power dynamics that exist in traditional classrooms.

Plural Futures
An approach to speculating futures that embraces the notion that the future is not singular or fixed; rather, there are endless potential futures, opening the doors for imagining scenarios we have not previously thought possible.

Dialogue
A primary tool for reflecting and furthering ideas collectively. Specifically, as stated by Shrewsbury in *What is Feminist Pedagogy*, to critically think, process, and proceed, it is critical to incorporate "a reflective process firmly grounded in the experiences of the everyday. It requires continuous questioning and making assumptions explicit, but it does so in a dialogue aimed not at disproving another person's perspective, nor destroying the validity of another's perspective, but a mutual exploration of implications of diverse experiences." (Shrewsbury 1987, 7).

Authenticity
Being genuine, vulnerable, and true-to-self allows students and educators to challenge and reach their fullest potential. As bell hooks states, "Any classroom that employs a holistic model of learning will also be a place where teachers grow, and are empowered by the process. That empowerment cannot happen if we refuse to be vulnerable while encouraging students to take risks." (1994, 21).

Even the act of rewriting definitions becomes an intentional act of "rule-breaking," or rather questioning the status quo, claiming agency, and coming together to imagine the world anew. The activity itself enacts almost all guiding principles and is an excellent example of the matriarchal design future approach in action. It took some time to get to these working principles, which are constantly redefined, but they first manifested as part of our initial proposal.

Our Initial Provocation
Providence, Rhode Island (2020) and Cologne, Germany (2021)

In 2020, during the early phases of the pandemic, our private conversations turned into a proposal. Although still hesitant about how to frame things, we were ready and agreed to embrace incompleteness and imperfection. We gathered our ideas in a shared document that felt like an angry and urgent plea for consideration. It read like this:

> What if we desire something else for future generations? What would happen if we start imagining and creating the futures we want? What would happen if we unlearn our patriarchal training? What would happen if we abandoned solutionism for the unknown? What would happen if we replaced human-centered design (aka design for consumption) and genuinely designed for the pluriverse? What would happen if we smashed the podium and instead created a non-hierarchical, non-linear approach to learning? Might we see that the lonely ladder to the top—the competitive, elitist approach to design study and practice could be abandoned for something more caring and restorative? And if we begin this at the root—at the very beginning of our students' studies—can the field change from singular and privileged to more open, collaborative, and anti-exceptional? Can we make design school, design studies, and the design field feel welcoming to all who desire to be there—not just those who already fit in? Is it even possible to de-couple design from whiteness, consumerism, capitalism, growth, and competition?
>
> We say yes—it is possible, but to do so means reconsidering much of what we know and have been taught. To do so, we must fully embrace who we are because although we exist in a creative field, we fail to realize how much we follow the old patriarchal rules; in doing so, we abandon what may be intuitive to us as humans to care for others. The new urgency of the Covid crisis, BLM movement, abortion ban, trans erasure, war, and natural disasters in recent years brought social inequity to the surface more than ever. In particular, caregivers (often mothers) are left to cope with the impossible challenge of balancing multiple responsibilities and emotional labor. We live in a state of unrest. Our lives are chaotic and unsettled, yet we thrive because we can and must multitask, and this new generation of students craves the real and the authentic. We have responsibilities to be vulnerable and lean into our intuition to practice matriarchal principles and teaching. The boundaries are removed, and we are no longer hiding. With the veil between work and life removed, the very fabric of society continues to change, and we hope to use that momentum to share and co-create matriarchal teaching methods and approaches in design and beyond.

The proposal was developed over a collaborative virtual session. Written quickly and with emotion, it broke the traditional rules of a conference abstract but was on point for the topic.

Our Approach

Reflection of Our Own Struggles & Current Constraints

When we began our dialogue, we were still determining the underlying cause of our frustrations and struggles and the successes we garnered as design educators in academic institutions. As a first step, we began identifying the obstacles and challenges we faced while attempting to practice our (then-undefined) teaching methodology, which centered on students and caregiving. While obvious, this exercise is a crucial foundation to name names, understand cause and effect, and connect the dots between societal constructs to our design education system (Figure 1).

For many, the state of society and the organizations we participate

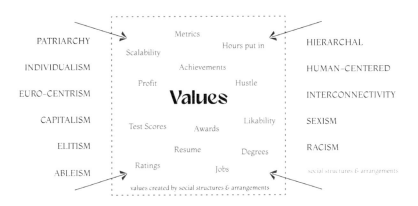

Fig. 1. Current societal values diagram.

in are not what we dream of. Yet, the patriarchal construct (as visualized in Figure 1) is prevalent in how we are trained and still practice as designers and educators. So much so it is often difficult to realize that struggles experienced are indeed due to constraints and oppressions created by societal constructs. bell hooks discusses the nature of the oppressor and oppressed relationship; "Under capitalism, patriarchy is structured so that sexism restricts women's behavior in some realms even as freedom from limitations is allowed in other spheres. The absence of extreme restrictions leads many women to ignore the areas in which they are exploited or discriminated against; it may even lead them to imagine that no women are oppressed" (hooks 2000, 5).

Speculating the Future

What could we practice differently to shift the paradigm then? What do we dream of? Reflecting on our favorite classroom design tool, we utilized a future cone (Figure 2) adapted from Hancock and Bezold (1994, 25) to visualize future scenarios. With the assumption that our future is never fixed, this tool engages with individual responsibilities and imaginations of identifying and reaching our preferred futures instead of simply moving forward with a status quo, a predictable, probable future. When we begin imagining our alternative and preferable futures without the patriarchal parameters we currently have, we return to

Imagining Futures/Futures Cone

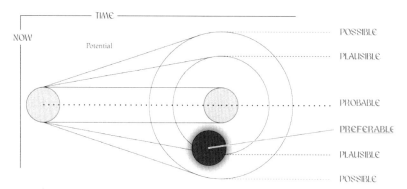

Fig. 2. A diagram based on the futures cone by Hancock and Bezold, 1994.

a future that centers its core values around care and joy—a result of our lived experiences that lean in on our intuition as caregivers and educators (Figure 3). The speculative imaginary of Matriarchal Design Futures counters the values and priorities created by white supremacy and capitalism. It values collectivism over individualism, cooperation over competition, inclusivity over elitism, and human rights over profit. It does not keep score or use metrics to measure success. Matriarchal Design Futures foregrounds identities and agencies beyond the binaries shaped by heteropatriarchy.

Matriarchal Design Future

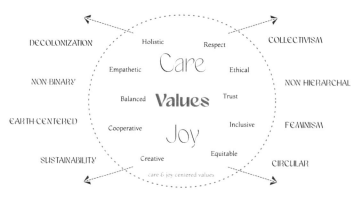

Fig. 3. Matriarchal design future values diagram.

To create more well-rounded and just opportunities for all, anti-exceptionalism and anti-elitism are at the core of Matriarchal Design Futures' values—countering existing patriarchal metrics, as seen in Figure 1. In this spirit, it is essential that *everyone,* whether one identifies as matriarchal or not, joins the co-creation of caring and restorative Matriarchal Design Futures by asking questions together. Therefore, we propose a collective work-in-progress to create matriarchal guiding principles which will help us lead, teach and learn, and continue examining the intersection of design education and the design industry through a matriarchal lens. We began simply—with a question: If we center our values and principles as matriarchal instead of patriarchal, how does

this change how we work, communicate, and think about the future?
Collective Workshopping—Approach and Findings
In keeping with our principle of collective action and creation, we brought our ideas into the public sphere via design education conferences. We wanted to validate and expand upon our individual reflections and assessments with other design educators and beyond.

We conducted our first workshop at the height of the pandemic in Feb of 2021 at AICAD (the Association of Independent Colleges of Art and Design). For background, "AICAD is a non-profit consortium of the leading specialized arts and design schools in the US and Canada …with students drawn from all 50 US states and more than 60 countries. Over 70% of these students receive financial aid to support their education" (AICAD.org). Originally proposed as an in-person gathering, the conference was moved online. We had over 75 attendees registered—a large number by any standard. It was clear we had hit a nerve with our theme, and we wondered if the pandemic had further exacerbated the need for new approaches to pedagogy.

Our final workshop had approximately 20 attendees from across the US and Canada. During the workshop, we walked through a slide deck of our high-level findings and ideas, and asked others to join us in a Google Jamboard for a virtual work session. During the work session, we proposed a series of prompts and questions about design pedagogy's current and preferable state. After our workshop, we discovered many design educators echoed our struggles and desire to work toward matriarchal design futures collectively—which was in keeping with our general assumptions.

After the AICAD conference, we wanted to gather feedback from an international audience, so we could determine if our findings were systematically American or global in nature. Our next step was to engage with educators at the *Attending [to] Futures* conference at The Köln International School of Design in Germany, which though also Western, would provide expanded insights. This was the first installation of the *Attending [to] Futures* conference, which is positioned as a conference for "design practitioners, researchers, educators, students, scholars, and activists who engage in a political reprogramming of design" (conference website). Our *Attending [to] Futures* workshop followed a similar format of lecture and work session. Our attendees were a small, diverse group, including a few who male-identified and both educators and practitioners. This work session further validated our findings. Key themes (Figure 4) include the need for more space to discuss matriarchal values in design education, challenges we face as practitioners, educators, and students, and ideas on how to practice matriarchal values in current systems. Statements from our participants are as follows:

> We need to start allowing ourselves to be vulnerable and uncomfortable.
> Remember that we have a choice.
> Co-creating syllabus with students
> See conflict as an opportunity for love and growth.
> Hold the community accountable to its own ideals.
> Are we supposed to not have life/family to take care of?
> Normalization of making mistakes
> Stop mythologizing artistic and design practice.
> Value local and small-scale work.
> Slow down to a human and nature pace!

Our work session further clarified the AICAD findings and validated our original hypothesis. With these significant discoveries, we wanted to bring this knowledge together and share it more broadly. In line with our philosophy of sharing and empowering collectively, we decided to disseminate our results through various platforms and media, including a workbook (both a printed publication and a free digital download).

Fig. 4. *Attending [to] Futures* workshop themes.

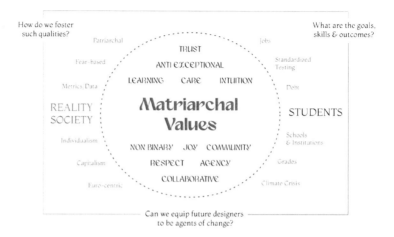

Synthesis of our Work and Workshop Experience

In synthesizing our original work with our findings from AICAD and *Attending [to] Futures,* we recognize that, especially for design educators who do not center activism or pedagogical development via research and professional practice, creating a space to reflect on how we practice and how we could practice matriarchal teaching is crucial. Additionally, those who naturally tend to get pulled into "care work" in the institutions to support students and peers need time to reflect on the tremendous importance of their matriarchal approach and roles in design education and to make this traditionally invisible work visible to themselves and others. Our findings justify how Matriarchal Design Futures as a pedagogical framework centers practices and values of caregiving and nurturing in design, and design education is necessary to counter the patriarchal constructs of the status quo. We collectively must validate, empower, and amplify our lived experiences and voices to make further paradigm shifts from patriarchal to matriarchal, elitism to inclusivity, consumption to sustainability, individualism to collectivism, and competition to cooperation.

Reality Versus Idealism—Challenges and Implications

We realize that challenges are inherent in bringing this approach into the design field; however, we see this as an opportunity. In the spirit of the designers at Superflux London, who state, "This work is not about predictions. It's about creating tools—tools that can help connect our present and our future selves so we become active participants in creating a future we want — a future that works for all." (Superflux) When we attempt to practice matriarchal design values in our patriarchal society, we often make smaller steps that, together, make longer strides. The authors, both design practitioners with over 25 years of working in design, are more than aware of the reality and constraints of industry work, as visualized in Figure 5—Reality versus Idealism. Despite those challenges, we remain optimistic. Our proposal is simple—keep taking small steps. We recognize, share, model, teach, learn, and influence, and we make change. We throw out top-down hierarchical approaches in the classroom and create a circular collective space (Figure 6). We nurture matriarchal values in the classroom and the design field to educate and influence students and practitioners. Envisioning matriarchal futures is critical because the alternative may be that we do not have any futures ahead of us. As stated In bell hooks' quote from *Feminism is for Everybody* "To be truly visionary we have to root our imagination in our concrete reality while simultaneously imagining possibilities beyond that reality" (2014, 110).

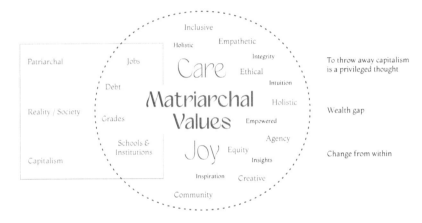

Fig. 5. Reality (current social state) versus idealism (matriarchal future values).

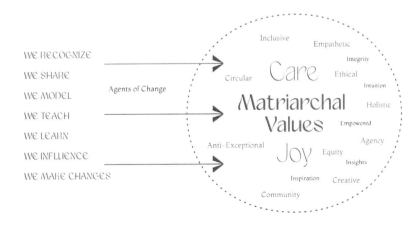

Fig. 6. Matriarchal Design Future actions.

1 Snyder-Quinn, Heather. Takase, Ayako. Matriarchal Design Futures: Workbook. 1st ed. 200. Providence, RI: Binch Press, 2022.

Provocations for the future

> Rather than providing specific conclusions, we wish to supply tools for provocation and reflection; therefore, we end with some of the questions we pose in our workshop and publication
>
> —Matriarchal Design Futures: Workbook.[1]

Reflection of the current state
What kind of qualities, skills, or traits are valued?
How is success measured?
What are the challenges & obstacles?

Preferable futures (matriarchal)
What skills or traits should be valued?
What are the things you do that are not recognized or valued?
How should success be measured?

Reaching our preferable futures
What changes & support do we need to see?
What can we do now?

These questions seek to provoke dialogue (internal and external), and we believe that small steps make big ripples when we take them collectively. Moving forward with this work, we will continue to co-create an open-source collective publication with participants—a set of holistic guiding principles, hopes, and aspirations for a collaborative, matriarchal, anti-exceptional design futures.

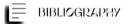

BIBLIOGRAPHY

Hancock, T and Bezold, C. "Possible Futures, Preferable Futures", *Healthcare Forum Journal*, vol. 37, no. 2, 1994, pp. 23-29.

hooks, bell. *Feminist Theory: From Margin to Center*. United Kingdom: Pluto Press, 2000.

---. *Teaching To Transgress*. Routledge, 1994.

International Academy HAGIA for Modern Matriarchal Studies. "Matriarchy" Accessed February 27, 2023.
https://www.hagia.de/en/matriarchy/.

Johnson, Allan G. *The Gender Knot*. Temple University Press, 2005.

Mareis, Claudia, and Paim, Nina, editors. *Design Struggles*. Valiz, 2021.

McIntosh, Peggy. "Feeling Like a Fraud." *Work in Progress by the Wellesley Centers for Women*, no. 18, 1985, all pages in series.

Shrewsbury, Carolyn M. "What Is Feminist Pedagogy?" *Women's Studies Quarterly*, vol. 15, no. 3/4, 1987, pp. 6-14.

Superflux. "Why We Need to Imagine Different Futures: Ted Talk" Accessed May 29, 2023.
https://superflux.in/index.php/work/why-we-need-to-imagine-different-futures-ted-talk/.

Additional Recommended Reading

This work would not be possible without all of those who came before us—paving the way for radical creativity and critical awareness to challenge the systems and structures ingrained in us.

Beauvoir, Simone de. *The Independent Woman: Extracts from the - Second Sex.* Knopf Doubleday Publishing Group, 2018.

Berg, Meggie, and Barbara K. Seeber. *The Slow Professor.* University of Toronto Press, 2016.

Bergman, Aeron, et al., editors. *Forms of Education.* INCA Press, 2016.

Brown, Adrienne Marie. *Emergent Strategy.* AK Press, 2017.

Brown, Stuart L. *Play.* Avery, 2009.

Clapp, Edward P., et al. *Maker Centered Learning.* Wiley, 2016.

Fry, Tony, and Adam Nocek, editors. *Design in Crisis.* Routledge, 2020.

Haraway, Donna. *Cyborg Manifesto.* Routledge, 1991.

Lindgren, Jacob. *Extra-curricular.* Onomatopee, 2018.

Meenadchi. *Decolonizing Non-Violent Communication.* Los Angeles Co—Conspirator Press, 2019.

Monteiro, Mike. *Ruined By Design.* Mule Design, 2019.

Place, Ali. *Feminist Designer: On the Personal and the Political in Design.* Cambridge, MA: MIT Press, 2023.

Russell, Legacy. *Glitch Feminism.* Verso Books, 2020.

Tuck E, Yang, Wayne K. "Decolonization is Not a Metaphor." *Decolonization: Indigeneity, Education & Society,* Vol. 1, No.1, 2012, pp.1-40.

Watson, Julia. *Lo–TEK. Design by Radical Indigenism.* Taschen, 2020.

IMAGES AND ILLUSTRATIONS

All images are screenshots of the virtual presentation held at the *Attending [to] Futures* conference in November 2021 and were created by the authors using Nari and Montaga.

Figure 1: Current societal values diagram.

Figure 2: A diagram based on the futures cone by Hancock and Bezold, 1994.

Figure 3: Matriarchal design future values diagram.

Figure 4: *Attending [to] Futures* workshop themes.

Figure 5: Reality (current social state) versus idealism (matriarchal future values).

Figure 6: Matriarchal Design Future actions.

Nari is an experiment in variable font technology created by Aasawari Kulkarni that attempts to answer the question, "what would it mean for a typeface to be feminist?". The result is an interactive variable typeface designed by a woman of color, one that has multiple voices that represent choice, expression, and inclusivity; it does not belong to any one extreme and is fluid in nature. It breaks away from the traditional "acceptable" proportions of letter design and is anything but neutral. (https://aasawarikulkarni.com/NARIVARIABLE)

Montaga is an Old Style font designed by Alejandra Rodriguez, a type designer from Mexico. Inspired by Venetian calligraphy, it is one of the only typefaces available on Google Fonts designed by a woman. With a strong inclination in the modulation axis, it generates shapes with marked stress—giving it a strong personality. Montaga is a work in progress and will be improved regularly.

WEIRD PROBLEMS

Rethinking Privileged Design?

(Sven Quadflieg)

WEIRD Problems

Everyday objects in industrialized societies are largely based on data that represents a WEIRD demographic. WEIRD is an acronym introduced into the discourse in the context of psychological studies by Joseph Henrich meaning: Western, educated, industrialized, rich, and democratic (Henrich, Heine, and Norenzayan 2010; Henrich 2020). It describes the phenomenon that scientists in the context of behavioral science publish psychological findings with the claim of universal validity, whereby the underlying data are collected exclusively in WEIRD societies. Thus, the claim is made—often implicitly—that these WEIRD standard subjects are representative, when in fact the "findings suggest that members of WEIRD societies, including young children, are among the least representative populations one could find for generalizing about humans" (Henrich, Heine, and Norenzayan 2010, 2). To grasp the problem, the actual figures are important: in the period of the study, 96% of the psychological sample came from WEIRD societies, which represent only 12% of the world population (ibid., 5). In this chapter I examine the WEIRD demographic that informs design artifacts and ask about the consequences of biased consumer surveys in everyday objects.

Design (often) accompanies structural disadvantage: the objects that surround us do not function equally for all people—conscious or unconscious exclusion or discrimination with and through design is ubiquitous. These objects that surround us are often designed *by* privileged people *for* privileged people and therefore manifest or reinforce existing social and political power structures. Following Peggy McIntosh, white privilege is "like an invisible weightless knapsack of special provisions, maps, passports, codebooks, visas, clothes, tools and blank checks" (McIntosh 1989, 10). McIntosh emphasizes that the advantage of this knapsack is not only unearned but often not perceived at all. Privilege can be understood to mean that certain characteristics (for example being white, cis-gender, male, able-bodied, etc.) lead to a structural advantage. However, this is only part of the problem, because it is above all also the combination of characteristics that lead to an advantage—in other words, discriminatory characteristics can be intersectionally reinforced, and, besides reflecting on possible privileges, this very understanding of this intersectionality[1] (or the matrix of domination[2]) is also of major significance.

Perceiving such privilege in design may not always be obvious—*if you don't have to think about it it's a privilege.*[3] If you are structurally advantaged, the desk in the office always has the right height, the website dropdown menu has a selection for your gender, you never have to wait in line of the public

1 Intersectionality is a term coined by Kimberlé Crenshaw (1989), who, starting from a legal context, argued that discriminatory features such as gender, race, and class are not always isolated from each other, but can overlap and reinforce each other.

2 The Matrix of Domination, formulated by Patricia Hill Collins (1990), likewise describes the interconnection of various discriminatory characteristics.

3 This sentence appears again and again in discussions about privileges. Since I could not find out who first said it, I unfortunately cannot quote it correctly.

restroom, and the band-aid matches your skin tone. Privilege guarantees that design is tailored to the already favored social groups—and that "white supremacy, cisnormativity, heteropatriarchy, capitalism, and settler colonialism [is] hardcoded into designed objects and systems" (Costanza-Chock 2021, 347). Privilege shows itself not only in the ways in which objects are specifically designed to cater to a certain group but also in the ways in which they are meant to specifically alienate others.

Imagine a train station. The bench lets me sit comfortably while I wait for the train, but people looking for a warm and dry place to sleep at night can't lie down because the armrests are strategically placed to prevent that. Such deprivations, also called *hostile* design, have a large presence in public spaces— and often serve to evict the homeless.

The train arrives. With ease I climb the steps and get in the carriage. Since 1991, Germany has been using *ICE* high-speed trains. These are not barrier-free—several steps have to be climbed when boarding. In order to be able to use such a train with a wheelchair, you must register the trip in advance with Deutsche Bahn's mobility service. This trip can only take place between 6am and 10pm, and sometimes only between 8 a.m. and 8 p.m., so that railroad employees can use a lift truck to enable boarding (see WDR 2022). In 2016, the *ICE* 4 was first deployed on long-distance services—this has a vehicle-based boarding aid that can theoretically be operated by on-board staff, which should make travel easier at stations that are not permanently staffed. However, this boarding aid is difficult to use and offers no real improvement (see Endres 2019). It's easy to think that this must be because of some technical reason or that there is just no better way to do this, yet, low-floor cars that allow step-free and wheelchair-accessible boarding will actually be used starting in 2024 (see WDR 2022). But even in these trains, there will only be a few wheelchair spaces and only one accessible toilet. Incidentally, there will be no wheelchair spaces in first class,[4] revealing how discriminations works intersectionally and are informed by hidden biases that surface even in concessional gestures. To give another example: While ergonomic considerations have meant that desks are often height-adjustable, the podium in the lecture hall, almost exclusively, is not. To illustrate, let me refer to a prominent photograph: Queen Elizabeth, on her visit to the United States in 1991, disappearing behind the White House podium so that only her hat peeks out over the microphones. The podium, as Kathryn H. Anthony puts it, a "symbol of power and prestige, creates a gendered space that all too often disempowers women and diminishes their credibility" (Anthony 2018). Such a podium does not necessarily limit technical functionality—it is a disadvantage on a symbolic level. The list could be continued almost endlessly, but already these examples show three important levels of discrimination: the ignoring of needs and wishes, the exclusion of a use and the symbolic disadvantage or insulting.

---

4 So far, there is only one type of *ICE* that offers wheelchair seats in first class.

The Issue of Standardization

The disregard of diverse needs, conditions, and structural disadvantages of social groups is also a result of standardization processes that were introduced with the mass production of consumer goods. Take an interior of a car: Here, in particular, the *white average male body* as a basis for design decisions is problematic—after all, the measurements put drivers at risk, whose bodies do not conform. The way cars are designed it makes it more likely for a cis-male body to survive a car accident.[5]

But standardization processes have shaped not only individual consumer products but whole systems and environments. An early known example from design history that assumes an *average male body* is Le Corbusier's Modulor system. With the aim of adapting architecture to a human dimension (cf. Frank 2003, 228), Le Corbusier determined a scale model based on a 175-cm-tall person (see Le Corbusier 2013, 43) that could be used to calculate for example the height and size of surfaces in the house. In the discussion about the elegant conversion of proportions from the metric system to feet and inches, the value 175cm was increased to 182.88 cm (6 feet), not because this was an estimated average, but an ideal height as suggested by literature. The Modulor specifically references English detective novels that usually describe their protagonist constable as male, good-looking, and 6 feet tall (see ibid., 56). Apart from the fact that the alleged average height does not represent a real average value, the problem with scale models is evident: large sections of society—especially women—are not considered. Standardization models such as the Modulor are supposedly centering the human and thus claim to be able to increase the quality of human lives, yet, they primarily account for built environments that disregard the majority of potential residents.[6]

Under the keyword "gender data gap" feminist writer Caroline Criado-Perez (2020), addresses the problem of patriarchal standardization in her book *Invisible Women. Exposing Data Bias in a World Designed for Men.* She discusses how especially in the U.S. and Europe anthropometric standards[7] further contributed to the manifestation of privilege, firstly because they disregard the lived realities of the already marginalized, and secondly because they demarcate what is "normal" and what is "deficient" embodiment. But data can also lead to problems in a much more subtle way—especially in the context of algorithms there are countless examples of intersectional discrimination, particularly in the context of race or gender (cf. for example Buolamwini and Gebru 2018; Benjamin 2019; Noble 2018): For example, objects are limited in their functionality—such as some fitness watches that fail to measure heart rate of People of Color correctly, but also work less well for people with elevated body mass indices (see Ajmal et al. 2021). This is an example of how hard- and software perpetuate intersecting forms of discrimination. The very algorithms that learn from datasets map the privileges of our society that can be found in these datasets.[8] The elimination of privileges in design requires that data sets are chosen that are appropriate to the users' diversity. The problem is not the data itself. The problem is its poor composition: Discrimination is based on unbalanced, incomplete, or WEIRD data and its lack of control.

---

5 For a summary, see Caroline Criado-Perez (2020, 252–260).

6 Le Corbusier's work has also been analyzed elsewhere with regard to sexism, exoticism, etc. (Frank 2003, 229–231). The brief paragraph on architecture also allows for a cross-reference to urban design, which often perpetuates unbalanced, gendered power relations (cf. Kern 2020).

7 See also, for example, Henry Dreyfuss' publication *The Measure of Man* (1960) (later: *The Measure of Man and Woman*) in which anthropometric standard values are mapped—and it is necessary to discuss whether this and subsequent works of this kind are sufficient, for example, in relation to gender, age, or ability.

8 In a few words: Image recognition algorithms, for example, can be trained on image datasets. If an algorithm has seen 1000 images of a cat, it can presumably recognize a cat, although it is usually not transparent how it recognizes the cat. With a cat, this is relatively unproblematic—with humans, however, it can contribute to an algorithm acting through the data in a racist or sexist way, for example. For example, if a dataset shows only white males in a certain subsection, then an algorithm is very likely to identify a Black woman as not belonging. To explain this with a simple example: If an algorithm is trained with images of doctors, then that algorithm will most likely see white men wearing white coats because the image datasets reflect the injustices of the world. Accordingly, it will most likely not recognize a Black woman as a doctor. This is a very truncated representation—the reality of algorithms is much more complex—but training data for algorithms is a major problem.

Marginalized people in design are also not adequately represented in decision-making structures: Designers often simply reproduce their view of the world—and the lack of reflection leads to a perception of one's own characteristics as neutral and one's own privileges as non-existent. This results in an image of a possible user—often

> "…raced, classed, and gendered within a worldview produced by the matrix of domination and internalized, then reproduced, by design teams. Designers most frequently assume that the unmarked user has access to a number of very powerful privileges, such as U.S. citizenship, English language proficiency, access to broadband internet, a smartphone, no disabilities, and so on. … Even with diverse design teams, the types and scope of "problem" addressed by most product design ends up limited to this tiny, but potentially highly profitable, subset of humanity." (Costanza-Chock 2021, 345–346)

So, especially when standardized solutions are developed, the focus is on a global minority that is overrepresented in the underlying data. What's more, the mechanisms of standardization in design don't just marginalize bodies, but also cultural practices via the establishment of normative, "cultivated" taste. The idea of modernist aesthetics produces global hierarchies and is racist at its core (see Recklies 2021, 107–109; Tlostanova 2017). Famous representatives of European architectural history, of *late colonial modernism* (see Göckede 2016), not only exported their design visions across cultural borders, they also—quite self-affirmatively—openly advocated a sense of cultural leadership. The architect and urban planner Ernst May, for example, not only disseminated his design ideas in the form of several buildings and plans in East African countries and thus influenced a transformation of the local architectural landscape (see Göckede 2016, 170–178; Sharp 1983)—he hoped, by the way, to create a new society and culture (see Gutschow 2012, 240)—, he also gave several lectures in which he self-evidently named a civilizational claim to leadership by Europe. In his work he shows, as Regina Göckede puts it, a colonial-racist attitude (see Göckede 2016, 226–235). Thus it is not surprising that his projects are partly characterized by racist segregation (see ibid., 146).[9]

The assertion of supposed Western supremacy is also evident in linguistic details—for example, the notion and subsequent formulation that a style could be "international," as implied by the designation of one of the most important architectural movements of the last century,[10] is problematic because it falsely presupposes that Eurocentrically formulated design qualities function in the same way across cultural boundaries (see Buzon 2020). In fact, the exhibition *Modern Architecture: International Exhibition,* presented in 1932 at New York's Museum of Modern Art, which serves as the basis of the concept of International Style, featured only works by white men from a few European countries and the United States.[11] This understanding of design and culture stems from the Eurocentric mindset of design modernism—and the habitus of its representatives, since well-known protagonists can be assumed to have a great lack of understanding of *different* cultures. Thus, apart from specific formulations, a "universal" understanding of design was established: "Colonialism, followed by imperialism, spread and installed Eurocentric epistemologies,

---

9 As Mara Recklies points out, however, the construction of style and taste also involves discrimination in the context of class (cf. Recklies 2021, 109–110)—in order not to go beyond the scope of the text, I will not go into this further.

10 Important is, of course, an imprecise term here—because the International Style was, of course, "important" only from a Eurocentric point of view.

11 Alfred Hamilton Barr Jr., founding director of the Museum of Modern Art, attests in the preface to the exhibition's publication to the four "founders of the International Style" (Walter Gropuis, Le Corbusier, Jacobus Johannes Pieter Oud, and Ludwig Mies van der Rohe) that their works had no "national characteristics"—from this, too, a kind of international validity of the style is inferred, although this is already difficult to argue geographically (Barr Jr. 1932, 16).

ontologies, and aesthetics over centuries by claiming them to be 'universal,' and this power has by no means disappeared" (Mareis and Paim 2021, 16). To this day, Western styles, generally speaking, are accepted as the global standard (see Recklies 2021, 111) and design is "still broadly regarded as something that belongs 'naturally' to the Global North" (Mareis and Paim 2021, 17)—WEIRD structures thus also play a role in the reception of design.

The Failure of Processes

Discrimination through imposed standards, exclusion through non-functional products—these are problem areas that, one would think, could be detected in the design process and reduced through a systematic engagement with potential users. Yet, we find that behind standardized products are standardized processes that are riddled with loopholes for bias to „ignore, bracket, or sideline questions of structural, historical, institutional, and/or systemic inequality" (Costanza-Chock 2020, 122). Since mid 20th century so-called human-centered design processes often start with an analysis of possible problems and focus on the needs of the users in order to guarantee functionality and strengthen the user experience. The word "human" should cause us to become skeptical: Who is the human whose supposed interests are at the center of such processes? Is there a way of designing that actually works for *everyone*?[12] Already the definition of interests causes ambiguity, because design decisions need to be justifiable and are based on potential profitability, which means that "most resources are dedicated to design problems that affect the wealthiest groups of people" (Costanza-Chock 2021, 347).

In what follows, I will outline why I think established design processes produce or manifest privilege. Generally speaking, they are characterized by a fundamental way of thinking that can be problematic, since the basic idea that design can solve problems—including the so-called wicked problems (cf. for example Rittel and Webber 1973; Buchanan 1992; Simon 1996)— is not wrong, but often leads to ignoring in real processes that this creates new problems. Focusing on problems created by purported solutions can help identify potential injustices that design can produce or reproduce. An example that can be used to explain this way of thinking can be found in the context of the Covid19 pandemic: In Germany, a privately developed Covid contact-tracking app was deployed in several regions, and its use was mandatory for participation in some events and even eating out. This app, *Luca,* has certainly solved one problem—contact tracing—but created a new one in the process, as it was simply not barrier-free at first (cf. Blinden- und Sehbehindertenverband Niedersachsen e.V. 2021) and thus excluded individuals from participating in events. The solution to the problem of contact tracing was applied for a majority while completely excluding a minority from the very possibility of returning to so-called "normal life," which is ethically unacceptable and demands change. Many solutions to supposed problems—if the processes are not designed in a diversity-sensitive way—often only work for a privileged target group, because this way of thinking is also not free of supposed averages and standards.

In light of the fact that design processes—especially in the context of so-called human-centered design—generally proclaim that the interests and needs of users are the focus, such an exclusionary design is troublesome.

12 Based on a publication by architect and designer Ron Mace (1985), seven rules—the principles of *Universal Design*—were formulated at the Center for Universal Design (1997, cf. Mitrasinovic 2008)—attempting to lay the groundwork for design that works for all possible users, with an emphasis on cognitive and physical abilities. Other names for similar approaches include *Design for Accessibility, Inclusive Design, Design for all,* and *Transgenerational Design* (cf. Mitrasinovic 2008). It can be criticized that these approaches are often quite vague in their statements. The normative attitude and the lack of understanding of intersectionality can also be questioned.

13 Incidentally, a connection can also be drawn here to the debate on the decolonization of design: Elisabeth (Dori) Tunstall has used the example of the Design for Social Impact Initiative (IDEO and Rockefeller Foundation) to explain how Western design processes and ways of thinking are framed as superior—and how, with the spread of design thinking and other nonnative principles, Indigenous forms of thinking are being overridden. She argues that the spread of such processes (using the example of the aforementioned initiative) are "another form of cultural imperialism that destabilizes and undermines indigenous approaches coming out of other traditions" (Tunstall 2013, 237).

14 There is a famous television report from the 1990s in which the IDEO design team is accompanied in the conception of a shopping cart. Divided into teams, interviews are conducted in supermarkets—with customers, sales assistants and those who push the carts together in the parking lots. Even though the research—as conveyed by the TV report—provides many important clues and the results are certainly impressive, the problem is: If such an undefined research does not happen to meet a marginalized person, then their needs are naturally not represented.

Processes such as design thinking, also due to clever marketing, achieved great attention beyond the design industry as well—ascribed a "superior epistemology", as Maggie Gram (2019) phrases it, although such processes are in reality rather oversimplified and merit more criticism.[13] For example, the design thinking process of the Institute of Design at Stanford formulates that one should "empathize," i.e. observe and communicate with people (Hasso Platner Institute of Design at Stanford n.d.), in order to produce sensible artifacts. while other design thinking processes refer to "observe" or "discover" instead of "empathize" (cf. Waidelich et al. 2018)—without defining exactly what that actually means (and without addressing that empathy tends to be subjective). Following Adrian Daub, such employments of empathy account for minimal observation of other people's behavior, and he concludes this can be described as a non-empathic person's conception of empathy (see Daub 2021, 143). Ethnographer Tim Seitz, who has investigated design thinking processes in field research, describes the vagueness of the concept of empathy as just imprecise enough to distract from methodological inconsistencies (see Seitz 2017, 55).

He concludes that empathy or observation are not methods, but rather vague ideas about engaging users that lead to inadequate, insufficient, and biased data sets.[14] Design thinking processes that rely on such ways of conducting research, as Sasha Costanza-Chock articulates, "erase certain groups of people: specifically, those who are intersectionally disadvantaged (or multiply burdened) under white supremacist heteropatriarchy, capitalism, and settler colonialism" (Costanza-Chock 2021, 337). In other words: design thinking is a fancy term for bad user research.

Problem-Causing Design

Rather than saying that design solves problems, I have argued that design is a problem-causing activity. Through standardized, vague, and methodologically flawed processes that systemically favor a WEIRD demographic and inform the production of artifacts that are optimized for this demographic, design contributes to the perpetuation of social inequalities.

Instead of following oversimplified processes, designers need to reckon with their own biases and positionality within social and cultural systems. The Design Justice Network, for example, has formulated principles such as "We center the voices of those who are directly impacted by the outcomes of the design process"[15] (Design Justice Network 2018), in order to account for the larger structures of oppression that design is embedded in. Yet, representation and inclusivity are only first steps towards making design (as a profession, as sets of objects, and ways of conducting research) more just and equitable.

BIBLIOGRAPHY

Ajmal, Tananant Boonya-Ananta, Andres J. Rodriguez, V. N. Du Le, and Jessica C. Ramella-Roman. "Monte Carlo Analysis of Optical Heart Rate Sensors in Commercial Wearables: The Effect of Skin Tone and Obesity on the Photoplethysmography (PPG) Signal." *Biomedical Optics Express* 12 (12) (2021): 7445. https://doi.org/10.1364/BOE.439893.

Anthony, Kathryn H. "Built-in Bias: Hidden Power and Privilege in Design." *The Architectual Review* (March 2018). https://www.architectural-review.com/essays/built-in-bias-hidden-power-and-privilege-in-design.

Barr Jr., Alfred H. "Foreword." In *Modern Architecture: International Exhibition, New York, Feb. 10 to March 23, 1932, Museum of Modern Art*, edited by Alfred H. Barr Jr., Henry-Russel Hitchcock, Philip Johnson, and Lewis Mumford, 12–17. New York City: The Museum of Modern Art, 1932. https://www.moma.org/documents/moma_catalogue_2044_300061855.pdf?_ga=2.60370093.1049633477.1661862040-261690467.1661862040.

Benjamin, Ruha. *Race after Technology: Abolitionist Tools for the New Jim Code*. Medford, MA: Polity, 2019.

Blinden- und Sehbehindertenverband Niedersachsen e.V. 2021. "Trauriges Bild bei der digitalen Barrierefreiheit." Last modified June 16, 2021. https://www.blindenverband.org/meldung/trauriges-bild-bei-der-digitalen-barrierefreiheit.html.

Buchanan, Richard. "Wicked Problems in Design Thinking." Design Issues, vol. 8, no. 2 (1992): 5–21.

Buolamwini, Joy, and Timnit Gebru. "Gender Shades: Intersectional Accuracy Disparities in Commercial Gender Classification." In *Proceedings of the 1st Conference on Fairness, Accountability and Transparency*, edited by Sorelle A. Friedler and Christo Wilson,

Proceedings of Machine Learning Research, PMLR 81 (2018): 77–91. https://proceedings.mlr.press/v81/buolamwini18a.html.

Buzon, Darin. 2020. "Design Thinking is a Rebrand for White Supremacy." *Medium* (blog). Last modified March 2, 2020. https://dabuzon.medium.com/design-thinking-is-a-rebrand-for-white-supremacy-b3d31aa55831.

Costanza-Chock, Sasha. "Design Justice. Towards an Intersectional Feminist Framework for Design Theory and Practice." In *Design Struggles: Intersecting Histories, Pedagogies, and Perspectives*, edited by Claudia Mareis and Nina Paim, 33–53. PLURAL 3. Amsterdam: Valiz, 2021. https://www.valiz.nl/images/DesignStruggles-DEF_978-94-92095-88-6single-28September22-VALIZ-def.pdf.

———. *Design Justice: Community-Led Practices to Build the Worlds We Need*. MIT Press, 2020.

Crenshaw, Kimberle. "Demarginalizing the Intersection of Race and Sex: A Black Feminist Critique of Antidiscrimination Doctrine, Feminist Theory and Antiracist Policies." *University of Chicago Legal Forum* (1) (1989): 139–67.

Criado-Perez, Caroline. *Unsichtbare Frauen: Wie eine von Daten beherrschte Welt die Hälfte der Bevölkerung ignoriert*. Translated by Stephanie Singh. Deutsche Erstausgabe. btb 71887. München: btb, 2020.

Daub, Adrian. *Was das Valley denken nennt: Über die Ideologie der Techbranche*. Translated by Stephan Gebauer. 2. Auflage. edition suhrkamp 2750. Berlin: Suhrkamp, 2021.

Design Justice Network. 2018. "Design Justice Network Principles." *Design Justice Network* (blog). Last modified summer 2018. https://designjustice.org/read-the-principles.

Dreyfuss, Henry. *The Measure of Man: Human Factors in Design*. New York City: Whitney Library of Design, 1960.

Endres, Bernhard. 2019. "Achillesferse: Fahrzeuggebundener Lift im ICE4." Last modified November 22, 2019. https://www.barrierefrei-unterwegs.de/achillesferse-fahrzeuggebundener-lift-im-ice-4/.

Frank, Susanne. *Stadtplanung im Geschlechterkampf: Stadt und Geschlecht in der Großstadtentwicklung des 19. und 20. Jahrhunderts*. Stadt, Raum und Gesellschaft, Bd. 20. Opladen: Leske + Budrich, 2003.

Göckede, Regina. *Spätkoloniale Moderne: Le Corbusier, Ernst May, Frank Lloyd Wright, The Architects Collaborative und die Globalisierung der Architekturmoderne*. Basel: Birkhäuser, 2016.

Gram, Maggie. 2019. "On Design Thinking." *N+1 Savior Complex* (35) (Fall 2019). https://www.nplusonemag.com/issue-35/reviews/on-design-thinking/.

Gutschow, Kai K. "Das Neue Afrika: Ernst May's 1947 Kampala Plan as Cultural Program." In *Colonial Architecture and Urbanism in Africa: Intertwined and Contested Histories*, edited by Fassil Demissie, 236–68. Design and the Built Environment. Farnham, Surrey, England ; Burlington, VT: Ashgate, 2012.

Hasso Platner Institute of Design at Stanford. n.d. "An Introduction to Design Thinking." Accessed August 16, 2022. https://web.stanford.edu/~mshanks/MichaelShanks/files/509554.pdf.

Henrich, Joseph. *The WEIRDest People in the World: How the West Became Psychologically Peculiar and Particularly Prosperous*. New York: Farrar, Straus and Giroux, 2020.

Henrich, Joseph, Steven J. Heine, and Ara Norenzayan. 2010. "The Weirdest People in the World?" *Behavioral and Brain Sciences* 33 (2–3) (2010): 61–83. https://doi.org/10.1017/S0140525X0999152X.

Hill Collins, Patricia. *Black Feminist Thought : Knowledge, Consciousness, and the Politics of Empowerment*. Boston: Unwin Hyman, 1990. https://search.library.wisc.edu/catalog/999621346002121.

Kern, Leslie. *Feminist City*. London; New York: Verso, 2020.

Le Corbusier. *Der Modulor. 1: Darstellung eines in Architektur und Technik allgemein anwendbaren harmonischen Maszes im menschlichen Maszstab*. 10. Aufl. (Faksimile-Wiedergabe der 2. Aufl. 1956). München: Dt. Verl.-Anst., 2013.

Mace, Ron. "Universal Design, Barrier-Free Environments for Everyone." *Designers West*, no. 33 (1) (1985): 147–52.

Mareis, Claudia, and Nina Paim. "Design Struggles. An Attempt to Imagine Design Otherwise." In *Design Struggles: Intersecting Histories, Pedagogies, and Perspectives*, edited by Claudia Mareis and Nina Paim, 11–22. PLURAL 3. Amsterdam: Valiz, 2021.

---

15 The other principles are: We use design to sustain, heal, and empower our communities, as well as to seek liberation from exploitative and oppressive systems. / We prioritize design's impact on the community over the intentions of the designer. / We view change as emergent from an accountable, accessible, and collaborative process, rather than as a point at the end of a process. (This principle was inspired by and adapted from https://www.alliedmedia.org/about/network-principles) / We see the role of the designer as a facilitator rather than an expert. / We believe that everyone is an expert based on their own lived experience, and that we all have unique and brilliant contributions to bring to a design process. / We share design knowledge and tools with our communities. / We work towards sustainable, community-led and -controlled outcomes. / We work towards non-exploitative solutions that reconnect us to the earth and to each other. / Before seeking new design solutions, we look for what is already working at the community level. We honor and uplift traditional, indigenous, and local knowledge and practices. (Design Justice Network 2018)

McIntosh, Peggy. "White Privilege: Unpacking the Invisible Knapsack." *Peace and Freedom* (August 1989); 10–12.

Mitrasinovic, Miodrag. "Universal Design." In *Wörterbuch Design: Begriffliche Perspektiven des Design*, edited by Michael Erlhoff and Tim Marshall, 418–21. Basel; Berlin: Birkhäuser, 2008.

Noble, Safiya Umoja. *Algorithms of Oppression: How Search Engines Reinforce Racism*. New York: New York University Press, 2018.

Recklies, Mara. "Kriterien für gutes Design, die den Schaden maximieren. Überlegungen zur Kriteriologie des Designs." In *Wie können wir den Schaden maximieren? Gestaltung trotz Komplexität: Beiträge zu einem Public Interest Design*, edited by Christoph Rodatz and Pierre Smolarski, 99–123. Public Interest Design, Band 2. Bielefeld: Transcript, 2021.

Rittel, Horst W. J., and Melvin M. Webber. "Dilemmas in a General Theory of Planning." *Policy Sciences* 4 (2) (1973): 155–69. https://doi.org/10.1007/BF01405730.

Seitz, Tim. *Design Thinking und der neue Geist des Kapitalismus: Soziologische Betrachtungen einer Innovationskultur*. Kulturen der Gesellschaft, Band 29. Bielefeld: Transcript, 2017.

Sharp, Dennis. "The Modern Movement in East Africa." *Habitat International* 7 (5–6) (1983): 311–26. https://doi.org/10.1016/0197-3975(83)90079-6.

Simon, Herbert Alexander. *The Sciences of the Artificial*. Cambridge, Mass.: MIT Press, 1996.

Tlostanova, Madina. "On Decolonizing Design." *Design Philosophy Papers* 15 (1) (2017): 51–61. https://doi.org/10.1080/14487136.2017.1301017.

Tunstall, Elisabeth (Dori). "Decolonizing Design Innovation: Design Anthropology, Critical Anthropology, and Indigenous Knowledge." In *Design Anthropology: Theory and Practice*, edited by Wendy Gunn, Ton Otto, and Rachel Charlotte Smith, 232–50. London; New York: Bloomsbury, 2013.

Waidelich, Lukas, Alexander Richter, Bernhard Kolmel, and Rebecca Bulander. "Design Thinking Process Model Review. A Systematic Literature Review of Current Design Thinking Models in Practice." In *2018 IEEE International Conference on Engineering, Technology and Innovation* (ICE/ITMC), 1–9. Stuttgart: IEEE, 2018. https://doi.org/10.1109/ICE.2018.8436281.

WDR. 2022. "Neuer ICE L: Kann die Bahn auch barrierefrei?" *WDR*. Last modified September 15, 2022. https://www1.wdr.de/nachrichten/bahn-ice-rollstuhl-behinderung-barrierefreiheit-100.html.

CHANGING THE HOW

First Steps Towards Critical Design Pedagogy

(Mira Schmitz)

This workshop documentation mobilizes critical pedagogy to reflect on a workshop I held at the *Attending [to] Futures* conference that examined discriminatory messages in advertising in order to encourage self-reflexivity in a potential future workspace setting.[1] Drawing on the works of bell hooks and Paulo Freire[2] my aim is to question not only *what* we teach graphic design students but also *how* we teach (see hooks 194, 29–30). Understanding that "the educator needs educating"[3] (Freire 2017, 27) and that education "as [a] practice of freedom is not just about liberatory knowledge, [but] about a liberatory practice" (hooks, 147) is crucial for creating more equitable, critical, and ethical classrooms.

Titled "Design: An Intersectional Entanglement – Redesigning Difference" the workshop's overall assignment was to analyze advertising with regard to its discriminatory content, using a variety of communication design parameters[4] to find out what exactly is *problematic, ambivalent,* or *positive* about them, and why. We focused on an advertising poster[5] for a retirement provision from a German bank.[6] In the next workshop phase, we created counter-designs, trying to flip the discriminatory message.

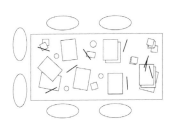

The 13 participants formed two groups and analyzed the given poster. After writing notes on the problematic, ambivalent, and positive aspects of the poster, and silently reading those of the others, the groups dissolved and reviewed all critiques in a common plenum. The aim was not to reach a consensus but to discuss and acknowledge diverging perspectives, understanding that there are different viewpoints that should be respected and that earlier

---

1. The above mentioned advertising functions as an instructive example, since the workshop's learnings can be transferred and adapted to other graphic design fields.

2. Both hooks and Freire were critical scholars in educational science. bell hooks (1952-2021) was a revolutionary Black author and social activist from the U.S., being mostly known for her intersectional work on race, feminism, and class struggles. Her first major work was *Ain't I a Woman? Black Women and Feminism* (1981), the title referring to the "Ain't I a Woman?" speech (1851) by Sojourner Truth. In her writings on education, she draws upon Freire's work, valuing and also criticizing his thoughts. Paulo Freire (1921-1997) was an educational theorist from Brazil who leaned on the works of Hegel, Marx, and anti-colonial thinkers. He "promoted the liberation of the working classes through a cooperative teacher-student educative model" (Freire 2017, 1).

3. Originally "himself" but I find it important to include every gender.

4. Pictures/illustration/graphic style, colors, room/space, element position/layout, messages, wording, context, typography/fonts, and effects

5. I chose this poster, because in an earlier similar workshop many groups decided independently from each other to tackle this one out of a multitude of posters. Initially, I had planned to include two additional posters with other intersections, one also being a refugee campaign. Nevertheless, the workshop showed that engaging with one poster was enough for the limited amount of time we had.

6. Attendee of the *Creative Representation of Difference* workshop, advertising for a retirement provision, Konstanz, 2021.

Fig 1: Workshop setting.

Fig 2: White board with parameters and post-its.

7 Poster description: The poster is vertically split into two parts. The upper part shows a skeptical-looking woman to the left, wearing casual clothes and having her arms crossed in front of her and to her right an older man, dressed in expensive clothes that is leaning over to her side, partly blocking her from the viewer's gaze. He is forming his lips for a kiss and reaching his hand with a diamond engagement ring towards her face. The header on the center of the page says: "We have the more attractive retirement provision for you!" The lower part is horizontally divided in two parts. To the left, beneath the woman is a white background with the bank's red logo turned into a high heel. To the right, beneath the man is a red background with a white text saying: "Quality pays off: The SV retirement provision. Stay flexible and independent." On the very bottom there is the website and logo of the bank's insurance.

Fig. 3. Counter-designs

8 Even though the ad gives the impression of wanting to change things, it leaves an odd message, since it suggests that this scenario (young woman marrying an old man for money) is the norm and the only other option for women to have a stable financial situation is to get the bank's retirement provision. It has a paternalistic tone and doesn't show the possibility of successful women or addresses systemic issues like the glass ceiling or gender pay gap, thus misplacing the fault on women, instead of engaging in an institutional critique.

9 *Womxn* is a term to include not only cis-gender women, but also trans women, non-binary people and every other gender identity which is not strictly male.

reflections can change due to constructive questioning and exchange. In a second step, the groups created drafts for a new poster, trying to rewrite the narratives they had identified as problematic. They could organize themselves, and everyone had the freedom to use their preferred method of creation: drawing, writing, mapping, etc. In the last phase of the workshop, participants reflected in a plenum again on their redesigns and the workshop itself.

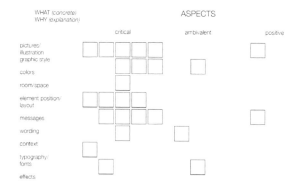

Looking for discriminatory content, the attendees detected several sexist messages in the poster[7] such as: *women wait passively until a man chases them, can't be independent, buy only shoes, are heterosexual by norm, choose their partner based on money.* Additionally, young women are reduced to their beauty whereas older men to their bank account.[8]

In their counter-design, one group showed old people of different genders having the possibility of a full fridge and time to relax, etc. in order not to work with inducing fear, but with visions of a better retirement future. Another group saw a chance to educate people and address issues like the gender pay gap, which is a structural problem. Some had the idea to show differently looking womxn[9] doing various jobs—being careful not to fall for racist and classist stereotypes. Others chose to omit pictures and work just with typography.

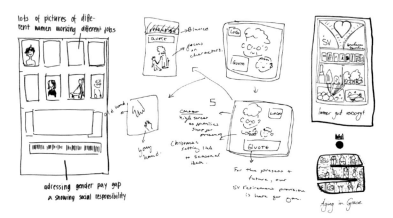

After having given a workshop overview and insight into attendees' thoughts, I would like to reflect on the workshop planning and implementation. The analogue form brought some advantages: scribbling roughly on paper instead of working digitally helped to put more focus on the concept, because no one lapsed into graphical details. Furthermore, the bodily presence of people created a certain closeness in a short time. My goal was to facilitate a communal atmosphere of trust and create a safer space that would enable participants to discuss sensitive subjects, while attending to a plurality of perspectives. This involved a careful preparation of the workshop setting and materials, taking into account the diverse[10] levels of experience and cultural backgrounds of the participants. Since most of the time not everything works out as smoothly as it does in theory[11] it can be useful to write down expectations and check the plan while being flexible with regard to timing and attending to the situation as it unfolds. Documenting everything[12] is crucial to evaluate and improve the workshop. It should be considered in advance that it can be harder to register and archive analog or verbal processes.

When noting that groups have diverging workflows, temporalities, and levels of experience, it becomes crucial to reflect upon the balance between guidance and liberty, so that no one feels patronized or lost.[13] Conducting the workshop, I made clear that I was not exempt from mistakes and open to criticism. A liberating pedagogy such as conceived by Paulo Freire, requires being aware of possible power imbalances in the room and trying not to impose your vision on the attendees but to value their reasoning and collective findings. Seeing myself as a facilitator rather than an all-knowing teacher, my aim was to work *with* participants, as they become "critical co-investigators" (Freire, 53–54). Facilitators are also taught by participants and attend to the mutual influence of both their reflections (ibid.). If we embrace that our ways of being and knowing are shaped by history and power relations, we understand that "no education is politically neutral" and that critical pedagogists conceive the classroom as a space "where we're all in power in different ways" (hooks, 30, 39, 152). Situating ourselves and others in an intersectional[14] way, seeing them as whole human beings without reducing them to their social position nor dismissing it, can be one method to respond to these specific and historic relations.

10 E.g., by asking the attendees to write down their names and pronouns if they feel comfortable with it, so that everyone can be addressed in an adequate manner.

11 There might be a long discussion, lots of intro-/extroverts or people with different levels of experience, etc.

12 Naturally, this implies that the permission is given by the attendees and that they know how this information might be used. Furthermore, I had planned for the attendees to write down feedback, but being busy dialoguing and writing, they did not, and the verbal one at the end was not recorded. This represented an important learning for me because there are e.g., various tools for digital workshops which facilitate documentation, but for the analogue one I hadn't planned this well enough.

13 In general, this relates to how much room and time pedagogists occupy, regarding the support or input they give. In specific, it can relate to communication: questions, for instance, should provoke reflections, without being too suggestive.

14 *Intersectional* refers to intersectionality—a term coined by Kimberlé Crenshaw—which is a lived reality, as well as a framework to analyze and account for intersecting forms of discrimination or power relations regarding race, gender, class, age, ability, etc., thus not treating these categories separately or additively, but perceiving their interrelations.

Fig. 4. Workshop Impressions

15 Using attendees' respective names and pronouns in interactions with them is also a way of hearing and seeing each other.

16 It's no shame for pedagogists to admit that they slipped some difficult words, yet they should try to minimize this risk and generate an atmosphere of trust that empowers the students to ask. This way, attendees will see that one values their questions and tries to learn from the situation, talking again at eye level.

17 In addition to letting the participants use their preferred methods of creation, I also asked them how much time they needed and made sure that we moved to the next phase if they wanted to or took more time for one task if they preferred it. They could always give me feedback during the workshop and didn't have to wait until the end, if it was urgent.

18 To deconstruct means to show the construction of something, and in this context it is related to exposing the discriminating messages that are embedded in the posters' design.

19 This was an attendee's important critique which generated a fruitful exchange.

20 Additionally, many public campaigns for good causes struggle with the same or similar underlying discriminatory messages. So if students learn to detect biases in posters which are perpetuated by graphic design principles, they can be more careful not to adopt these in their own work, no matter if they're engaging in activist campaigns, advertising or any other field related to graphic design.

21 Across disciplines, cultures, genders, etc.

Following bell hooks, the objective of an engaging pedagogy should be to "teach students *how to listen, how to hear one another*" (ibid., 149) and to act exemplarly of how to listen seriously[15] (see ibid., 150). This also helps to address people in a more appropriate way. In a similar way, Freire criticizes educators who do not adjust their language to those of the attendees (see 69). Striving to speak in simple terms, sometimes, facilitators still have to explain a few words upon request.[16] To attune to the attendees not only in terms of language, it is useful to think of what they could be afraid of to reduce their fears from the start. Furthermore, pedagogists should try to imagine what participants could be wishing for and include these ideas while leaving enough room for everyone's voice.[17]

The workshop was intended to critically engage with the problematic aspects of advertising in public space which shapes the communication landscapes we inhabit. Attendees conversationally combined their disciplinary knowledge and personal experience to deconstruct[18] the poster and flip the script of communication design principles. I'm aware that these counter-designs are still designs helping to sell products[19], but not every design student has the luxury to do purely non-commercial work.[20] A critical examination of the underlying messages that constantly surround us, enabled us to expose the ways in which normative gender roles, racial stereotypes, or classist assumptions are deeply embedded in and perpetuated by the designs that define public spaces.

Combining academic approaches with everyday experiences, we critically engaged with the ways in which advertising shapes our understanding of the world (see hooks, 15). Many students noted that they had walked by public ads before without perceiving their normative and discriminatory implications. The dominant narrative becomes invisible due to its omnipresence in the way that it masks itself as *normal* and therefore *legitimate*. It gets internalized and disseminated, if there's no point of rupture, a moment of pause in which the message is analyzed and actively opposed with counter-designs. Drawing on critical pedagogy scholarship that not only challenges the *content* of (design) education but also re-thinks and transforms educational structures (see Freire, 47), teachers can enable students to detect biases in their own practices and can additionally learn from the students' findings and exchange.

Questioning established ways of knowing and teaching is a dialogical and collaborative effort. It is not a theorizing of and in an abstract space, but rather an aspiration "for the *emergence* of consciousness and *critical intervention* in reality" (ibid., 54). Equal exchange is crucial for student-teacher relationships, but also for the dialogue between critical pedagogists for further development and dissemination of alternative pedagogies. Educators who want to change established practices need to collaborate in a boundary-crossing[21] way and discuss their visions (see hooks, 15, 130). This is why it is pivotal to create platforms and publications where different perspectives can occupy room and be archived for posterity: to un-learn, re-learn, and envision. Following Freire, education is an "ongoing activity" and constantly remade in the praxis. In order to be, it must become" (57). In fact, its fluid, dialogical nature is its source of power.

BIBLIOGRAPHY

Freire, Paulo. *Pedagogy of the Oppressed.* Penguin Classics, 2017. Originally published in 1970.

hooks, bell. *Teaching to Transgress. Education as the Practice of Freedom.* Routledge, 1994.

IMAGES AND ILLUSTRATIONS

Figure 1: Mira Schmitz, workshop setting, Konstanz, 2022.

Figure 2: Mira Schmitz, white board with parameters and post-its, Konstanz, 2022.

Figure 3: Mira Schmitz, counter designs, Köln, 2021.

Figure 4: Courtesy of *Attending [to] Futures,* workshop impressions, Köln, 2021.

AN OPTICAL DECOY FOR THE MACHINE

Automatic Policing of Trademarks Online

(Chris Hamamoto) (Federico Pérez Villoro)

We waited until midnight to walk to the market. The address was not marked on our VPN-powered Google Maps, but the receptionists of our hotel told us how to get there. The reason for our visit to Putian was not surprising to them. The city's reputation as a counterfeit shoe capital is an open secret and the Anfu market was an obvious destination for travelers interested in it.

    The market expands a few blocks as a network of storefronts distributed within narrow streets lit up only by the LED signage that distinguishes vendors, in many cases with names and logos recognizable as knockoffs of Western brands. Some businesses are more established and rely on glossy displays to promote their latest products. Others are informal and feel more like storage rooms with hundreds of shoe boxes piled up and no clear way to sort through them. It is a hectic environment, only intensified by riders of electric scooters moving quickly through the streets looking for better deals. Anfu is not a shopping center for consumers, but rather a source of supply for third party vendors. Nothing is labeled with prices or sold on site.

    A few vendors asked for our WeChat ID, and for the remainder of our time in China we were sent promotions for wholesale shoes. But we weren't looking to purchase as much as we wanted to understand the images that had taken us there in the first place. Months before we got to China, we noticed online product shots advertising replica shoes with their logos digitally modified. The alterations were subtle enough to not confuse customers looking for specific models, yet the logos were just different enough to trick machines: The images were modified to avoid being detected by software policing the web for counterfeits. So, there we were, texting with strangers 450 miles away from our studio in Shenzhen trying to get access to the bootlegging industry in order

Fig. 1. DHgate product photo, digitally altered product shot of a Nike Vapormax with a modification to the swoosh logo.

to explore the technical limits of images—their encoded properties that enable their tracking and prevent them from freely circulating online. As machines capable of segmenting contents within images are developed, the material nature of digital images evolves from being passive objects of representation to components of procedural operations.

In the 1980s and '90s, Putian was an official manufacturing hub for foreign shoe brands such as Nike, Adidas, and Puma. Previously, these companies' factories were concentrated in Taiwan, but after the production costs there—particularly workers' wages—rose beyond what companies were willing to pay, Putian's close proximity to Taiwan and lower cost of living made it an attractive site to relocate in order to boost profits. But as costs of living there increased along with the minimum wage, the shoe brands again relocated their manufacturing—this time to Vietnam, Cambodia, and India.

Unlike most post-industrial cities, however, when big brands decided to leave, workers in Putian were able to maintain their shoe industry by pivoting towards replica production. The know-how was there and the production infrastructure was locally preserved. Sometimes replica shoes are constructed with the same machines and in the same factories as those that were used to make "authentic" shoes years before. They are often sold explicitly as replicas—at times even under the premise of being "technically improved"—and typically at the same retail prices as their "legitimate" references, which sell out quickly and demand an inflated price on the resell market.

Anfu opens only at night and operates as showrooms with transactions to be conducted online. After the 2021 amendment to the Criminal Law of the People's Republic of China, producing counterfeits and infringing on trademarks can be sanctioned with up to ten years imprisonment. However, it isn't a "black market" per se, since authorities are well aware of it—rather the coordination among buyers and sellers is orchestrated within enough layers of opaqueness that it allows them to avoid being shut down. Considering that it was indeed the production of shoes that boosted Putian's economy years ago, regulating it for the benefit of Western companies is understandably not in the local interest.

Although the replica industry increasingly runs the risk of government seizures, as private prosecutions filed by trademark owners build pressure, generations of shoemakers sustain an important part of the city's economy. The International Consumers Union estimates that factory costs for popular shoes compose only 2% of gross profit made on sales, with only 0.4% of the total gross profit going to workers' wages. In the replica shoe market, the factory's share of the profit is far greater—up to 36% (see China Sourcing Agent 2020). With those numbers in mind, it is not hard to imagine why companies protect their logos aggressively as their brand becomes their primary resource to manufacture "value" through marketing, design, and new technologies. With increasingly distributed manufacturing processes, Western companies have to develop acute monitoring processes to secure control over their branding features.

Image property

Logos are images with a high recognition value. As a legacy of the heraldry system during the High Middle Ages, these symbols communicate the provenance of services and products and visually organize labor groups within industrial societies. With the creation of laws in the 19th century to require registration and protect the use of simple images as a corporate identification system, logos were intended to create an ecosystem of accountability and regulated competition. Images were turned into instruments to legitimize companies and assure consumers of quality standards for their products.

Expanding outward from the single logo as identifier to a graphic system, companies now use branding both to operate internally and to communicate externally. As scientific management took hold of manufacturing in early 20th century America, standardization proved itself to the managerial and owner class. By reducing derivation in the production process, including everything from the parts used to make a good to the movements used to construct it, new levels of efficiency were unlocked. This ethos went hand-in-hand with branding, which through visual language helped businesses to deploy and replicate themselves across the globe.

Fig. 2. McDonalds, "Speedee" the anthropomorphic hamburger, the corporate mascot long before the creation of "Ronald McDonald".

An early confluence of these strategies can be found in McDonald's "Speedee System," which incorporated a Fordist assembly line into their food preparation. While franchising the business, their workflow reputation also became a marketing tool, and their "Speedee System" a communication gimmick adorning signs and packaging. McDonald's even had a Speedee mascot—a chef with a hamburger head in a leaping position—before adopting Ronald McDonald.

The McDonald's brand wasn't conveyed by the flavor of its hamburger but by the possibility of homogenizing it: an idea that was embedded into their visual identity. However, in a context of corporate rivalry, the ownership of recognizable visual identities has resulted in brands being inflated with manufactured social meanings. Currently, the cost of products depends less on their ability to satisfy a specific need than on their ability to communicate complex cultural codes. Maurizio Lazzarato identified this some time ago: the value of work can be understood as the production of "information and cultural content of products" (Lazzarato et al. 1996, 138). This information is coded and decipherable and, under the logic of intellectual property, marketable.

Intellectual property does not however attribute the property rights of actual images, but rather rights over their reproduction. Yet, in a quest for efficiency, corporate symbols result in increasingly reductive compositions. Companies turn away from distinctive elements in their logos—propelled by modernist aesthetics entangled with normative principles. While designs keep evolving towards generic outcomes, trademarks continue to be litigated. Yet, our legal system does not truly protect authorship; rather, it establishes priority of a given image to those who officially register it and have the resources to protect its registration.

Fig. 3. Wikipedia, a product bearing „Linux" name, but not infringing the trademark owned by Linus Torvalds, because it falls into a different category.

But if images can be owned, how can we understand their visual boundaries? If the ability to enforce ownership over graphics requires establishing the limit of an idea, how can we do so with fuzzy objects such as images that seem similar? In order to register a logo in the U.S. Patent and Trademark Office, it has to be sufficiently distinct from other registered symbols within a particular business category. The new brand must be deemed "inherently distinctive" and legible enough as its own endeavor as to not confuse consumers about its possible connection with another party, purposely or accidentally. In reverse, there can be similar logos for companies that are dedicated to different things. But, as expected, companies encompass broad operating categories within their structures, covering the widest possible range of legal categories.

Ownership over images is unstable. Beyond the objective geometries of a given logo, their limits are defined by interpretive assessments of those who issue legal judgments within intellectual property courts. The ability to prevent unauthorized reproductions of a brand depends on whether or not the trademark is registered, the formal proximity between the images in question, the similarity of the type of businesses and above all the extent to which customers recognize the brand as an indicator of origin of the product or service. But what criteria is used to distinguish between symbols? Are technical processes being implemented today meant to measure formal distances among abstract shapes?

Corporate pastiche

In the 20th century, companies embraced new production methods to efficiently expand their brands across territories—transforming the colonial project into a softer transnational business effort. The ways companies presented themselves were tied to the reproductive capacities of industries—under the ultimate premise of consistent growth fueled by productive "function" over cultural concerns. Today, as modernism's commitment to disciplined consistency is fracturing, branding reflects more iterative production cycles—from design to manufacture to consumption and back to design. This is not to say that design responds less to the logic of capital, on the contrary: as manufacturing becomes more agile, companies have the ability to quickly adjust to markets. This results in a less direct relationship between design intent and consumers' feedback. While visual standardization was a given within an inflexible supply chain, more flexible approaches to design are being adopted by established brands, despite the practice potentially undermining their ability to litigate IP. Styles were previously incubated in regional subcultures before being appropriated by major corporations; now it is much more common for graphic trends to circulate widely online, through a plethora of hosts, before exhausting themselves and taking hold with specific industries.

Compared to Nike, with its years-long production and research and development cycles, this new approach is best embodied by Shein, a fast-fashion company which focuses on rapid recreation of burgeoning designs in small batches to test market responses before producing larger inventories. While this model has made them one of the largest fashion retailers worldwide with a $100 billion valuation (although it is rumored they have since lost a significant portion of their value due to stagnating growth), it has also garnered them the reputation for stealing other designers' ideas. Shein recreates garments copying boutique designers' social media posts and then popularizes them on social media by sending influencers "hauls" of clothing to try on and post about. Shein's tactics exploit both the potential of new production cycles and how visual information circulates today.

These more fluid strategies behind branding and product development are not lost on consumers, who have embraced self-conscious knockoffs that gain notoriety through their antagonism of big brands. When our lives are dominated by generic signifiers (the Kleenex effect), there is an appeal in challenging those who hold control over such fragile claims.

Fig. 4. NSS Magazine, Menthol 10's product shot, nssmag.com, March 15, 2019, Photo: Ari Saal Forman, Drawing a comparison between Nike shoes and Newport cigarettes targeting of the African American consumer, Ari Saal Forman used the Newport Spinnaker logo on a custom-made shoe resembling Nike's Air Force 1 as a commentary on their business practices.

In the case of sneakers, this often takes shape in smaller brands co-opting logos and silhouettes from large companies and using the modern supply chain's increased accessibility to create bootlegs. Recent examples that brought about litigation are by designers Warren Lota, MSCHF, OMI Hellcat, Kool Kiy, and John Geiger, who have all been sued by Nike for IP infringement. But again, larger companies will also self-reference their own designs to create tiers of exclusivity within their product lines. An example of this gone awry gained visibility when Ye (formerly known as Kanye West) promoted boycotting a design by Adidas similar to his Yeezy Foam Runners, which is also owned by Adidas. In both cases, it's questionable what "value" is being offered to consumers, yet such exercises are profitable enough that the practice persists. For instance, New York based "art collective" MSCHF, founded by former Buzzfeed employee Gabriel Whaley, has attracted at least $11.5 million dollars in venture funding claiming a valuation of over $200 million dollars. MSCHF's output include "drops" such as sandals made out of luxury Birkin bags called "Birkinstocks," and a shoe inspired by Gobstopper candies that was a collaboration with late night talk show host Jimmy Fallon.

Fig. 5. LOVE (@diddy), "Since the era of Run-DMC @adidas has always used Hip Hop to build its brand and make billions off of our culture. BUT WE ARE MORE THAN JUST CONSUMERS NOW, WE'RE THE OWNERS. @KanyeWest and YEEZY are the reason Adidas is relevant to culture. WE KNOW OUR VALUE! I'm done wearing Adidas products until they make this right! We have to support each other!! Everybody repost this please!!", instagram.com, September 6, 2022, Photo: Ye (formerly known as Kanye West) accuses Adidas of copying his designs, also manufactured and funded by Adidas, sparking protests by media personalities such as Sean Combs aka Diddy.

We felt a similar sense of distortion when comparing the images with altered logos online to those in the Anfu market later. Upon arriving, we noticed that many of the strategies we encountered on e-commerce websites were also being practiced in the physical marketplaces. But beyond that there was a familiarity with such a pastiche sensibility: As if the counterfeit goods had seeped back into the "originals," their aesthetic approaches that had emerged as a way to resist intellectual property regimes in places like Putian were now being surfaced in high fashion markets, seemingly inspired by the instability of branding, sometimes a trendy cultural nod towards bootlegs, always without clarity of their origins.

In some cases, we would see the intentional deformation of brand signifiers, such as the extension of a Nike swoosh where the tip of the swoosh folded back on itself to create a closed shape, or the complete removal of the Adidas three stripes "mountain" logo from the soles of Yeezy shoes. The storefronts too mimicked the disorganization of the online posts, with their level of formality seeming to have an inverse correlation between the perceived authenticity of their products. Shoes that looked like Nike Air Jordan 1s, but with intentionally deformed swooshes, were prominently displayed in what seemed like permanent showrooms, whereas authentic-looking Nike shoes were shown in unadorned, seemingly temporary spaces. We also found the purposeful misbranding of products with brands such as Nev Buylane and Panix—technically legal, but unabashedly derivative, which take their design cues from more established brands such as New Balance and Adidas.

The echoes between the distorted logos we encountered online and those we found in Anfu market were striking. In both cases, the brand modifications appeared to not only undermine policing of these gray markets but also to embody new production and communication methods—responding more to the logics of production processes and online platforms today than they were beholden to the more rigid logics of 20th century manufacturing and communications.

Universal Logo Detector

As consumer experiences move online, the flow of trademarks becomes a threat for companies that fear losing control over their brands. More than three million images are uploaded daily on Amazon alone, and at least one million different logos circulate within its platform. In this context, platforms have turned to machine vision technologies to monitor violations.

Computers learning to detect logos within images have recently become a powerful tool to prevent unlicensed vendors from advertising counterfeits. These programs can infer an image's contents as they compare it with large datasets of pre-labeled materials. As humans, we can intuitively detect a logo when we see it. But this distinction is strongly provided by context—we recognize logos when we see them perform as logos. However, how does the concept of a logo translate into computational space? Any system capable of identifying logos would have to account for a variety of placements, sizes, angles from which they are photographed, surfaces in which they are imprinted, and be sensitive to real life distortions, obstructions, and evolutions on a brand.

Recently, Amazon developed an internal computer vision system that has the needed sensibility to do just that. The model was engineered as a "class-agnostic universal logo detector" working from the hypothesis that there is an underlying structure of where these tend to sit within images. Given the lack of public libraries of logos, Amazon used their own catalog of images uploaded by users to train their models. After processing a million images associated with two thousand brands within different categories, they generated a library of 300,000 images classifying logo positions that were manually annotated by Amazon Mechanical Turk workers.

Following the resulting heat map of common placements, an additional system matches these regions with corresponding logos. The model is capable of processing up to 1500 images per second and can detect brands it has never seen. Given the sheer number of images that get uploaded to Amazon it wouldn't be computationally feasible to treat each new logo as a new class and re-train models for each of them. Instead, the model "learns the similarity among arbitrary groups of data" and puts together images with formal proximity within a multidimensional "latent space." Think of clouds of images that look similar to each other organized by measure of a large number of mathematical variables. The model computes the statistical distance between distinct branding features and establishes thresholds for what should be recognized as a single class.

The process is then enriched through the Amazon Brand Registry, where vendors can submit information about their brands and protect them against infringement. Users are invited to upload trademarks, symbols, names, and other branding elements to boost automated tools that scan over eight billion listings per day, as they aim to prevent fraudulent ones from going live before they are posted. Suspected items are monitored and reported by "true" brand owners via a verification system to be later investigated by Amazon. In fact, as part of their anti-bootlegging efforts, Amazon created the Counterfeit Crimes Unit (CCU) to work directly with law enforcement, conduct investigations, and pursue litigation. While big companies develop precise tools that aim mathematically to synthesize the properties of images, logos are elusive by nature and not always an easy thing to capture.

Branding in Reverse

These tools might help Amazon ensure trust in their platform, but it's important to recognize their secondary uses. The permanent analysis of branding elements within uploads enhances semantic searches, personalized product recommendations, and contextual ads. This data is used not only for the protection of users' brands but also benefits the algorithmic economy that sustains Amazon. The information collected through anti-counterfeiting programs feeds back into the operation of the platform to increase consumption.

Furthermore, Amazon owns and collects information in the same marketplace in which it competes—giving them a strong advantage. Amazon has more than 150 brands registered with the U.S. Patent and Trademark Office through which it sells hundreds of thousand items on its site. While in 2019 the company assured the U.S. Congress that it does not advantage its own brands within the platform, many sellers believe that Amazon gives itself better placement within organic search results—making it difficult for smaller vendors to position their products. This was the central claim of a letter that The National Association of Wholesaler-Distributors, representing over 30,000 distributors, sent to Congress in 2020 regarding Amazon's "monopolistic mistreatment of its third-party sellers" (see Adami 2022).

A recent investigation conducted by The Markup confirmed this claim. Amazon prioritizes its own brands and those exclusive to the platform, even when their competitors have better ratings and more sales. In 2021, the agency studied search results on Amazon for nearly 3,500 popular queries and analyzed what the platform placed as the top listing. Around 60% of such cases were sold to advertisers as "sponsored" content. But half of the leftover 40% was reserved to Amazon's brands and brand exclusives to the site. Only 20% ended up being open to the rest of competitors. This even when Amazon's brands and brand exclusives to the site made up only 6% of the whole pool within the survey and the rest of the competitors made up 77% (see Jeffries and Yin 2021).

While Amazon advocates for its sellers to protect their brands' consistency as a form of trust-building with consumers, its own market strategies differ. Instead of centralizing its products to a single recognizable brand, Amazon spreads them through a multiplicity of names, labels, and seemingly unaffiliated enterprises. By doing so, the platform disassociates itself from its own products, diluting its accountability over their quality and betting on quick adjustments and product placement at scale rather than on brand loyalty. A sort of branding in reverse, the potential success of its products is built on inconsistent labeling, on the Amazon brand going unnoticed.

Fig. 6. Left: Our Amazon Brands (@OurAmazonBrands), Sponsored Post, instagram.com, Right: Allbirds, Men's Wool Runner product photograph, allbirds.com. Allbirds co-CEO Joey Zwillinger wrote an open letter to Jeff Bezos when Amazon's 206 Collective brand copied his company's wool sneaker, urging Amazon to adopt Allbirds' sustainability practices in addition to its design, November 25, 2019.

The ultimate form of marketing camouflage is copying. Amazon has been consistently accused by multiple smaller manufacturers of knocking off their products, sneaking their house brands products suddenly into search results as such items grow in popularity. In the case of most "illegitimate" replicas, it is signaled to their audience that they are in on the ploy; whereas it would seem as the Amazon unbranded products intend to deceive their audience based on deluge and attempt to short circuit IP by preying on lack of awareness. However, compared to the bootleg resellers who operate at the fringes, Amazon's foray into permissible copies has limitless capital and legal protections at their disposal. On the one hand, Amazon develops robust technical defenses against trademark infringement while also implementing marketing techniques that are at odds with their anti-counterfeit programs. In such an asymmetric competitive context, the development of counter policing tools, such as the altered Nike images, are meaningful examples beyond the computational limits imposed by platforms.

Mathematical Logos

With technologies capable of inferring meaning out of visual contents, it is increasingly necessary to account for logos' statistical dimension. We have to consider images, mathematically. The systems that monitor graphic relationships online work from precise processes of inspection and comparison. The geometry of a logo is not only an aesthetic factor but also an operational one. It is, then, necessary to ponder on whether, as the mathematics of images are overseen, the mechanisms of property attribution might also be recalibrated under new logics of computational supervision.

The possibility of ownership relies on technologies of enforcement—this has been the historical function of contracts and laws to protect property. In an online context, the policing of imagery, and by extension visual culture, has become yet another means to secure it. In addition to the shaky premises that underlie intellectual property, handing over the authority to police images online to a burgeoning regime of private corporate surveillance risks relying on the supposed objectivity of biased computational infrastructures. While the products offered by private technology companies are touted as relying on neutral data, there is an inherent conflict of interest when the companies regulating the exchange of visual information also generate profit from what visual information is circulated.

The relationship between the policing of information and who benefits from said policing is further complicated, as the expertise and resources needed to enforce images' boundaries is dropping rapidly. For instance, as part of a 2018 #100DaysOfMLCode challenge, now research scientist and then student Conner Shorten built an image classifier to detect the difference between Adidas and Nike shoes. With a very small, low-resolution dataset—140 images which were distorted to fit into a square format—resulted in image detection with 99.7% accuracy (see Shorten 2018). Considering the contrast between a one-day student experiment and the resources of technology companies like Amazon and Google (who distribute a "Nike Swoosh Compilation" through their machine learning community website Kaggle), it is safe to say that the "intellectual property" of logos can be heavily monitored.

With these systems in place, we can no longer consider images, or logos, only as content and form relationships. Rather these compositions are now indivisible from their programmatic dimension. As researchers Ingrid Hoelzl and Remi Marie elaborate on the evolution of images: "With digitalization, the mathematics underlying the image is no longer merely geometric but increasingly algorithmic: protocols that regulate when/how an image (or image element) is displayed on screen, when/where/how it is being sent to/how it changes if a user clicks on it (an ad for instance) or what is considered a suspicious visual pattern and how it is detected etc." (Hoelzl and Marie 2021, 236)

There is an active feedback loop between what we see and the infrastructures set in place to make our seeing possible. Images today are no longer objects of representation but rather are tools that interface human and machine interactions. A logo today might not just serve to signal to possible consumers the provenance of a product and secure proper brand attribution, but rather it be an artifact meant to be processed computationally in order to execute tasks—such as making it easier for automatic IP infringement bots to detect it, trigger contextual ads as it gets scanned, or embedding within its form alternative text solutions in case it finds its way into a social media post. Therefore, beyond focusing on their graphic qualities, an in-depth analysis of the ways in which logos perform has to account for the ways in which they compute.

Fig. 7. A McDonald's filter pops up on Snapchat as users scan one of their golden arches, 2015.

It's worthwhile to insist on the shifting nature of images' value within this framework too. While the story of Carolyn Davidson, who as a student designed one of the most impactful logos in history—the Nike swoosh—for $35, is well documented (Davidson was later awarded shares in the company now speculated to be worth over 5 million dollars), how does the value of a logo evolve when it becomes data? In the mindset of scientific management and branding as a step towards standardization to increase market reach, a logo is a key piece in disseminating products and services. When we consider a logo's technical potential, however, it takes on new scales. Within this context, a logo expands its usefulness to become an instrument to police misuse of IP as well or serve as an input in predictive design software. Although designers understand their clients will continue to use their work far into the future, it is hard to believe any designer could have predicted these outcomes.

While computers have long been able to process images, the possibility for code to detect an image within another image—to segment a logo within a photo—requires precise semantic training, augmenting the authority of computers in processes that have been historically social. Machine vision technologies are used in products that scrape the web looking for counterfeits, in security cameras that read license plates and recognize peoples' identities in crowds, among many other applications. Not only do the images we exchange online nurture private surveillance products without our knowledge or explicit consent, but such systems retrofit back into our consuming, social, and political lives. Online platforms are increasingly opaque infrastructures that capitalize on our attention and digital behaviors—designed as personalized experiences catered through robust extraction of collective and personal data.

Optical Decoys

An optical decoy for the machine, the altered logos escape the codified order of property algorithmically protected online. However, just as companies expand their trademarks, bots policing them have become more precise.

When we first found these images on e-commerce platforms like dhgate.com, Taobao, and Wanelo, the Nike swooshes were graphically diverse—often doubled up upon themselves or with portions elongated to produce doppelganger logos that made the shoes look like bizarro versions of the "original" products they referenced. Today the same products can be found, but in their promotional images their logos are almost entirely removed—instead of the more boisterous graphics, we can find small remnants of the logos within the images with swooshes abruptly cut off at their stems, or covered by thoughtfully placed hang tags. Any presence of the logo's recognizable geometry is at risk of detection.

The visual approach found in the product listing's logo manipulation are also present in their product descriptions. Generic keywords that describe the shoes in question identify the products: "casual," "low top," "sports." As well as misspelling or abbreviations of popular model names or brand collaborators: "dunkes" for Nike "dunks" and "OW" for popular fashion brand "Off-White." However, what was not present were direct references to the brands the products seemed to implicitly evoke such as "Nike," "Adidas," or "New Balance." It seems that the textual brand signifier cannot be evoked either.

As the technologies that protect IP become more granular, so does the possibility to assert ownership over images. Control over things depends on the possibility to describe and delimit them. If it is possible to measure the thresholds of logos circulating online, what will stop companies from designing towards determining their IP based on increasingly expanded visual codes? Can the image of a whole shoe become an algorithmic trademark? Identifying the formal distance between similar images for legal reasons had been an interpretative exercise so far. Logos, likewise, have been sufficiently subjective concepts. In the end, it may not really be as clear, for the human eye, to recognize the boundaries between the elements that compose an image... but it is safe to say that the machine will always find them.

The day after our visit to Anfu, we arranged to meet up with a replica shoe maker that had become popular on Reddit. We sat down in a nondescript apartment and were offered tea and cigarettes while they shared sample materials and breakdowns of popular shoe silhouettes with their component pieces deconstructed. Indeed, to our untrained eye, the difference between their offerings and their "references" was indistinguishable. When we asked about the images we had found online, they claimed to never have seen them. Instead, they had carved out a seemingly thriving business using other evasive tactics such as an ever-changing website URL, occasional passwords, semi-coded language, informal payment structures, and direct communication on WeChat.

The seller apologized that their factory was closed that day, but offered us some shoe models they had on hand. We left Putian wearing replicas of NikeCraft Mars Yard Shoe 1.0, a collaboration with Tom Sachs. The swooshes were intact.

BIBLIOGRAPHY

Jeffries, Adrianne, and Leon Yin. 2021. "Amazon Puts Its Own 'Brands' First Above Better-Rated Products." The Markup. October 14, 2021; Accessed October 16, 2022. https://themarkup.org/amazons-advantage/2021/10/14/amazon-puts-its-own-brands-first-above-better-rated-products.

Adami, Blake. 2022. "NAW Voices Support of Anti-Trust Legislation, Addressing 'Amazon's Abuses'". Industrial Distribution, January 19, 2022; Accessed October 16, 2022. https://www.inddist.com/associations/news/22005741/naw-voices-support-of-antitrust-legislation-addressing-amazons-abuses.

Shorten, Connor. 2018. "Python: How to Build a Convolutional Network Classifier: Nike vs Adidas Shoes." Medium, July 14, 2018; Accessed October 16, 2022. https://towardsdatascience.com/how-to-build-a-convolutional-network-classifier-81eef880715e.

Hoelzl, Ingrid and Remi Marie. "The Martian Image (On Earth)". In *The Palgrave Handbook of Image Studies,* edited by Purgar, Krešimir, 233 – 246. Cham: Springer International Publishing, 2021. https://doi.org/10.1007/978-3-030-71830-5.

Lazzarato, Maurizio, Paul Colilli, Ed Emory, Maurizia Boscagli, Cesare Casarino, and Michael Turits. "Immaterial Labor." In *Radical Thought in Italy: A Potential Politics,* edited by Paolo Virno and Michael Hardt, NED-New edition, 7:133–48. University of Minnesota Press, 1996.

China Sourcing Agent. 2020. "The Secret of Fake Sneakers Workshop Capital ---- Putian," Mysourcify, August 1, 2020; Accessed October 16, 2022. https://mysourcify.com/the-secret-of-fake-sneakers-workshop-capital-putian/.

Yin, Leon. 2021. "Introducing Amazon Brand Detector." The Markup, November 29, 2021; Accessed October 16, 2022. https://themarkup.org/amazons-advantage/2021/11/29/introducing-amazon-brand-detector.

IMAGES AND ILLUSTRATIONS

Figure 1: DHgate, product photo, dhgate.com, c. 2016.

Figure 2: McDonald's, Burger Head, Gentilly section of New Orleans, Chris Hamamoto and Federico Pérez Villoro, June 2011.

Figure 3: Photo: StromBer, LinuxWasch3, March 22, 2008. Accessed May 2023. https://commons.wikimedia.org/wiki/File:LinuxWasch3.jpg.

Figure 4: Ari Saal Forman, Ari Menthol 10s, 2006, in: NSS Magazine, "Menthol 10's product shot", March 15, 2019.

Figure 5: Diddy (@diddy) 2022. "Since the era of Run-DMC @adidas has always used Hip Hop to build its brand and make billions off of our culture. BUT WE ARE MORE THAN JUST CONSUMERS NOW, WE'RE THE OWNERS. @KanyeWest and YEEZY are the reason Adidas is relevant to culture. WE KNOW OUR VALUE! I'm done wearing Adidas products until they make this right! We have to support each other!! Everybody repost this please!!" Instagram, September 6, 2022.

Figure 6: Left: Our Amazon Brands, Sponsored Post, instagram.com/OurAmazonBrands, Right: Allbirds, Men's Wool Runner product photograph, allbirds.com, Photographer Unknown, November 25, 2019. Accessed May 2023.

Figure 7: Khushbu Shah/Eater, 2015. Accessed May 2023. https://www.eater.com/2015/6/18/8806759/mcdonalds-snapchat-filters

VARIANT OF CYBERFEMINISM(S)

(Mindy Seu)

This is an edited transcription of a lecture and performative reading by Mindy Seu.

> I have long been a gatherer. Though we rarely hear this word used literally anymore, we do hear its sister gathering, as in gathering people, gathering information, gathering place. … But the term gatherer we more immediately associate with our origins as hunter-gatherers … We went, we gathered goods, and then we returned home to our kin, sharing as survival.
>
> — Mindy Seu, "On Gathering", 2021.

These were some of the opening lines from my essay "On Gathering" for *Shift Space,* the inaugural publication by the Knight Foundation and United States Artists to celebrate their 2021 Artist Fellows. The paper considered variations of material and social gathering: Material gathering brings together disparate objects, while social gathering activates this collection through an event. Written during the pandemic, the gatherings discussed focused on creating this sense of communion online.

> Before the tool that forces energy outward, we made the tool that brings energy home. Prior to the preeminence of sticks, swords and the Hero's killing tools, our ancestors' greatest invention was the container: the basket of wild oats, the medicine bundle, the net made of your own hair, the home, the shrine, the place that contains whatever is sacred. The recipient, the holder, the story. The bag of stars.
>
> — Ursula K. Le Guin, "The Carrier Bag Theory of Fiction", 1988.

In her essay "The Carrier Bag Theory of Fiction", Le Guin posits that the first tool was the basket, a tool of gathering, rather than the spear, a tool of dominance. If we rethink the history of technology, we might reframe some of these ancestral tools, thereby shifting our focus from the individual hero towards the community.

Today, I'll focus on the *Cyberfeminism Index* as an example of material and social gatherings, as well as the different containers for sharing them. Gathering is ultimately about collecting items and sharing them with your kin.

There are multiple definitions of cyberfeminism. To think about this term, we can break apart the word itself. This prefix "cyber" comes from Norbert Wiener's "cybernetics" from the 1940s. "Cyber" was then fixed to "space," as in cyberspace, a term that first appeared in William Gibson's sci-fi novel Neuromancer (1984). While this fiction has been said to have predicted networked sensory landscapes that are in discussion today, his cyberspace was characterized by the male gaze, with fembabes, cyberbots, and women of the male techno-fantasy. When "cyber" finally merged with "feminism"—creating cyberfeminism—in 1991, it was a provocation: How could those who identify as feminist reclaim what cyberspace and its corresponding techno-utopia or -dystopia could be? Moving again from the spear to the basket, we can reconsider our history of technology to not only uplift the women who co-developed internet technologies, but also highlight the application layer of the stack. Thinking back to the basket instead of a spear, we can refocus the stories that emerge when we proceed with a feminist lens on the histories of technology.

The *Cyberfeminism Index* is a sourcebook, an annotated chronology, and a collection of online activism and net art from the past three decades. Using the *Cyberfeminism Index* as a proxy, its translation into three different containers—spreadsheet, catalog, and website—express new modes of reading with the affordances of each media.

Container 1: Spreadsheet

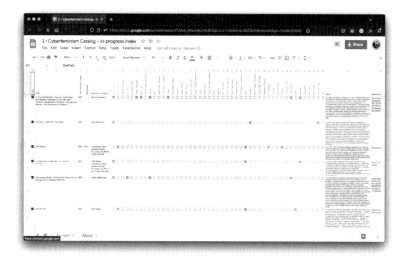

Fig. 1. *Cyberfeminism Index* spreadsheet (2019)

This open-access, crowd-sourced spreadsheet was the first container for the *Cyberfeminism Index*. The labels at the top display ways of categorizing each entry. Judy Malloy, an early cyberfeminist media artist who created hypertext fictions, informed me of a useful distinction: YACK / HACK to note theory vs. practice, respectively. The blue terms are the various topics: affective computing, open source software, hacktivism, glitch, digital diasporas, et cetera. And the green ones are the media: directories, manifestos, organizations, et cetera. When you zoom out and scroll, you'll find that entries do not fit cleanly into singular categories.

While spreadsheets have existed since the written ledger, the first digital spreadsheet was VisiCalc, included in IBM's P.C. in the 1980s. The first GUI-based spreadsheet appeared in 1985 with Excel 1.0. GUI, Graphical User

Interface, utilizes skeuomorphism so readers can understand the intended function of desktop tools without using the Command Line. The trash appears as a waste bin, and so on.

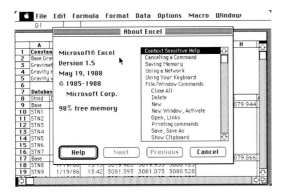

Fig. 2. Microsoft Excel 1.5 (1988)

When the first digital spreadsheets first came out, it was considered a liberatory technology. It was considered "functional programming for the masses." (Peyton Jones, Burnett and Blackwell 2014) Anyone with access to a personal computer and Excel could do fairly complex computations. However, as noted by Ted Nelson, "Conventional data structures, especially tables and arrays, are confined structures, created from a rigid top-down specification that enforces regularity and rectangularity." (Nelson 2011) Nelson, the father of the concept of hypertext, developed ZigZag, an *n*-dimensional spreadsheet. *Rectangularity* and *regularity:* if you are only plotting things on an x- and y-axis, you lose access to depth and blurry taxonomies. It removes the possibility of imagining new identification schemas because they are rigid and predetermined.

Container 2: Catalog, a Brief Reading

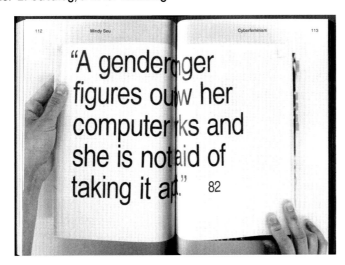

Fig. 3. A spread from Harvard Graduate School of Design's *ADPD Annual* (2019) showing a spread from *Cyberfeminism Catalog* (2019)

The catalog is structured as an encyclopedia, rather than an essay anthology, with an annotated chronology of hundreds of entries of internet activism and net art from 1991 to the present. With cross-references embedded in each entry, the reader moves through the book in a nonlinear sequence, jumping from texts that complement or juxtapose the respective entry's theme.

(1) "A Cyborg Manifesto: Science, Technology and Socialist Feminism in the Late Twentieth Century." Donna Haraway. Essay published in *Simians, Cyborgs and Women: The Reinvention of Nature,* Routledge 1991.

(2) "A Cyberfeminist Manifesto for the 21st Century." VNS Matrix, 1991.

We are the modern cunt
positive anti reason
unbounded unleashed unforgiving
we see art with our cunt we make art with our cunt
we believe in jouissance madness holiness and poetry
we are the virus of the new world disorder
rupturing the symbolic from within
saboteurs of big daddy mainframe
the clitoris is a direct line to the matrix
the VNS MATRIX
terminators of the moral code
mercenaries of slime
go down on the altar of abjection
probing the visceral temple we speak in tongues
infiltrating disrupting disseminating
corrupting the discourse
we are the future cunt (Cross-reference, 86)

(86) Courageous cunts. courageouscunts.com. 2012.

This is a protest page! We're a group of girls that got quite angry about the growing propaganda to surgically "improve" the female genitalia. Don't get us wrong: we're not blaming any woman for her conscious, informed decision. If you really want labiaplasty, go ahead. It's the alliance between porn and the medical industry we're opposed to. It's about their campaign to sell us the perfect labia. Here we try to raise a voice against it!

(87) "Introduction: Subaltern Empowerment, Socioeconomic Globalization, and Digital Divides." Radhika Gajjala, *Cyberculture and the Subaltern.* Lexington Books, 2012.

This maps how voice and silence shape online space in relation to offline actualities. Thus it weaves the virtual unreal. (Cross-reference, 74)

(74) Prema Murthy, Bindigirl, https://artbase.rhizome.org/wiki/Q4304, 2001.

According to Prema Murphy, Bindi is a girl born out of the exotic and erotic. She is the embodiment of desire for and of the other, the desire of wanting to be known or to know at an intimate level. And at the same time, finding safety, even power, in distance. In being mysterious, liberation, and not being easily categorized. Bindi girl is the product of a colonialist mentality. She is aware that she is being watched and asks for something in return for being looked at—to mimic the symbiotic relationship that exists in the real world between the colonized and the colonizer.

Not only does the desire to conquer the other exist in colonialism, but a longing by the other for his conqueror and his or her capitalist ideas exist as well. This pattern of desire and longing must be re-evaluated before we can move on into a post-colonial territory. Bindi is Murthy's avatar.

Container 3: Website

When my collaborator Angeline Meitzler and I began the third container of the *Cyberfeminism Index*—the website—we considered two primary questions: How do we visualize citations? How do we consider the lifespan of a website?

Proto-internets were largely informed by analog forms. Xanadu, conceived of by Ted Nelson but never mainstream, was influenced by the Talmud, the theological doctrine of Judaism. The structure of the page is built around a dialectic of different voices. The Mishnah is the central column that holds the primary religious text. Surrounding this is commentary or analysis of the Mishnah. And the outermost column is commentary on the commentary. How would the World Wide Web be different if co-authorship and citations were built into its infrastructure?

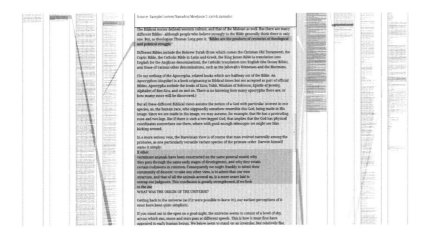

Fig. 4.   Ted Nelson's Xanadu (1960s)

In some ways, Xanadu feels quite similar to the web pages that we know of today, with a long scrolling central column that's rather flat. However, when there is a link, it pulls up the page of the original source with a two-way link. The World Wide Web uses one-way links that are very susceptible to link rot. With two-way links, a pseudo-archival method is built into the infrastructure because you have two links holding hands, always referring back to the original citation. With one-way links, we need to take extra care in order to maintain this connection—to slow down, provide attribution, and preserve the original source.

Fig. 5. *Cyberfeminism Index* website (2020), developed by Angeline Meitzler

We also asked ourselves how websites age. Angeline and I wanted to make a website that would be online and working for as long as possible. To do so, we referred to earlier sites that were still running and seemed durable. The 100 Anti-Theses manifesto by the Old Boys Network (OBN) first went live in 1997 and works nearly perfectly today, 25 years later, due to its hardcoding in HTML and CSS, the backbone of the internet. The site was built with tags like <h1> (header one), <h2> (header two), <li> (list items), CSS elements like <dropdown> and the system font Arial. (Arial is one of the few system fonts co-designed by a woman: Patricia Saunders for IBM in the early 1980s). By hardcoding it, OBN did not rely on third-party JavaScript libraries or Flash, which were quick to degrade over time. "Defaults" are designed by people. And by embracing this styling, it allows the website to restyle as the browser is updated.

With these two primary questions in mind—"How do we visualize citations?" and "How do websites age?"—we built the cyberfeminismindex.com, commissioned by Rhizome and presented at the New Museum in October 2020. When you first arrive, you are greeted with green blurred text. When it sharpens, it appears to be a standard table. But as you interact with the page, elements are made unusual: Dropdowns glow and extend to the width of the page, drawers open to reveal more information, and titles are added to a side panel "trail." Whether the visitor is clicking intuitively or intentionally, your selections build into a collection, creating associative links. This collection can then be downloaded as a PDF. Each of the entries also includes cross-references that push and pull you throughout the site in a non-linear way.

> **Author's note:**
>
> *Since this lecture and subsequent transcription was published, the newest publication of the* Cyberfeminism Index *was published by Inventory Press in January 2023.*

# BIBLIOGRAPHY

Courageous Cunts. 2012. courageouscunts.com.

Gajjala, Radhika. "Introduction: Subaltern Empowerment, Socioeconomic Globalization, and Digital Divides." In *Cyberculture and the Subaltern,* edited by Radhika Gajjala. Lexington Books, 2012.

Gibson, William. *Neuromancer.* Ace, 1984.

Haraway, Donna. "A Cyborg Manifesto: Science, Technology and Socialist Feminism in the Late Twentieth Century." In *Simians, Cyborgs and Women: The Reinvention of Nature,* Routledge, 1991.

Le Guin, Ursula K. "The Carrier Bag Theory of Fiction." In *Women of Vision,* edited by Denise Dipont. St Martins Pr, 1988.

Murthy, Prema. "Bindigirl." Rhizome/ArtBase. 2001. https://artbase.rhizome.org/wiki/Q4304.

Nelson, Ted. "The ZIGZAG® DATABASE and VISUALIZATION SYSTEM." Presentation video, 2011. https://archive.org/details/zigzagpresentation.

———. *Project Xanadu.* 1960. https://xanadu.com/.

Peyton Jones, Simon, Margaret Burnett, and Alan Blackwell. "Spreadsheets: functional programming for the masses." Presentation, 2014. https://www.slideshare.net/kfrdbs/peyton-jones.

Seu, Mindy. *Cyberfeminism Index.* ADPD Annual, Harvard Graduate School of Design, 2019.

Seu, Mindy. "On Gathering." In *Shift Space 1.0.* Knight Foundation and United States Artists, 2021. https://issue1.shiftspace.pub/on-gathering-mindy-seu.

Seu, Mindy and Angeline Meitzler. "Cyberfeminism Index." 2020. cyberfeminismindex.com.

VNS Matrix. "A Cyberfeminist Manifesto for the 21st Century," 1991.

Wiener, Norbert. *Cybernetics.* MIT Press, 1948.

IMAGES AND ILLUSTRATIONS

Figure 1: Mindy Seu and Angeline Meitzler, *Cyberfeminism Index* spreadsheet, 2019.

Figure 2: Microsoft Corporation, Microsoft Excel 1.5, 1988.

Figure 3: Mindy Seu, *Cyberfeminism Index,* 2019, in: *ADPD Annual,* Harvard Graduate School of Design, 2019.

Figure 4: Ted Nelson, Xanadu, 1960s.

Figure 5: Angeline Meitzler, *Cyberfeminism Index* website, 2020.

BIO NOTES

BIO NOTES

Editor Biographies

Johanna Mehl (she/her) is a designer, scholar, and educator interested in the politics and relations that take shape through and around design practices. She holds a B.A. in Communication Design from the Niederrhein University of Applied Science and an M.A. in Art and Design Studies from the University of the Arts Folkwang, Essen. Besides her design, artistic and curatorial practice, she has taught in the fields of digital media, culture studies, and design theory at different design schools across Europe. She holds a research associate position at TU Dresden where she is a PhD candidate at the Chair for Digital Cultures researching the cultural history of environmental design practices. She is an editorial board member of the Design+Posthumanism Network and part of the research group *Against Catastrophe.*

Prof. Dr. Carolin Höfler (she/her) is Professor of Design Theory and Research at Köln International School Design of TH Köln. She studied art history, modern German literature, and theater & film as well as architecture at universities in Cologne, Vienna, and Berlin. Since 2022, she is a member of the research training group "connecting – excluding: Cultural Dynamics Beyond Globalized Networks", a collaborative venture between the University of Cologne, the Academy of Media Arts Cologne and TH Köln, funded by the German Research Foundation (DFG). Next to her spatial practice, she works in the team of "oza _studio for architecture and scenography" in Berlin. She is co-editor of the publication (with Philipp Reinfeld): *Mit weit geschlossenen Augen. Virtuelle Realitäten entwerfen.* Paderborn: Brill | Fink 2022

Author Biographies

A

Frederick M.C. van Amstel is an Assistant Professor and complicator in the Laboratory of Design against Oppression (LADO), UTFPR, Brazil. His recent research deals with the contradiction of oppression and the possibility of designing for liberation. Together with Lesley-Ann Noel and Rodrigo Gonzatto, he guest edited the special issues on Design, Oppression, and Liberation for the Diseña Journal (21 and 22).

Rafaela Angelon is a Master student at the Graduate Program in Technology and Society - PPGTE at UTFPR, Brazil. Her research combines intersectional art, design, theater and fashion, paying particular attention to the work of women artists and activists. Her work appeared in Art, Design & Communication in Higher Education journal and DRS2022: Bilbao.

Tomás Corvalán Azócar (they/he) is a Chilean designer, researcher and facilitator interested in queer, feminist and critical approaches to (design) academia. Born and raised in the land nowadays known as Santiago de Chile, Tomás first steps into design were inside a school strongly influenced by the Bauhaus educational system. They hold a B.A. Hons in Design from Pontificia Universidad Católica de Chile and a M.A. in Integrated Design at the Köln International School of Design. While looking for an answer to the question *How can textile practices improve design education under queer perspectives?* Tomás' recent Master thesis suggests that textile practices can expand design education by recovering traditional Chilean rituals, embracing and bolstering the power of deviating from western ontologies. Their interests lie in design politics, decolonialism, (design) activism and textiles.

B _____

Lisa Baumgarten is a critical design mediator working in design, research, as writer and as teacher/learner. She is the co-creator of the participatory research platform Teaching Design which focuses on design education from intersectional feminist perspectives. Lisa has been teaching design theory and practice as adjunct lecturer at German and international design universities since 2017. From Oct 2021–Sept 2022 Lisa was part of the Institute of Design Research at HBK Braunschweig as interims professor of Design Sciences where she facilitated seminars in the MA program Transformation Design. Since Oct 2022 Lisa is a guest professor at Studiengruppe Informationdesign (Communication Design) at Burg Giebichenstein, University of Art and Design Halle. Her current research focuses on design mediation as critical practice and the potentials and shortfalls of institutional critique within design study programs. Lisa's research and writing has been published and presented amongst others at Creative Bodies—Creative Minds Conference, Graz (AU), Designsymposium "Kompliz*innen" at BURG Halle (DE), the German Society for Design Theory and Research (DGTF) as well
as formdesign magazine.

Prof. Dr. **Tom Bieling** is a professor of Design Theory and Vice Dean at HfG Offenbach University of Art and Design, and teaches Design Studies at HAWK Hildesheim. At the Centre for Design Research at HAW Hamburg (2019–2022) he held the professorship for design theory and research. Guest professorships at the University of Trento and GUC Cairo. Head of research cluster Social Design at Design Research Lab of Berlin University of the Arts (2010–2019). Previously research assistant at T-Labs / TU Berlin (2007–2010). He is editor of the DESIGNABILITIES Design Research Journal, co-editor of the book series Design Meanings (Mimesis), co-editor of the BIRD series (Birkhäuser/DeGruyter), part of the Board of International Research in Design, co-host of the NERD conference for New Experimental Research in Design, and initiator of designforschung.org. Books: "Inklusion als Entwurf" (2019), "Design (&) Activism" (2019), "Gender (&) Design" (2020) and „Gender Puppets" (2007).

Frieder Bohaumilitzky is a designer and political scientist. He designs objects and spaces, creates exhibitions, and intervenes in structures. In doing this, he examines the socio-political context of design, its methods and its application in politics. He studied Political Science at the Universität Hamburg and Design at the HFBK Hamburg and the Bezalel Academy of Arts and Design in Jerusalem. From 2020-2023 he was a research assistant at the Zentrum für Designforschung at the HAW Hamburg, and from 2017-2019 he was a part of the Projektbüro Friedrich von Borries in Berlin. Currently he is completing a PhD at the HFBK Hamburg on the connection of design with right-wing populism and right-wing extremism.

Isabella Brandalise, Quizzical Superintendent, is a PhD candidate at RMIT University investigating ways in which institutional structures can be opened up and re-configured through imagination exercises. She holds a master's degree in Transdisciplinary Design from Parsons School for Design and in Art from the University of Brasília. In 2021, she co-founded the Patadesign School.

Following the first edition of the Patadesign School, **Brandalise**, **Eira** and **Rosenbak** published the zine Patadesign School 1: Ethernity (2022), a pataphysical experiment of its own, which documents the first edition of the School. This publication is an addition to the body of work the co-founders have produced in recent years, including articles and presentations for design conferences, the book Patadesign: notas pendentes de soluções imaginárias (Brandalise and Eira, 2019) and the PhD thesis The Science of Imagining Solutions: Design Becoming Conscious of Itself through Design (Rosenbak, 2018).

C

Cerrato – Halls is a collaborative practice between **Jaione Cerrato** and **Jon Halls**, socially engaged designers and artists focused on the concept of value and its creation in contemporary society. Our multidisciplinary explorations aim to practically apply the potential inclusivity of art in helping inspire future paths forward for our society, by creating frameworks for audiences and participants to contribute. With this belief in mind, for the last five years we have worked together on projects across Europe and collaborated with a range of independent collectives and institutions with the aim of generating meaningful discussion. Some of these institutions include: Antiuniversity Now, Baltan Laboratories, Royal College of Art and Akademie Schloss Solitude.

D

Adam DelMarcelle's prints and social art actions have been made in Pennsylvania, on the frontlines of the exploding overdose epidemic and have functioned to educate and mobilize community response through compelling his viewers to ask better questions of themselves by considering the part of the problem they are responsible for. After losing a brother to an overdose, DelMarcelle has committed his life to the betterment of his community through his work as an educator and artist. He travels widely activating communities through outreach, activism, and educating anyone who will listen to the power art possesses to disrupt, resist, and document our human existence. DelMarcelle's work has been extensively written about and exhibited and is included in several collections across the United States including the Library of Congress, The Cushing Whitney Medical Library at Yale University, Syracuse University, Letterform Archive and many more.

E _____

Henrique Eira, Superliminal Composer, is an independent graphic designer and design teacher based in Brasília. He holds an MA degree from the University of Brasília and an MFA degree from CalArts, and investigates political, poetic and experimental approaches to graphic design and typography. In 2021, he co-founded the Patadesign School.

F _____

Marius Förster works at the intersection of design, research and art. Through the amalgamation of theory and practice he aims at working his way through contemporary issues of the anthropocene, such as the climate catastrophe, more-than-human relationships and their transformations. He is part of RIBL (Research Institute of Botanical Linguistics) and co-initiated the speculative and participative project 3000 Peaks, a critical mediation that addresses consequences and effects of the global climate catastrophe for Switzerland. He is co-editor of the publication Un/Certain Futures (transcript, 2018) and cofounder of the design studio operative.space.

G _____

Imad Gebrael is a Lebanese designer, educator, and researcher based in Berlin. He has produced visual and theoretical works around identity representation and self-Orientalism in Arab* design, counter-mapping, and archiving. He has also collaborated with several journalistic platforms on exploring common grounds between design and media outlets across Europe. Imad has lectured at several academic institutions including Humboldt University of Berlin, Berlin University of the Arts, Hochschule für Künste Bremen, The University of Art and Design Linz, and Design Akademie Berlin. He has co-founded cultural and urban projects centering Arab-migrant experiences and is currently undertaking ethnographic research on the negotiations of Arab-Arab identifications in Sonnenallee, Berlin, as part of his doctoral project within the Department of European Ethnology at the Humboldt University of Berlin.

H _____

Prof. Dr. **Anke Haarmann** is a philosopher, artist, and design theoretician. 'She founded the "Centre for Design Research" at the University of Applied Sciences in Hamburg and has led the research project "Speculative Space" (2019-2022). Haarmann is currently Director of PhDArts at the Academy of Creative and Performing Arts (ACPA), Professor of Practice and Theory of Research in the Visual Arts at the Leiden University and Research Lector Art Theory and

Practice at the Royal Academy of Art The Hague. Recent publications are: „Künstlerische Forschung. Ein Handbuch" ed. by Badura, Dubach, Haarmann et al. Zürich/Berlin: diaphanes, 2015 "Artistic Research: Eine epistemologische Ästhetik", Bielefeld: transcript Verlag, 2019; "Theater of Research" in: The Routledge Companion to Performance Philosophy. Eds. Cull Ó Maoilearca/Alice Lagaay. London: Routledge, 2020. „Der erweiterte Designbegriff" in: „Philosophie des Designs" ed. by Feige, Arnold, Rautzenberg, Bielefeld: transcript, 2020.

Chris Hamamoto and **Federico Pérez Villoro**'s collaborative work investigates the impact of emerging technologies in contemporary culture and politics. It often includes computer-based media, publications, video, writing, and pedagogical initiatives. They both hold MFAs from the Rhode Island School of Design, where they met in 2011. Chris is based in Seoul, South Korea and works as a designer and educator. He is an assistant professor at the Seoul National University, while maintaining an independent graphic design practice. Federico is an artist and researcher living and working in Mexico City. He has advanced various independent educational programs and has served as a faculty at the Rhode Island School of Design and the California College of the Arts. Their work together has been exhibited internationally and recognized by institutions such as Printed Matter, the Walker Art Center, OCAT Shenzhen, and the Yerba Buena Center for the Arts.

J

Dorsa Javaherian (she/her) is an Iranian designer based in Cologne, holding a Bachelor's degree in Industrial Design from the University of Tehran and a Master's degree in Integrated Design from Köln International School of Design. Dorsa's interest lies at the intersections of design, education, inclusion, and community building, and she believes in plural futures. As a designer, she inspires her practice by understanding diaspora experiences and undertaking community building initiatives. Besides pursuing her design career in the corporate environment, she has actively contributed to social innovation work in various grassroots organizations in Cologne.

K

Jiye Kim (she/her) was born and raised in Seoul, South Korea. She goes by the name 'Jane' too. She has been on a journey of finding her own identity as a designer since moving from Korea to the United Kingdom, and is now living in Köln, Germany. Her identity has been gradually changing due to several multicultural experiences and constant self-reflection. She joined a Masters Program, 'Integrated Design' at Köln International School of Design (KISD) in March, 2021, and graduated in Feb, 2023 with a master thesis focused on ethical design processes for technological services.

Torben Körschkes is part of the design and research collective HEFT, which explores questions of socio-political spaces. He studied design at Folkwang Universität der Künste in Essen and HFBK Hamburg, where he completed his MFA on contemporary salons in 2018. Current grants and residencies include

O Instituto (Porto) funded by the EU, Goethe Institute and the City of Hamburg (2023), Hamburger Zukunftsstipendium (2021), Elbkulturfonds (2020), Bibliothek Andreas Züst (2019). He is currently working towards a PhD on the relationship between complexity and community at TU Berlin.

L

Edith Lázár is a Romanian writer, curator and fashion theorist based in Cluj-Napoca. A dropout academic in the field of philosophy, her research focuses on fictions, aesthetic politics, speculative design and the troublesome socio-political threads of fashion. She is the co-founder of the curatorial collective Aici Acolo, showcasing young artists and cultivating collaborative models. In 2019, she was an Akademie Schloss Solitude fellow (Design/Fashion Theory) exploring practices of writing that merge theory, storytelling and fiction in writing one's narrative. Afterwards, she initiated Out of Stock, a speculative journal for fashion and design grounded in Eastern European sensibilities. Lately, she's been working on a Sci-Fi audio-novel. Recent publications include: "Fashion Feels. When Clothing Becomes an Eco-Skin" - Contemporary Lynx 16 (2) and a series of inserts for the artist publication Post-Human Exercises (Christina Maria Pfeifer, 2022).

Chris Lee is a graphic designer and educator based in Lenapehoking (Brooklyn, NY). He is a graduate of OCADU and the Sandberg Instituut. His research/studio practice explores graphic design's entanglement with capitalism and colonialism/ity through the banal genre of the document. He recently published his first book, Immutable: Designing History, with Onomatopee. He is also currently developing a typographical project that narrates the oscillating racialization of the "East-Asian" between the "model minority" and "yellow peril" and its role in consolidating Euro-American settler identity. Chris is an Assistant Professor in the Undergraduate Communications Design Department at the Pratt Institute.

Sally Loutfy (she/her) is a Lebanese Architect and Designer interested in the influence of human psychology in architecture and urban space. She was born and raised in Beirut, Lebanon; a place that she shares a bitter-sweet relationship with. Her country and the experiences she lived there influence both her work and designs in a very core way. Sally came to Germany in 2021 to pursue her Master's Degree at KISD in Integrated Design research. Her academic work has revolved for a few years around the effects of trauma and political conflict on the ways in which we design for our built environment. At the moment, Sally is working as a 3D Innovation Architect in Berlin.

N

Becky Nasadowski is a designer, educator, and researcher seeking ways to intervene in the design field's liberal, often business-oriented, approaches to social justice. She works toward a design pedagogy that embraces existing research from humanities disciplines and directly engages questions about power, oppression, and histories of violence. Select publications include an experimental book with Heath Schultz titled i hate war, but i hate our enemies even more (Minor Compositions, 2019) and the essay "On Design Pedagogy and Empty Pluralism" in the collection Feminist Designer: On the Personal and the Political in Design (ed. Ali Place, MIT Press, 2023). Nasadowski has an MFA in Design from the multidisciplinary program at The University of Texas at Austin and is an Assistant Professor in the Department of Art at The University of Tennessee at Chattanooga.

César Neri is a Brooklyn-based designer playing somewhere between interaction design and architecture. His personal work explores the role of design and technology in the pursuit of decolonizing collective memory and identity in contemporary Latin American culture. Specifically focusing on living Maya cosmologies and ontologies as a way to question our institutionalized values and conceptualizing alternatives. He is currently working on building software solutions to help decarbonize the planet at scale.

O

Luiza Prado de O. Martins is an artist, writer, educator, and researcher investigating plant-human relations, reproduction, herbal medicine, and radical, decolonising care. Her body of artistic work spans video, food, performance, and sculpture, examining questions of reproductive rights from a feminist and anti-colonial lens, with a particular interest in herbalist medicinal practices. Her ongoing artistic research project, "Un/Earthings and Moon Landings" narrates the extinction and later reappearance of an ancient contraceptive, aphrodisiac and spice, called silphium, through a series of artworks. The project explores the limits of archival practices in landscapes affected by anthropogenic climate change. In the past, Prado has exhibited work at the Art Institute of Chicago, the Museum of Modern Art Warsaw, Haus der Kulturen der Welt, Savvy Contemporary, Akademie Schloss Solitude, and Kampnagel, among others.

Q

Sven Quadflieg studied design at the Folkwang University of the Arts and the Zurich University of the Arts and earned his doctorate at the HFBK Hamburg. He works as a professor at the University of Applied Sciences in Lippstadt, having previously taught at various German universities. In his research he is interested in political and social design and the mutual influences and dependencies between design and society. Current publications are the monograph Mit erhobener Faust (Adocs 2021) and the anthology (Dis)Obedience in Digital Societies. Perspectives on the Power of Algorithms and Data (Transcript 2022).

Heather Snyder Quinn (she/her) is usually where she "isn't supposed to be." You will find her playing in unexpected places, physical or virtual, and collaborating with people from an array of backgrounds. Her work uses design fiction to empower communities to imagine possible futures and understand technology's impact on human freedoms. The World Economic Forum, MIT Press, Yale Law School, The Washington Post, Hyperallergic, and NASA have recognized her work. Currently, she is editing Technologies of Deception, a publication bringing together art, design, technology, ethics, futurism, and policymaking. Heather is an Assistant Professor of Design Futures at Washington University and a mother of two daughters.

R

Dr. **Søren Rosenbak**, Superseding Umpire, is a designer, researcher and educator working at Laerdal Medical, where he designs for the future of healthcare education. He is driven by design's capacity for giving us a sense of what is possible in this world, and holds a PhD in pataphysically infused design from Umeå Institute of Design. In 2021, he co-founded the Patadesign School.

Zoë R. Rush is a designer and researcher based in Kerry, Ireland whose practice explores the role of education and community participation in imagining place-based, sustainable futures. She is a co-founder of *Patio International*, a collective of designers from Europe and Latin America that explore how design as a discipline can foster creative collaboration and solidarity with people from different communities and backgrounds.

S

Carmem Saito is a PhD candidate at the Royal College of Art (London, UK). Her research explores fashion consumption, tacit knowledge and material mediation in digital contexts, exploring the complexities and contradictions of the fashion industry with a specific focus on the sensing body, touch, and materials. The project takes a critical look at how systems of consumption are imagined, designed, and used by consumers, exploring how material tacit knowledge can contribute to rethinking the technologies and apparatuses that currently support and promote contemporary cultures of consumption.

Dr. **Ina Scheffler** received her Master's degree in Cultural Anthropology, Modern English Literature, and Scandinavian Studies from the University of Bonn in 2007, subsequently completing State Examinations I and II in Art and English and teaching at high school level between 2012 and 2014. She held a teaching position in art didactics at the Staatliche Kunstakademie Düsseldorf and substitute professorships at the Kunsthochschule Mainz and the University of Siegen. Since October 2019, she is a postdoc at the University of Siegen with research interests and publications on school architecture, educational spaces, and children's drawing, among others in "Hier und Jetzt. Presence, Contemporary Art, and Artistic Thinking as Fruitful Educational Moments" in Lerchenfeld 46/2018.

Mira Schmitz (mira, they), a junior design researcher at KITE Design Research, questions hierarchical structures and likes to blur disciplinary boundaries. Their thematic focus is on sustainable transformation, critical design and intersectionality which emerged during their communication design studies, especially in Mira's bachelor's thesis at FH Aachen and master's thesis "Mach[t]arten" at HTWG Konstanz. Having been active in diverse eco-social voluntary initiatives and projects, mira was often involved in developing alternative structures; e.g.

in the HTWG student group Offen_Für which created various formats for sensitization, empowerment and exchange against discrimination. Previously, Mira worked as a research assistant in the HTWG's diversity project and Green Office, the University of Konstanz' field experiment related to class discrimination and held design workshops and a talk about intersectionality.

Abigail Schreider (she/her) holds a BA in Industrial design from the University of Buenos Aires and a Masters in Integrated design at Köln International School of Design. Originally from Entre Rios, Argentina and now based in Cologne where she works as a service designer. Her work, motivation and struggle lies in bringing discussion to the workplace around issues such as care, diversity, inclusion and belonging. As a designer and immigrant, Abigail navigates between corporate workplaces where critical agendas make their way and academic spaces for research and reflection. This dialogue builds and reflects her daily thinking and doing. She has organized several design jams and is also a member of Hay Futura, a collective of design workers in Argentina.

Bibiana Oliveira Serpa holds a PhD in Design from the School of Industrial Design of the University of the State of Rio de Janeiro (ESDI/UERJ). She is a feminist activist and a co-founder of the Design and Oppression network. Her research associates participatory and critical design approaches with politicizing actions within social movements, thus seeking to understand paths for an engaged design practice grounded on popular education and feminism.

Mindy Seu is a designer and technologist based in New York City, currently teaching as an Assistant Professor at Rutgers Mason Gross School of the Arts and Critic at Yale School of Art. Her expanded practice involves archival projects, techno-critical writing, performative lectures, and design commissions. Seu's ongoing Cyberfeminism Index gathers three decades of online activism and net art, and it was commissioned by Rhizome and presented at the New Museum.

T

Ayako Takase (she/they) is a gender non-conforming Asian mother/parent in the US who is never perfectly here nor there. Ayako is a fluid designer and educator who centers their practice on creating experiences and objects that foster meaningful, emotive connections with people, culture, and audiences. Ayako is a co-founder and director of Observatory, a multi-disciplinary design studio based in Providence, RI. Observatory relies foremost on an intuitive process that allows a natural interplay of form and function in their designs. The studio's work has earned numerous awards with leading companies such as Herman Miller, Google, and Procter & Gamble. Ayako is also an Associate Professor at Rhode Island School of Design and graduate program director of the Industrial Design department. She teaches hands-on studios focusing on audience-centric, emotive, and iterative design.

ngọc triêu (b. 1994, Vietnam) is a design researcher who practices design and research as an intervention to address and reform asymmetrical power relations through the lenses of decoloniality and decentralization. Her work focuses on the intersection of digital design, human rights, and public-interest technology. ngọc is passionate about user advocacy, co-creation, and equal access to knowledge. Whether ngọc is distilling data into insights that inform design decisions or conceptualizing information architecture, she collaborates closely with tech funders, designers, developers, and researchers to ensure usability, security, and dignity for vulnerable communities.

W

Lauren Williams (she/her) is a Detroit-based designer, researcher, and educator. She works with visual and interactive media to understand, critique, and reimagine the ways social and economic systems distribute and exercise power. Through her creative practice and research, she often investigates social fictions like race and the myths that uphold oppressive systems like capitalism. Themes of trust and the transformations enabled by social engagement shape both her approaches and the questions she examines surrounding power and oppression, social relations, and social movements. Lauren has taught design + interdisciplinary studios and intensives at CCS, ArtCenter College of Design, CalArts and elsewhere. Previously, she managed programs and policy aimed at cultivating economic justice at Prosperity Now in DC. Going forward, she's finding ways to align her capacities with revolutionary movements that build toward different socioeconomic systems entirely and usher in new dimensions of power and freedom altogether.

Z

Dr. **Bonne Zabolotney** is an interdisciplinary designer, educator, and researcher focusing on Canadian design culture — particularly anonymous and unacknowledged works— and the political economy of design. She holds a PhD Design from RMIT in Melbourne, Australia, an MA Liberal Arts from Simon Fraser University in Vancouver, BC, and a BDes from Alberta University of the Arts. She teaches critical studies and communication design at Emily Carr University of Art + Design.

Language Editor Biography

Aside from conducting research in the sociology of the senses—see his edited volume Sensing Collectives – Aesthetics and Politics Intertwined (transkript 2023)—**Jacob Watson** is a freelance translator and editor in Berlin. He studied philosophy and languages before obtaining his Diplôme avancé d'etudes françaises & traduction at the Université Marc Bloch, Strasbourg (2002). His fields are philosophy and law, sociology and history, art and film, most notably as house translator for the law journal Ancilla Luris of Zürcher Hochschule für Angewandte Wissenschaften. Recent book translations are Work – the Last 1000 Years (Verso, 2018) by Andrea Komlosy and Eros, Lust and Sin by Franz X Eder (forthcoming).